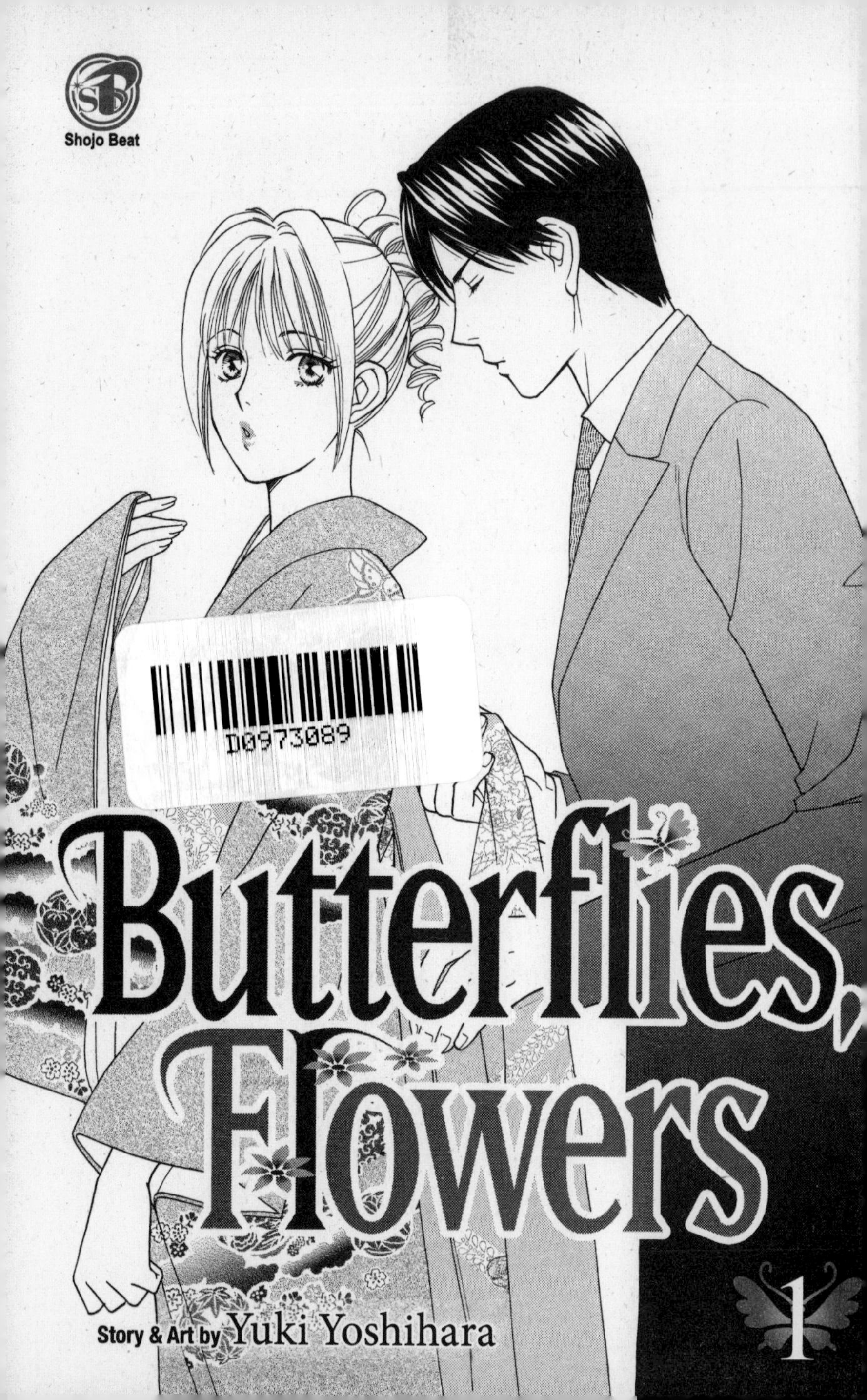
Shojo Beat
Butterflies, Flowers
1
Story & Art by Yuki Yoshihara

Butterflies, Flowers

Contents

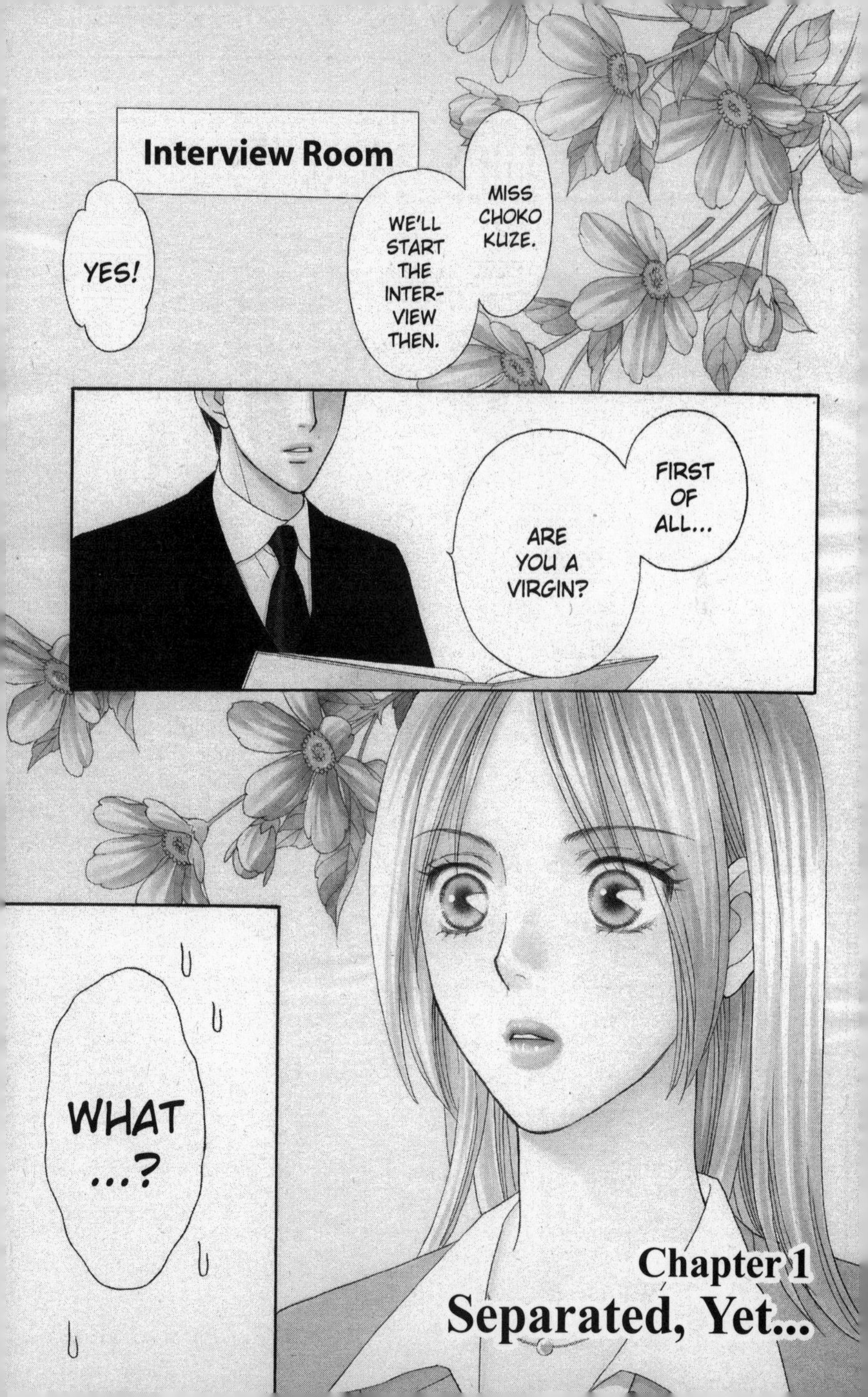

Interview Room
MISS CHOKO KUZE.
WE'LL START THE INTER-VIEW THEN.
YES!
FIRST OF ALL...
ARE YOU A VIRGIN?
Chapter 1
Separated, Yet...
WHAT ...?

Chapter 1
Separated, Yet...

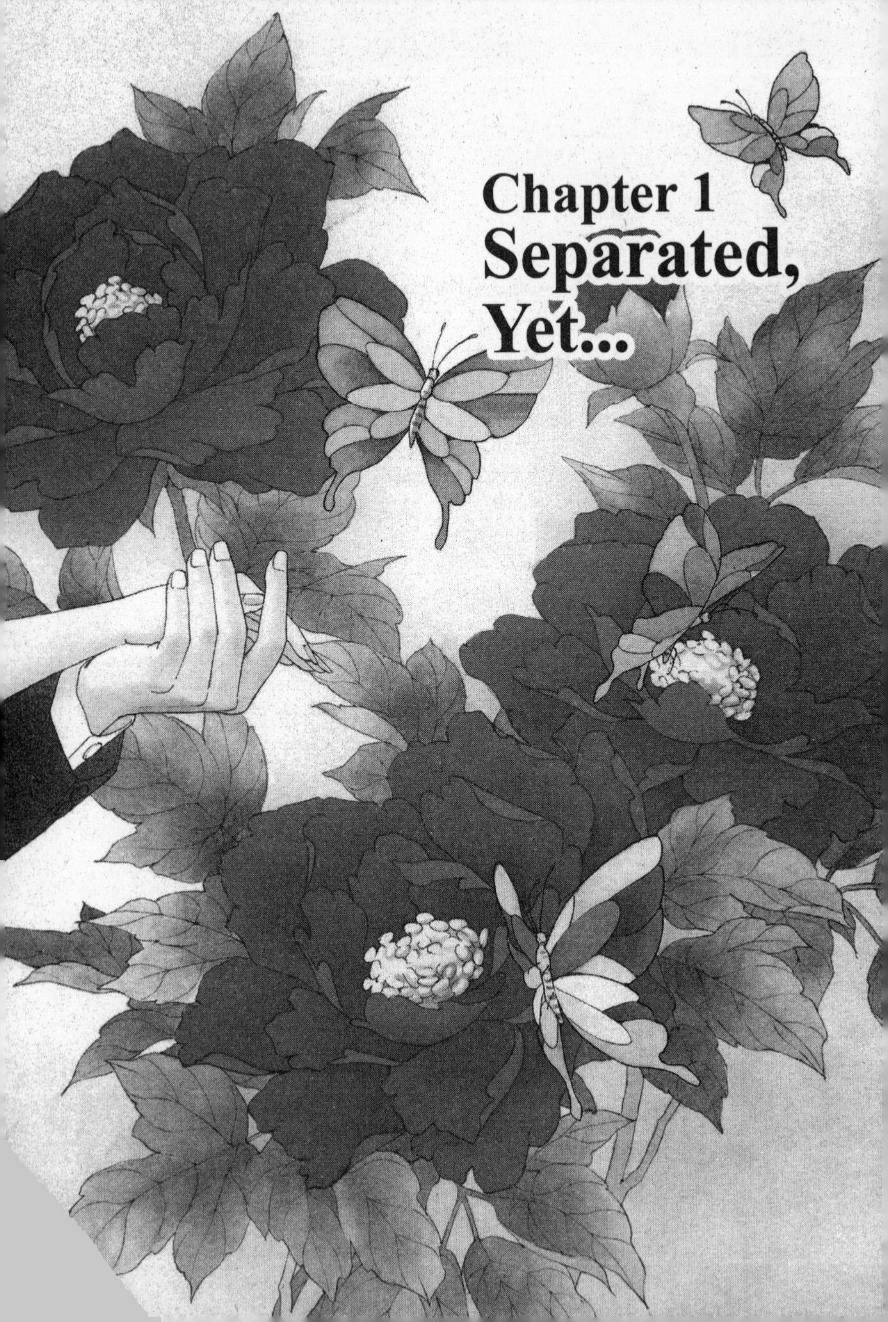

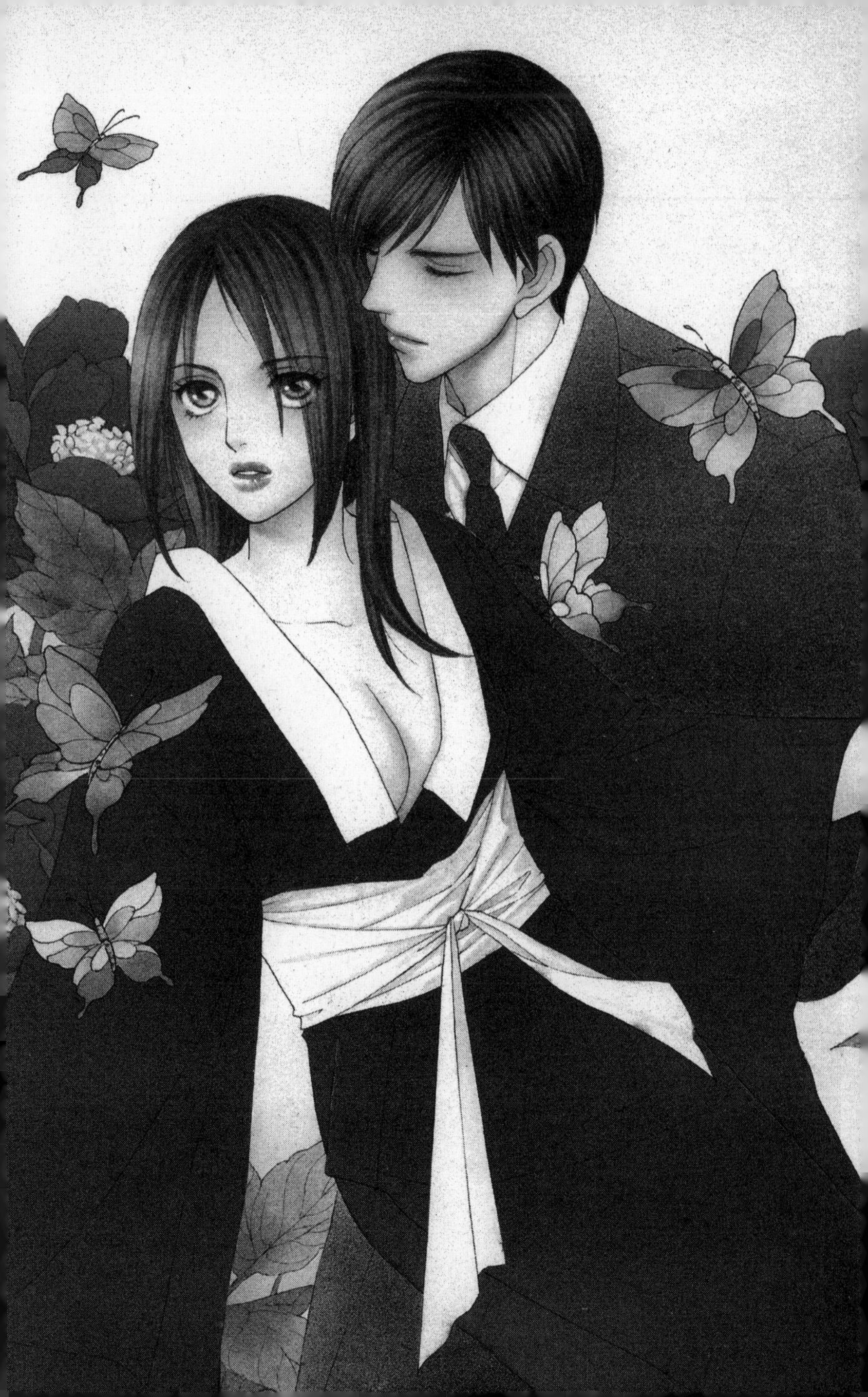

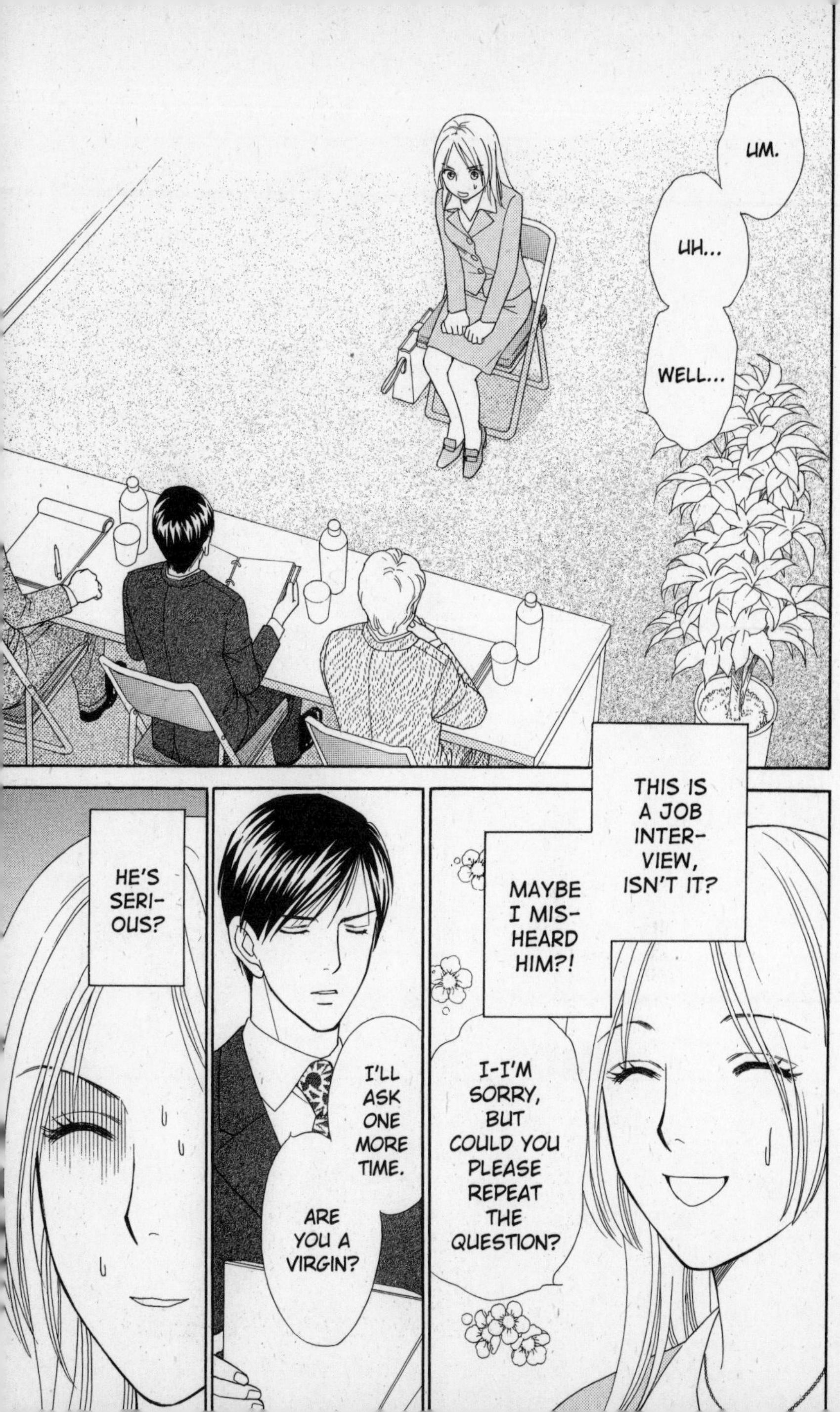
UM.
UH...
WELL...
THIS IS A JOB INTERVIEW, ISN'T IT?
MAYBE I MISHEARD HIM?!
I-I'M SORRY, BUT COULD YOU PLEASE REPEAT THE QUESTION?
I'LL ASK ONE MORE TIME.
ARE YOU A VIRGIN?
HE'S SERIOUS?

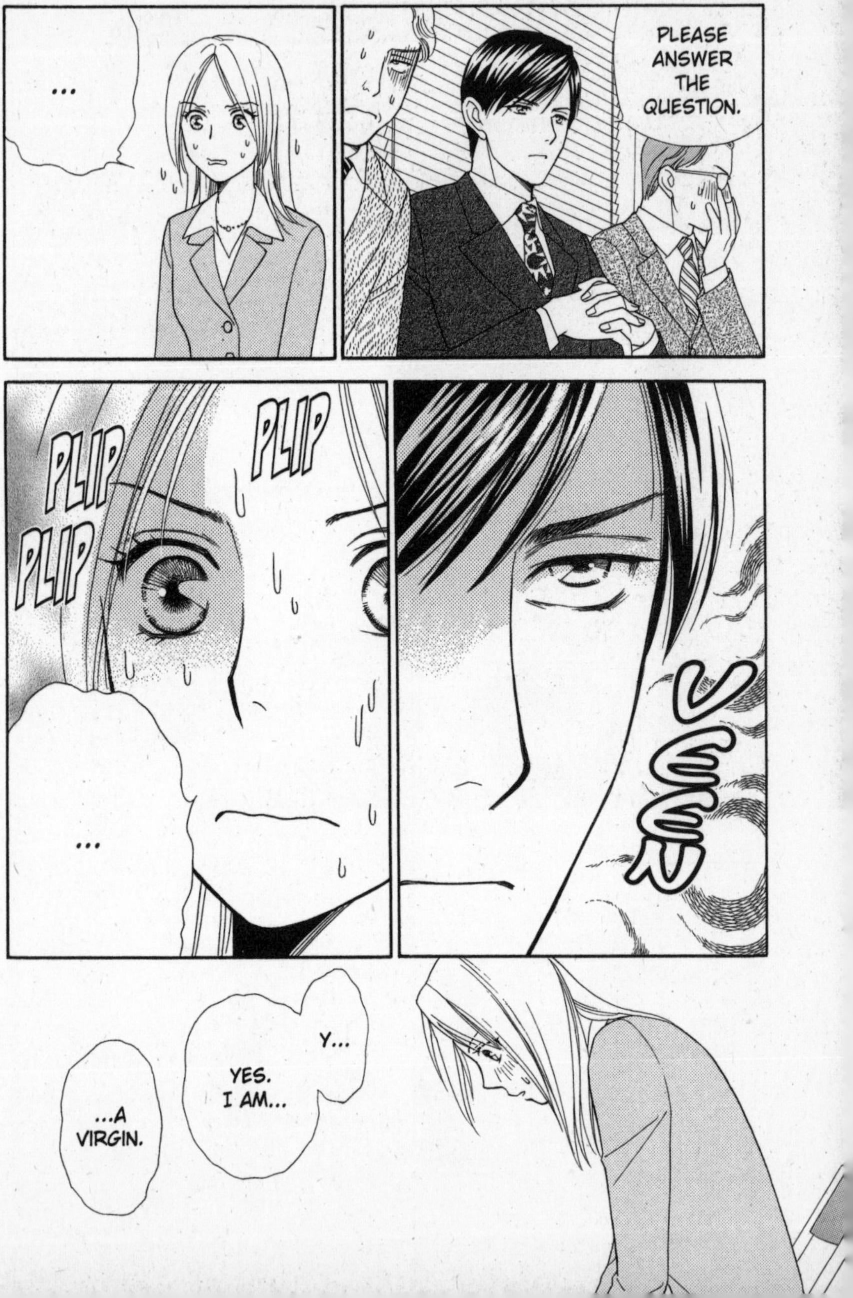
PLEASE ANSWER THE QUESTION.
...
VEER
PLIP
PLIP PLIP
...
Y...
YES. I AM...
...A VIRGIN.

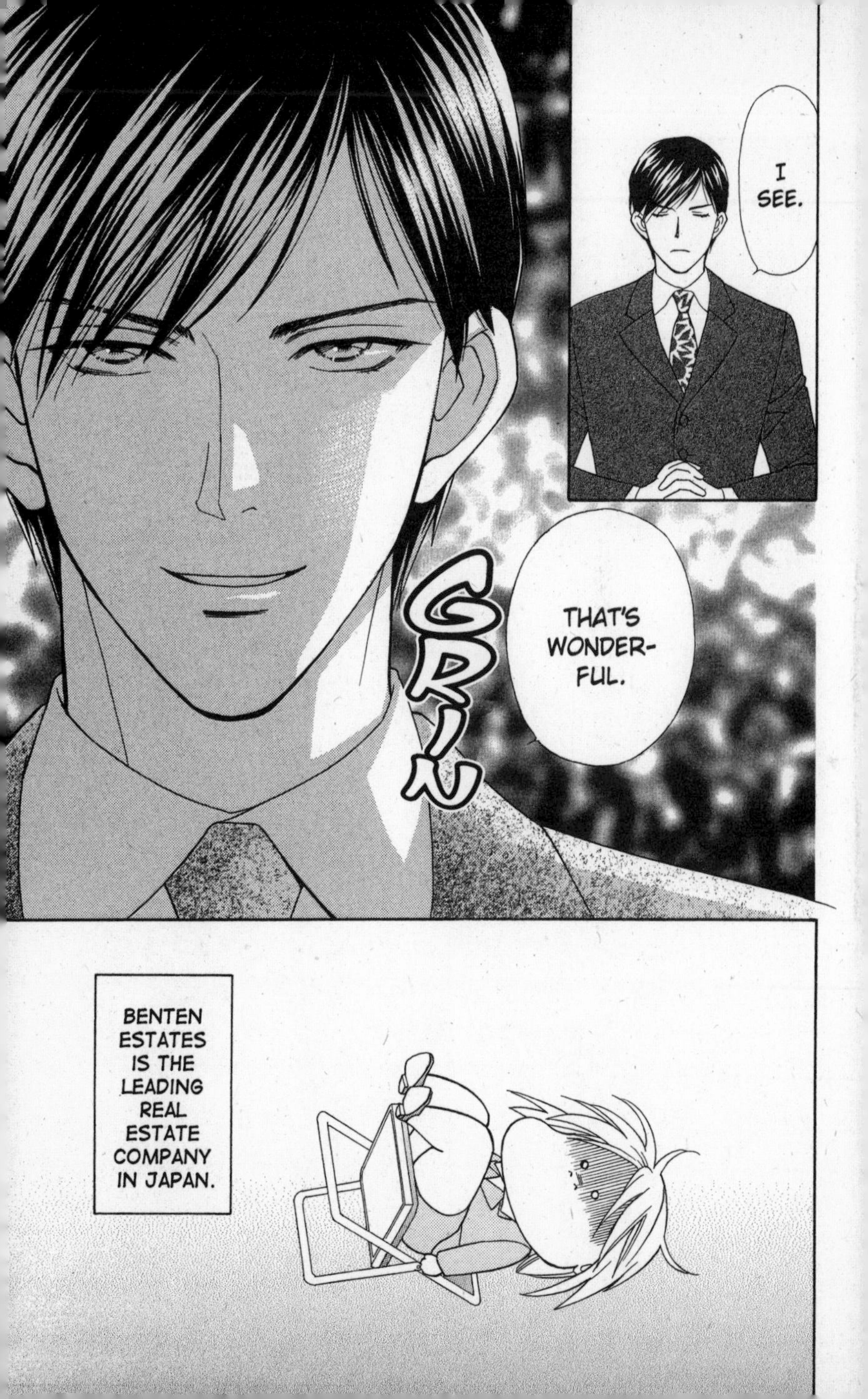
I SEE.
THAT'S WONDER-FUL.
GRIN
BENTEN ESTATES IS THE LEADING REAL ESTATE COMPANY IN JAPAN.

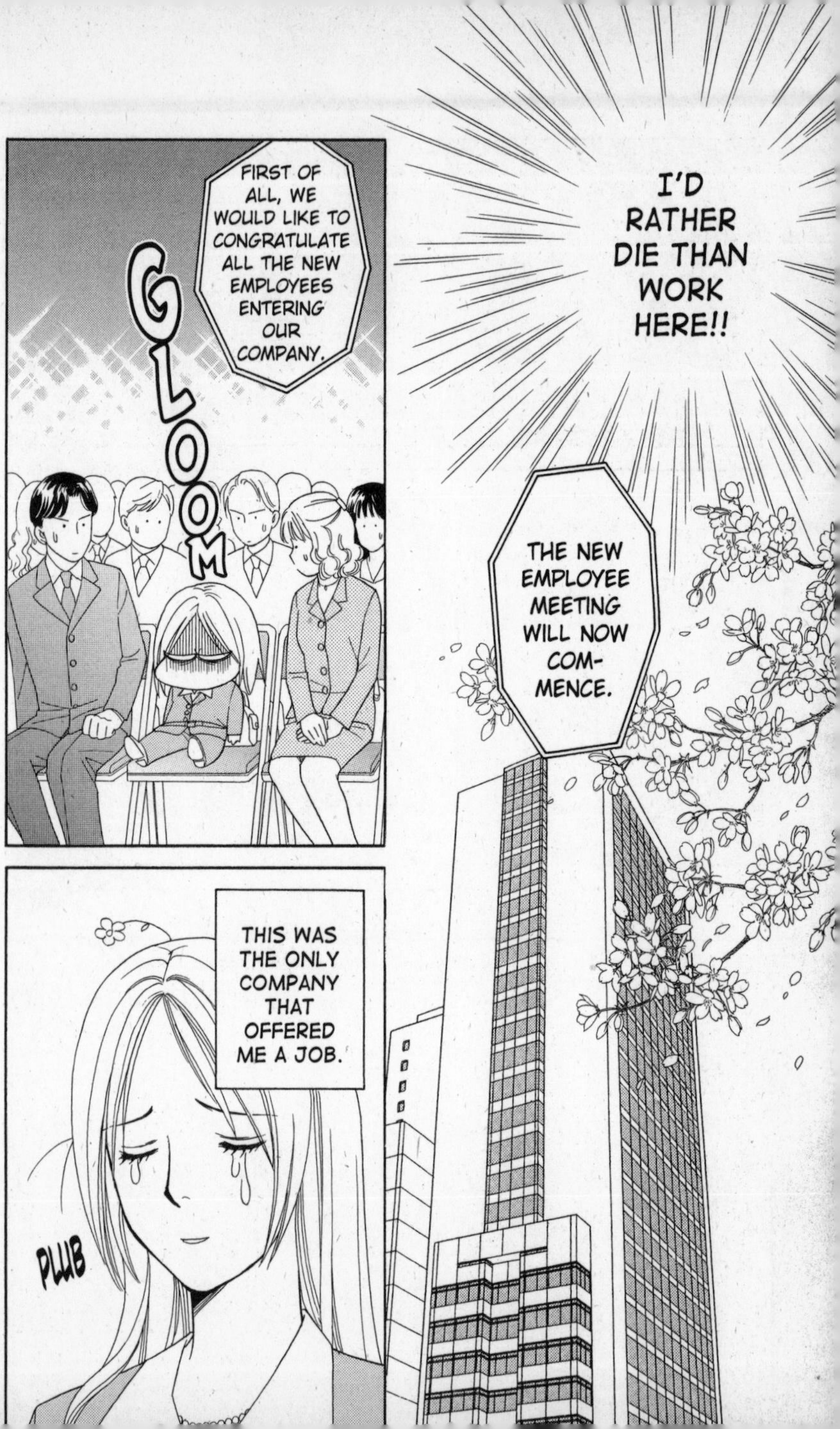
I'D RATHER DIE THAN WORK HERE!!
THE NEW EMPLOYEE MEETING WILL NOW COM-MENCE.
FIRST OF ALL, WE WOULD LIKE TO CONGRATULATE ALL THE NEW EMPLOYEES ENTERING OUR COMPANY.
GLOOM
THIS WAS THE ONLY COMPANY THAT OFFERED ME A JOB.
PLUB

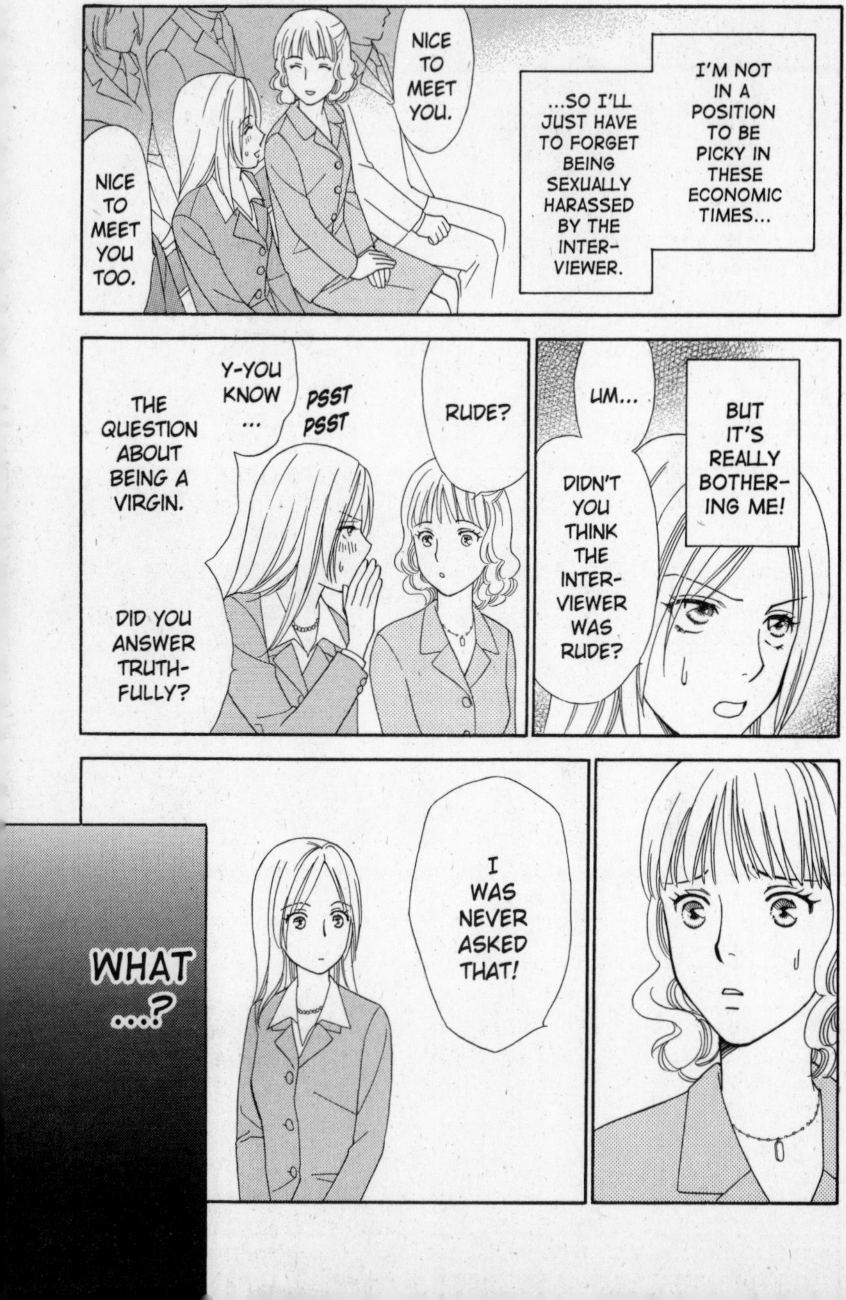
I'M NOT IN A POSITION TO BE PICKY IN THESE ECONOMIC TIMES...
...SO I'LL JUST HAVE TO FORGET BEING SEXUALLY HARASSED BY THE INTER-VIEWER.
NICE TO MEET YOU.
NICE TO MEET YOU TOO.
BUT IT'S REALLY BOTHER-ING ME!
UM...
DIDN'T YOU THINK THE INTER-VIEWER WAS RUDE?
RUDE?
PSST PSST
Y-YOU KNOW ...
THE QUESTION ABOUT BEING A VIRGIN.
DID YOU ANSWER TRUTH-FULLY?
I WAS NEVER ASKED THAT!
WHAT ...?

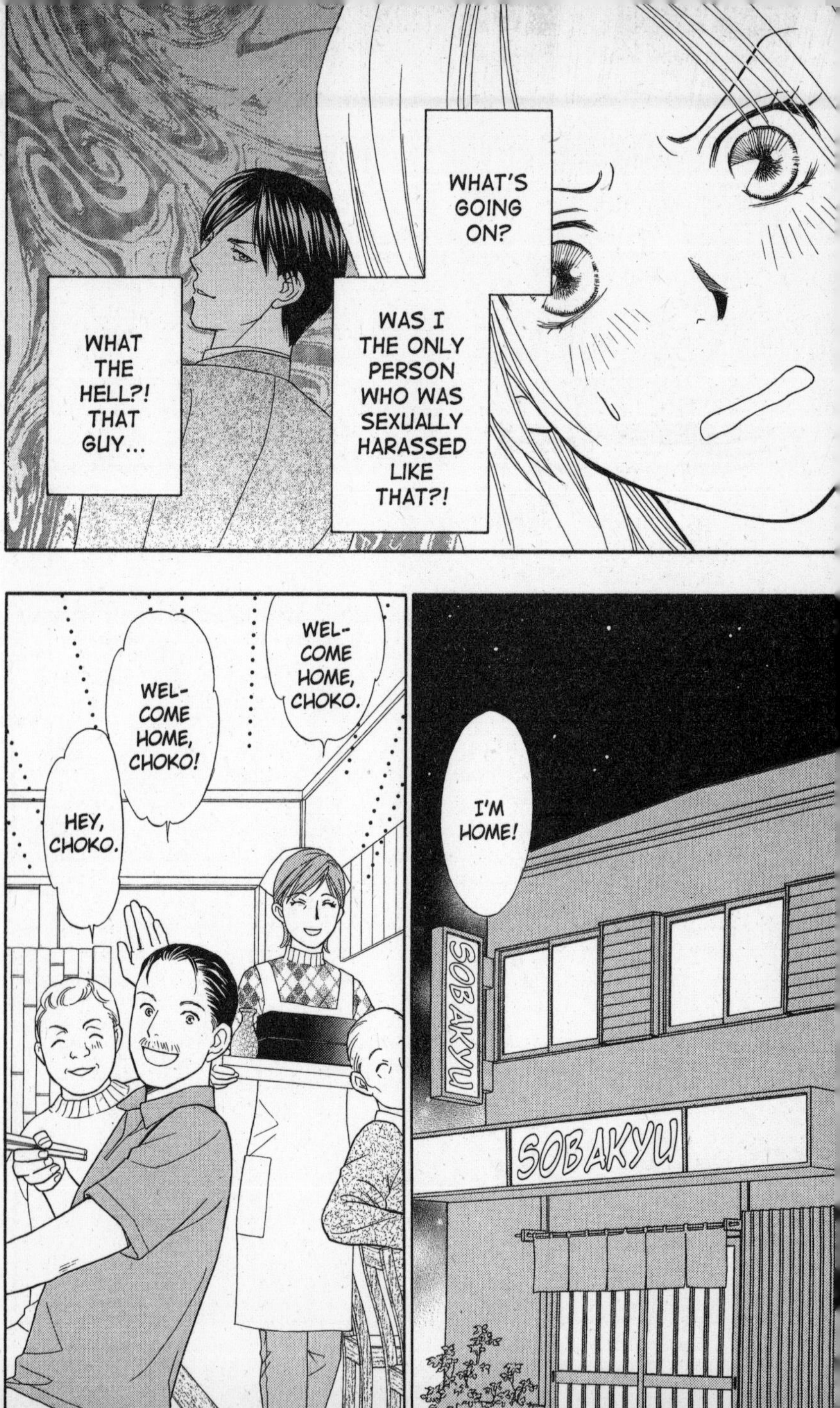

WHAT'S GOING ON?
WAS I THE ONLY PERSON WHO WAS SEXUALLY HARASSED LIKE THAT?!
WHAT THE HELL?! THAT GUY...
I'M HOME!
SOBAKYU
SOBAKYU
WEL-COME HOME, CHOKO.
WEL-COME HOME, CHOKO!
HEY, CHOKO.

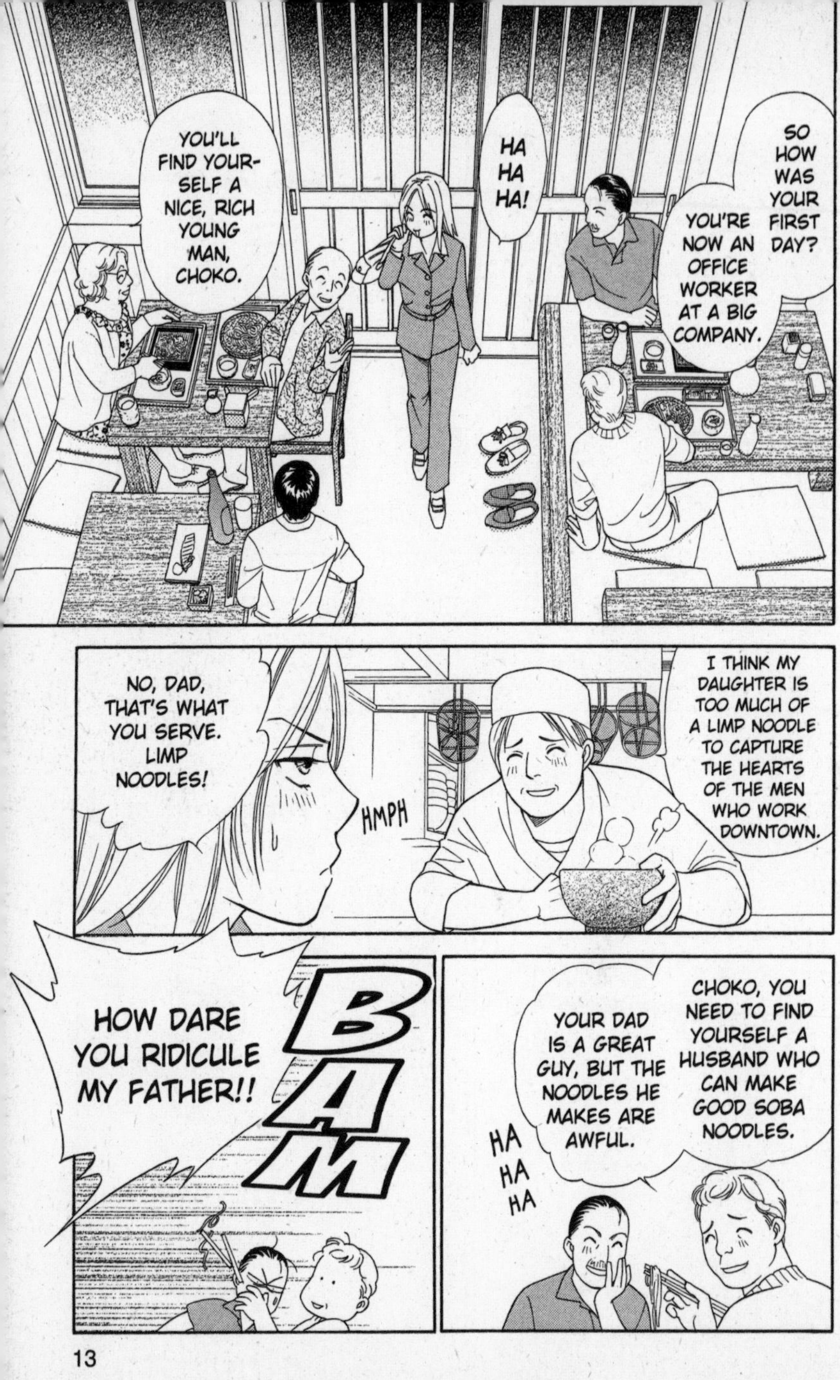
SO HOW WAS YOUR FIRST DAY?
YOU'RE NOW AN OFFICE WORKER AT A BIG COMPANY.
HA HA HA!
YOU'LL FIND YOUR-SELF A NICE, RICH YOUNG MAN, CHOKO.
I THINK MY DAUGHTER IS TOO MUCH OF A LIMP NOODLE TO CAPTURE THE HEARTS OF THE MEN WHO WORK DOWNTOWN.
HMPH
NO, DAD, THAT'S WHAT YOU SERVE. LIMP NOODLES!
CHOKO, YOU NEED TO FIND YOURSELF A HUSBAND WHO CAN MAKE GOOD SOBA NOODLES.
YOUR DAD IS A GREAT GUY, BUT THE NOODLES HE MAKES ARE AWFUL.
HA HA HA
BAM
HOW DARE YOU RIDICULE MY FATHER!!

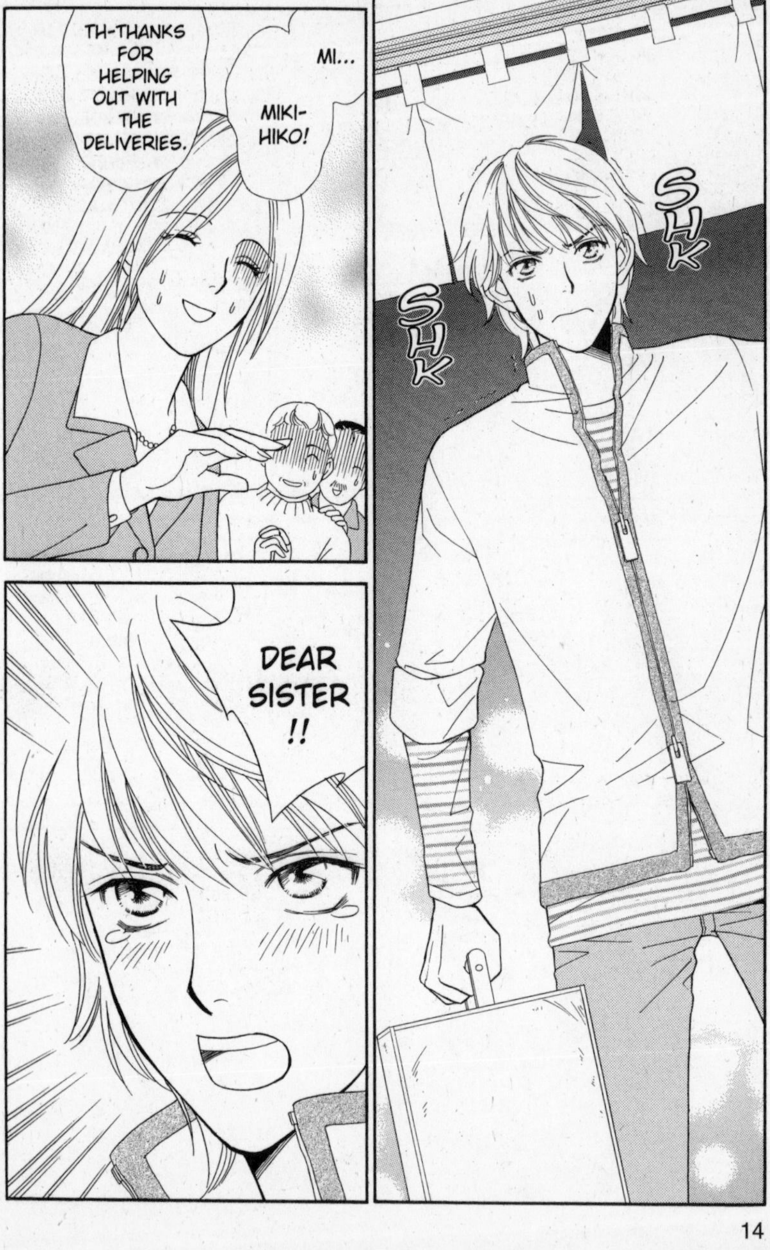
SHK
SHK
MI...
MIKI-HIKO!
TH-THANKS FOR HELPING OUT WITH THE DELIVERIES.
DEAR SISTER !!

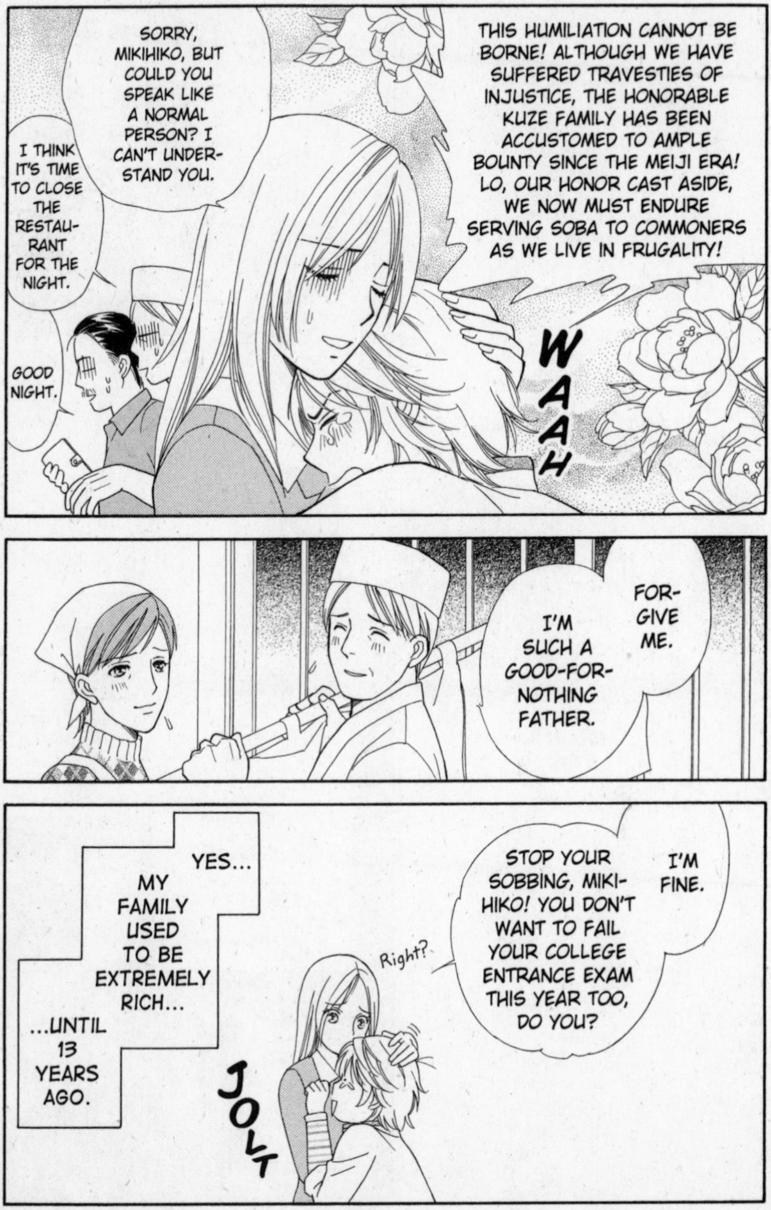
THIS HUMILIATION CANNOT BE BORNE! ALTHOUGH WE HAVE SUFFERED TRAVESTIES OF INJUSTICE, THE HONORABLE KUZE FAMILY HAS BEEN ACCUSTOMED TO AMPLE BOUNTY SINCE THE MEIJI ERA! LO, OUR HONOR CAST ASIDE, WE NOW MUST ENDURE SERVING SOBA TO COMMONERS AS WE LIVE IN FRUGALITY!
WAAAH
SORRY, MIKIHIKO, BUT COULD YOU SPEAK LIKE A NORMAL PERSON? I CAN'T UNDERSTAND YOU.
I THINK IT'S TIME TO CLOSE THE RESTAURANT FOR THE NIGHT.
GOOD NIGHT.
FORGIVE ME.
I'M SUCH A GOOD-FOR-NOTHING FATHER.
I'M FINE.
STOP YOUR SOBBING, MIKIHIKO! YOU DON'T WANT TO FAIL YOUR COLLEGE ENTRANCE EXAM THIS YEAR TOO, DO YOU?
Right?
YES... MY FAMILY USED TO BE EXTREMELY RICH... ...UNTIL 13 YEARS AGO.
JOLT

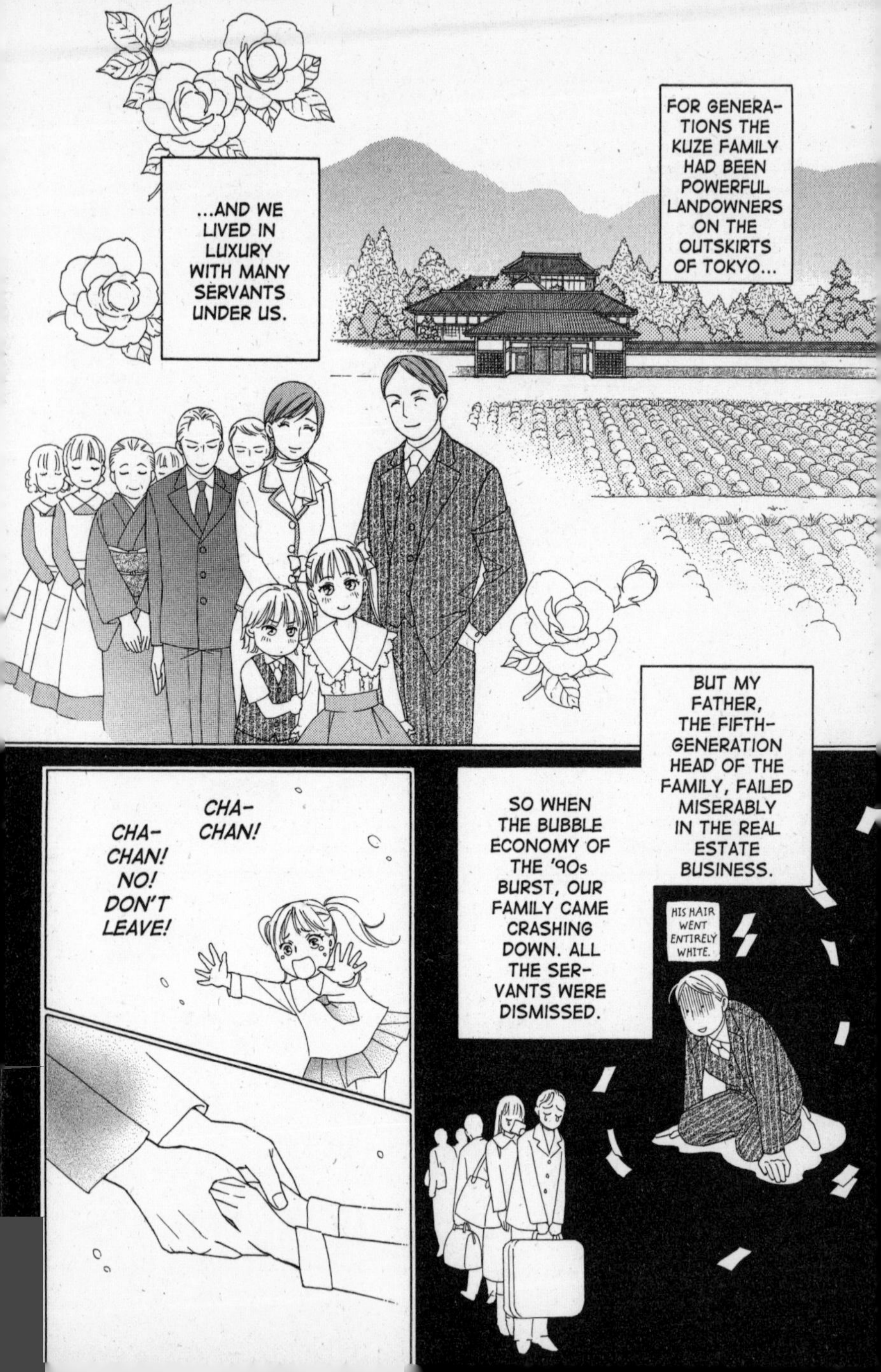
FOR GENERATIONS THE KUZE FAMILY HAD BEEN POWERFUL LANDOWNERS ON THE OUTSKIRTS OF TOKYO...
...AND WE LIVED IN LUXURY WITH MANY SERVANTS UNDER US.
BUT MY FATHER, THE FIFTH-GENERATION HEAD OF THE FAMILY, FAILED MISERABLY IN THE REAL ESTATE BUSINESS.
SO WHEN THE BUBBLE ECONOMY OF THE '90s BURST, OUR FAMILY CAME CRASHING DOWN. ALL THE SERVANTS WERE DISMISSED.
HIS HAIR WENT ENTIRELY WHITE.
CHA-CHAN!
CHA-CHAN! NO! DON'T LEAVE!

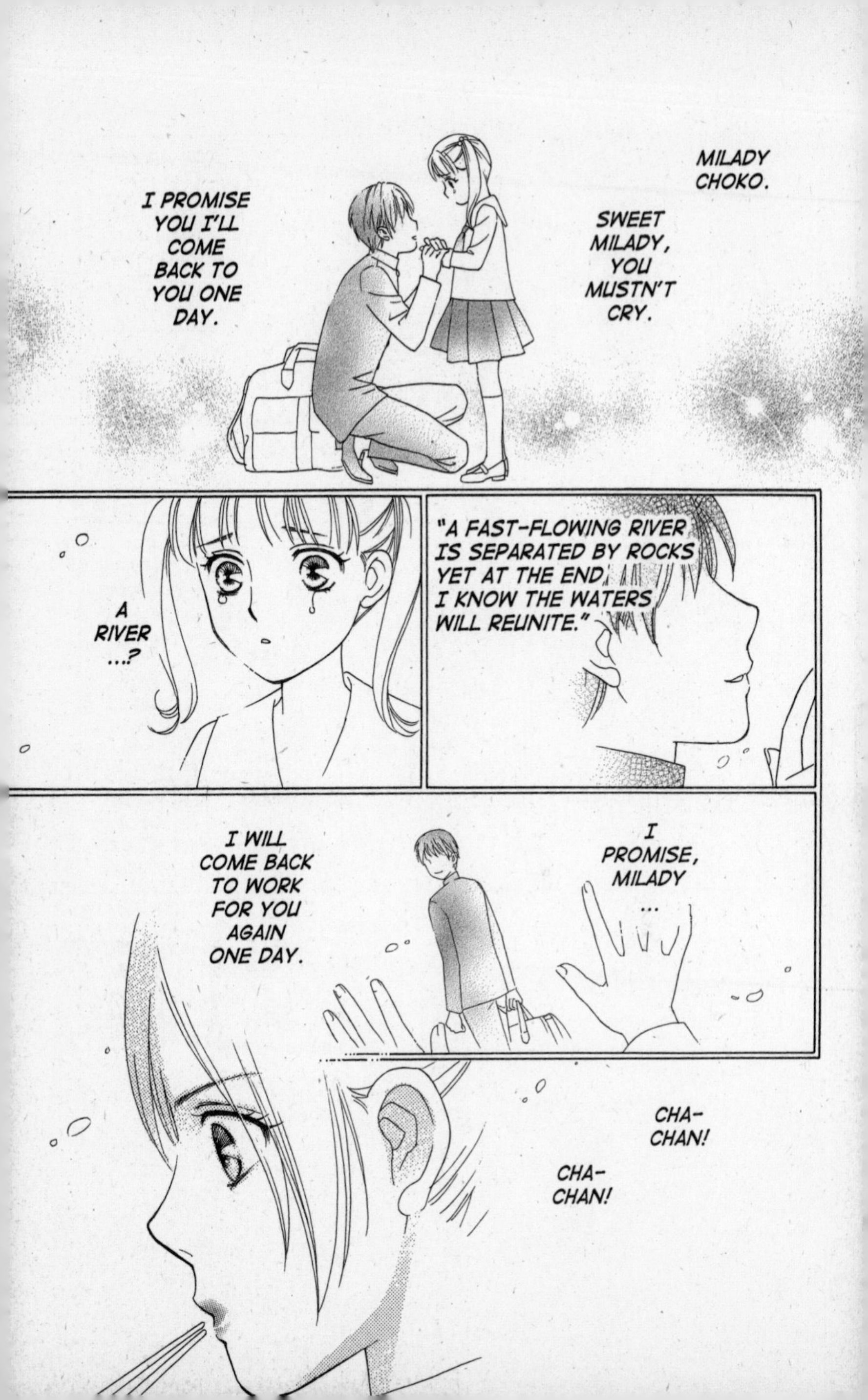
MILADY CHOKO.
SWEET MILADY, YOU MUSTN'T CRY.
I PROMISE YOU I'LL COME BACK TO YOU ONE DAY.
"A FAST-FLOWING RIVER IS SEPARATED BY ROCKS YET AT THE END, I KNOW THE WATERS WILL REUNITE."
A RIVER ...?
I PROMISE, MILADY ...
I WILL COME BACK TO WORK FOR YOU AGAIN ONE DAY.
CHA-CHAN!
CHA-CHAN!

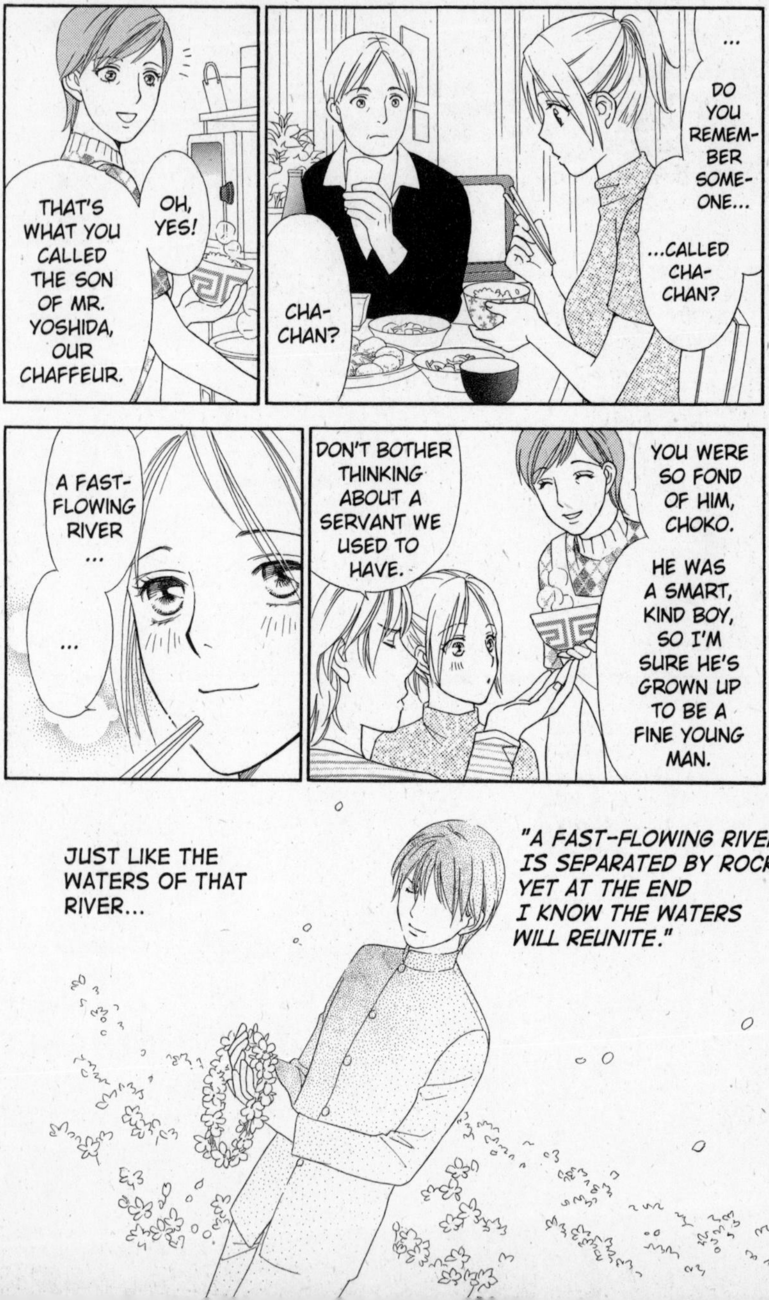
...
DO YOU REMEMBER SOMEONE...
...CALLED CHA-CHAN?
CHA-CHAN?
OH, YES!
THAT'S WHAT YOU CALLED THE SON OF MR. YOSHIDA, OUR CHAFFEUR.
YOU WERE SO FOND OF HIM, CHOKO.
HE WAS A SMART, KIND BOY, SO I'M SURE HE'S GROWN UP TO BE A FINE YOUNG MAN.
DON'T BOTHER THINKING ABOUT A SERVANT WE USED TO HAVE.
A FAST-FLOWING RIVER ...
...
"A FAST-FLOWING RIVER IS SEPARATED BY ROCKS YET AT THE END I KNOW THE WATERS WILL REUNITE."
JUST LIKE THE WATERS OF THAT RIVER...

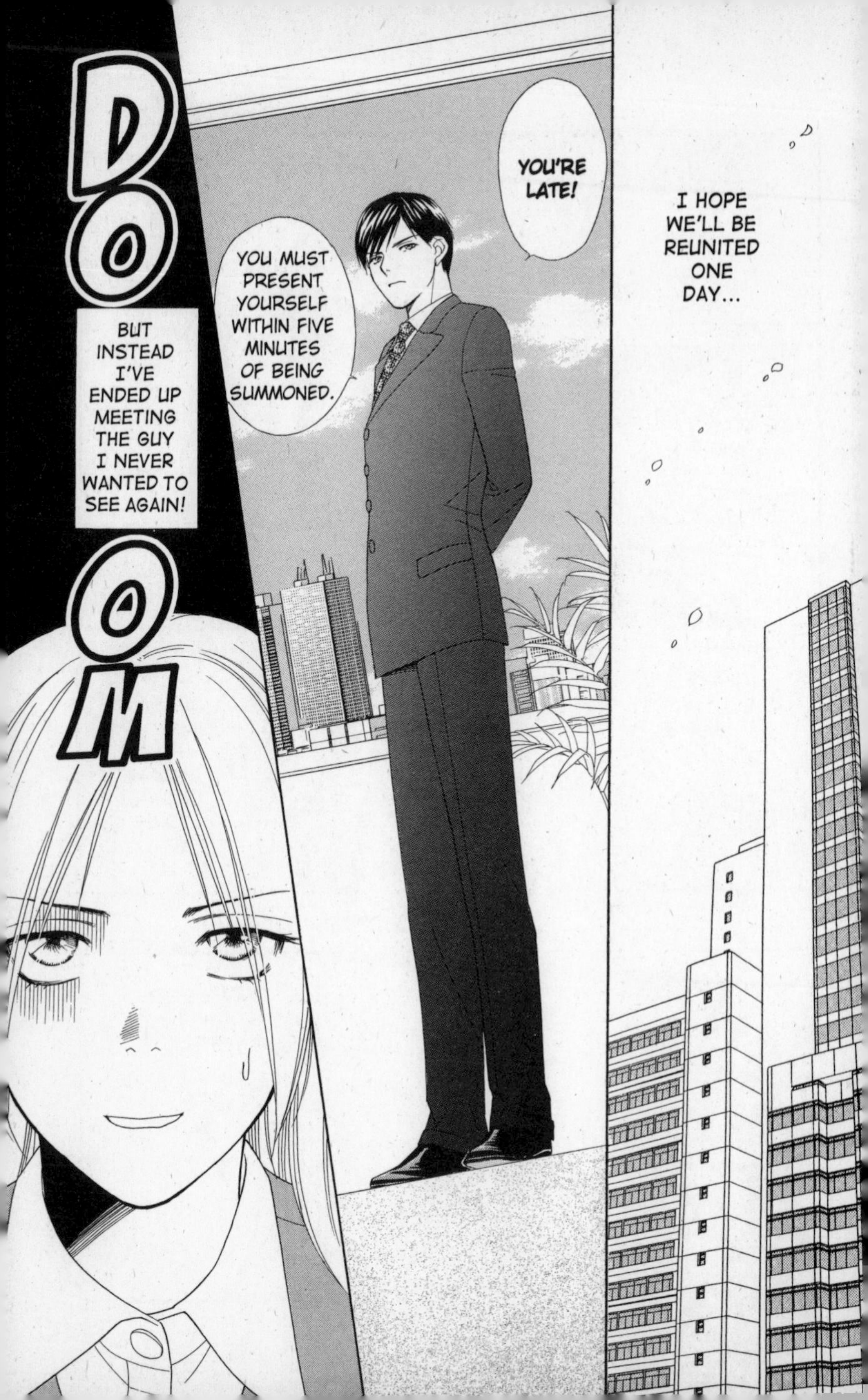
I HOPE WE'LL BE REUNITED ONE DAY...
YOU'RE LATE!
YOU MUST PRESENT YOURSELF WITHIN FIVE MINUTES OF BEING SUMMONED.
BUT INSTEAD I'VE ENDED UP MEETING THE GUY I NEVER WANTED TO SEE AGAIN!
DOOM

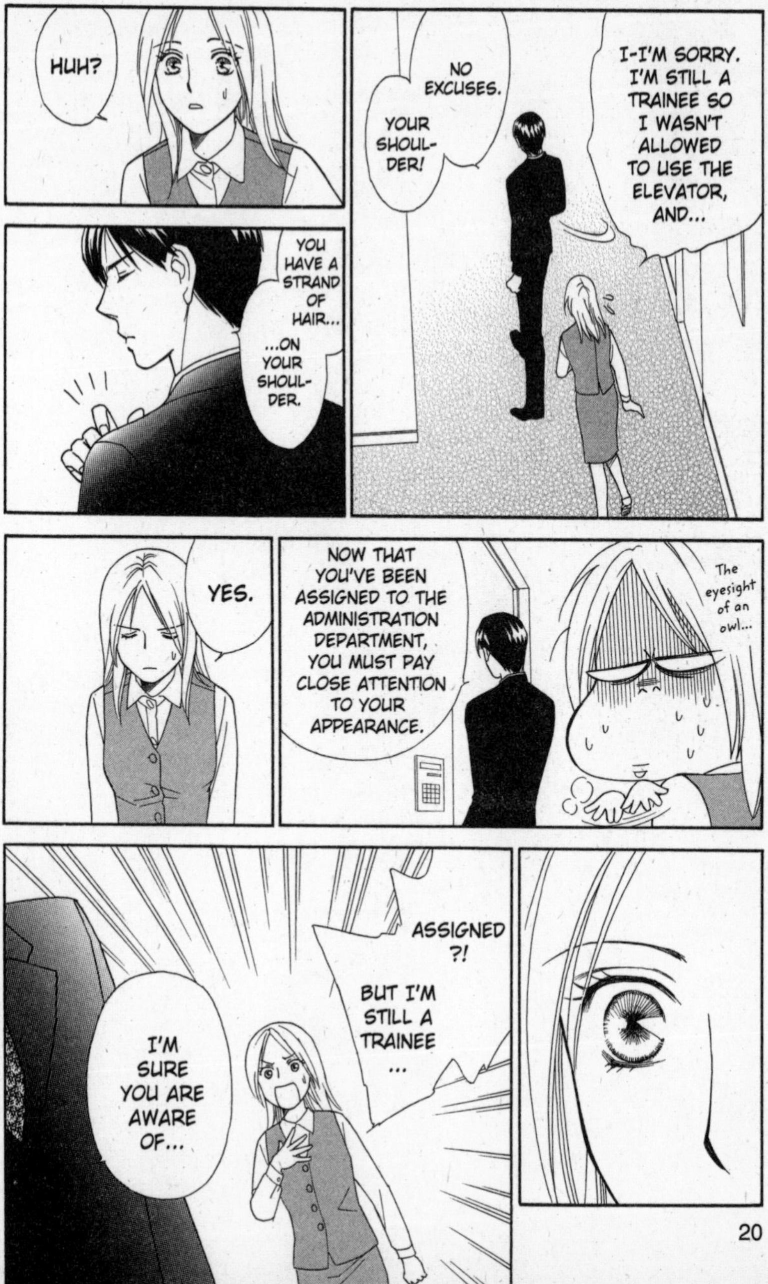
I-I'M SORRY. I'M STILL A TRAINEE SO I WASN'T ALLOWED TO USE THE ELEVATOR, AND...
NO EXCUSES.
YOUR SHOULDER!
HUH?
YOU HAVE A STRAND OF HAIR...
...ON YOUR SHOULDER.
The eyesight of an owl...
NOW THAT YOU'VE BEEN ASSIGNED TO THE ADMINISTRATION DEPARTMENT, YOU MUST PAY CLOSE ATTENTION TO YOUR APPEARANCE.
YES.
ASSIGNED ?!
BUT I'M STILL A TRAINEE ...
I'M SURE YOU ARE AWARE OF...

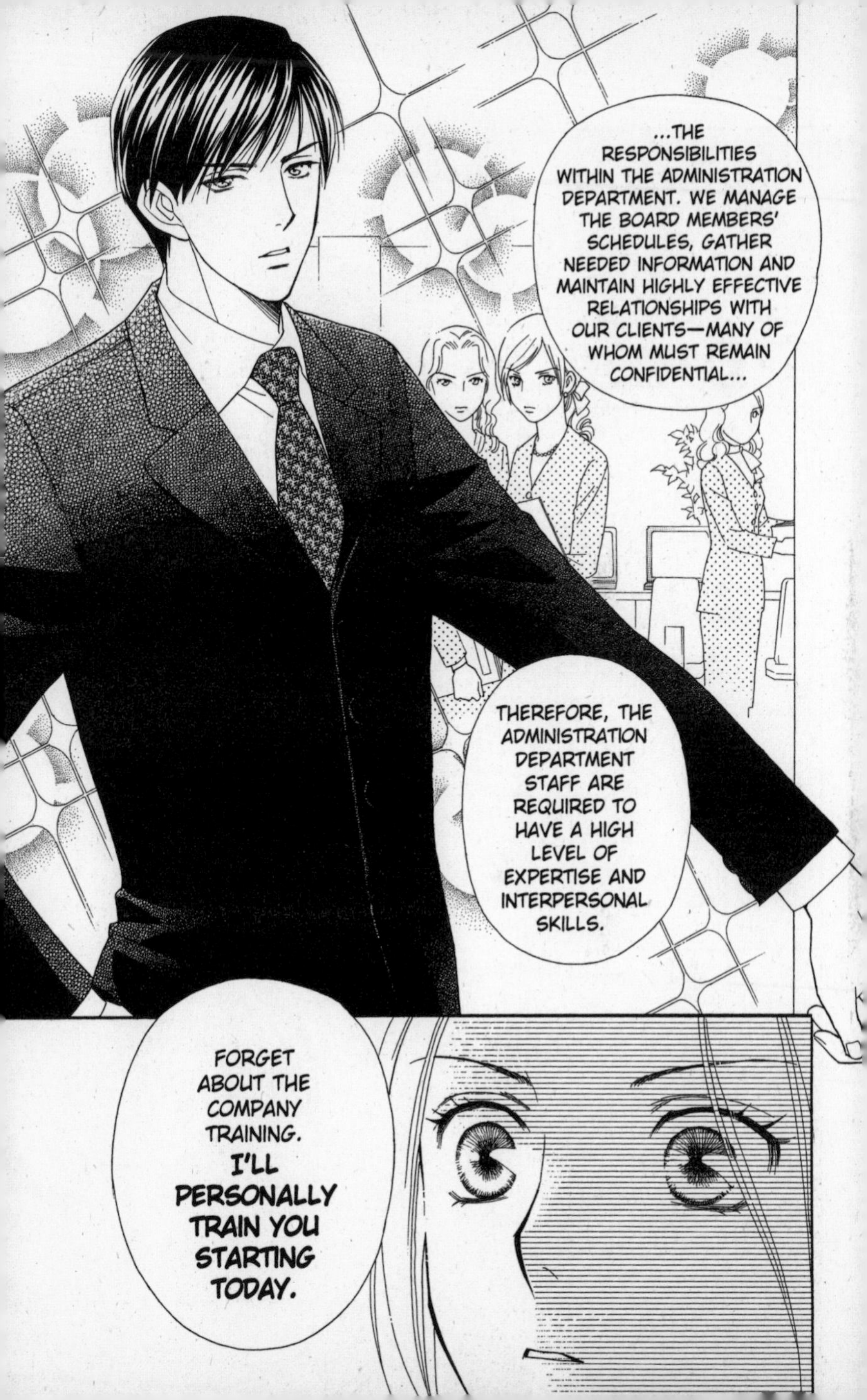
...THE RESPONSIBILITIES WITHIN THE ADMINISTRATION DEPARTMENT. WE MANAGE THE BOARD MEMBERS' SCHEDULES, GATHER NEEDED INFORMATION AND MAINTAIN HIGHLY EFFECTIVE RELATIONSHIPS WITH OUR CLIENTS—MANY OF WHOM MUST REMAIN CONFIDENTIAL...
THEREFORE, THE ADMINISTRATION DEPARTMENT STAFF ARE REQUIRED TO HAVE A HIGH LEVEL OF EXPERTISE AND INTERPERSONAL SKILLS.
FORGET ABOUT THE COMPANY TRAINING. I'LL PERSONALLY TRAIN YOU STARTING TODAY.

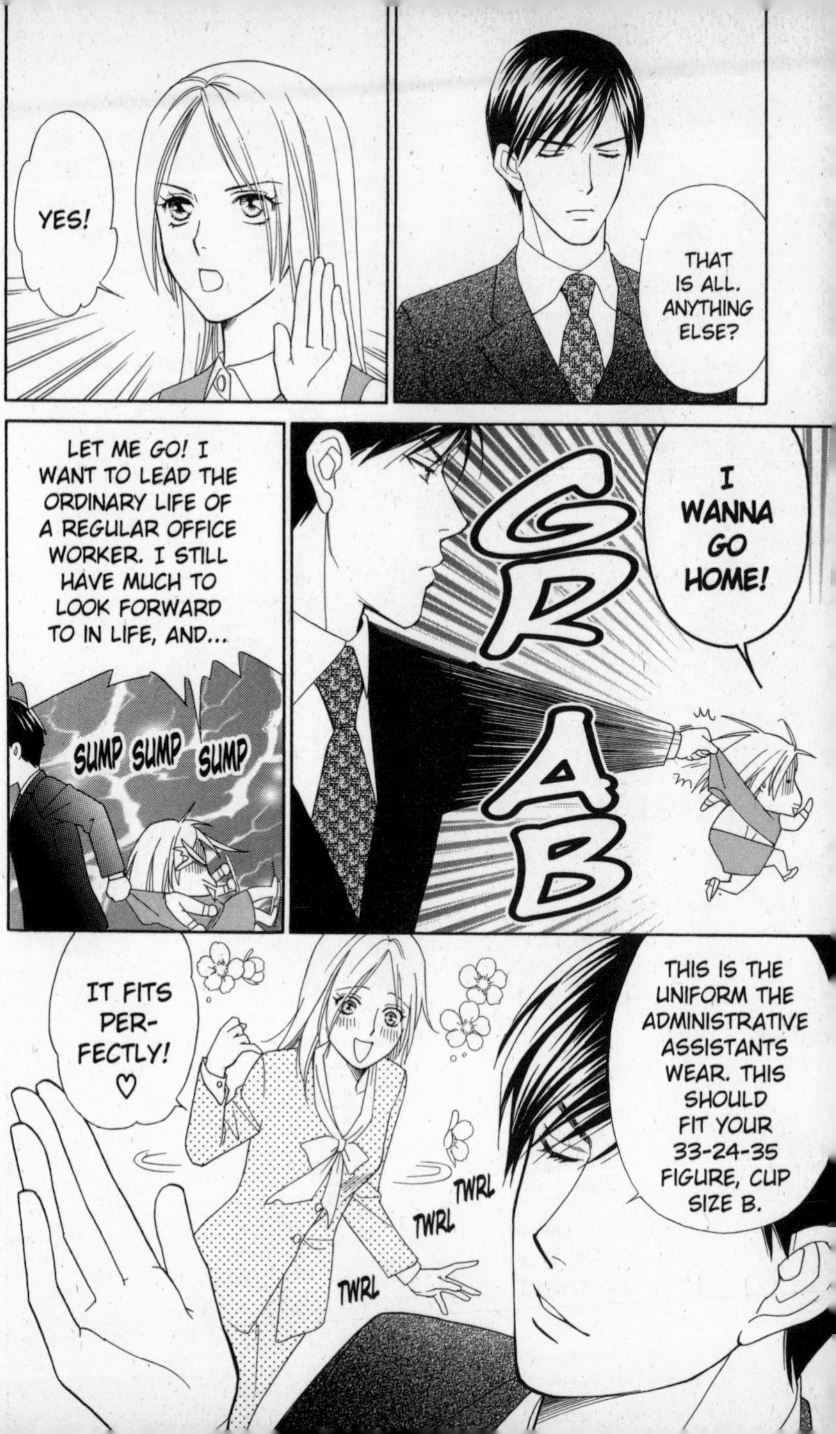
THAT IS ALL. ANYTHING ELSE?
YES!
I WANNA GO HOME!
GRAB
LET ME GO! I WANT TO LEAD THE ORDINARY LIFE OF A REGULAR OFFICE WORKER. I STILL HAVE MUCH TO LOOK FORWARD TO IN LIFE, AND...
SUMP SUMP SUMP
THIS IS THE UNIFORM THE ADMINISTRATIVE ASSISTANTS WEAR. THIS SHOULD FIT YOUR 33-24-35 FIGURE, CUP SIZE B.
TWRL TWRL TWRL
IT FITS PER-FECTLY! ♡

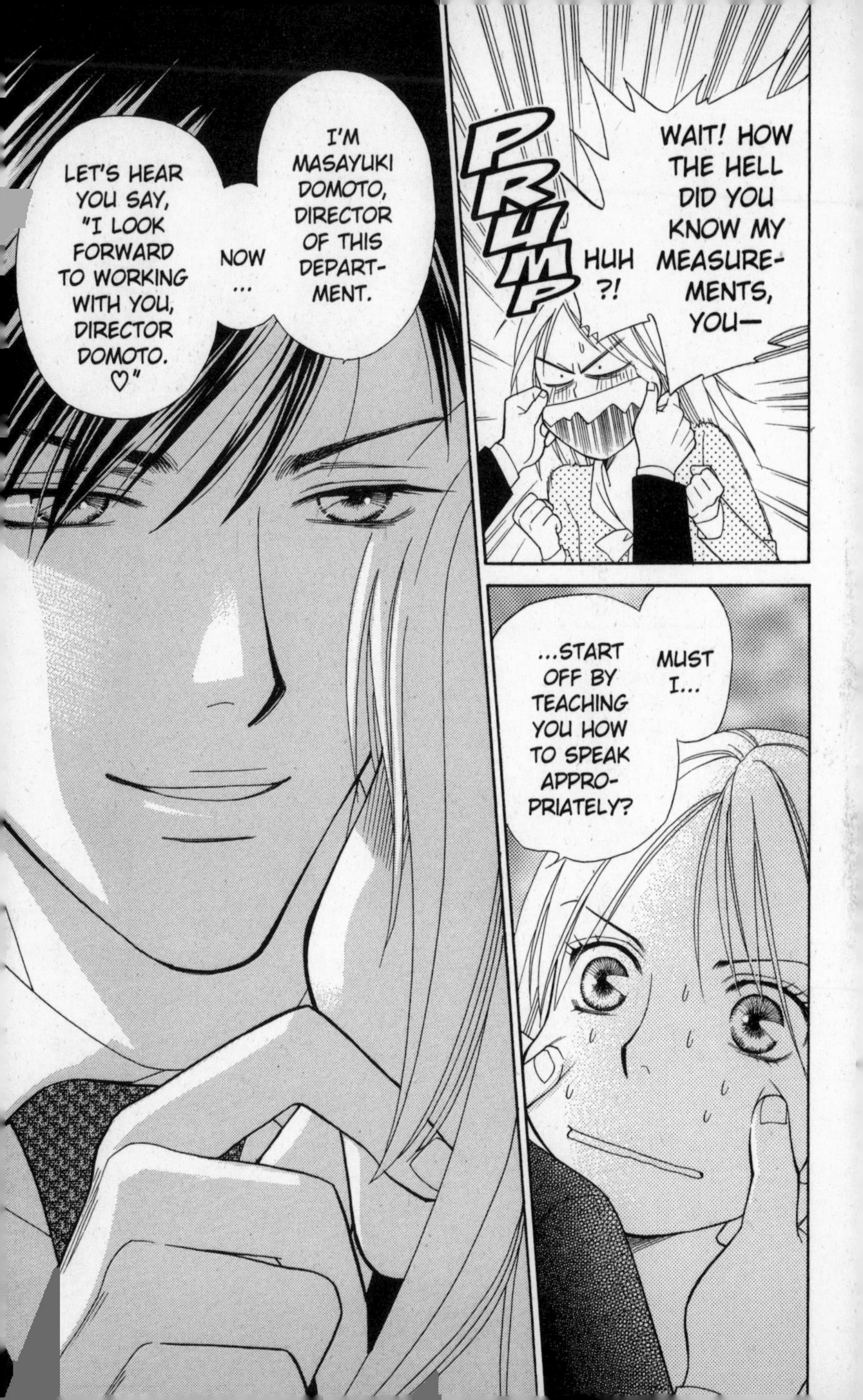
PRUMP
HUH ?!
WAIT! HOW THE HELL DID YOU KNOW MY MEASUREMENTS, YOU—
MUST I...
...START OFF BY TEACHING YOU HOW TO SPEAK APPROPRIATELY?
I'M MASAYUKI DOMOTO, DIRECTOR OF THIS DEPARTMENT.
NOW ...
LET'S HEAR YOU SAY, "I LOOK FORWARD TO WORKING WITH YOU, DIRECTOR DOMOTO. ♡"

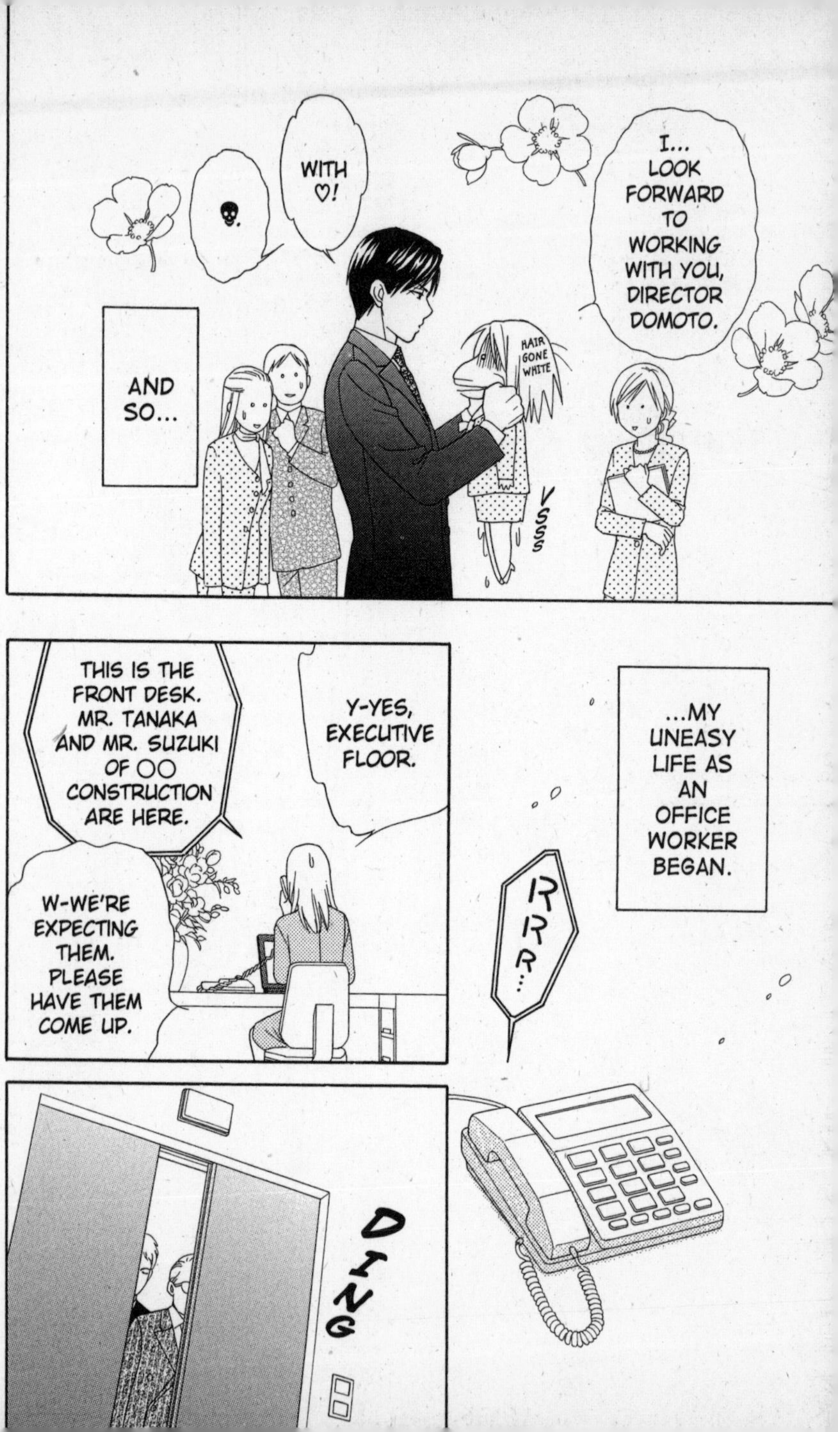
I... LOOK FORWARD TO WORKING WITH YOU, DIRECTOR DOMOTO.
WITH ♡!
☠.
HAIR GONE WHITE
AND SO...
VSSS
...MY UNEASY LIFE AS AN OFFICE WORKER BEGAN.
RRR...
Y-YES, EXECUTIVE FLOOR.
THIS IS THE FRONT DESK. MR. TANAKA AND MR. SUZUKI OF ○○ CONSTRUCTION ARE HERE.
W-WE'RE EXPECTING THEM. PLEASE HAVE THEM COME UP.
DING

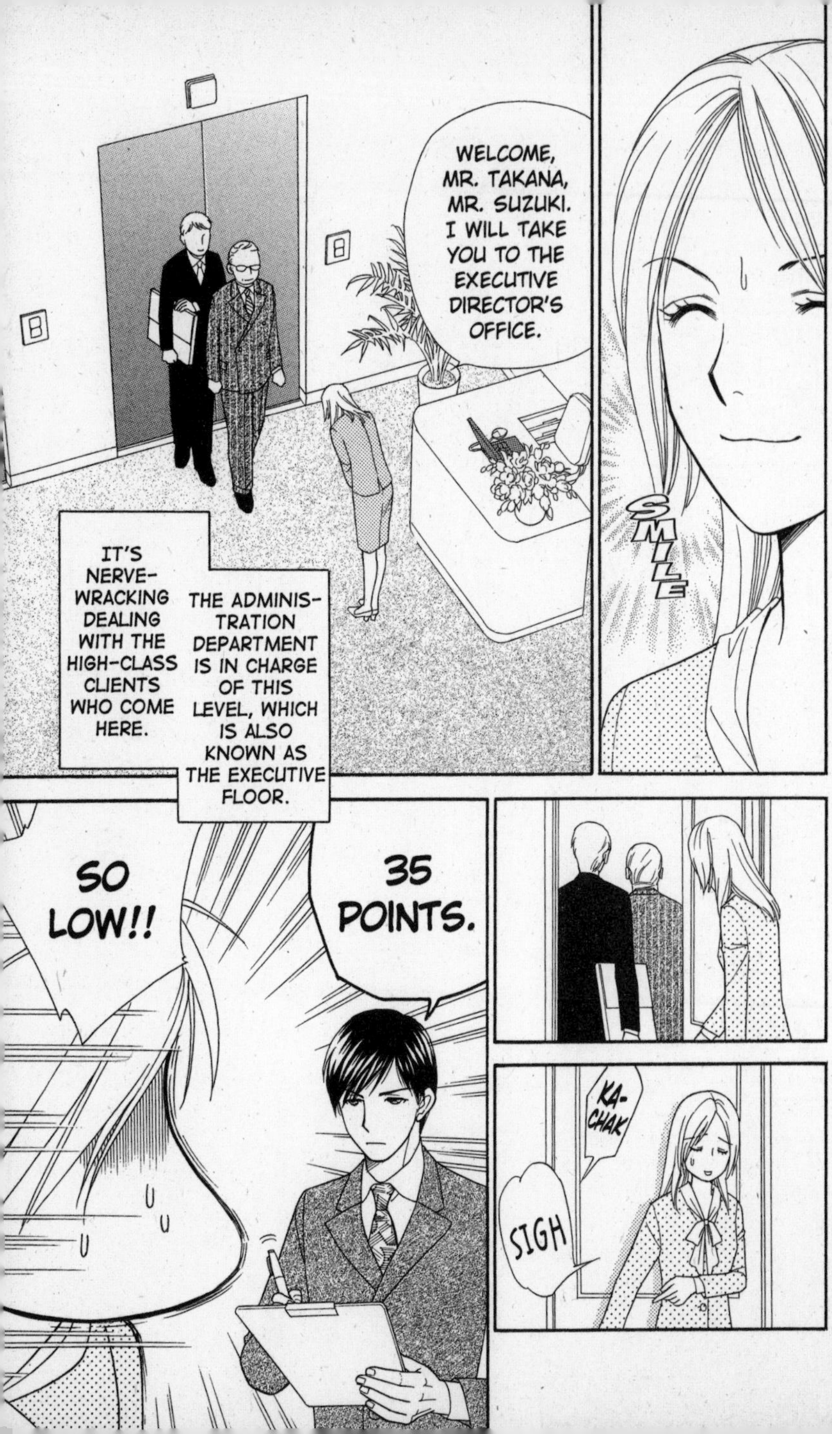
SMILE
WELCOME, MR. TAKANA, MR. SUZUKI. I WILL TAKE YOU TO THE EXECUTIVE DIRECTOR'S OFFICE.
THE ADMINIS-TRATION DEPARTMENT IS IN CHARGE OF THIS LEVEL, WHICH IS ALSO KNOWN AS THE EXECUTIVE FLOOR.
IT'S NERVE-WRACKING DEALING WITH THE HIGH-CLASS CLIENTS WHO COME HERE.
KA-CHAK
SIGH
35 POINTS.
SO LOW!!

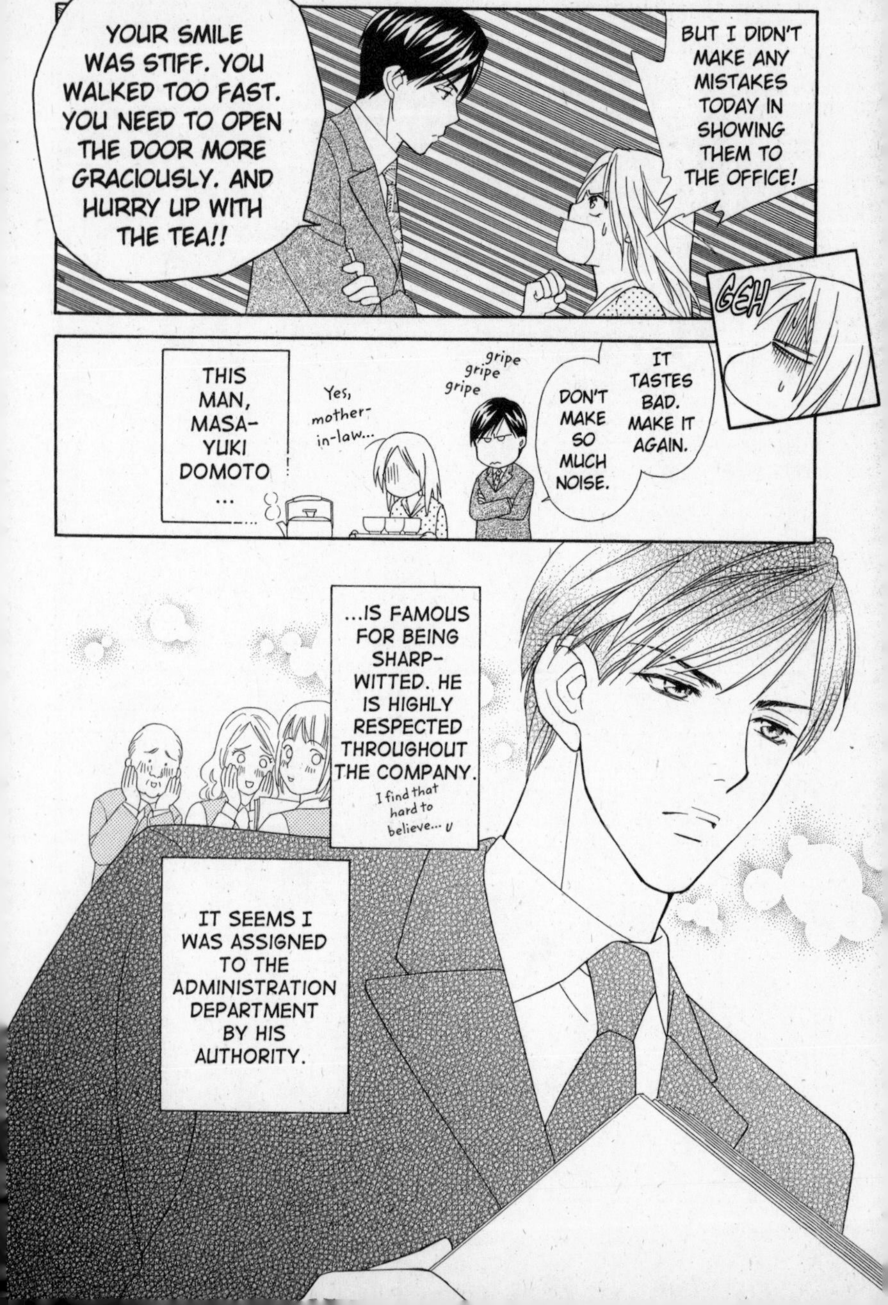
BUT I DIDN'T MAKE ANY MISTAKES TODAY IN SHOWING THEM TO THE OFFICE!
YOUR SMILE WAS STIFF. YOU WALKED TOO FAST. YOU NEED TO OPEN THE DOOR MORE GRACIOUSLY. AND HURRY UP WITH THE TEA!!
GEH
IT TASTES BAD. MAKE IT AGAIN.
DON'T MAKE SO MUCH NOISE.
gripe gripe gripe
Yes, mother-in-law...
THIS MAN, MASA-YUKI DOMOTO ...
...IS FAMOUS FOR BEING SHARP-WITTED. HE IS HIGHLY RESPECTED THROUGHOUT THE COMPANY.
I find that hard to believe...
IT SEEMS I WAS ASSIGNED TO THE ADMINISTRATION DEPARTMENT BY HIS AUTHORITY.

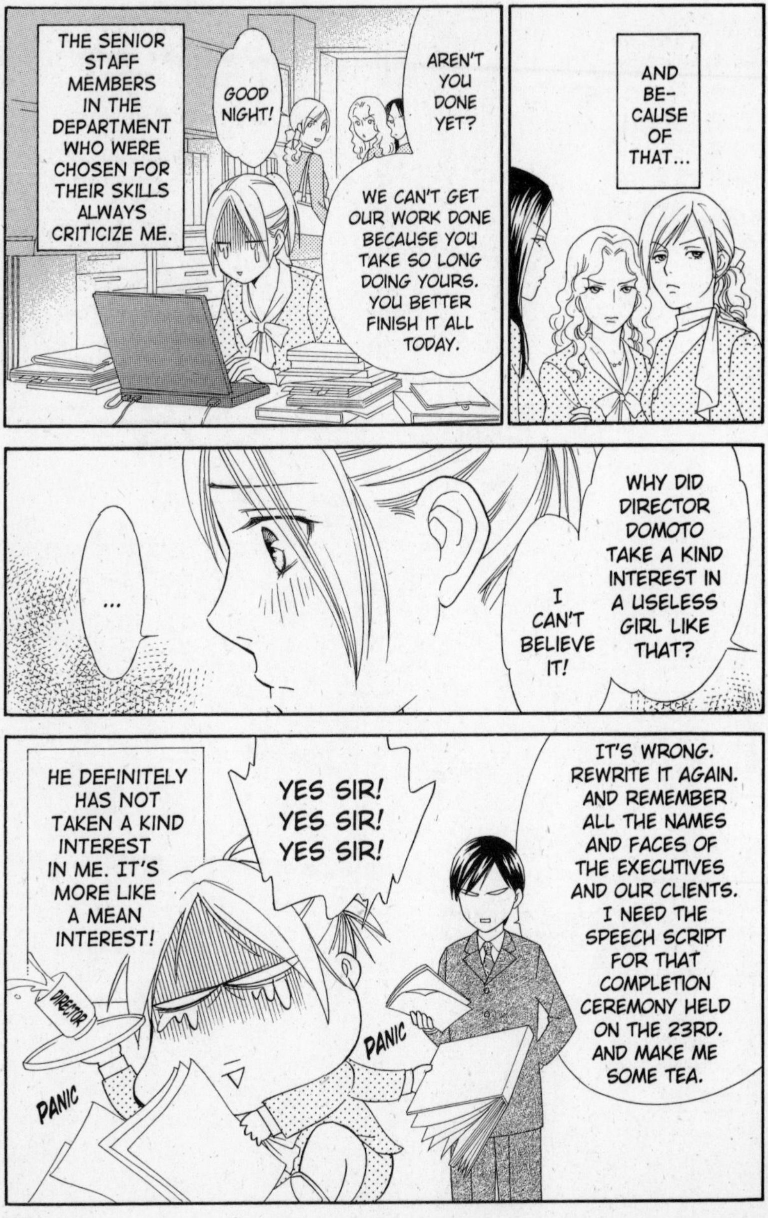
AND BE- CAUSE OF THAT...
AREN'T YOU DONE YET?
WE CAN'T GET OUR WORK DONE BECAUSE YOU TAKE SO LONG DOING YOURS. YOU BETTER FINISH IT ALL TODAY.
GOOD NIGHT!
THE SENIOR STAFF MEMBERS IN THE DEPARTMENT WHO WERE CHOSEN FOR THEIR SKILLS ALWAYS CRITICIZE ME.
WHY DID DIRECTOR DOMOTO TAKE A KIND INTEREST IN A USELESS GIRL LIKE THAT?
I CAN'T BELIEVE IT!
...
IT'S WRONG. REWRITE IT AGAIN. AND REMEMBER ALL THE NAMES AND FACES OF THE EXECUTIVES AND OUR CLIENTS. I NEED THE SPEECH SCRIPT FOR THAT COMPLETION CEREMONY HELD ON THE 23RD. AND MAKE ME SOME TEA.
PANIC
YES SIR! YES SIR! YES SIR!
DIRECTOR
PANIC
HE DEFINITELY HAS NOT TAKEN A KIND INTEREST IN ME. IT'S MORE LIKE A MEAN INTEREST!

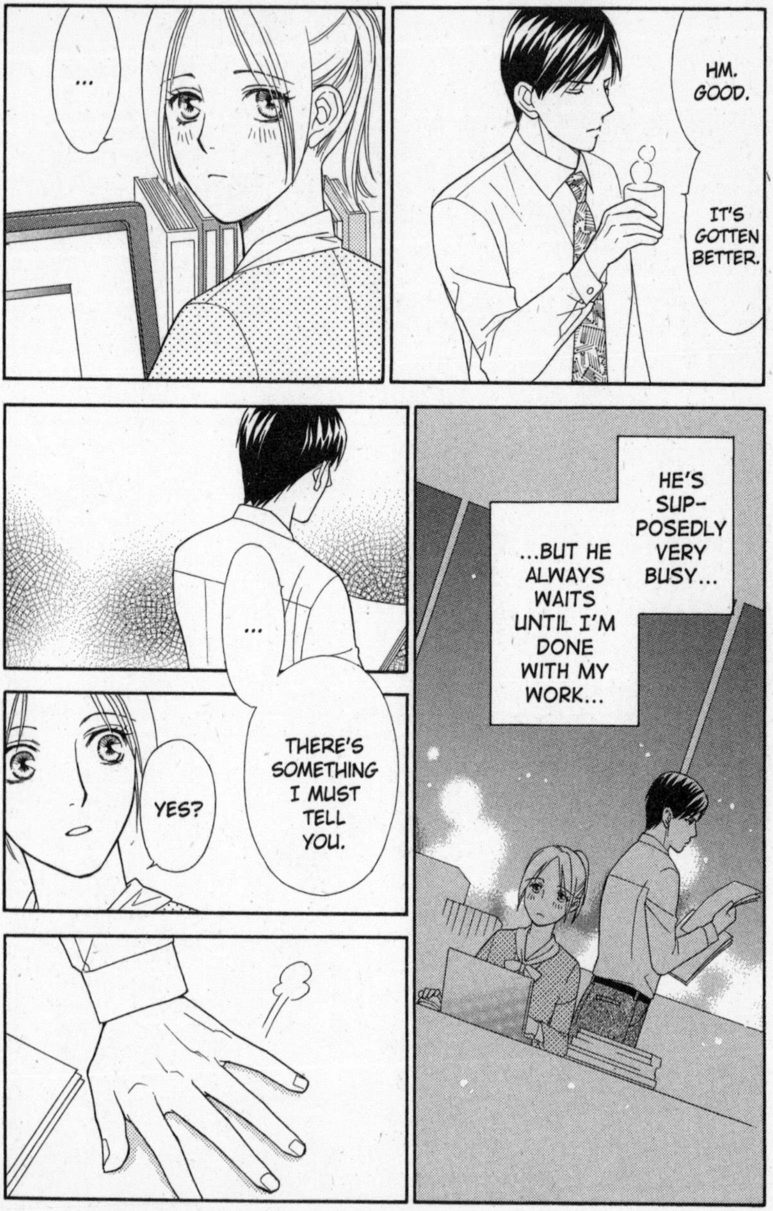
HM. GOOD.
IT'S GOTTEN BETTER.
...
HE'S SUP-POSEDLY VERY BUSY...
...BUT HE ALWAYS WAITS UNTIL I'M DONE WITH MY WORK...
...
THERE'S SOMETHING I MUST TELL YOU.
YES?

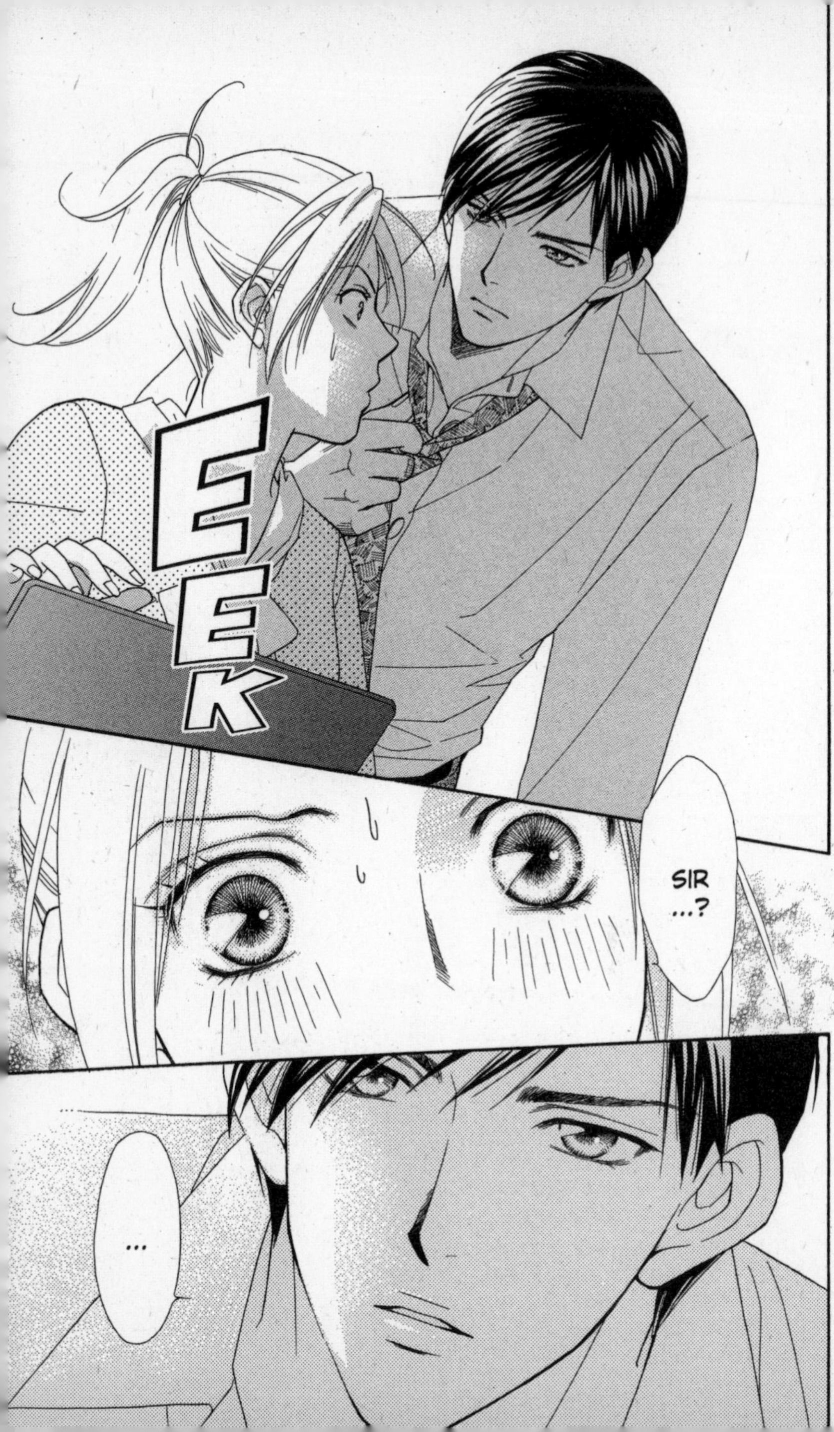
EEEK
SIR ...?
...

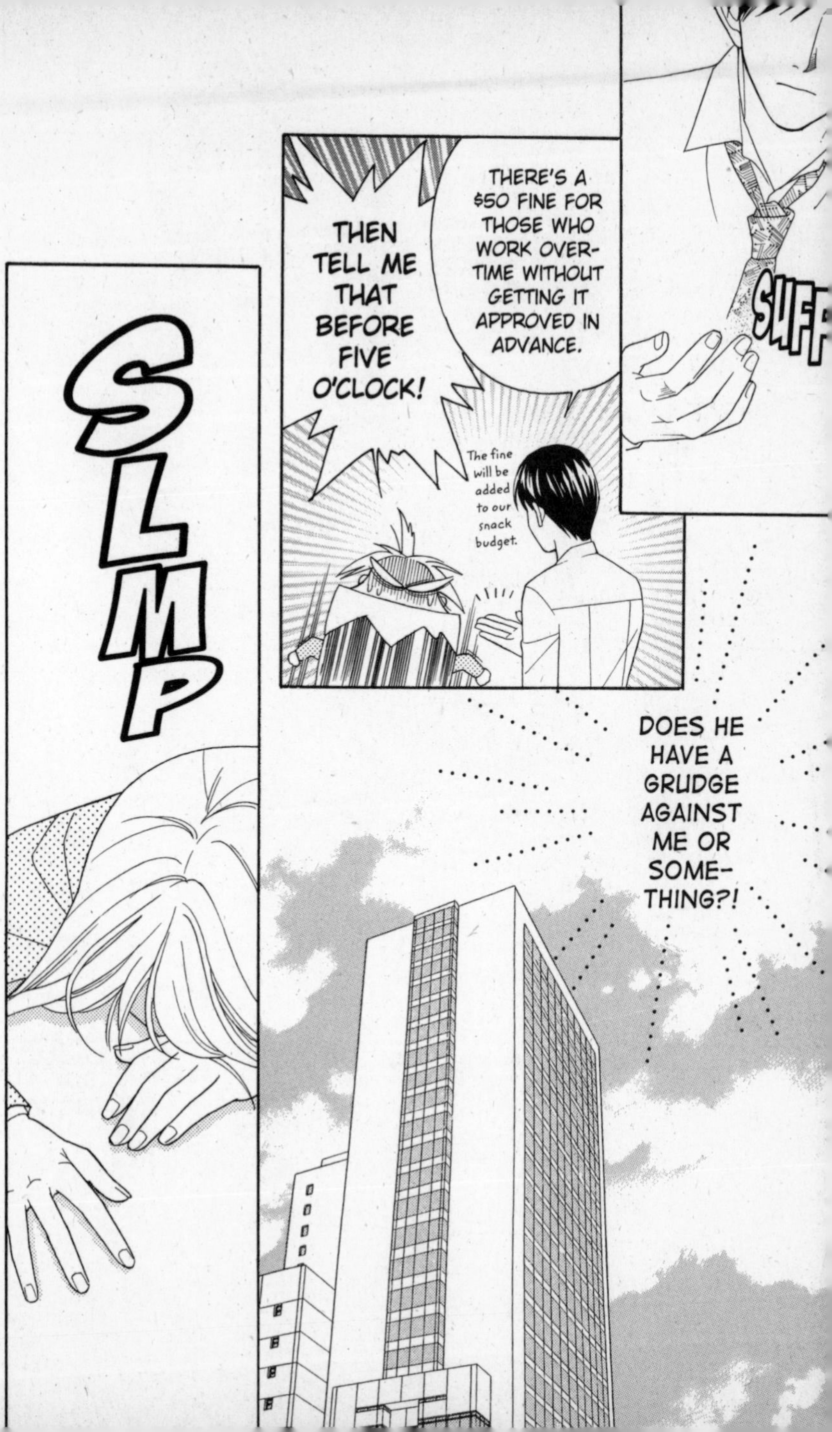
SUFF
THERE'S A $50 FINE FOR THOSE WHO WORK OVER-TIME WITHOUT GETTING IT APPROVED IN ADVANCE.
THEN TELL ME THAT BEFORE FIVE O'CLOCK!
The fine will be added to our snack budget.
DOES HE HAVE A GRUDGE AGAINST ME OR SOME-THING?!
SLMP

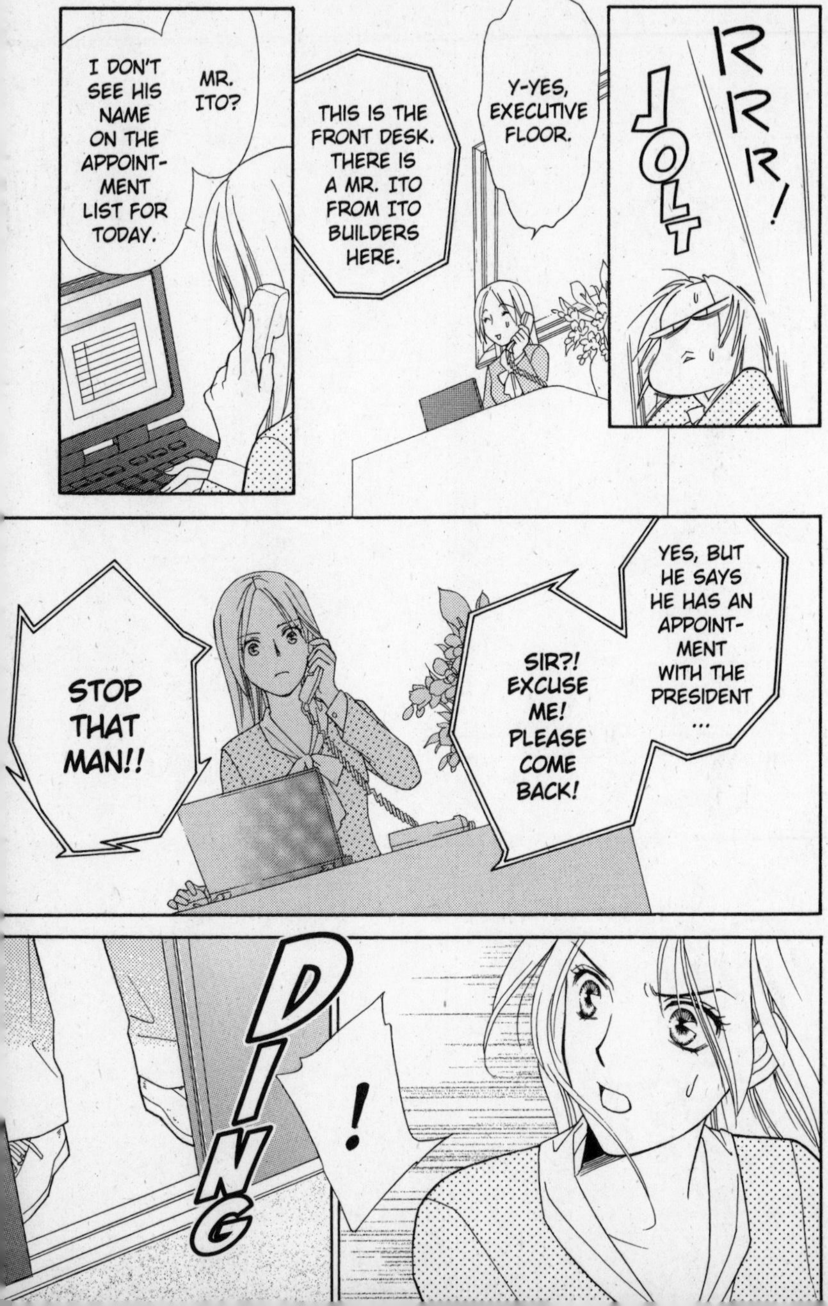
RRR!
JOLT
Y-YES, EXECUTIVE FLOOR.
THIS IS THE FRONT DESK. THERE IS A MR. ITO FROM ITO BUILDERS HERE.
MR. ITO?
I DON'T SEE HIS NAME ON THE APPOINT-MENT LIST FOR TODAY.
YES, BUT HE SAYS HE HAS AN APPOINT-MENT WITH THE PRESIDENT ...
SIR?! EXCUSE ME! PLEASE COME BACK!
STOP THAT MAN!!
DING
!

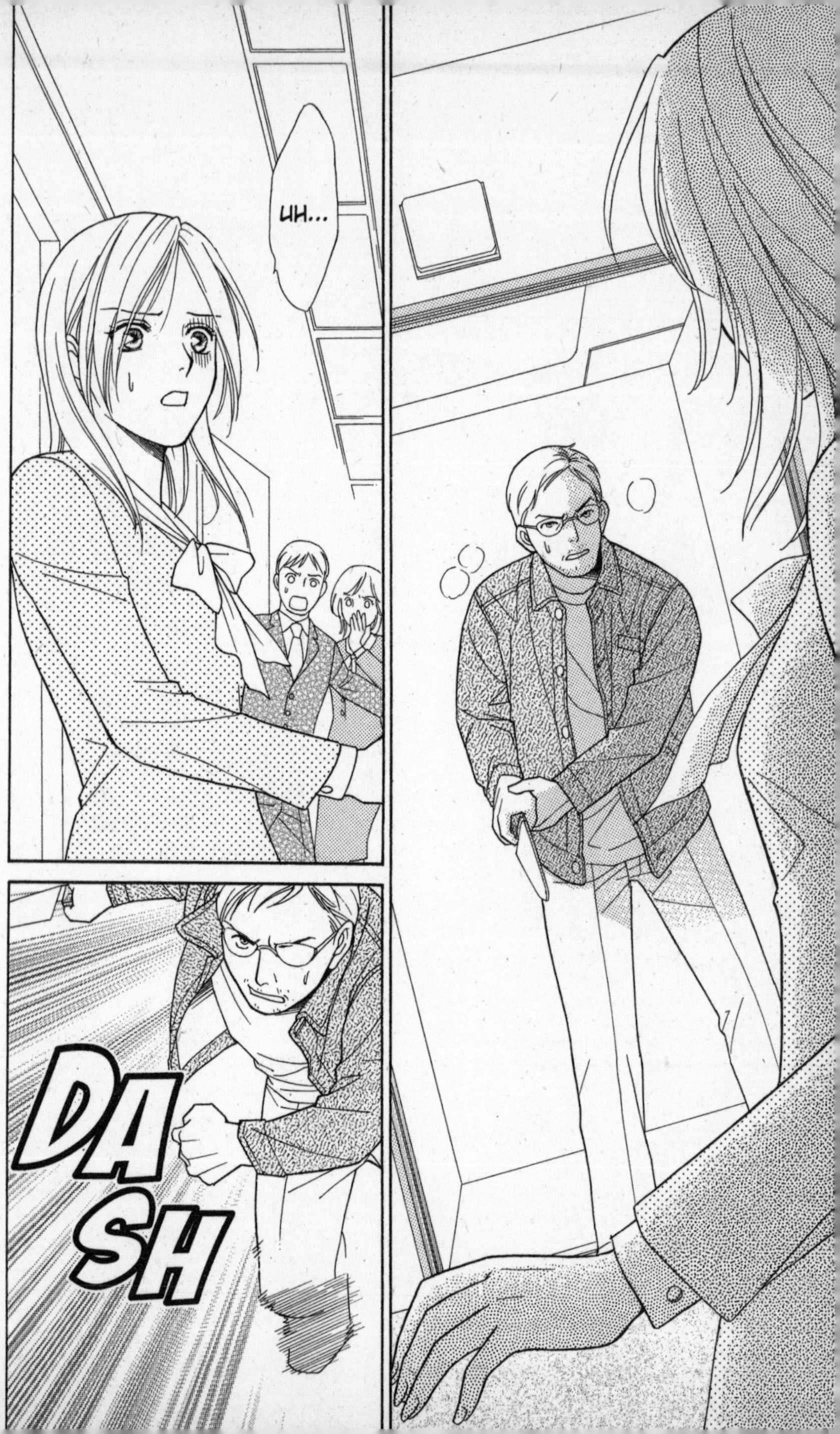
UH...
DASH

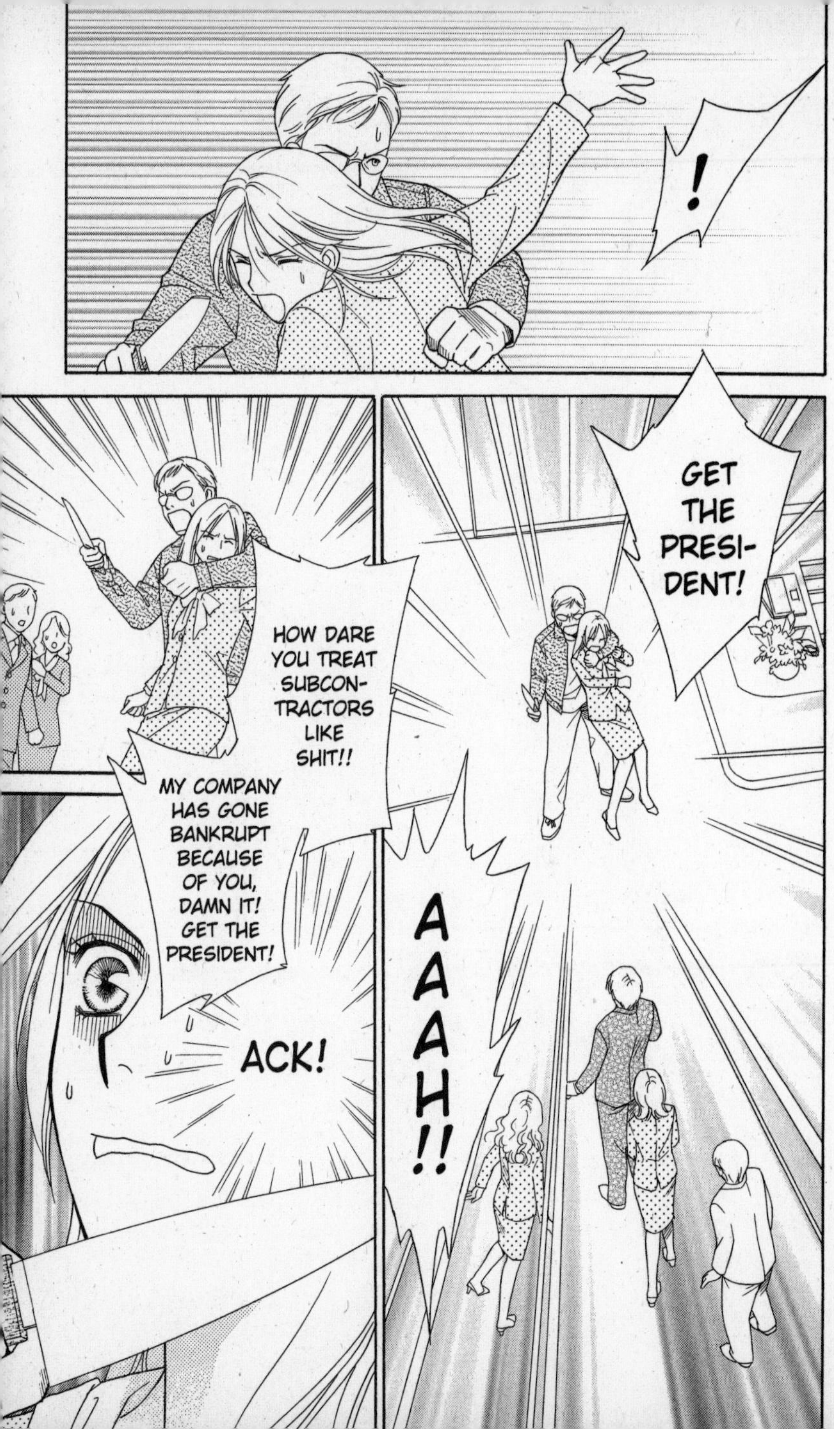
!
GET THE PRESI-DENT!
AAAH!!
HOW DARE YOU TREAT SUBCON-TRACTORS LIKE SHIT!!
MY COMPANY HAS GONE BANKRUPT BECAUSE OF YOU, DAMN IT! GET THE PRESIDENT!
ACK!

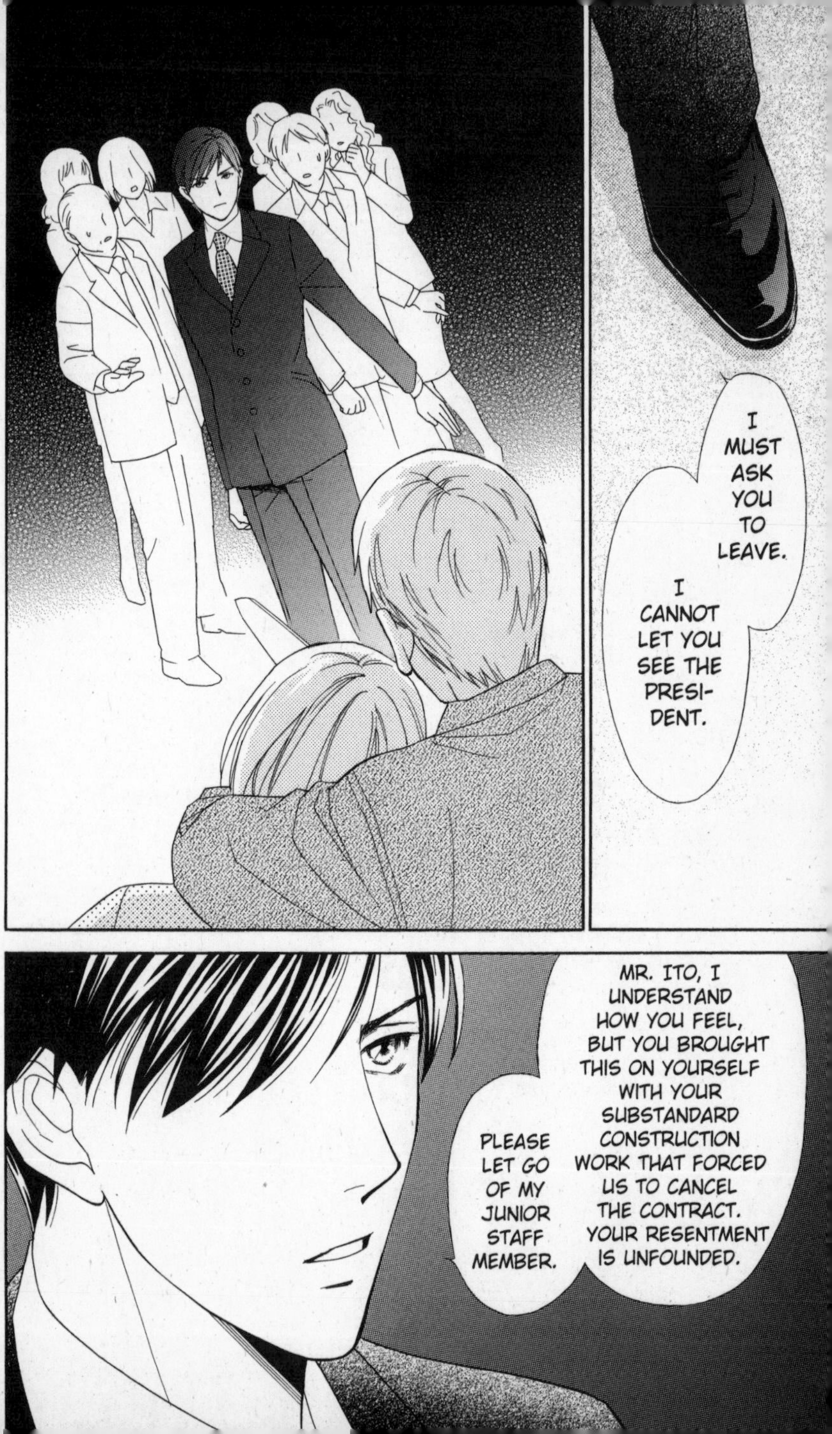
I MUST ASK YOU TO LEAVE.
I CANNOT LET YOU SEE THE PRESIDENT.
MR. ITO, I UNDERSTAND HOW YOU FEEL, BUT YOU BROUGHT THIS ON YOURSELF WITH YOUR SUBSTANDARD CONSTRUCTION WORK THAT FORCED US TO CANCEL THE CONTRACT. YOUR RESENTMENT IS UNFOUNDED.
PLEASE LET GO OF MY JUNIOR STAFF MEMBER.

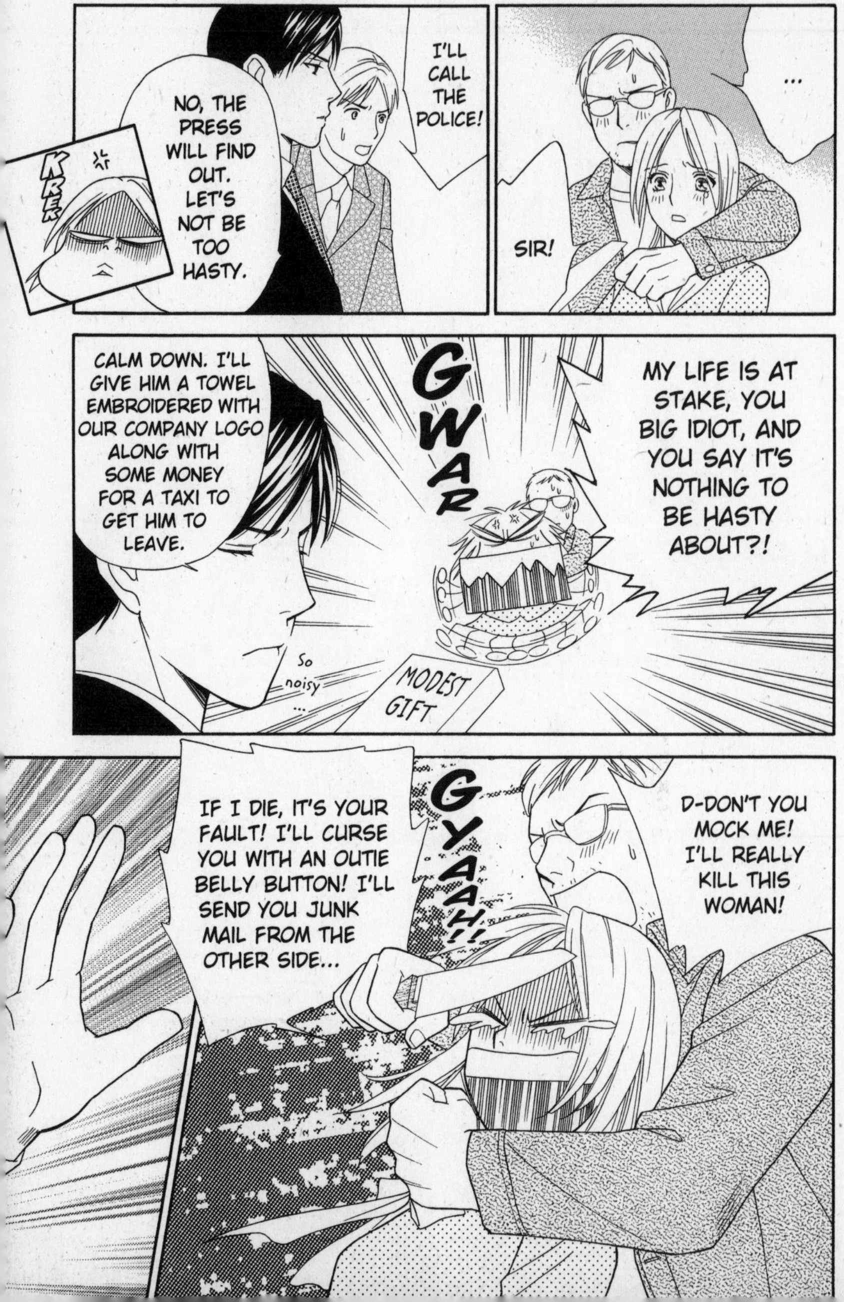
...
SIR!
I'LL CALL THE POLICE!
NO, THE PRESS WILL FIND OUT. LET'S NOT BE TOO HASTY.
KREK
MY LIFE IS AT STAKE, YOU BIG IDIOT, AND YOU SAY IT'S NOTHING TO BE HASTY ABOUT?!
GWAR
CALM DOWN. I'LL GIVE HIM A TOWEL EMBROIDERED WITH OUR COMPANY LOGO ALONG WITH SOME MONEY FOR A TAXI TO GET HIM TO LEAVE.
So noisy...
MODEST GIFT
D-DON'T YOU MOCK ME! I'LL REALLY KILL THIS WOMAN!
GYAAH!!
IF I DIE, IT'S YOUR FAULT! I'LL CURSE YOU WITH AN OUTIE BELLY BUTTON! I'LL SEND YOU JUNK MAIL FROM THE OTHER SIDE...

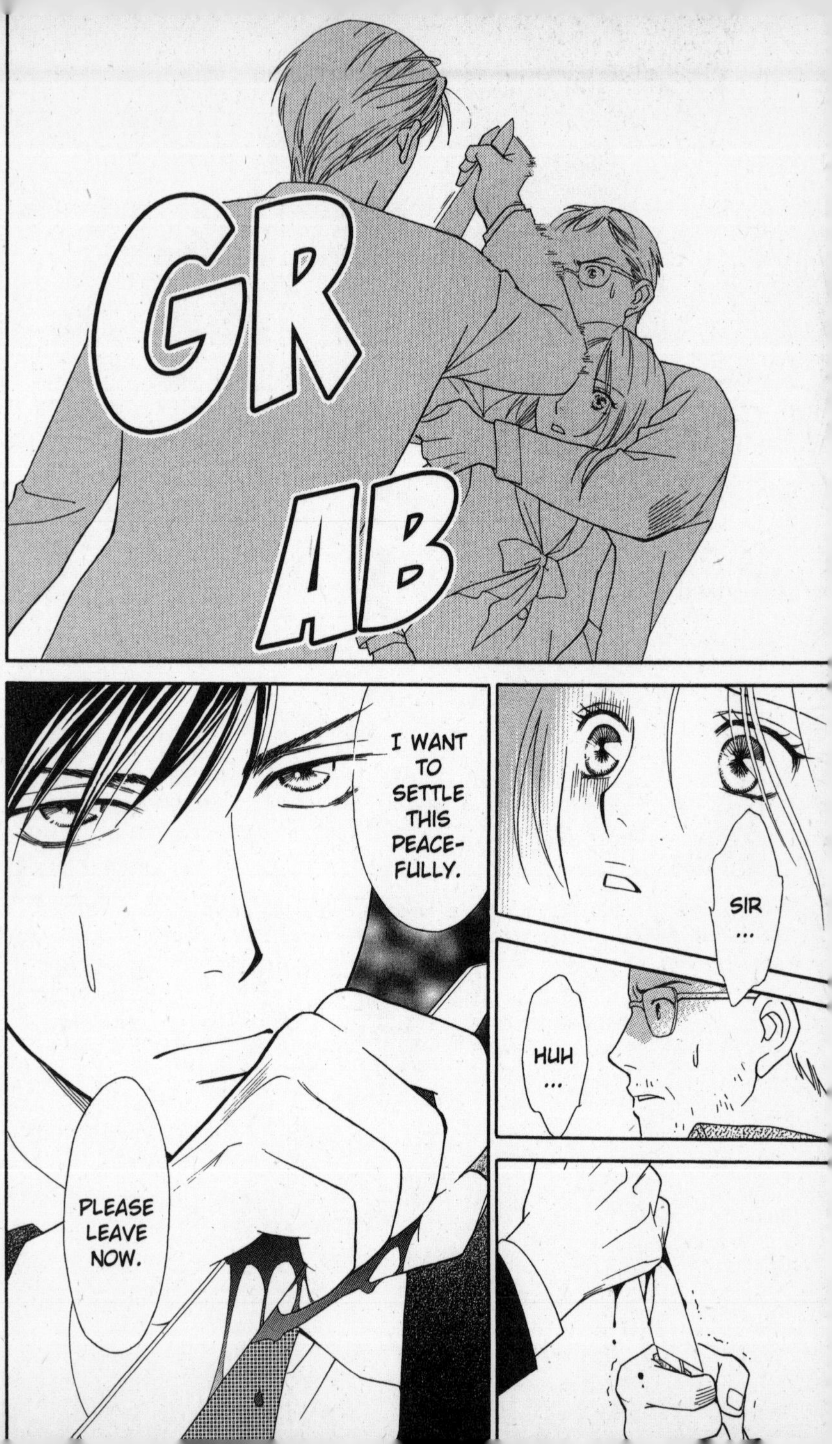
GRAB
SIR ...
HUH ...
I WANT TO SETTLE THIS PEACE-FULLY.
PLEASE LEAVE NOW.

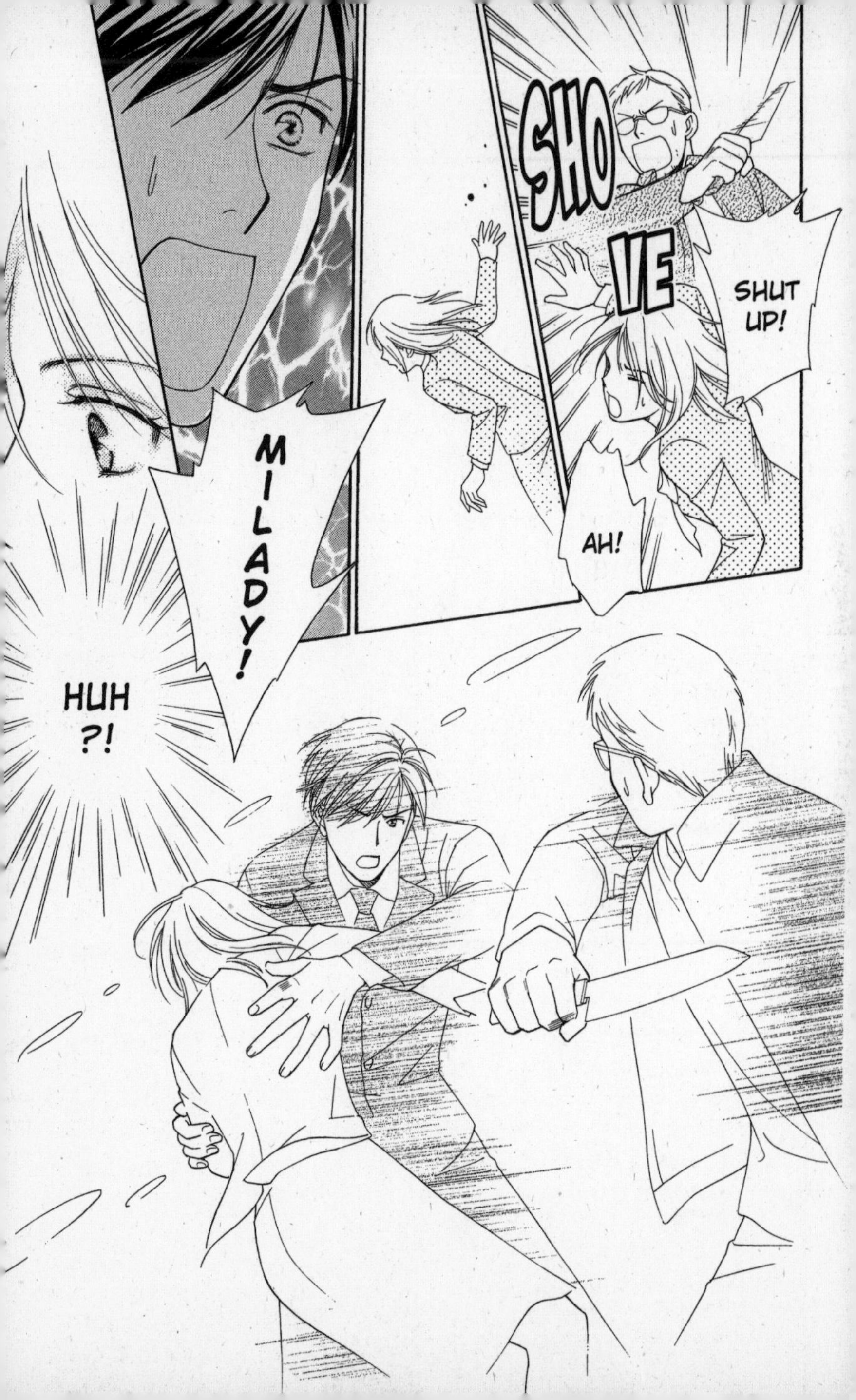
SHUT UP!
SHOVE
AH!
MILLADY!
HUH?!

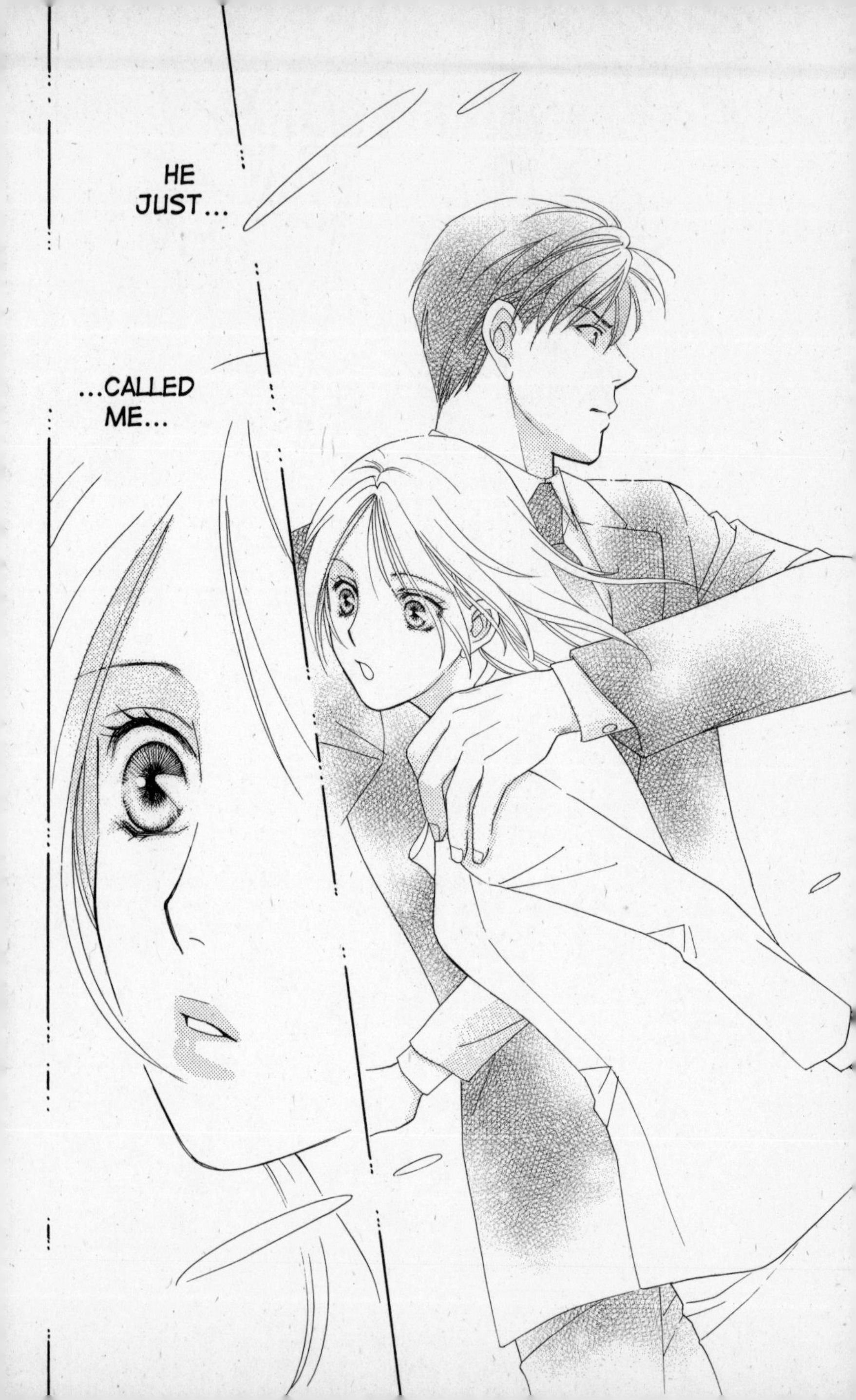
HE JUST...
...CALLED ME...

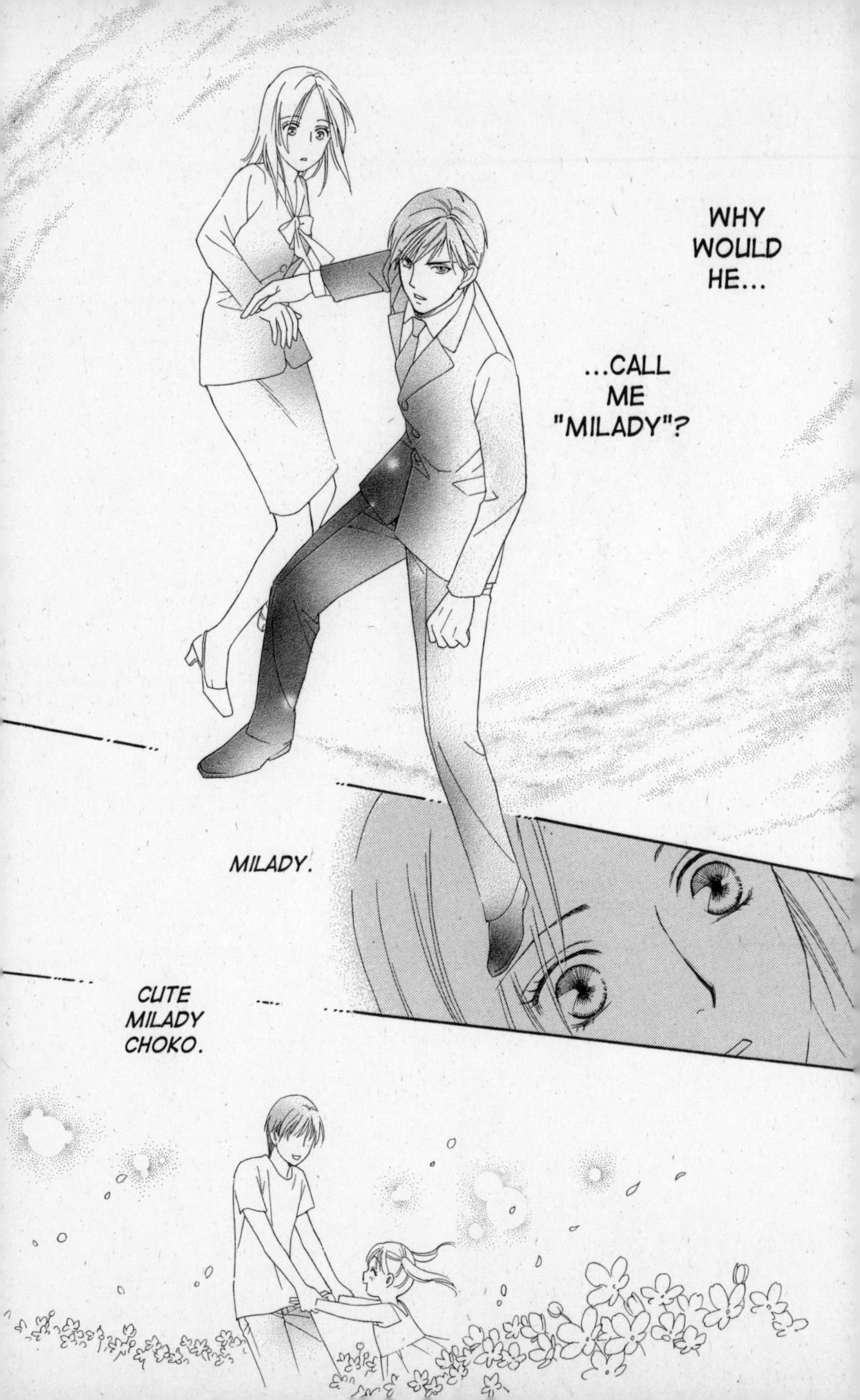
WHY WOULD HE...
...CALL ME "MILADY"?
MILADY.
CUTE MILADY CHOKO.

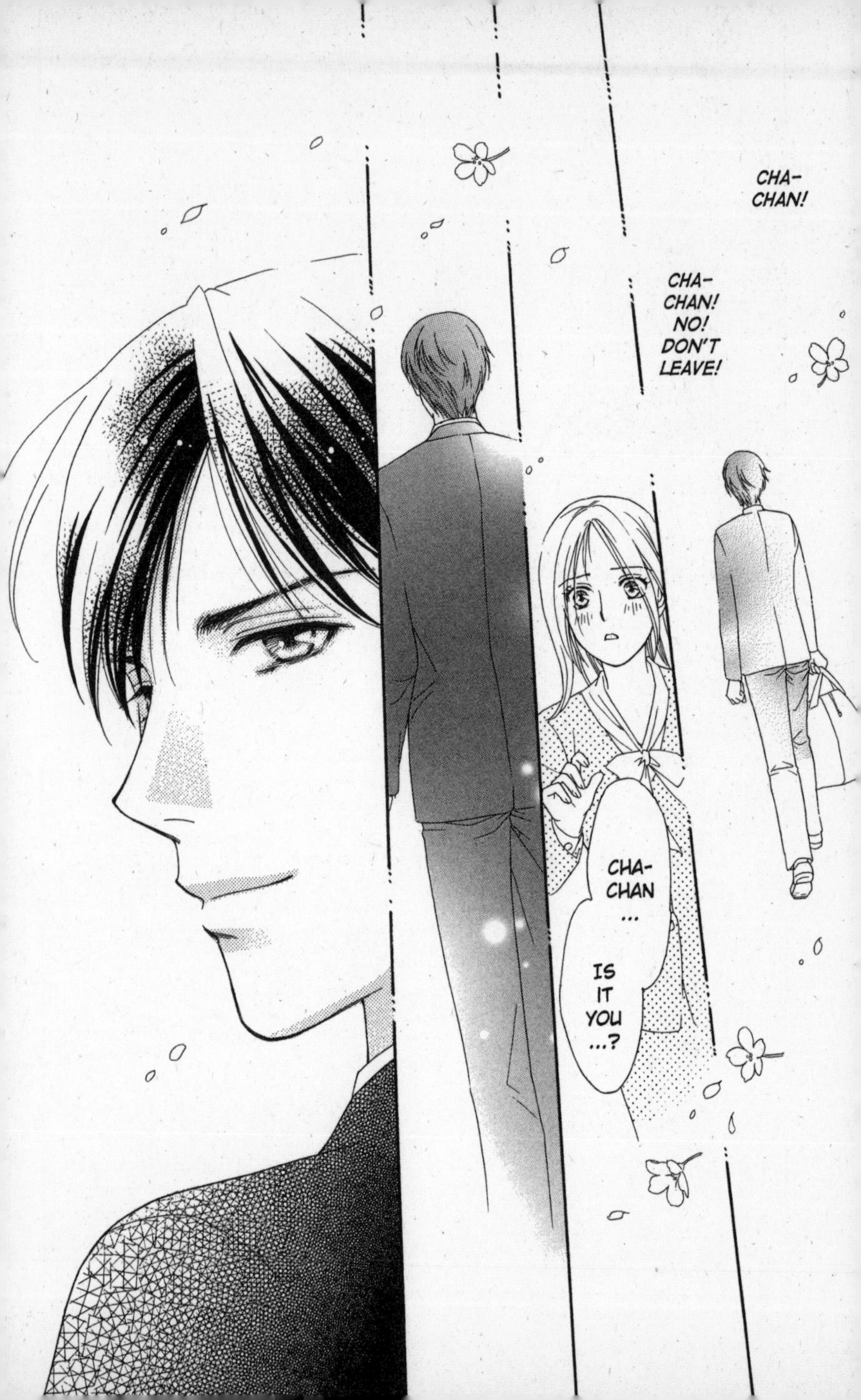
CHA-CHAN!
CHA-CHAN! NO! DON'T LEAVE!
CHA-CHAN... IS IT YOU...?

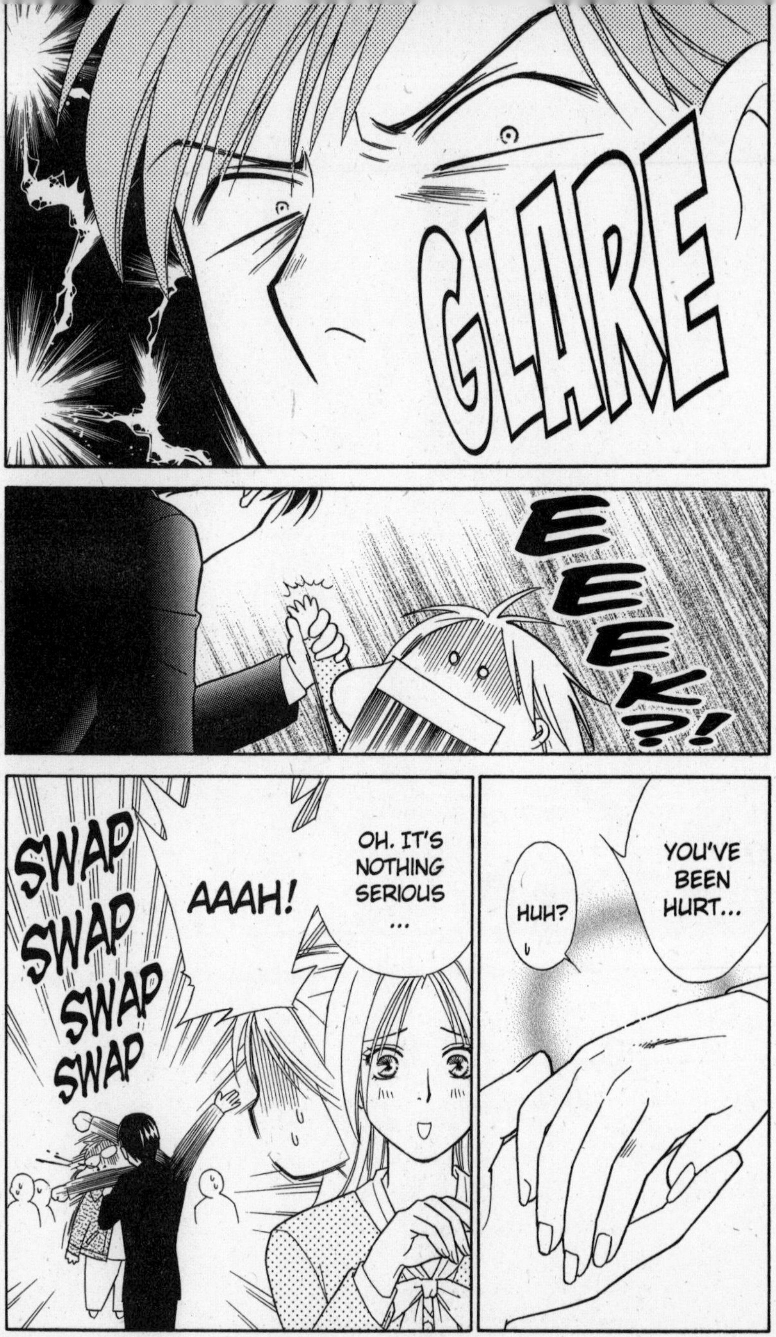
GLARE
EEEEK?!
YOU'VE BEEN HURT...
HUH?
OH. IT'S NOTHING SERIOUS ...
AAAH!
SWAP SWAP SWAP SWAP

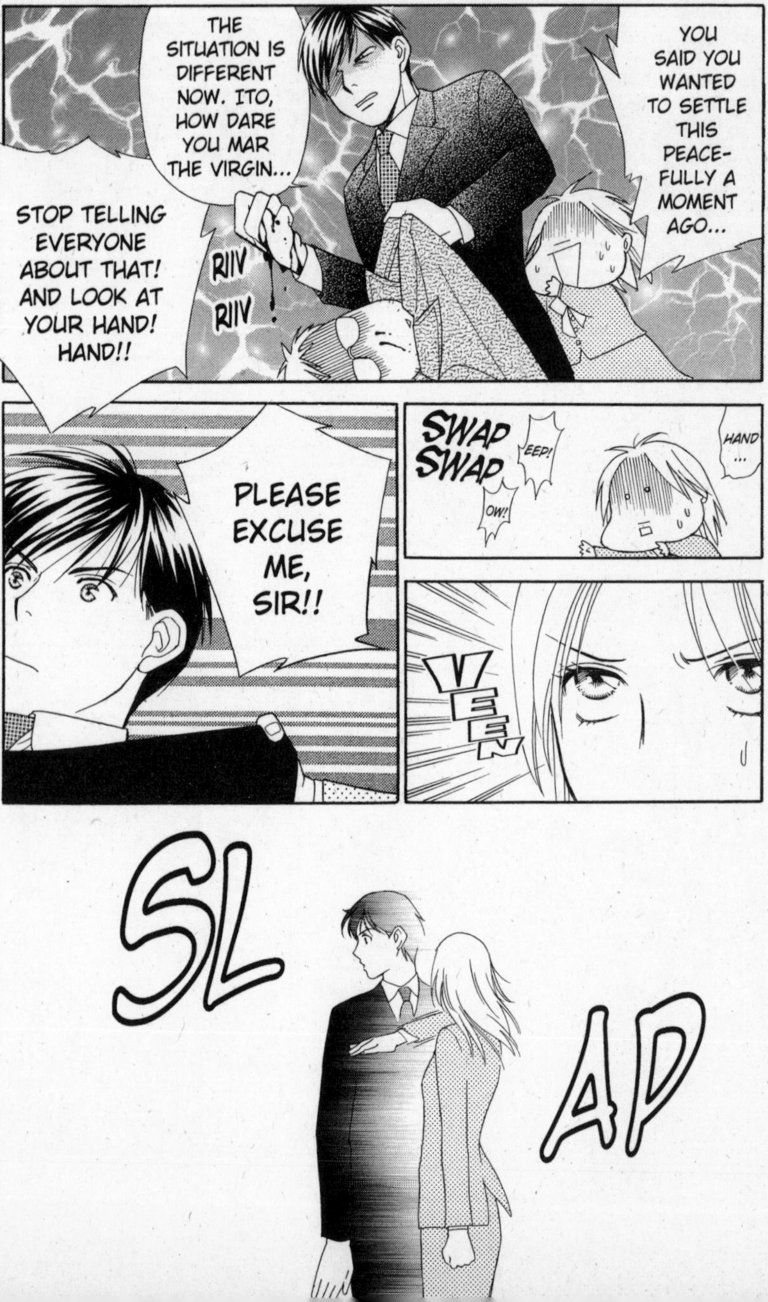
YOU SAID YOU WANTED TO SETTLE THIS PEACE-FULLY A MOMENT AGO...
THE SITUATION IS DIFFERENT NOW. ITO, HOW DARE YOU MAR THE VIRGIN...
RIIV RIIV
STOP TELLING EVERYONE ABOUT THAT! AND LOOK AT YOUR HAND! HAND!!
HAND ...
SWAP SWAP
EEP!
OW!
VEEN
PLEASE EXCUSE ME, SIR!!
SLAP

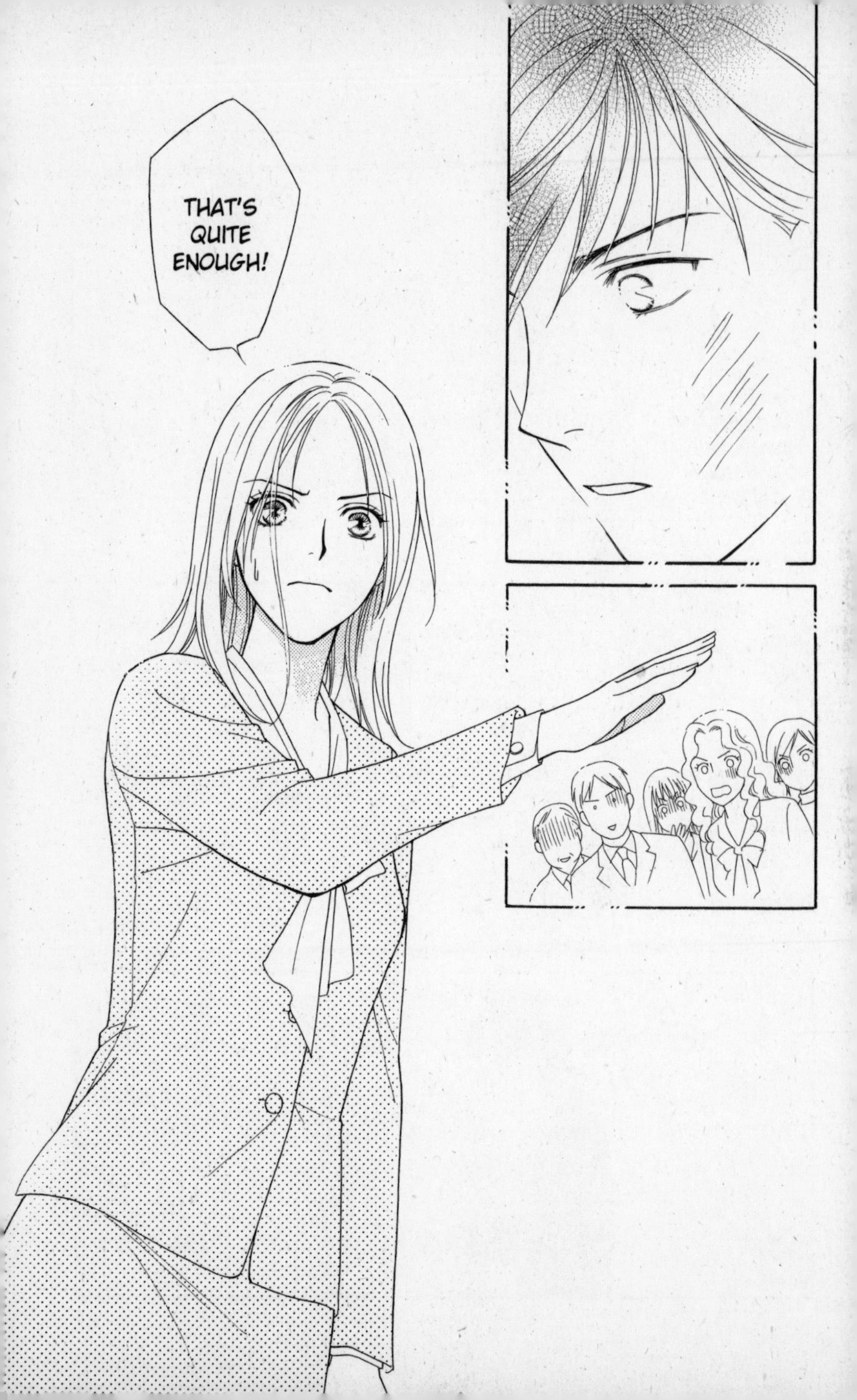
THAT'S QUITE ENOUGH!

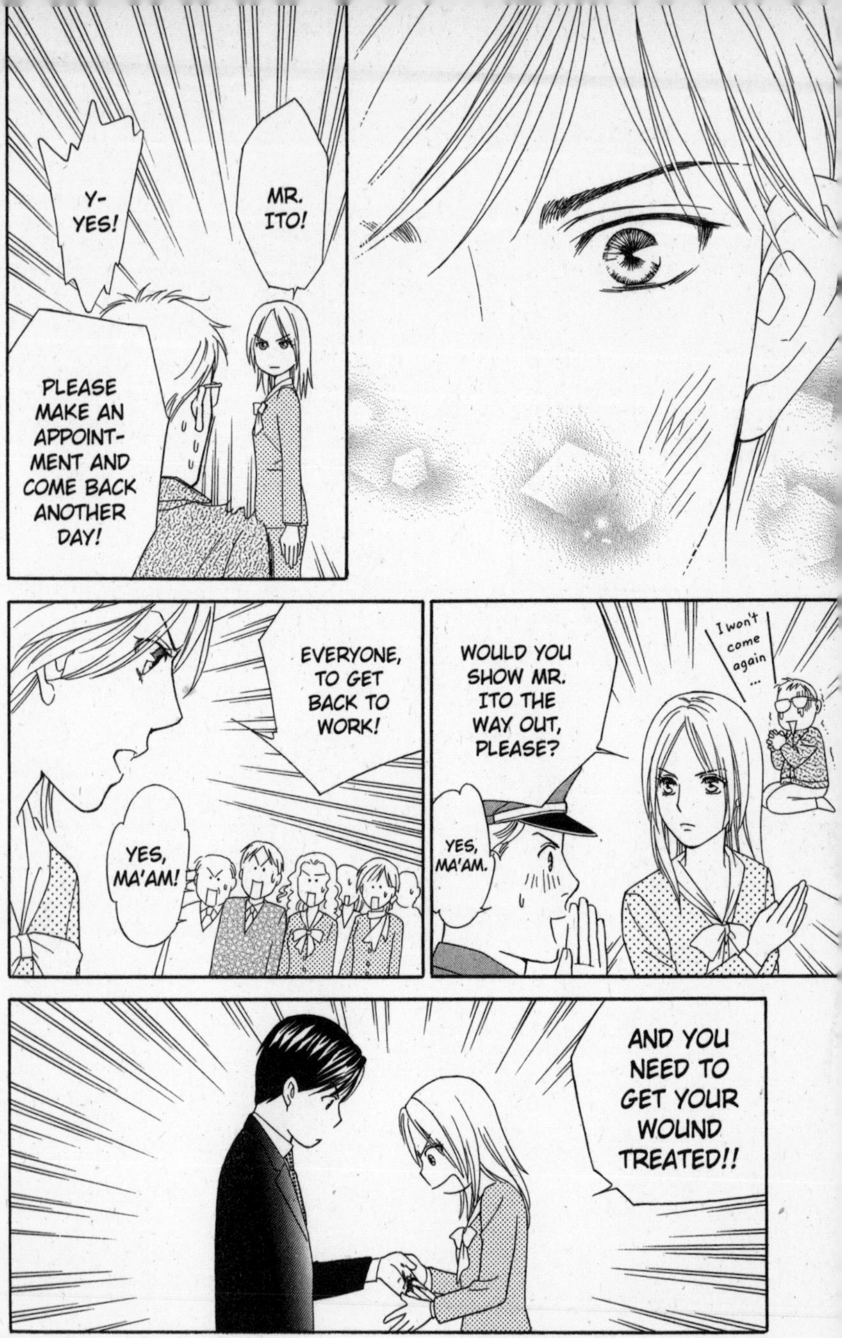
MR. ITO!
Y-YES!
PLEASE MAKE AN APPOINTMENT AND COME BACK ANOTHER DAY!
WOULD YOU SHOW MR. ITO THE WAY OUT, PLEASE?
I won't come again ...
YES, MA'AM.
EVERYONE, TO GET BACK TO WORK!
YES, MA'AM!
AND YOU NEED TO GET YOUR WOUND TREATED!!

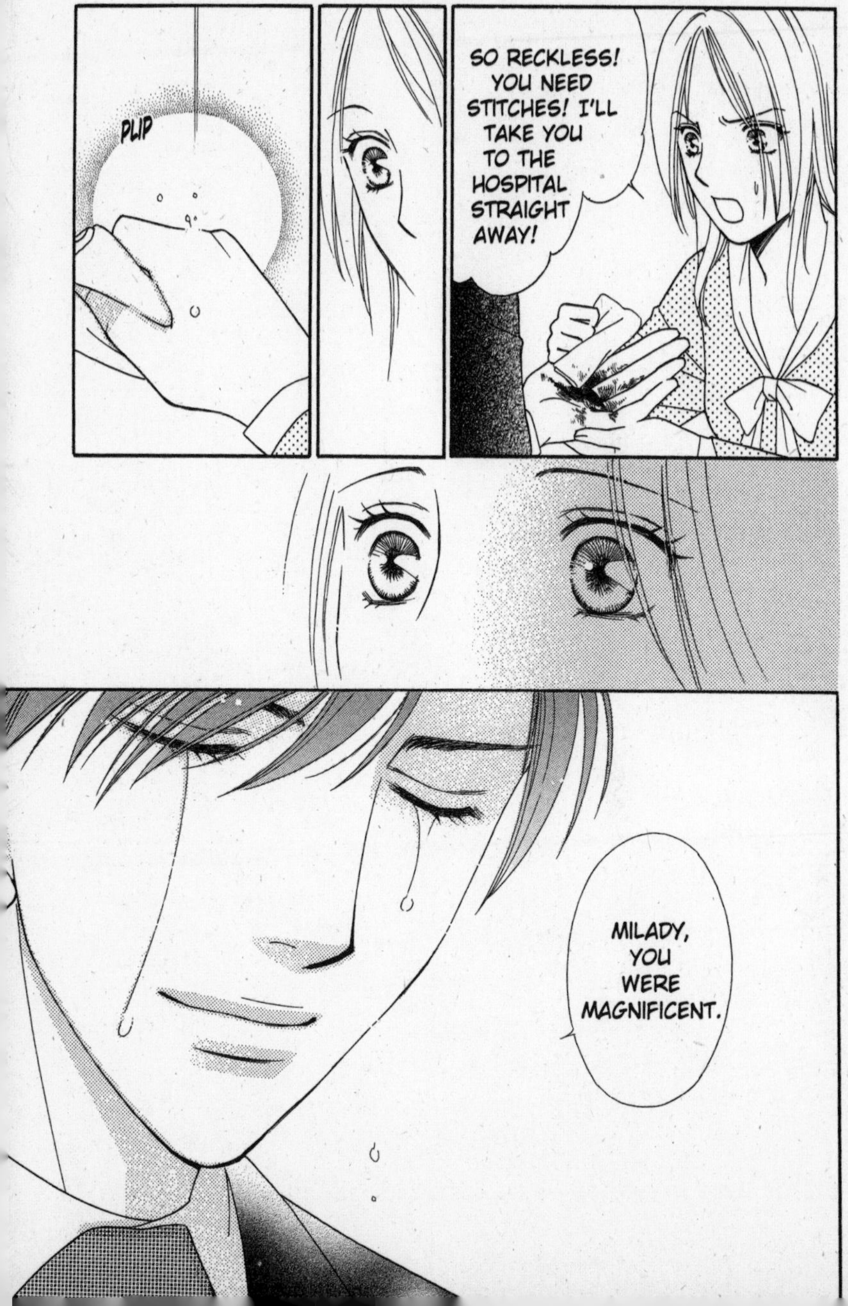
SO RECKLESS! YOU NEED STITCHES! I'LL TAKE YOU TO THE HOSPITAL STRAIGHT AWAY!
PLIP
MILADY, YOU WERE MAGNIFICENT.

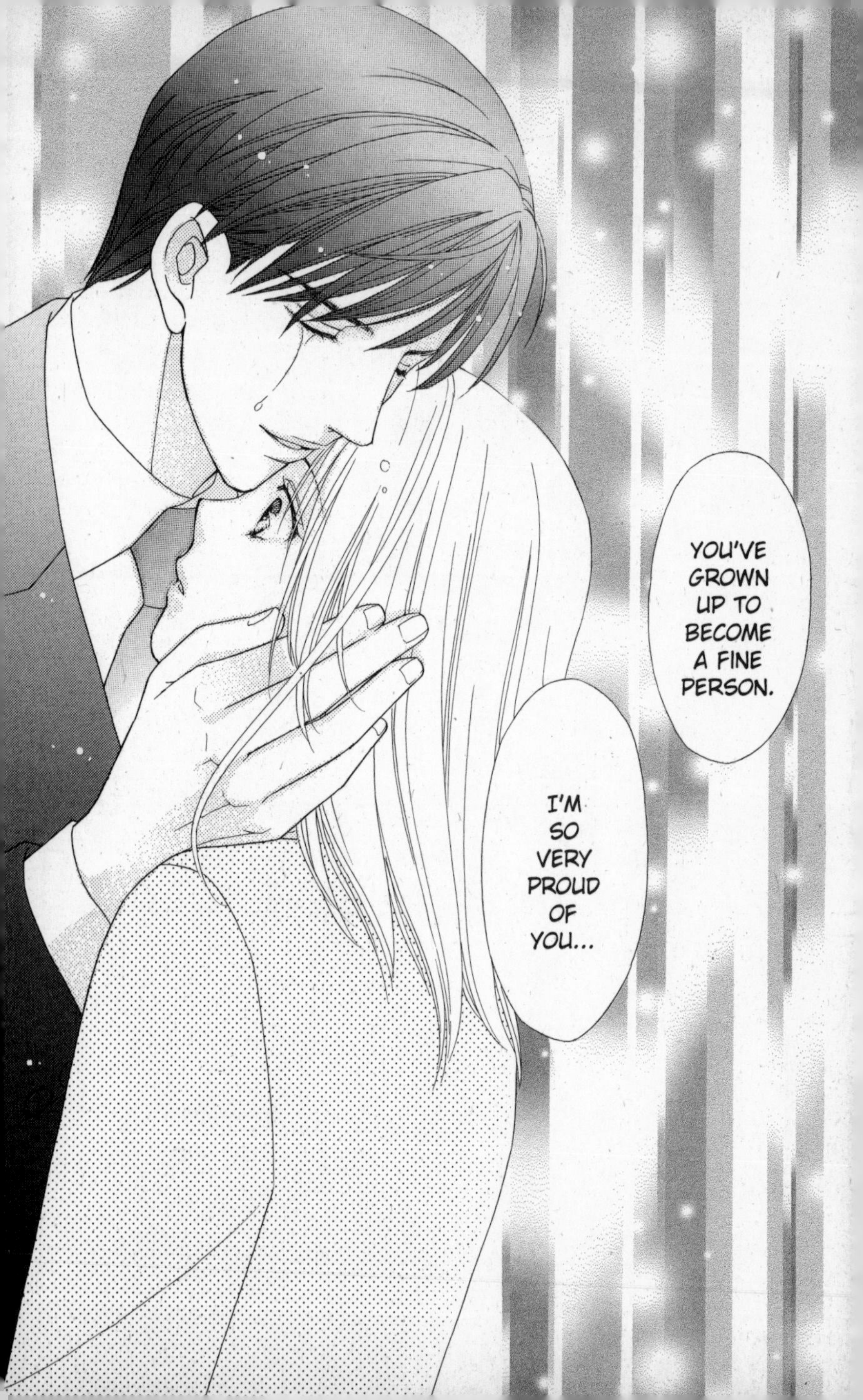
YOU'VE GROWN UP TO BECOME A FINE PERSON.
I'M SO VERY PROUD OF YOU...

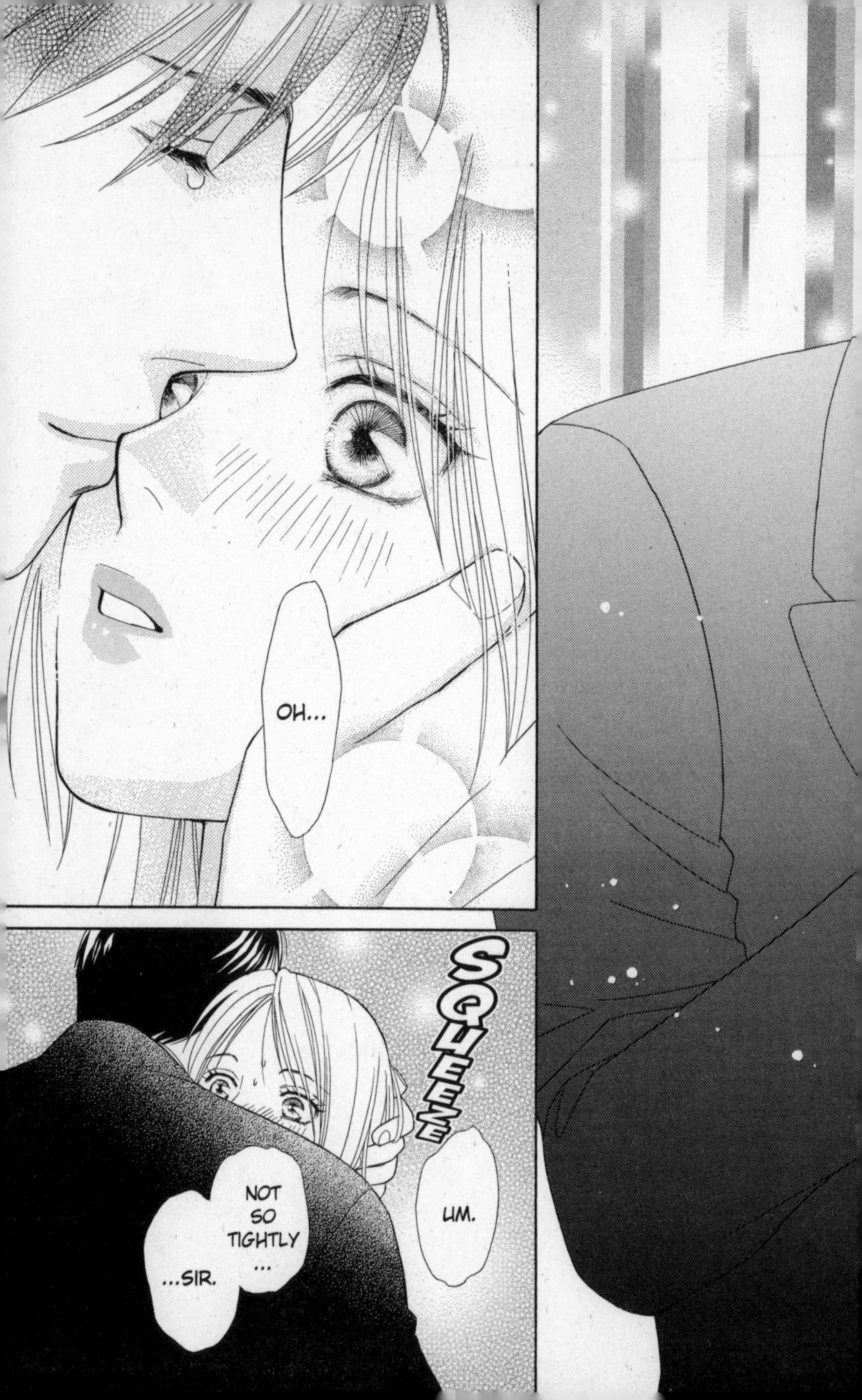
OH...
SQUEEZE
UM.
NOT SO TIGHTLY ...
...SIR.

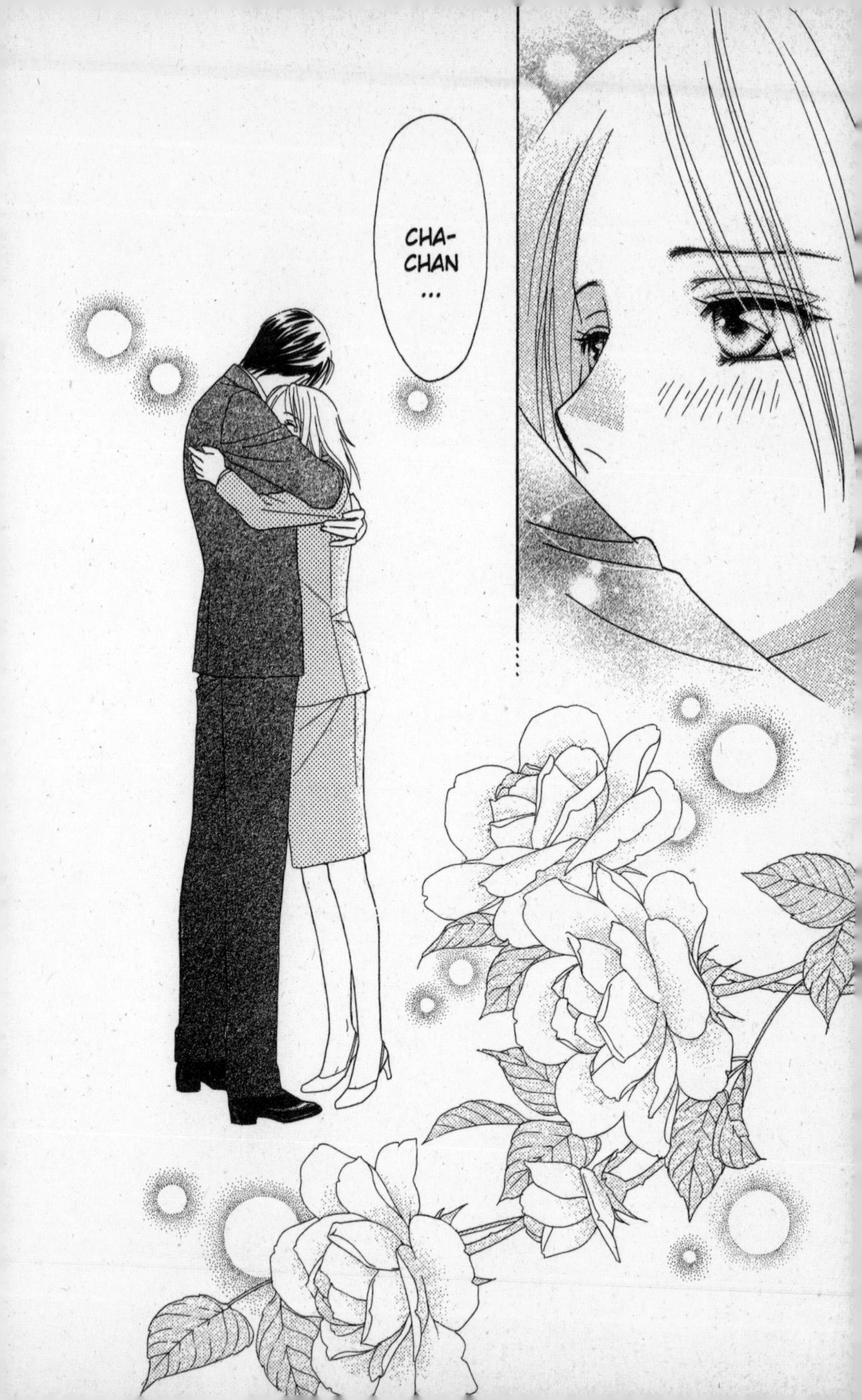
CHA-
CHAN
...

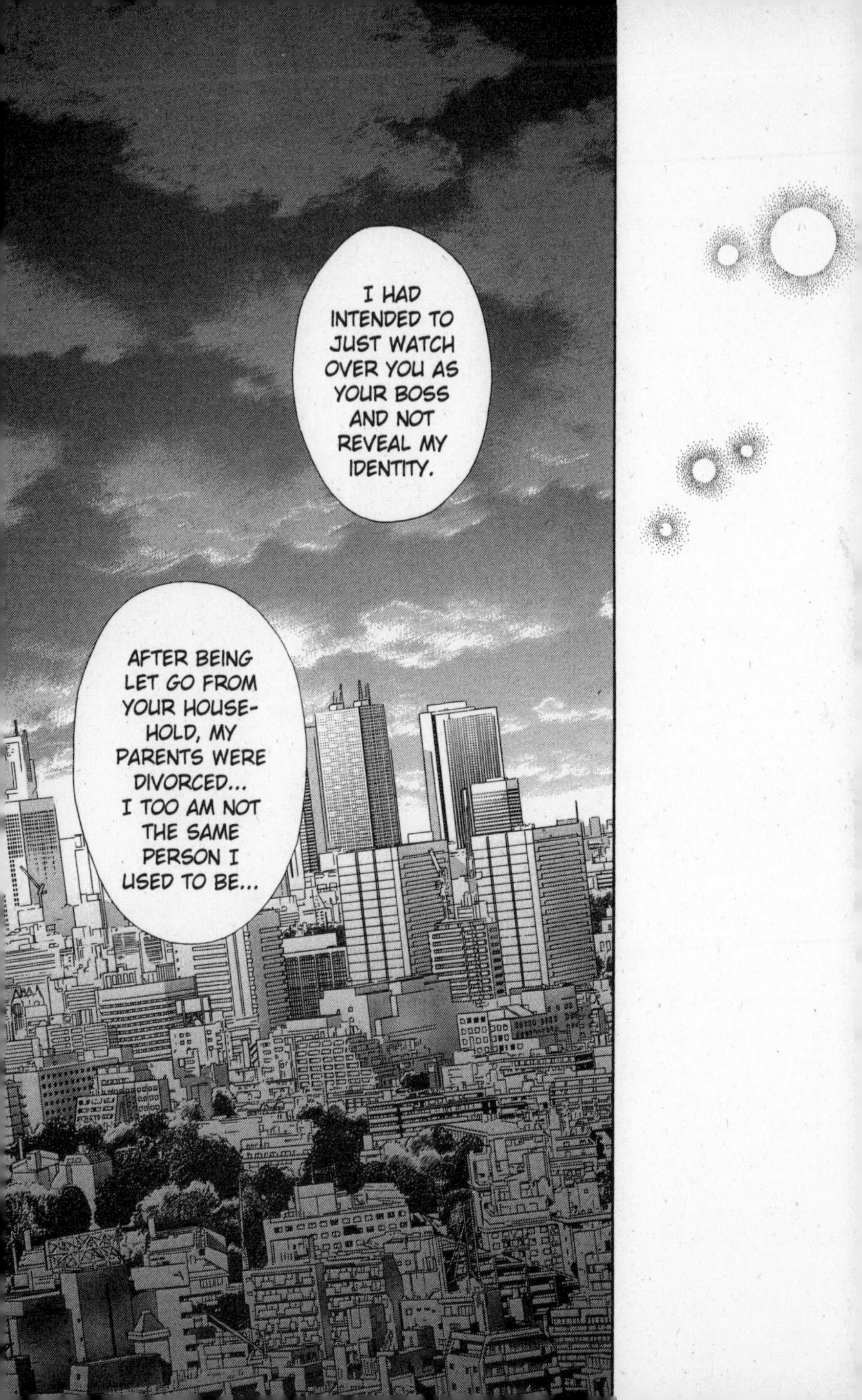
I HAD INTENDED TO JUST WATCH OVER YOU AS YOUR BOSS AND NOT REVEAL MY IDENTITY.
AFTER BEING LET GO FROM YOUR HOUSE-HOLD, MY PARENTS WERE DIVORCED... I TOO AM NOT THE SAME PERSON I USED TO BE...

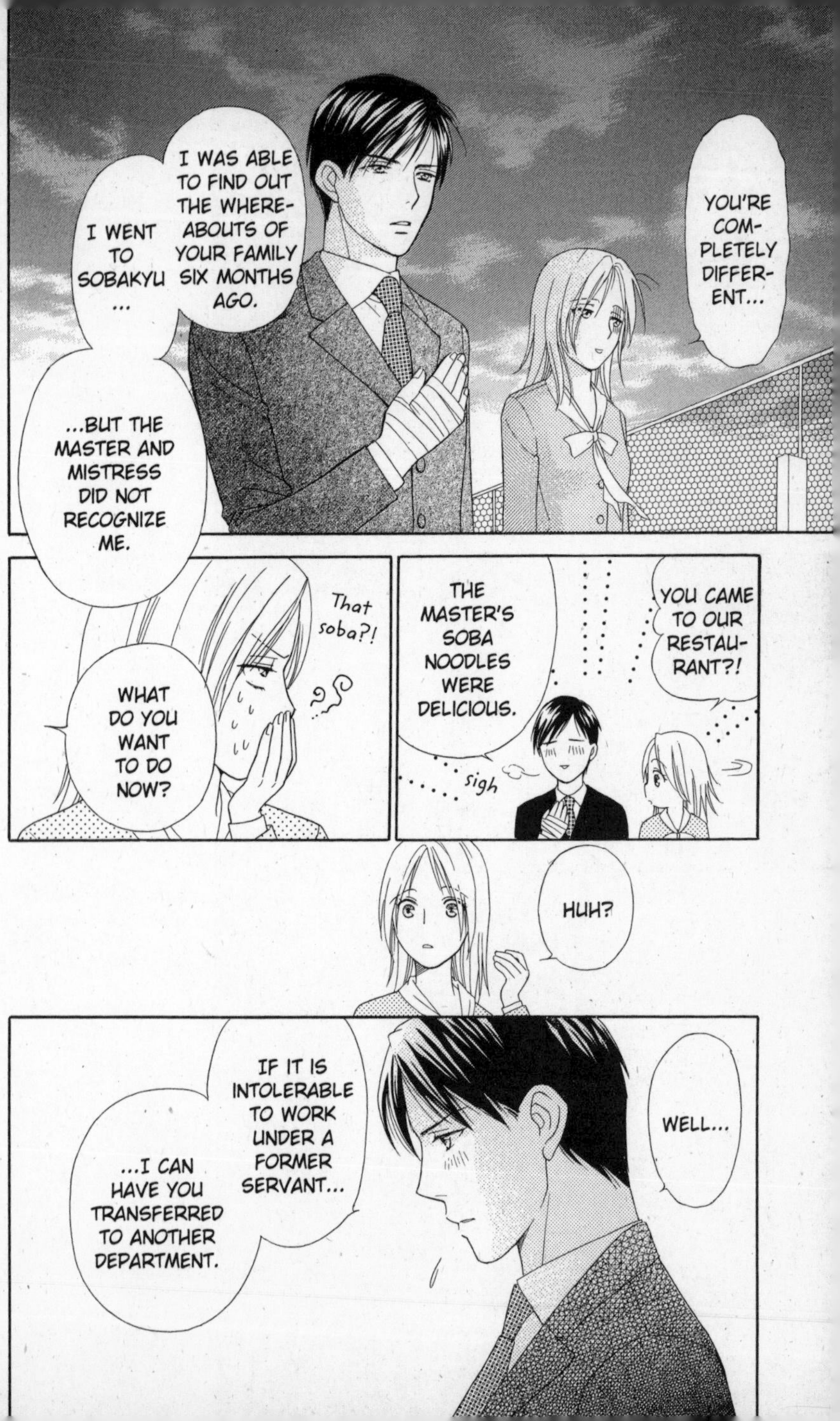
YOU'RE COMPLETELY DIFFERENT...
I WAS ABLE TO FIND OUT THE WHEREABOUTS OF YOUR FAMILY SIX MONTHS AGO.
I WENT TO SOBAKYU...
...BUT THE MASTER AND MISTRESS DID NOT RECOGNIZE ME.
YOU CAME TO OUR RESTAURANT?!
THE MASTER'S SOBA NOODLES WERE DELICIOUS.
sigh
That soba?!
WHAT DO YOU WANT TO DO NOW?
HUH?
WELL...
IF IT IS INTOLERABLE TO WORK UNDER A FORMER SERVANT...
...I CAN HAVE YOU TRANSFERRED TO ANOTHER DEPARTMENT.

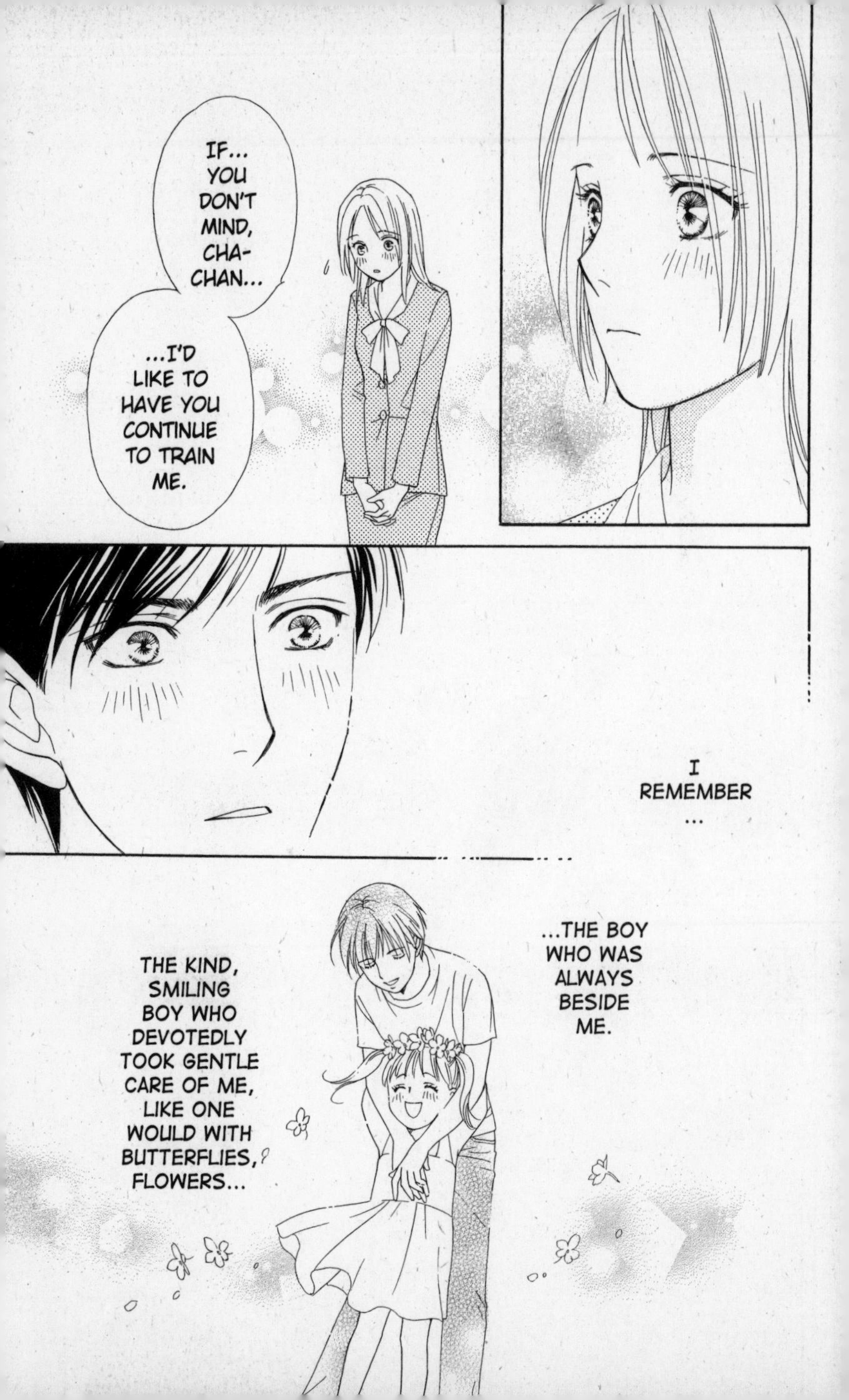
IF... YOU DON'T MIND, CHA-CHAN...
...I'D LIKE TO HAVE YOU CONTINUE TO TRAIN ME.
I REMEMBER...
...THE BOY WHO WAS ALWAYS BESIDE ME.
THE KIND, SMILING BOY WHO DEVOTEDLY TOOK GENTLE CARE OF ME, LIKE ONE WOULD WITH BUTTERFLIES, FLOWERS...

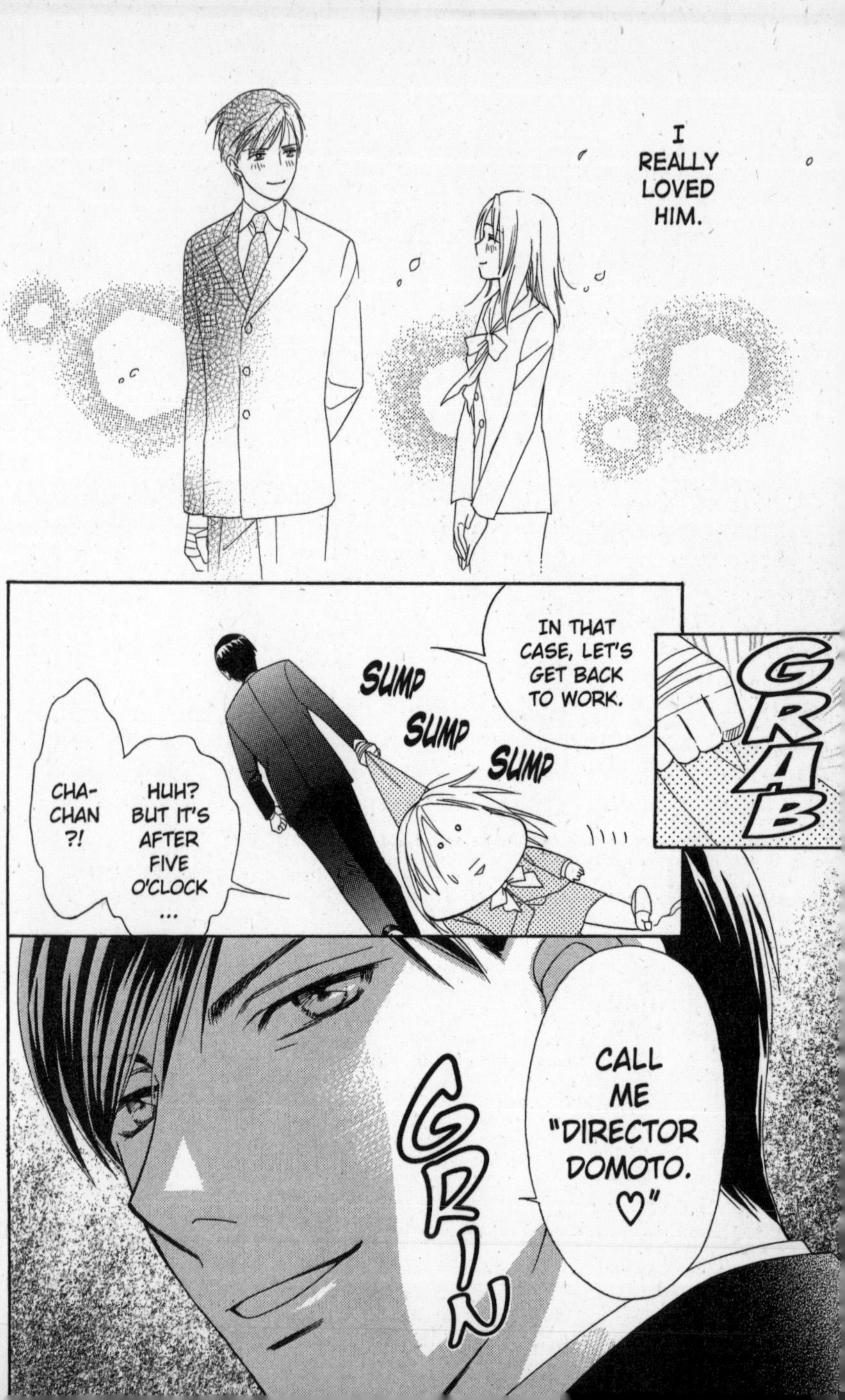
I REALLY LOVED HIM.
GRAB
IN THAT CASE, LET'S GET BACK TO WORK.
SUMP SUMP SUMP
HUH? BUT IT'S AFTER FIVE O'CLOCK...
CHA-CHAN?!
CALL ME "DIRECTOR DOMOTO. ♡"
GRIN

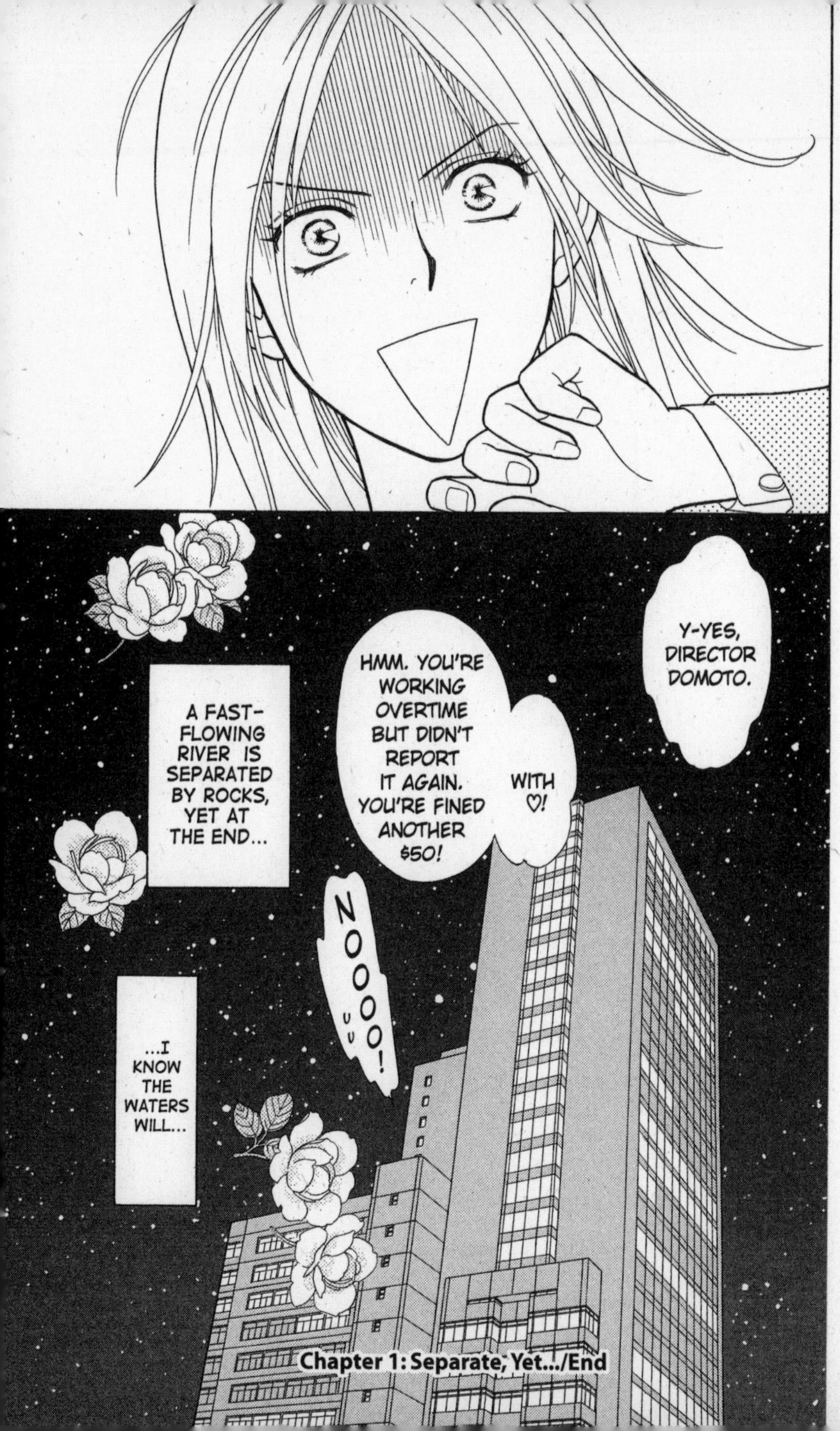
Y-YES, DIRECTOR DOMOTO.
HMM. YOU'RE WORKING OVERTIME BUT DIDN'T REPORT IT AGAIN. YOU'RE FINED ANOTHER $50!
WITH ♡!
A FAST-FLOWING RIVER IS SEPARATED BY ROCKS, YET AT THE END...
NOOOO!
...I KNOW THE WATERS WILL...
Chapter 1: Separate, Yet.../End

DIRECTOR!!

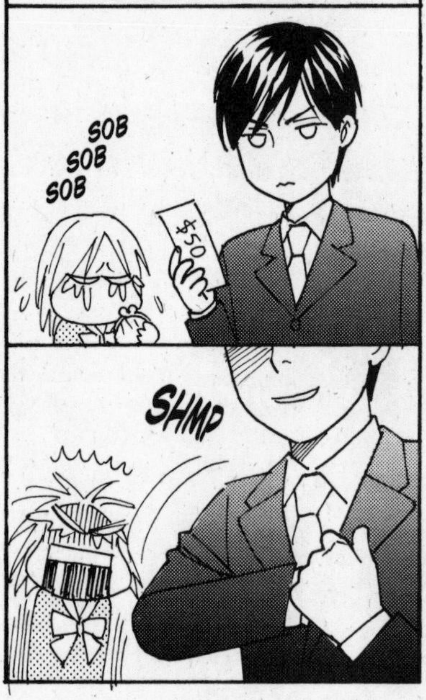
SOB
SOB
SOB
$50
SHMP

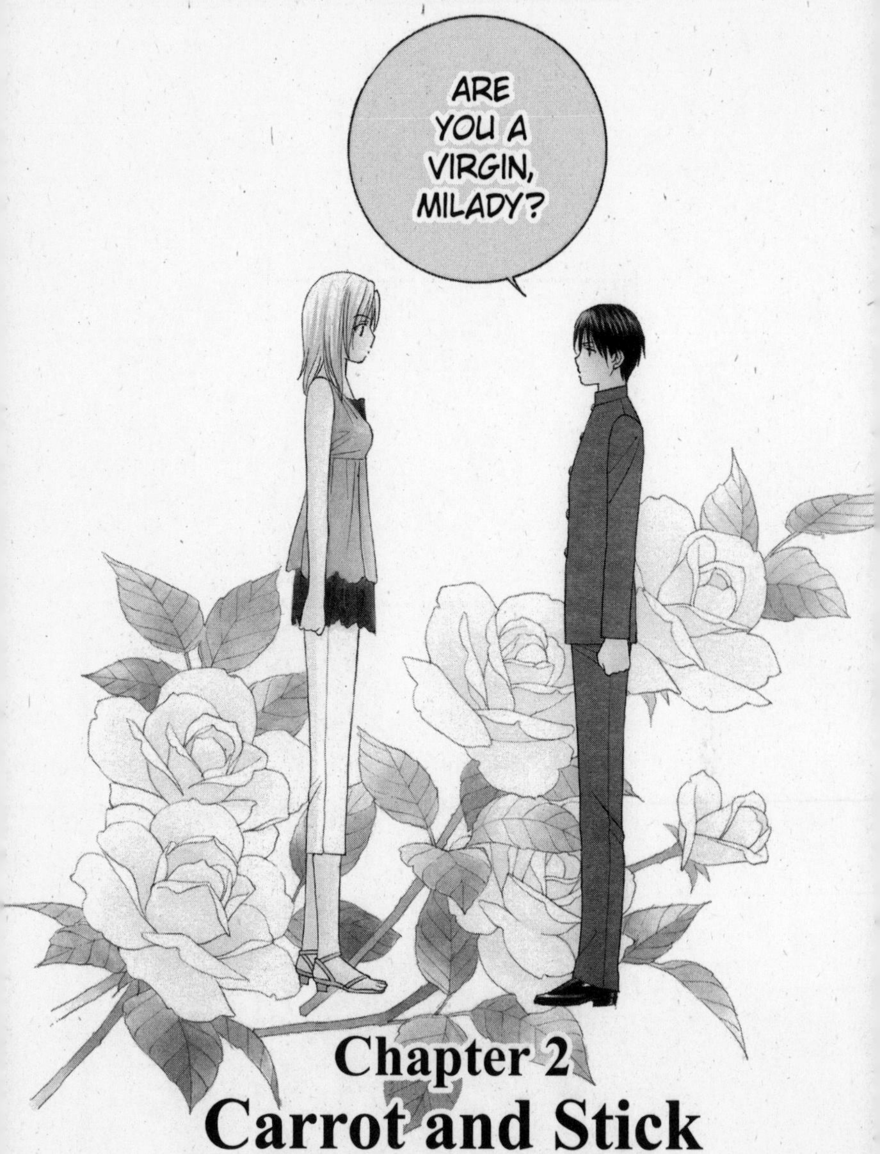
ARE YOU A VIRGIN, MILADY?

Chapter 2
Carrot and Stick and Caramel

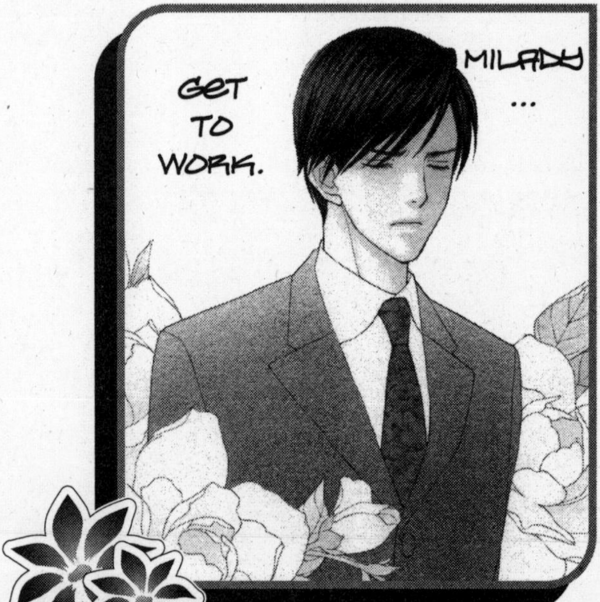
MILADY ...
GET TO WORK.

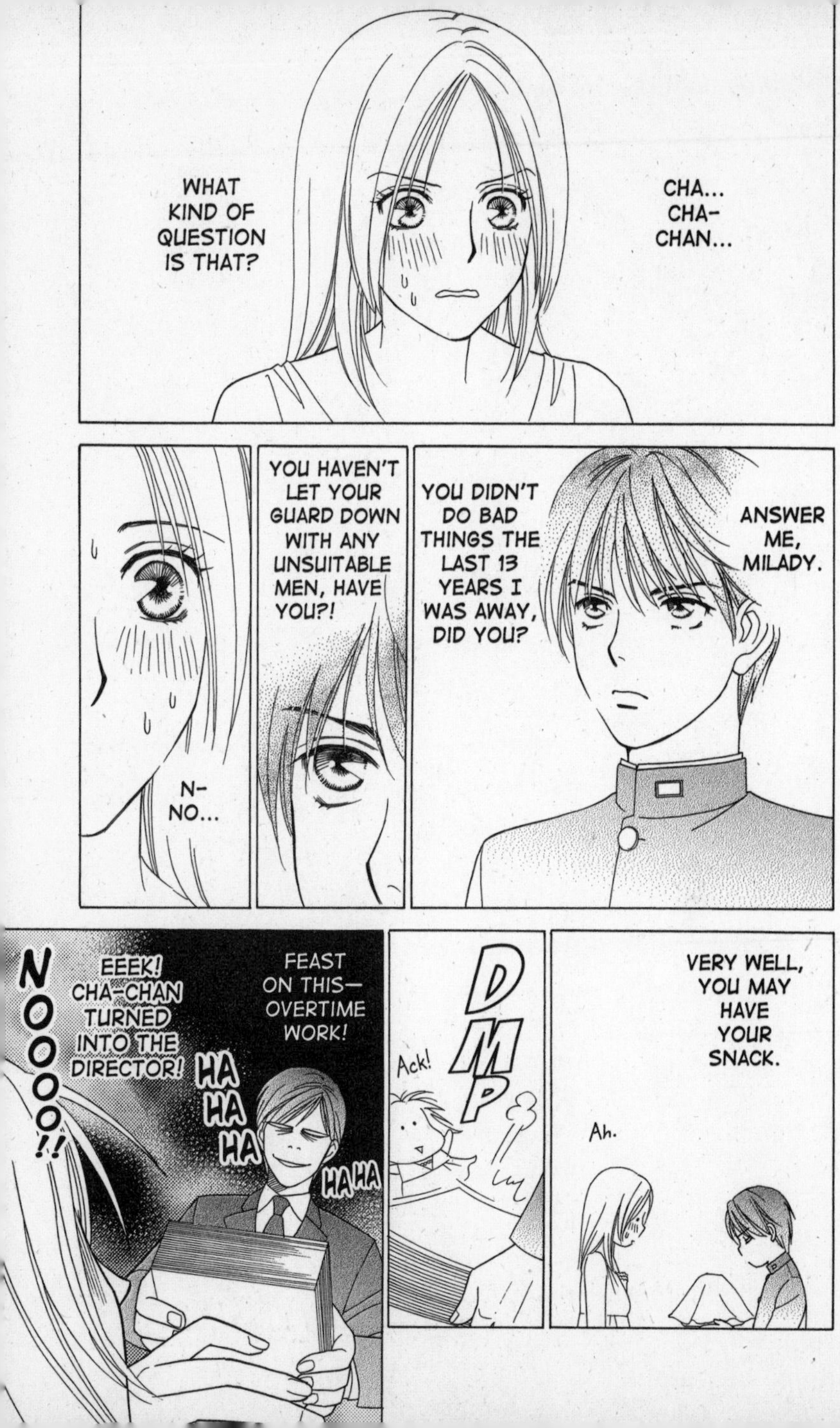
CHA... CHA-CHAN...
WHAT KIND OF QUESTION IS THAT?
ANSWER ME, MILADY.
YOU DIDN'T DO BAD THINGS THE LAST 13 YEARS I WAS AWAY, DID YOU?
YOU HAVEN'T LET YOUR GUARD DOWN WITH ANY UNSUITABLE MEN, HAVE YOU?!
N- NO...
VERY WELL, YOU MAY HAVE YOUR SNACK.
Ah.
DMP
Ack!
FEAST ON THIS—OVERTIME WORK!
EEEK! CHA-CHAN TURNED INTO THE DIRECTOR!
HA HA HA
HAHA
NOOOOO!!

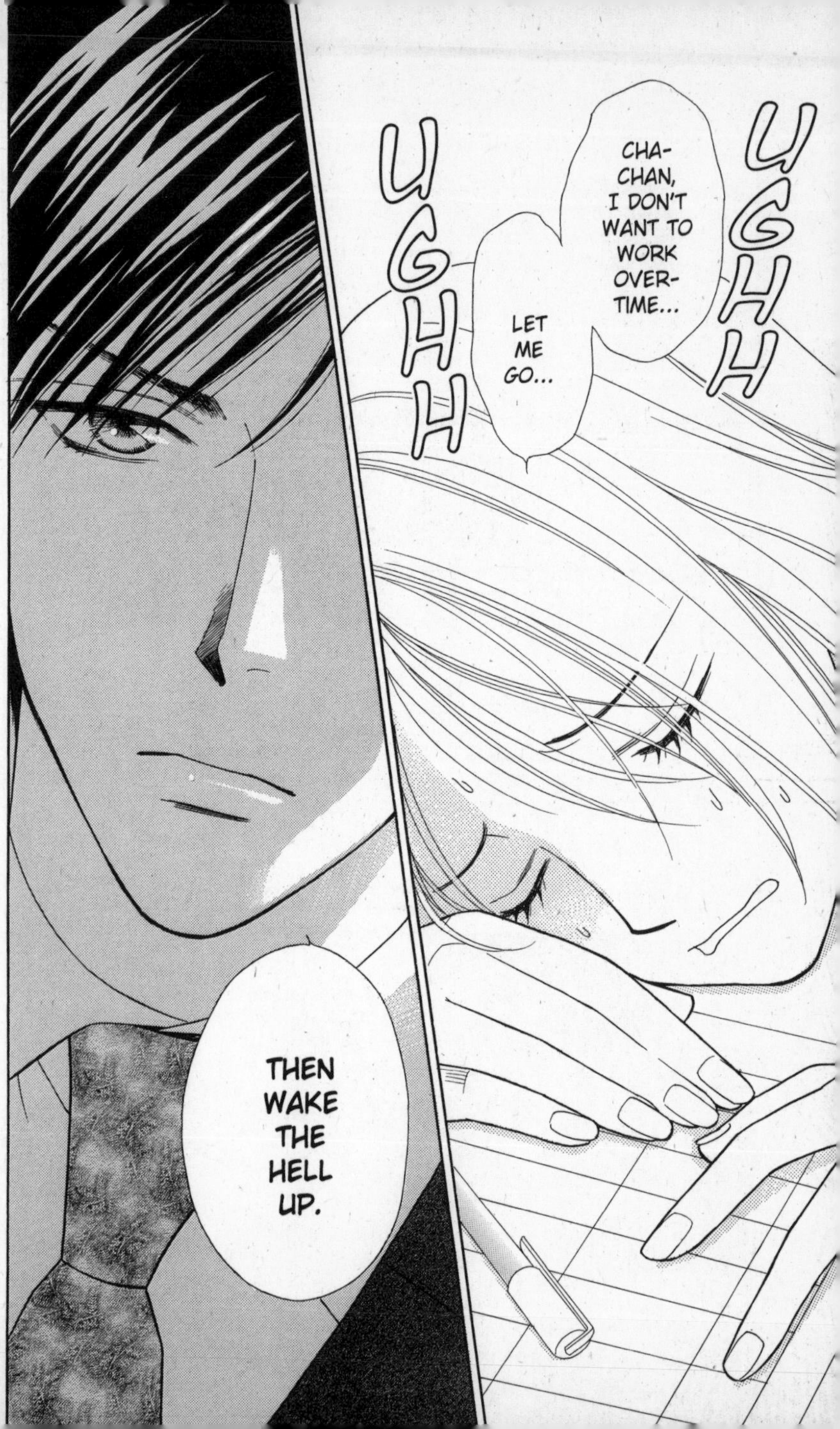
UGHH
CHA-CHAN, I DON'T WANT TO WORK OVER-TIME...
LET ME GO...
UGHH
THEN WAKE THE HELL UP.

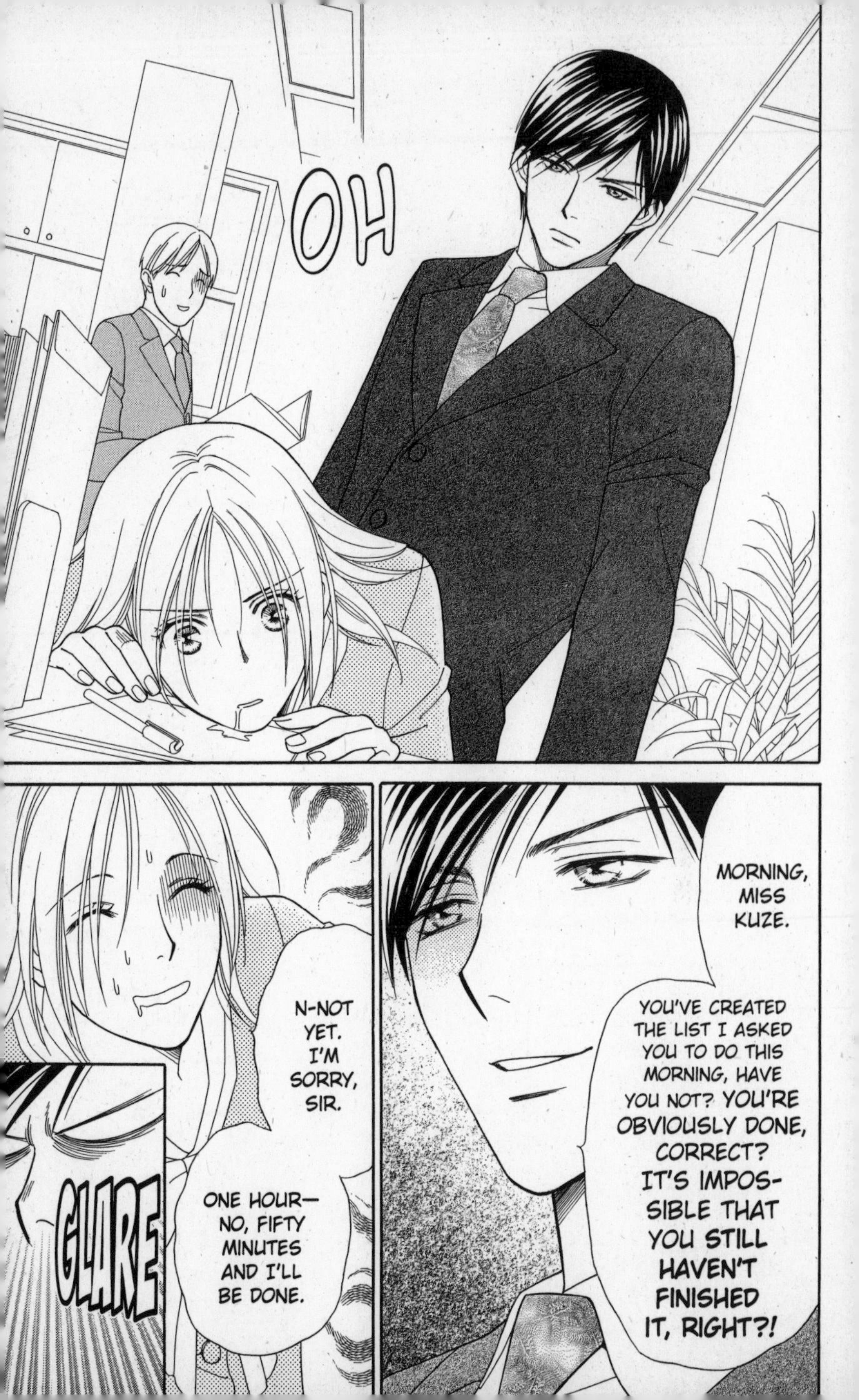
OH
MORNING, MISS KUZE.
YOU'VE CREATED THE LIST I ASKED YOU TO DO THIS MORNING, HAVE YOU NOT? YOU'RE OBVIOUSLY DONE, CORRECT? IT'S IMPOS-SIBLE THAT YOU STILL HAVEN'T FINISHED IT, RIGHT?!
N-NOT YET. I'M SORRY, SIR.
GLARE
ONE HOUR—NO, FIFTY MINUTES AND I'LL BE DONE.

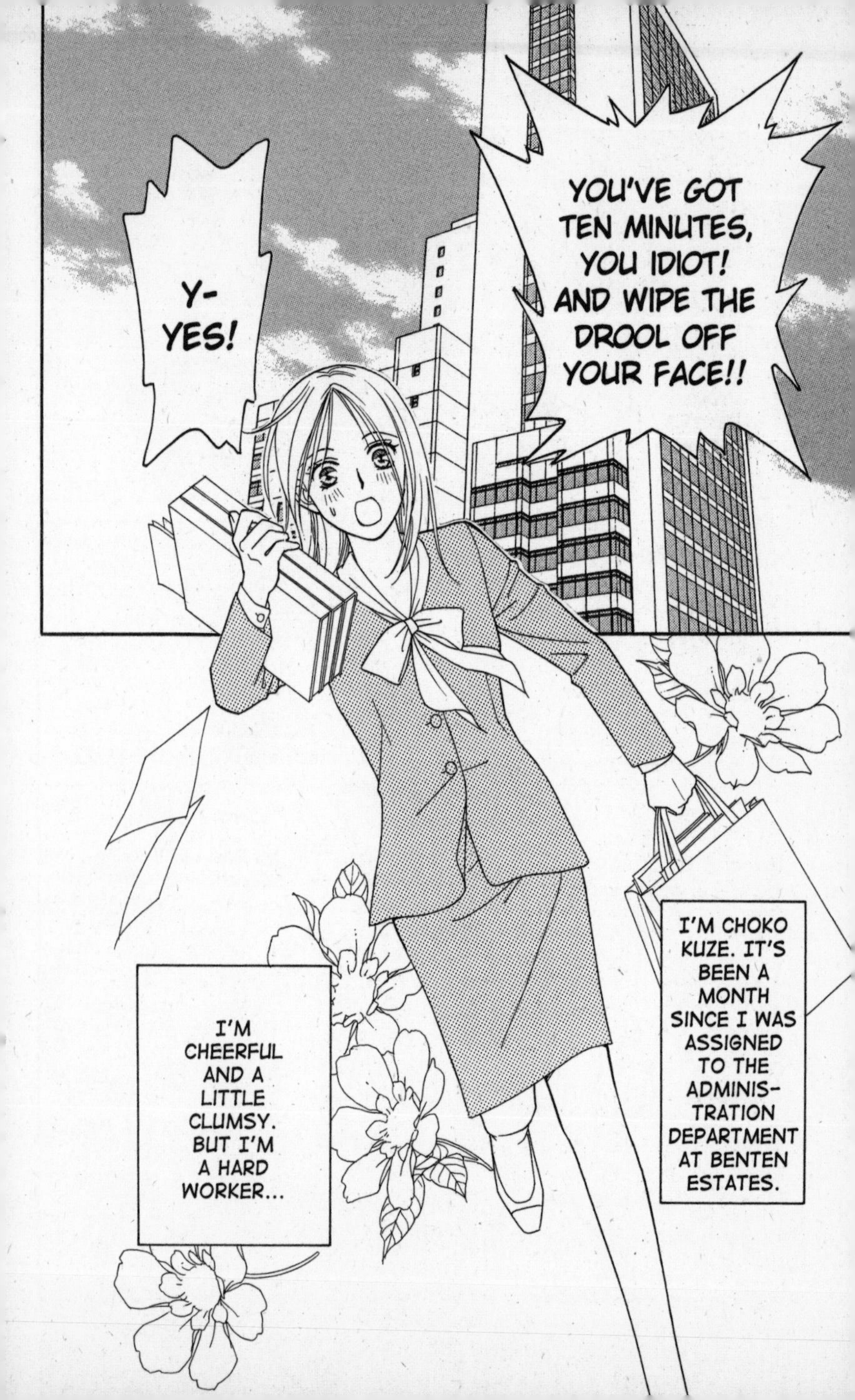
YOU'VE GOT TEN MINUTES, YOU IDIOT! AND WIPE THE DROOL OFF YOUR FACE!!
Y-YES!
I'M CHOKO KUZE. IT'S BEEN A MONTH SINCE I WAS ASSIGNED TO THE ADMINIS-TRATION DEPARTMENT AT BENTEN ESTATES.
I'M CHEERFUL AND A LITTLE CLUMSY. BUT I'M A HARD WORKER...

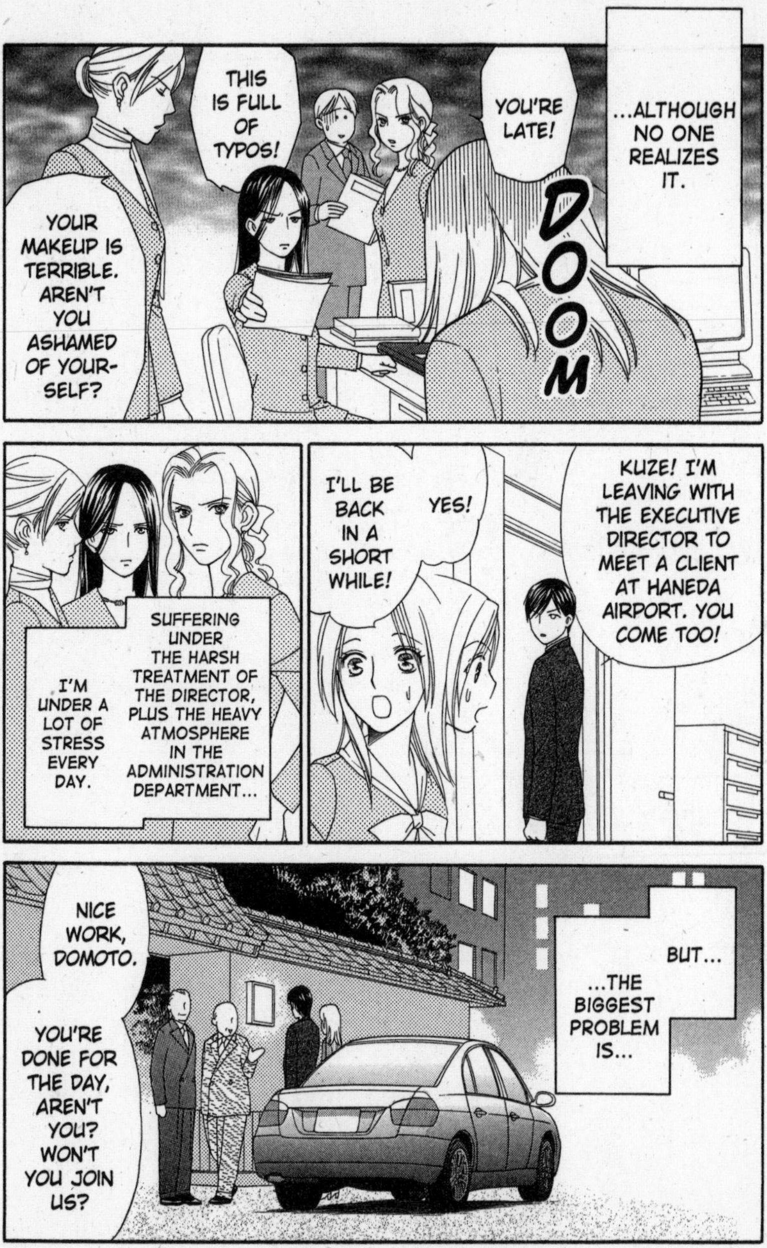
...ALTHOUGH NO ONE REALIZES IT.
YOU'RE LATE!
DOOM
THIS IS FULL OF TYPOS!
YOUR MAKEUP IS TERRIBLE. AREN'T YOU ASHAMED OF YOURSELF?
KUZE! I'M LEAVING WITH THE EXECUTIVE DIRECTOR TO MEET A CLIENT AT HANEDA AIRPORT. YOU COME TOO!
YES!
I'LL BE BACK IN A SHORT WHILE!
SUFFERING UNDER THE HARSH TREATMENT OF THE DIRECTOR, PLUS THE HEAVY ATMOSPHERE IN THE ADMINISTRATION DEPARTMENT...
I'M UNDER A LOT OF STRESS EVERY DAY.
BUT...
...THE BIGGEST PROBLEM IS...
NICE WORK, DOMOTO.
YOU'RE DONE FOR THE DAY, AREN'T YOU? WON'T YOU JOIN US?

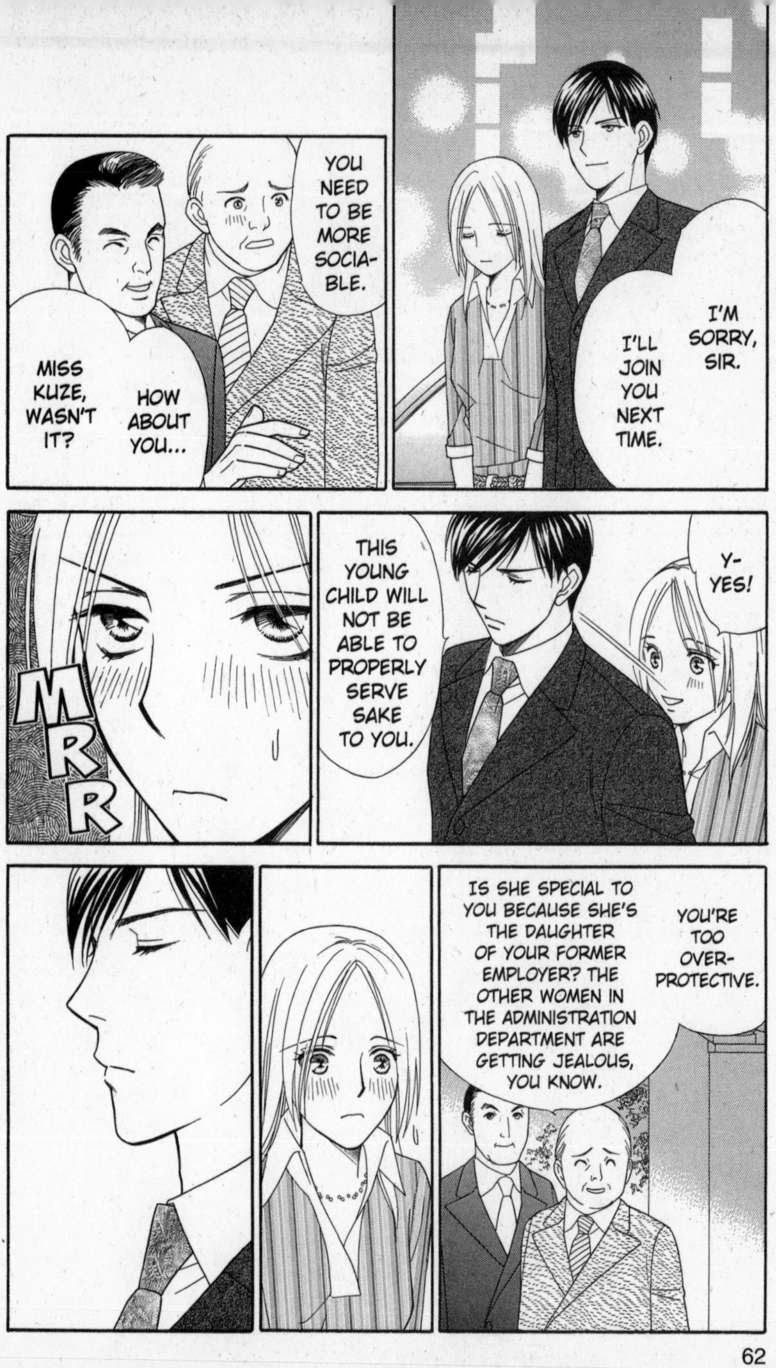
I'M SORRY, SIR.
I'LL JOIN YOU NEXT TIME.
YOU NEED TO BE MORE SOCIABLE.
HOW ABOUT YOU...
MISS KUZE, WASN'T IT?
Y-YES!
THIS YOUNG CHILD WILL NOT BE ABLE TO PROPERLY SERVE SAKE TO YOU.
MRR
YOU'RE TOO OVER-PROTECTIVE.
IS SHE SPECIAL TO YOU BECAUSE SHE'S THE DAUGHTER OF YOUR FORMER EMPLOYER? THE OTHER WOMEN IN THE ADMINISTRATION DEPARTMENT ARE GETTING JEALOUS, YOU KNOW.

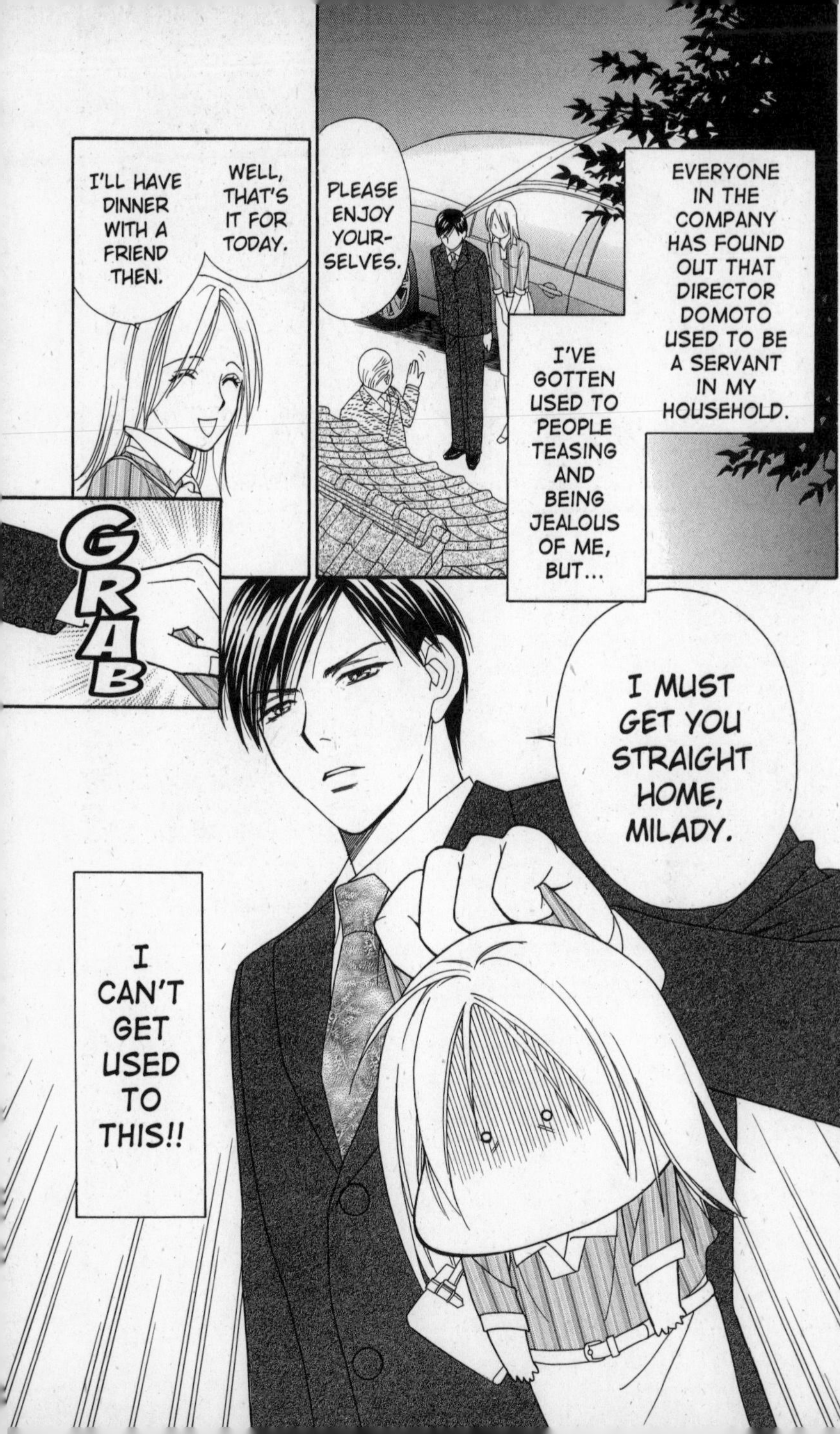
EVERYONE IN THE COMPANY HAS FOUND OUT THAT DIRECTOR DOMOTO USED TO BE A SERVANT IN MY HOUSEHOLD.
PLEASE ENJOY YOUR-SELVES.
I'VE GOTTEN USED TO PEOPLE TEASING AND BEING JEALOUS OF ME, BUT...
WELL, THAT'S IT FOR TODAY.
I'LL HAVE DINNER WITH A FRIEND THEN.
GRAB
I MUST GET YOU STRAIGHT HOME, MILADY.
I CAN'T GET USED TO THIS!!

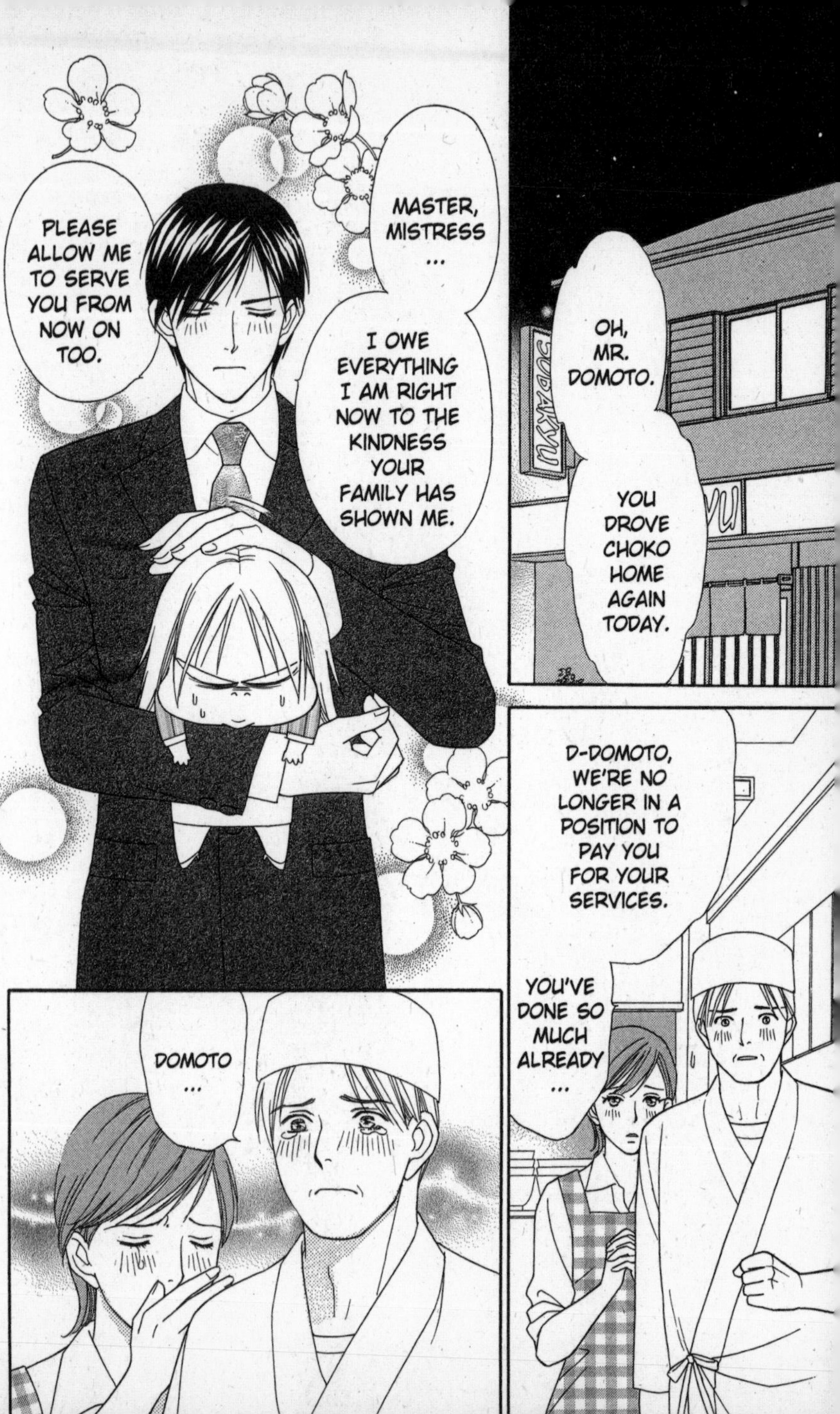
OH, MR. DOMOTO.
YOU DROVE CHOKO HOME AGAIN TODAY.
D-DOMOTO, WE'RE NO LONGER IN A POSITION TO PAY YOU FOR YOUR SERVICES.
YOU'VE DONE SO MUCH ALREADY ...
MASTER, MISTRESS ...
I OWE EVERYTHING I AM RIGHT NOW TO THE KINDNESS YOUR FAMILY HAS SHOWN ME.
PLEASE ALLOW ME TO SERVE YOU FROM NOW ON TOO.
DOMOTO ...

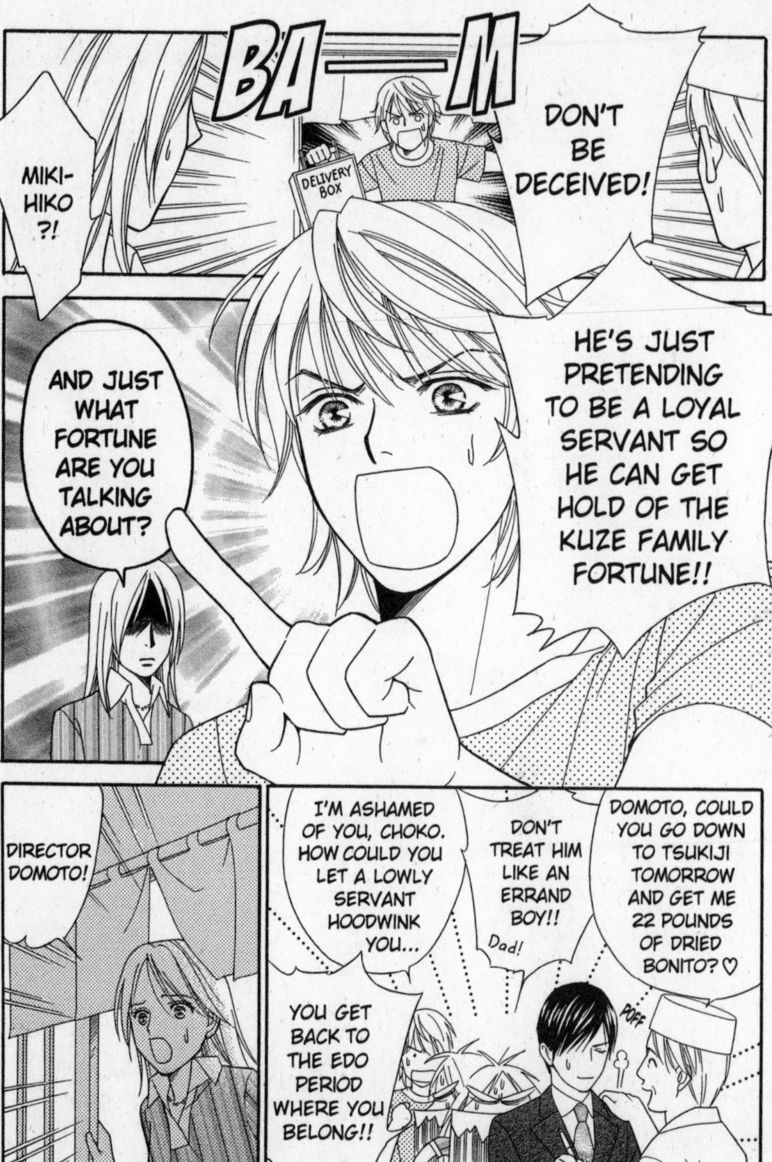
BA—M
DON'T BE DECEIVED!
DELIVERY BOX
MIKI-HIKO?!
HE'S JUST PRETENDING TO BE A LOYAL SERVANT SO HE CAN GET HOLD OF THE KUZE FAMILY FORTUNE!!
AND JUST WHAT FORTUNE ARE YOU TALKING ABOUT?
DOMOTO, COULD YOU GO DOWN TO TSUKIJI TOMORROW AND GET ME 22 POUNDS OF DRIED BONITO? ♡
POFF
DON'T TREAT HIM LIKE AN ERRAND BOY!!
Dad!
I'M ASHAMED OF YOU, CHOKO. HOW COULD YOU LET A LOWLY SERVANT HOODWINK YOU...
YOU GET BACK TO THE EDO PERIOD WHERE YOU BELONG!!
DIRECTOR DOMOTO!

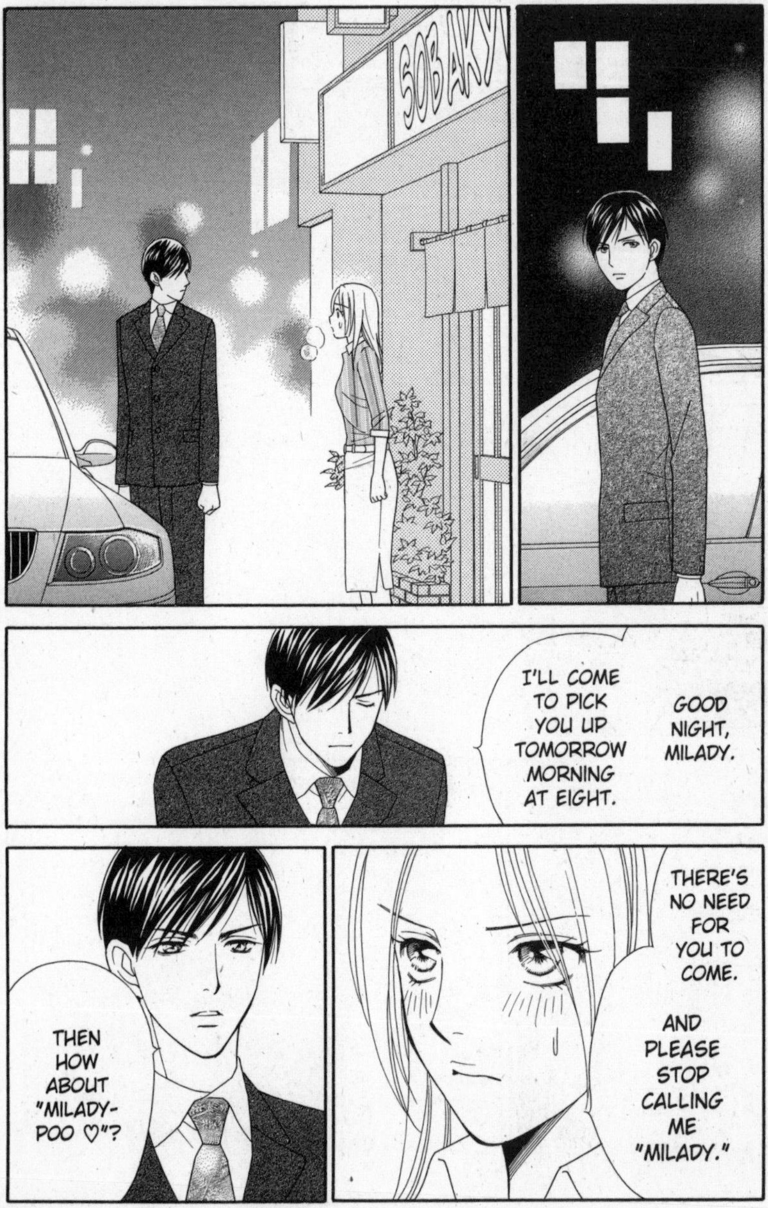
SOBAKY
GOOD NIGHT, MILADY.
I'LL COME TO PICK YOU UP TOMORROW MORNING AT EIGHT.
THERE'S NO NEED FOR YOU TO COME.
AND PLEASE STOP CALLING ME "MILADY."
THEN HOW ABOUT "MILADY-POO ♡"?

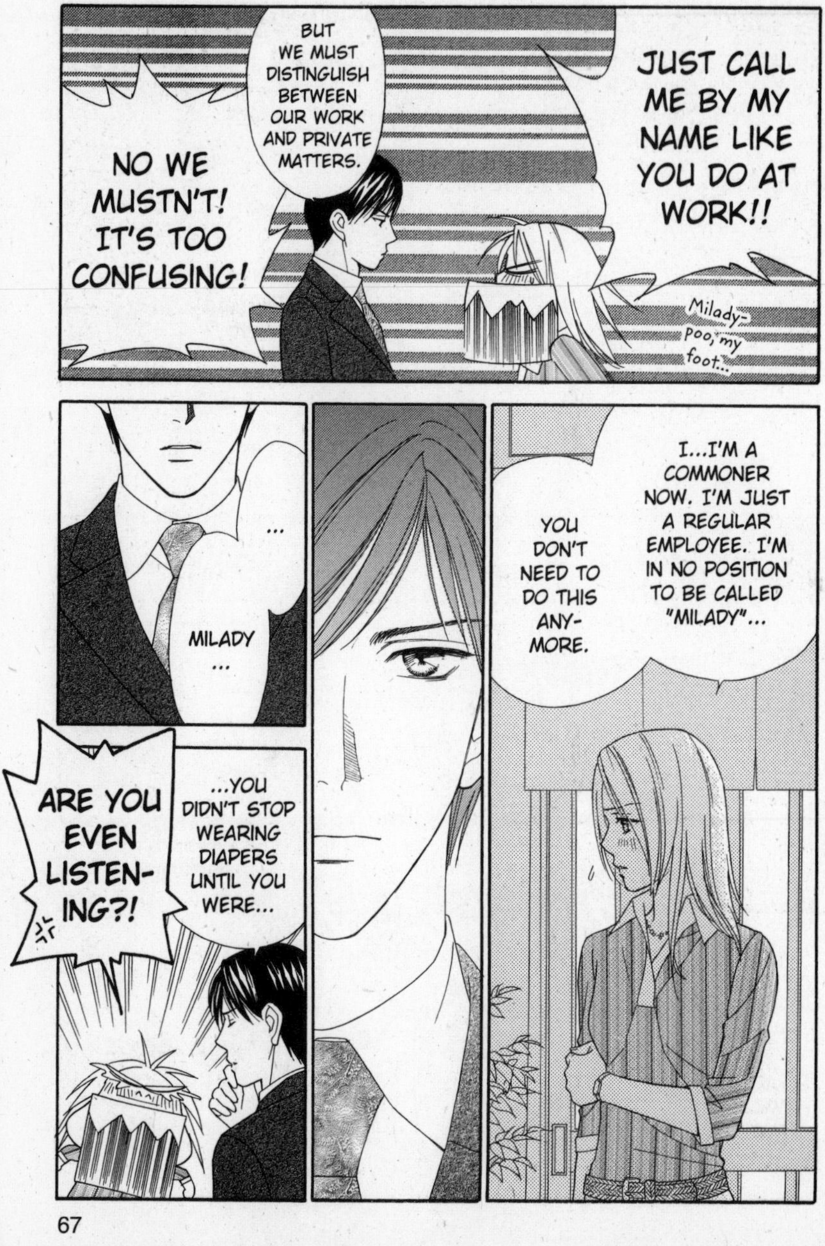
JUST CALL ME BY MY NAME LIKE YOU DO AT WORK!!
BUT WE MUST DISTINGUISH BETWEEN OUR WORK AND PRIVATE MATTERS.
NO WE MUSTN'T! IT'S TOO CONFUSING!
Milady-poo, my foot...
I...I'M A COMMONER NOW. I'M JUST A REGULAR EMPLOYEE. I'M IN NO POSITION TO BE CALLED "MILADY"...
YOU DON'T NEED TO DO THIS ANY-MORE.
...
MILADY ...
...YOU DIDN'T STOP WEARING DIAPERS UNTIL YOU WERE...
ARE YOU EVEN LISTEN-ING?!

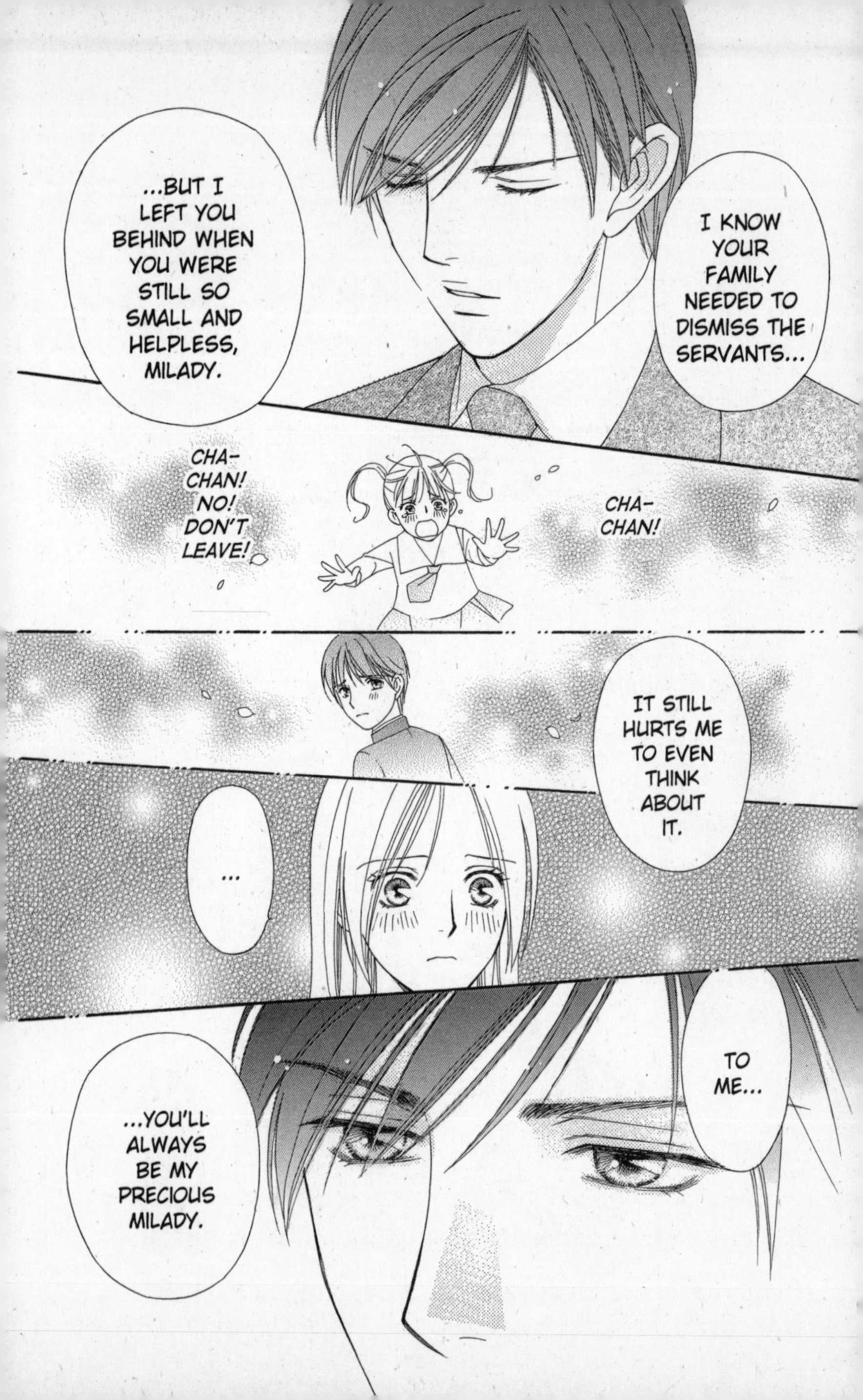
I KNOW YOUR FAMILY NEEDED TO DISMISS THE SERVANTS...
...BUT I LEFT YOU BEHIND WHEN YOU WERE STILL SO SMALL AND HELPLESS, MILADY.
CHA-CHAN!
CHA-CHAN! NO! DON'T LEAVE!
IT STILL HURTS ME TO EVEN THINK ABOUT IT.
...
TO ME...
...YOU'LL ALWAYS BE MY PRECIOUS MILADY.

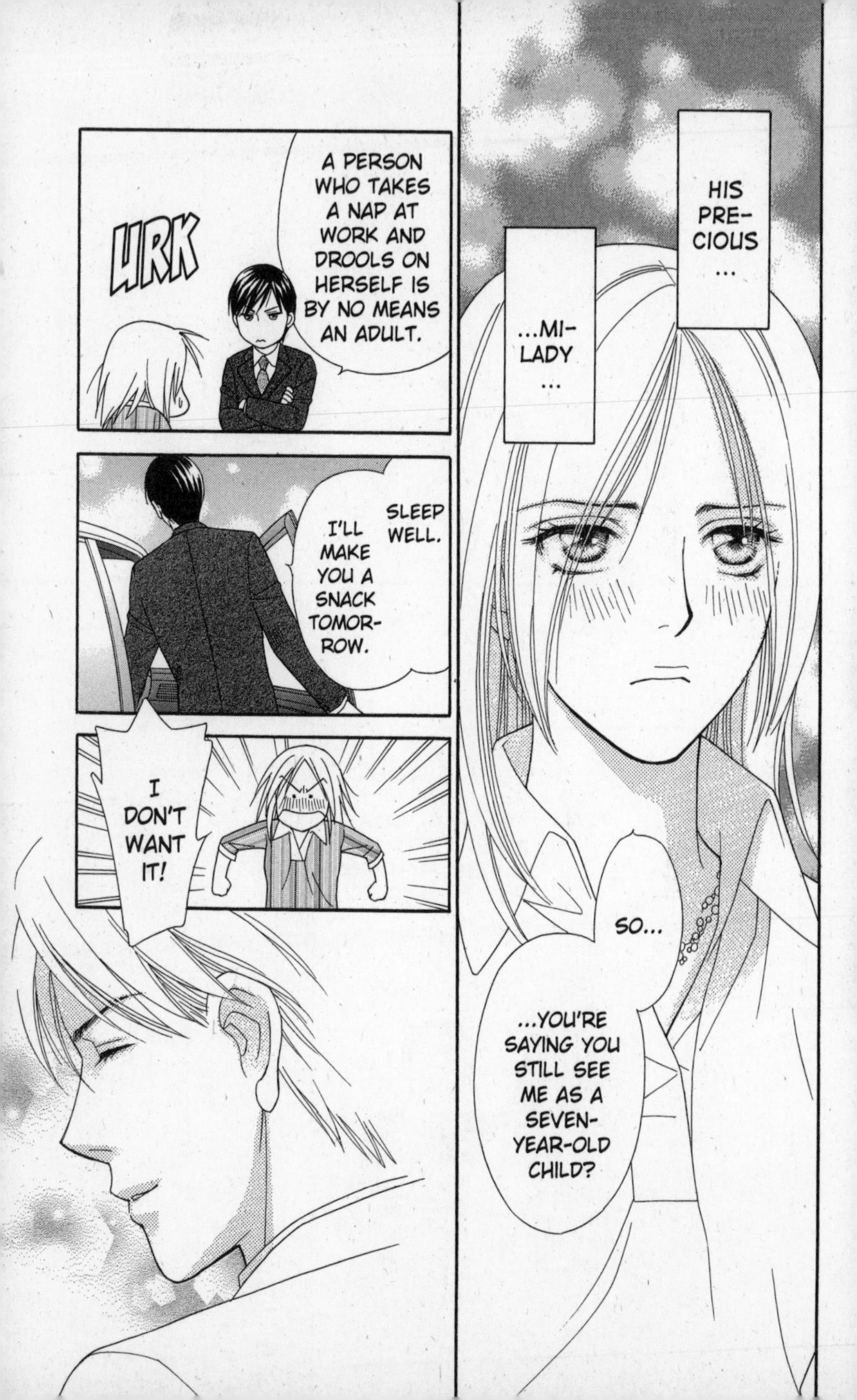
HIS PRE-CIOUS ...
...MI-LADY ...
SO...
...YOU'RE SAYING YOU STILL SEE ME AS A SEVEN-YEAR-OLD CHILD?
A PERSON WHO TAKES A NAP AT WORK AND DROOLS ON HERSELF IS BY NO MEANS AN ADULT.
URK
SLEEP WELL.
I'LL MAKE YOU A SNACK TOMOR-ROW.
I DON'T WANT IT!

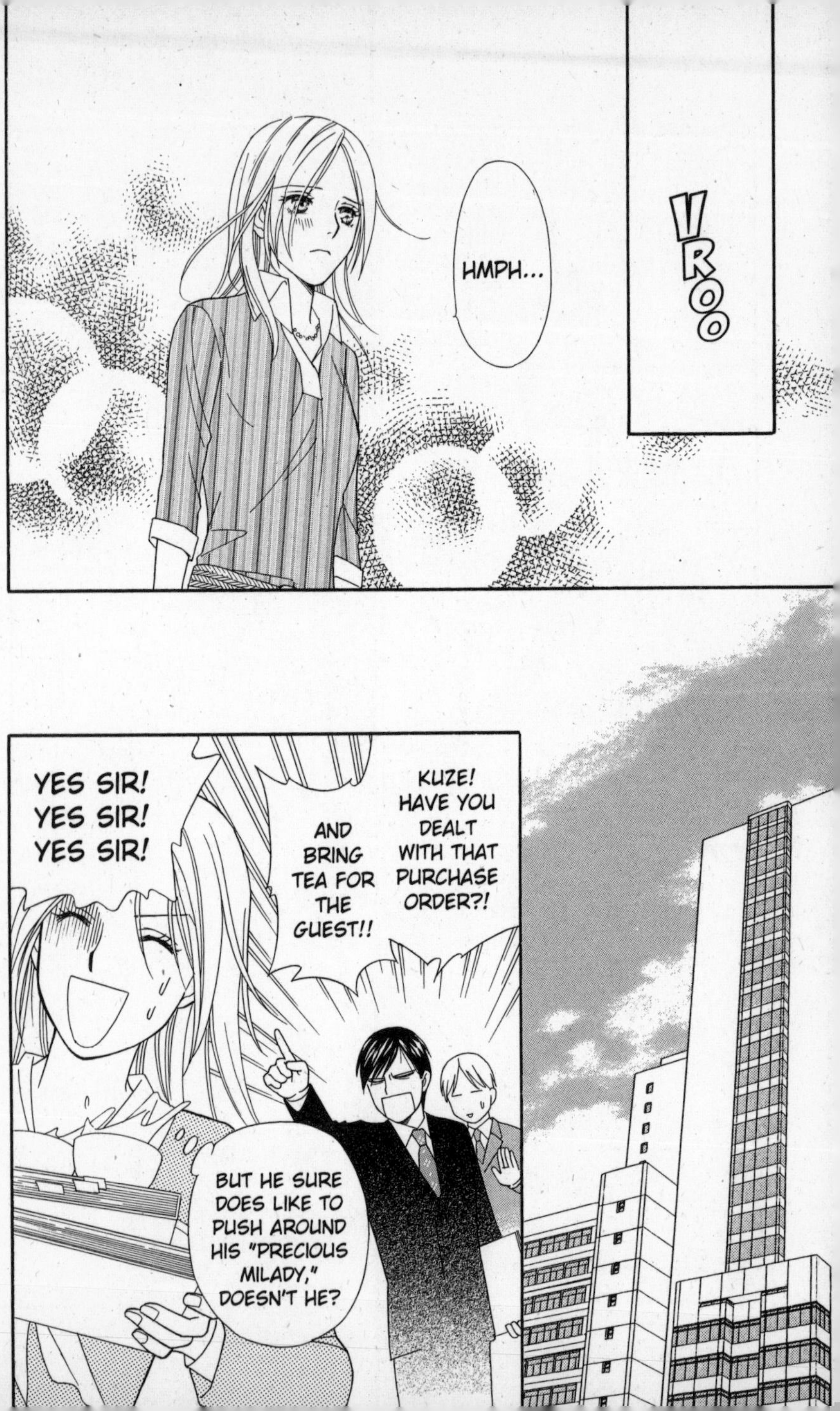
VROO
HMPH...
KUZE! HAVE YOU DEALT WITH THAT PURCHASE ORDER?!
AND BRING TEA FOR THE GUEST!!
YES SIR! YES SIR! YES SIR!
BUT HE SURE DOES LIKE TO PUSH AROUND HIS "PRECIOUS MILADY," DOESN'T HE?

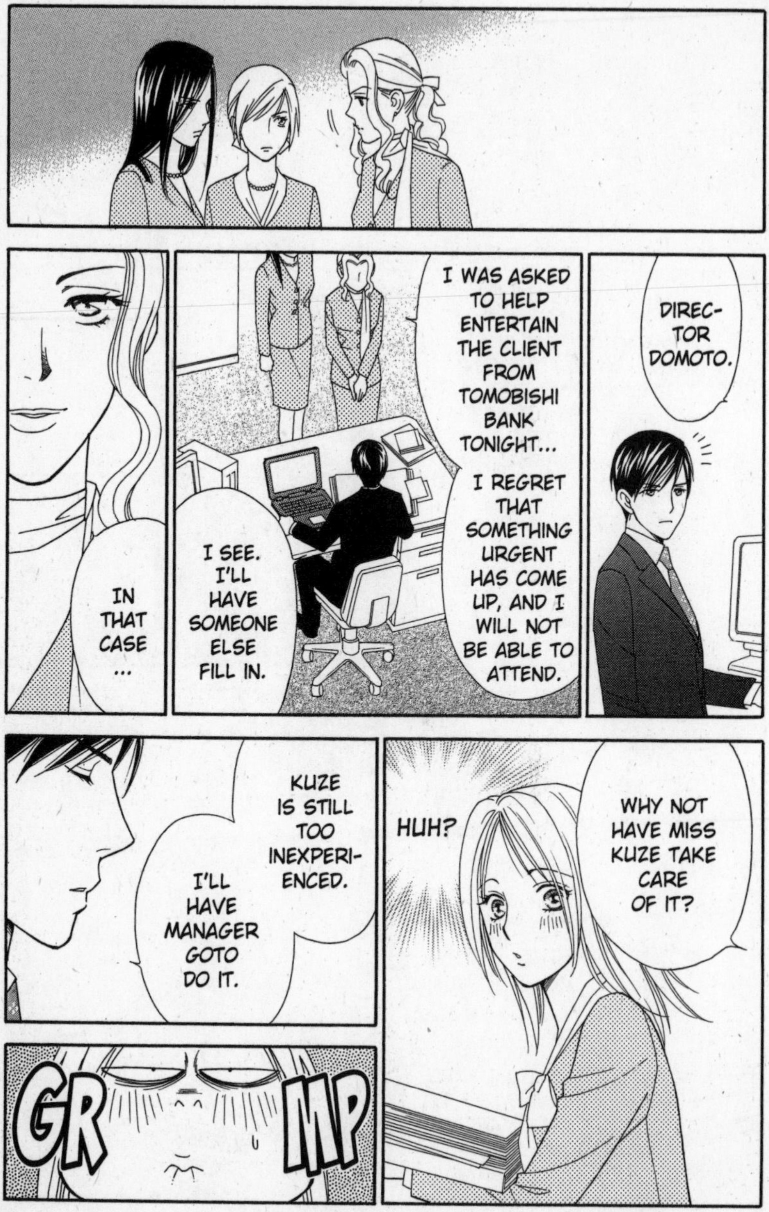
DIRECTOR DOMOTO.
I WAS ASKED TO HELP ENTERTAIN THE CLIENT FROM TOMOBISHI BANK TONIGHT...
I REGRET THAT SOMETHING URGENT HAS COME UP, AND I WILL NOT BE ABLE TO ATTEND.
I SEE. I'LL HAVE SOMEONE ELSE FILL IN.
IN THAT CASE ...
WHY NOT HAVE MISS KUZE TAKE CARE OF IT?
HUH?
KUZE IS STILL TOO INEXPERIENCED.
I'LL HAVE MANAGER GOTO DO IT.
GRMP

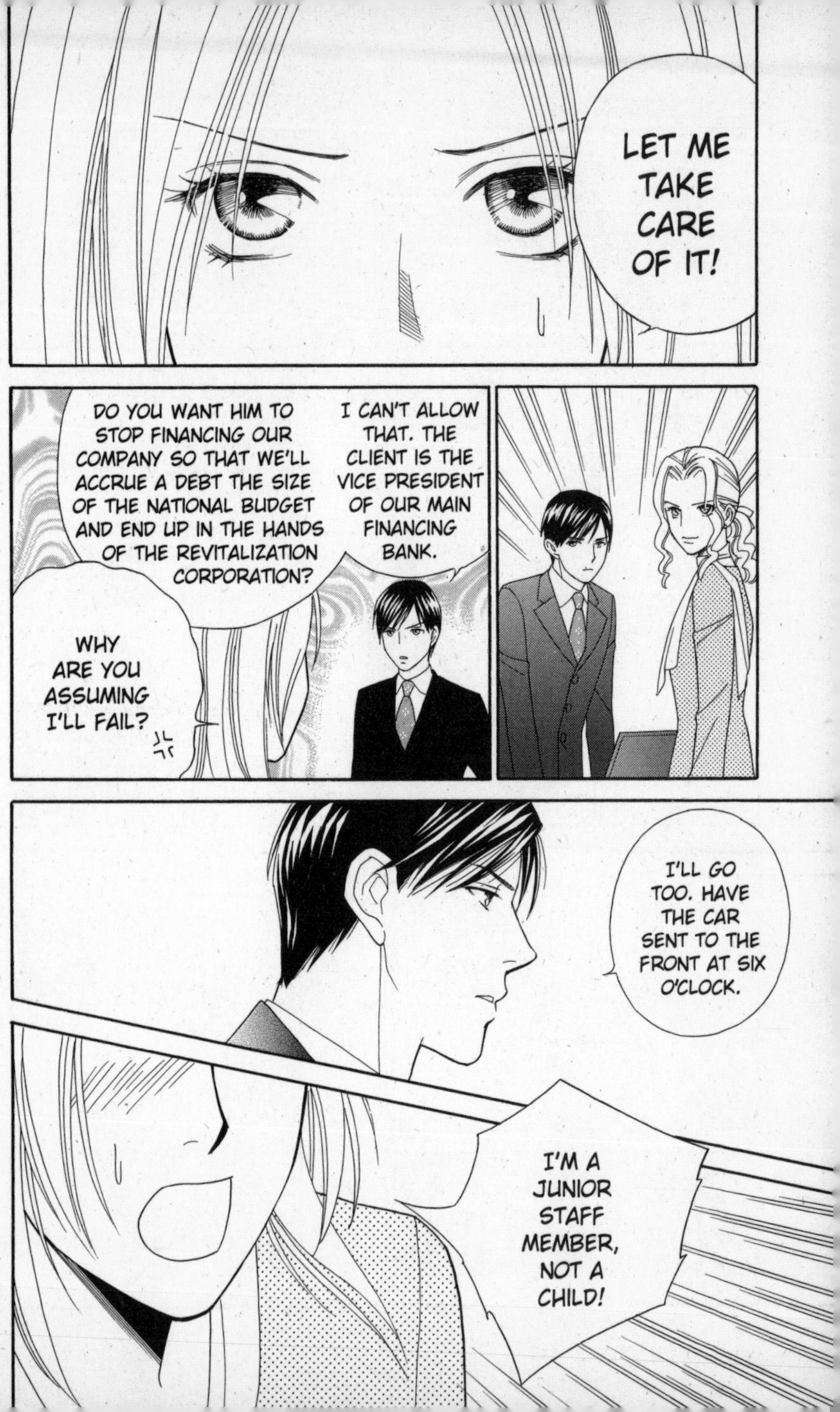
LET ME TAKE CARE OF IT!
I CAN'T ALLOW THAT. THE CLIENT IS THE VICE PRESIDENT OF OUR MAIN FINANCING BANK.
DO YOU WANT HIM TO STOP FINANCING OUR COMPANY SO THAT WE'LL ACCRUE A DEBT THE SIZE OF THE NATIONAL BUDGET AND END UP IN THE HANDS OF THE REVITALIZATION CORPORATION?
WHY ARE YOU ASSUMING I'LL FAIL?
I'LL GO TOO. HAVE THE CAR SENT TO THE FRONT AT SIX O'CLOCK.
I'M A JUNIOR STAFF MEMBER, NOT A CHILD!

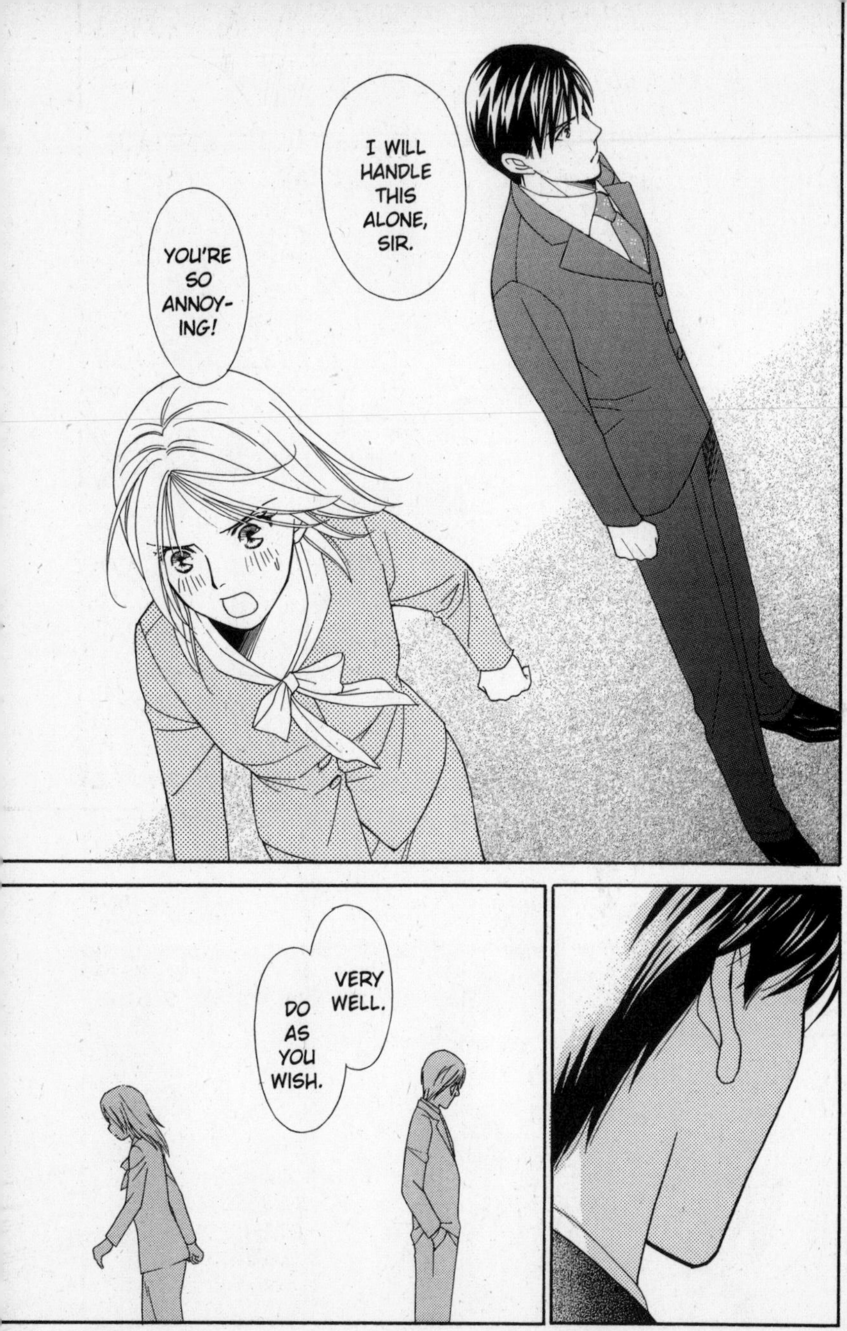
I WILL HANDLE THIS ALONE, SIR.
YOU'RE SO ANNOY-ING!
VERY WELL. DO AS YOU WISH.

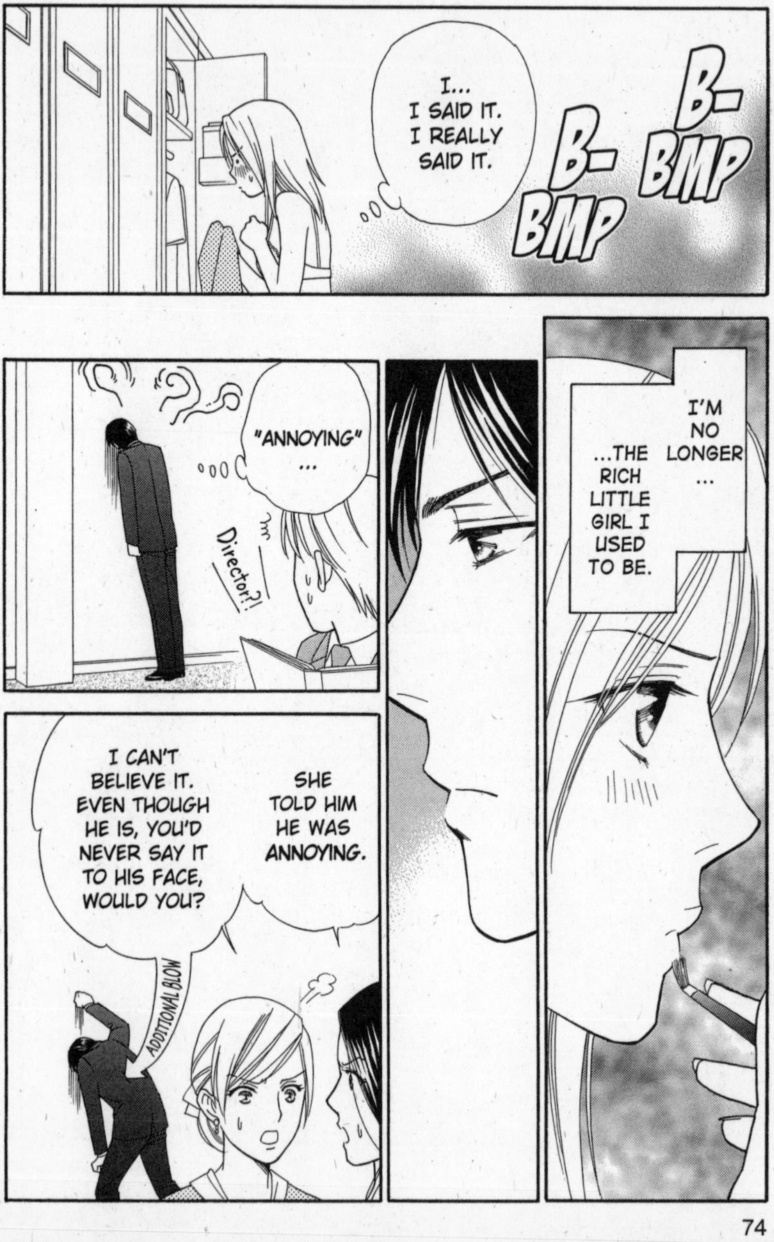
B-BMP
I... I SAID IT. I REALLY SAID IT.
B-BMP
I'M NO LONGER...
...THE RICH LITTLE GIRL I USED TO BE.
"ANNOYING"...
Director?!
SHE TOLD HIM HE WAS ANNOYING.
I CAN'T BELIEVE IT. EVEN THOUGH HE IS, YOU'D NEVER SAY IT TO HIS FACE, WOULD YOU?
ADDITIONAL BLOW

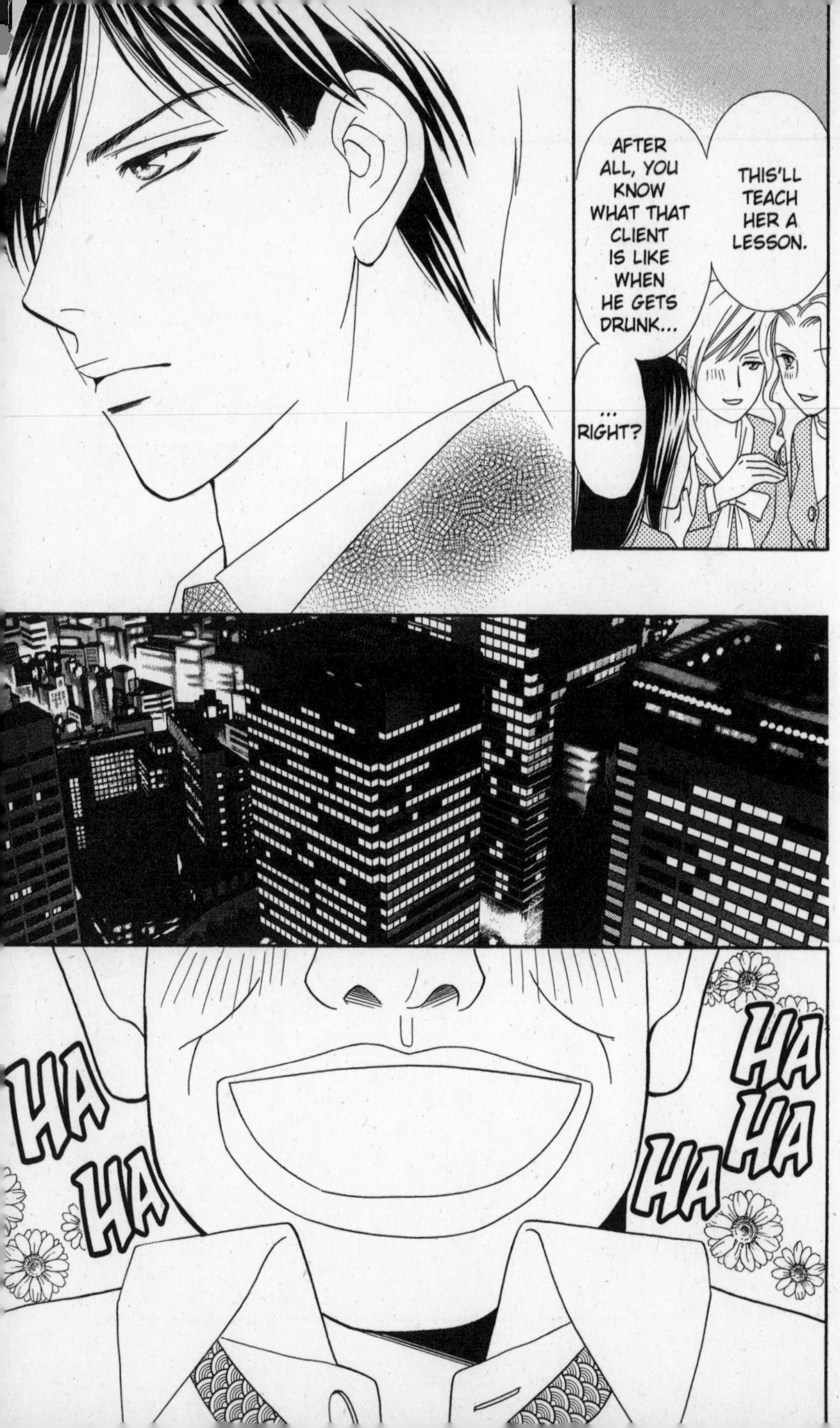
THIS'LL TEACH HER A LESSON.
AFTER ALL, YOU KNOW WHAT THAT CLIENT IS LIKE WHEN HE GETS DRUNK...
... RIGHT?
HA HA HA
HA HA

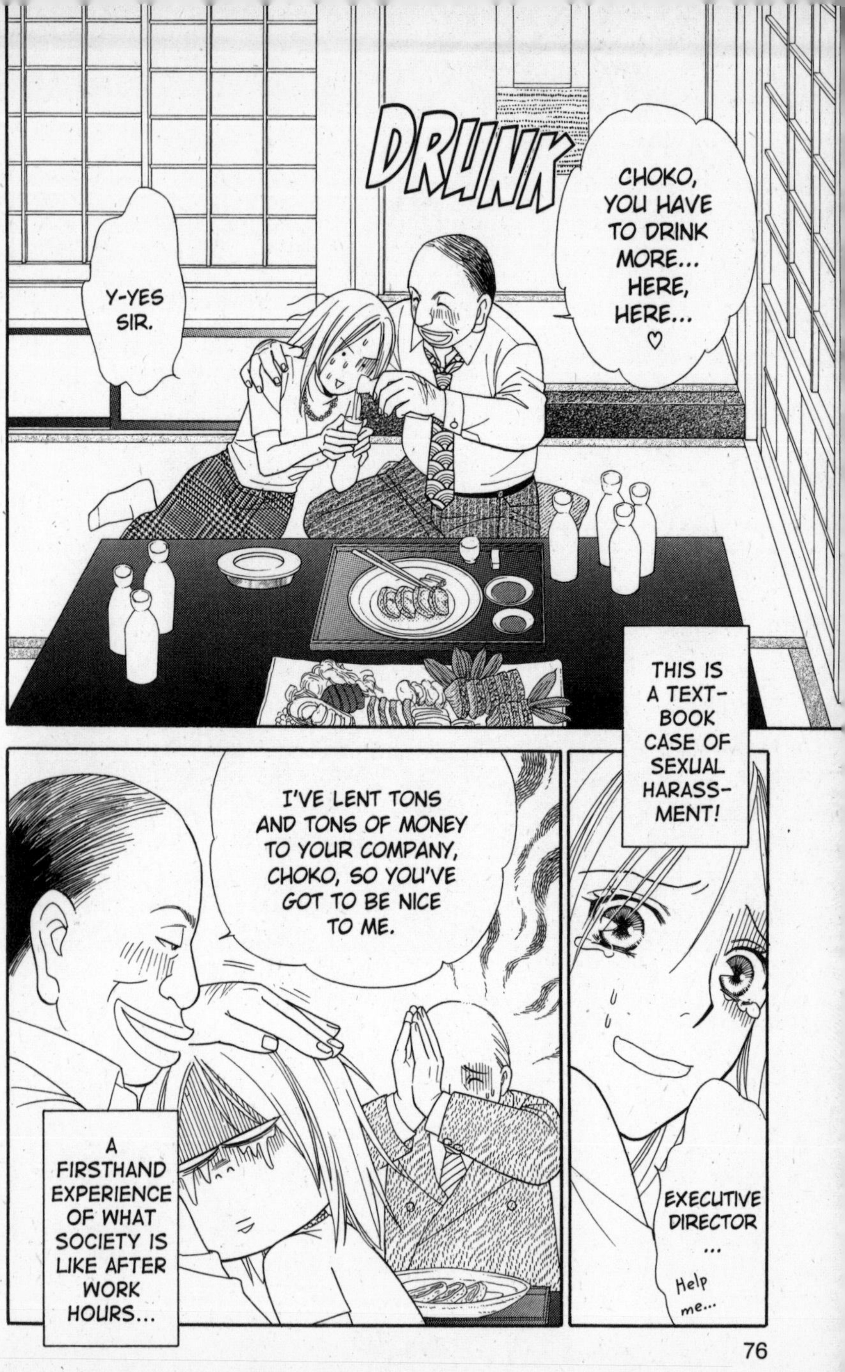
CHOKO, YOU HAVE TO DRINK MORE... HERE, HERE... ♡
DRUNK
Y-YES SIR.
THIS IS A TEXT-BOOK CASE OF SEXUAL HARASS-MENT!
EXECUTIVE DIRECTOR ...
Help me...
I'VE LENT TONS AND TONS OF MONEY TO YOUR COMPANY, CHOKO, SO YOU'VE GOT TO BE NICE TO ME.
A FIRSTHAND EXPERIENCE OF WHAT SOCIETY IS LIKE AFTER WORK HOURS...

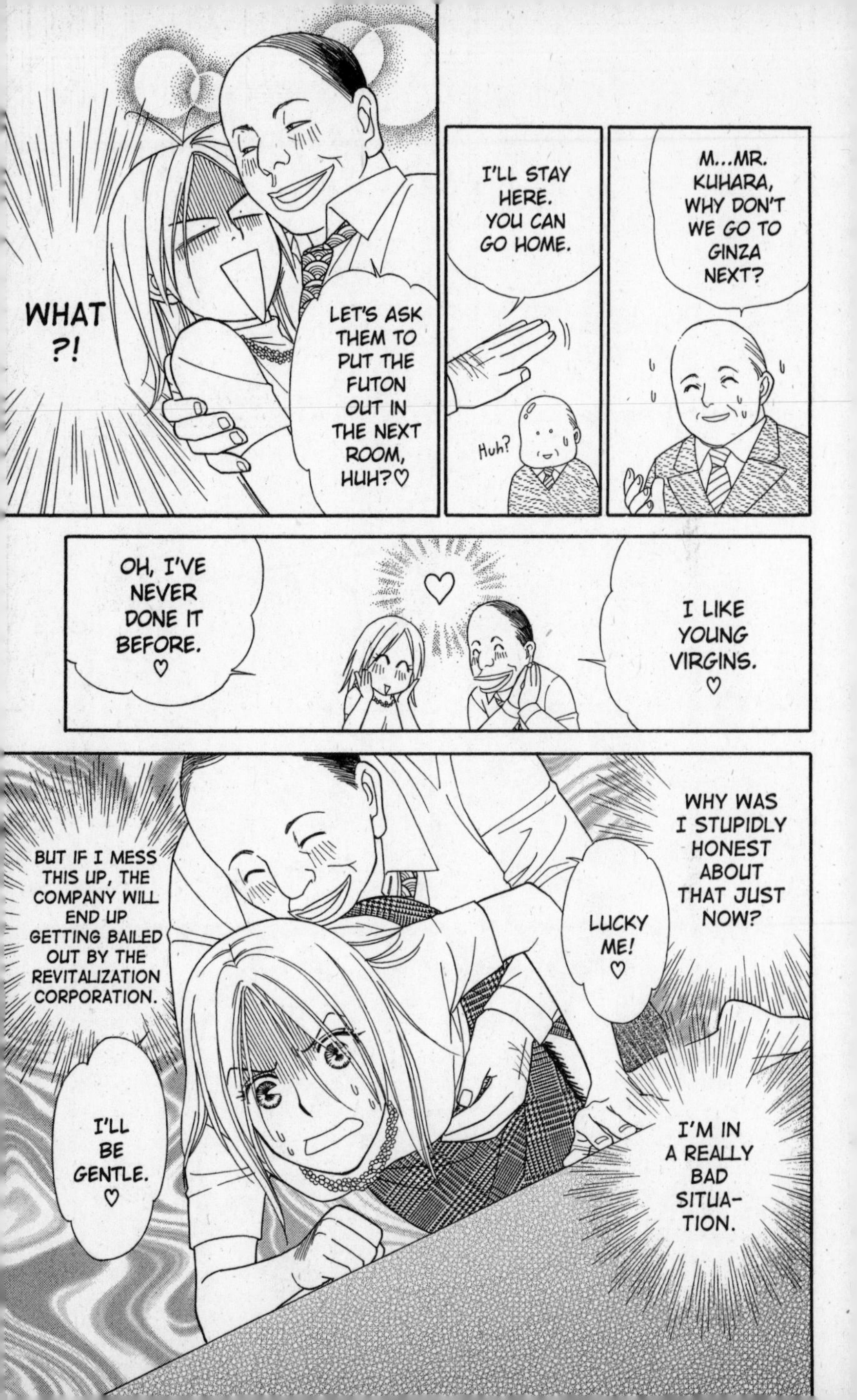
M...MR. KUHARA, WHY DON'T WE GO TO GINZA NEXT?
I'LL STAY HERE. YOU CAN GO HOME.
Huh?
LET'S ASK THEM TO PUT THE FUTON OUT IN THE NEXT ROOM, HUH?♡
WHAT?!
I LIKE YOUNG VIRGINS. ♡
OH, I'VE NEVER DONE IT BEFORE. ♡
WHY WAS I STUPIDLY HONEST ABOUT THAT JUST NOW?
LUCKY ME! ♡
BUT IF I MESS THIS UP, THE COMPANY WILL END UP GETTING BAILED OUT BY THE REVITALIZATION CORPORATION.
I'M IN A REALLY BAD SITUATION.
I'LL BE GENTLE. ♡

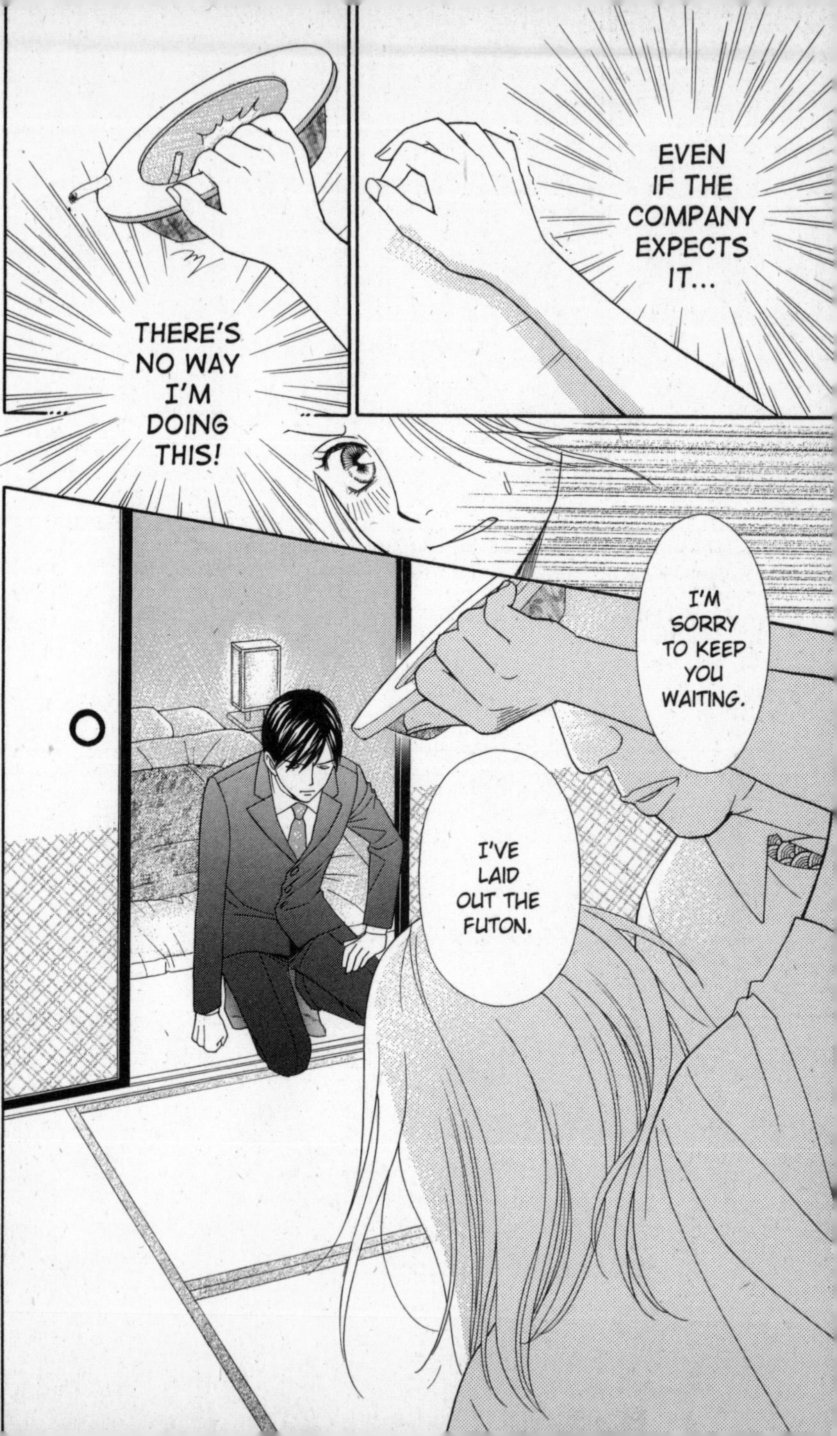
EVEN IF THE COMPANY EXPECTS IT...
THERE'S NO WAY I'M DOING THIS!
I'M SORRY TO KEEP YOU WAITING.
I'VE LAID OUT THE FUTON.

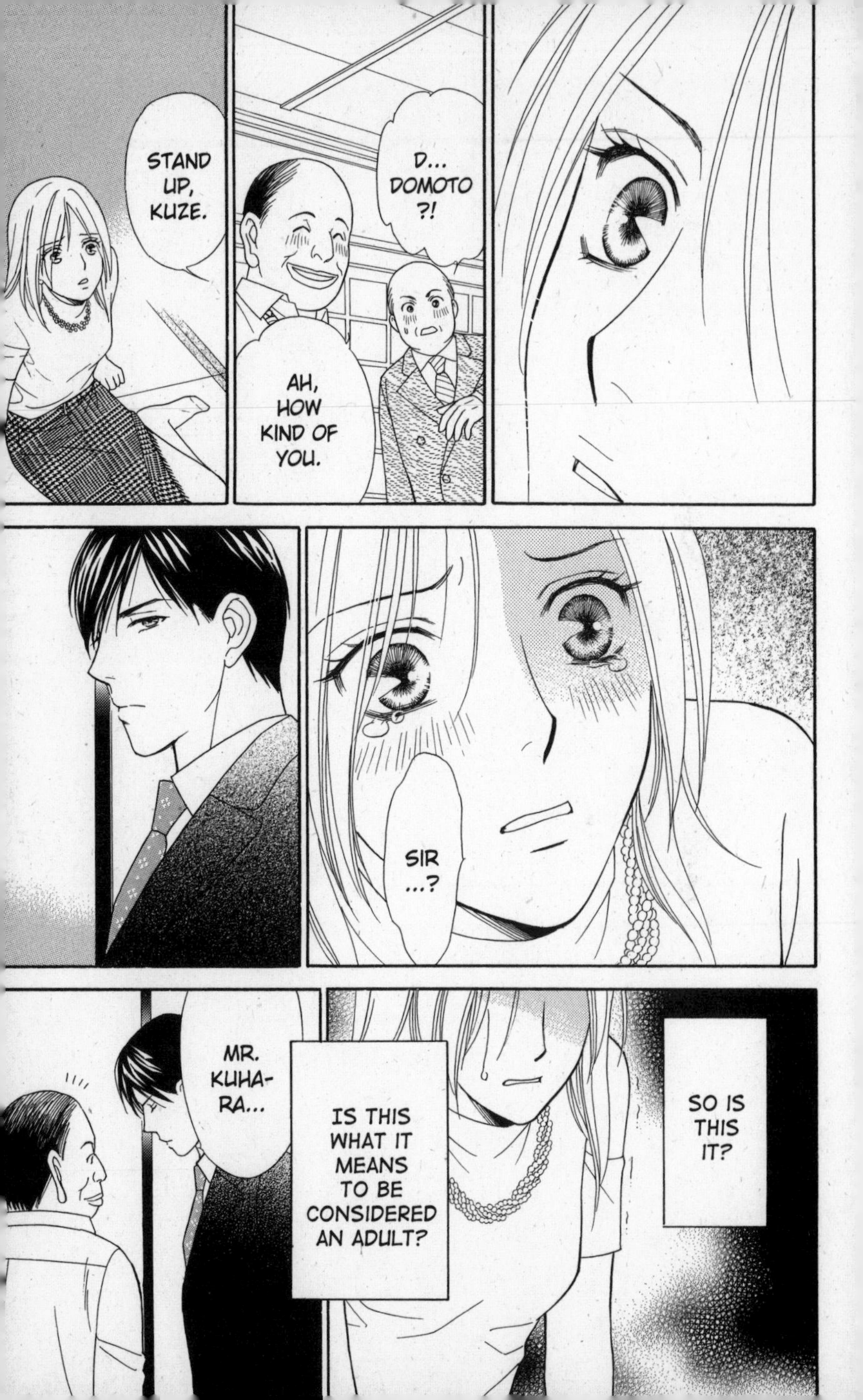
D... DOMOTO ?!
AH, HOW KIND OF YOU.
STAND UP, KUZE.
SIR ...?
SO IS THIS IT?
IS THIS WHAT IT MEANS TO BE CONSIDERED AN ADULT?
MR. KUHA-RA...

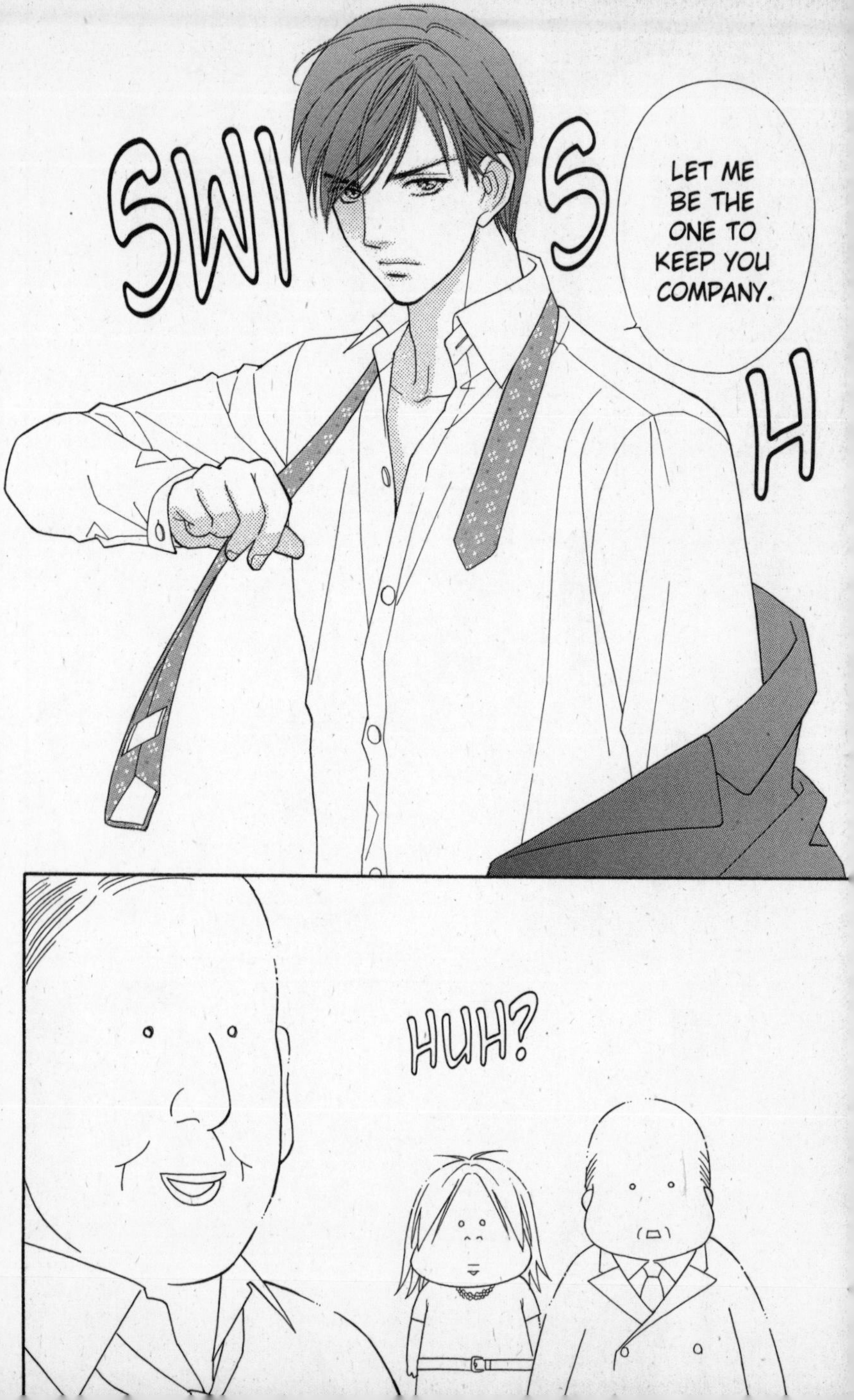
LET ME BE THE ONE TO KEEP YOU COMPANY.
SWISH
HUH?

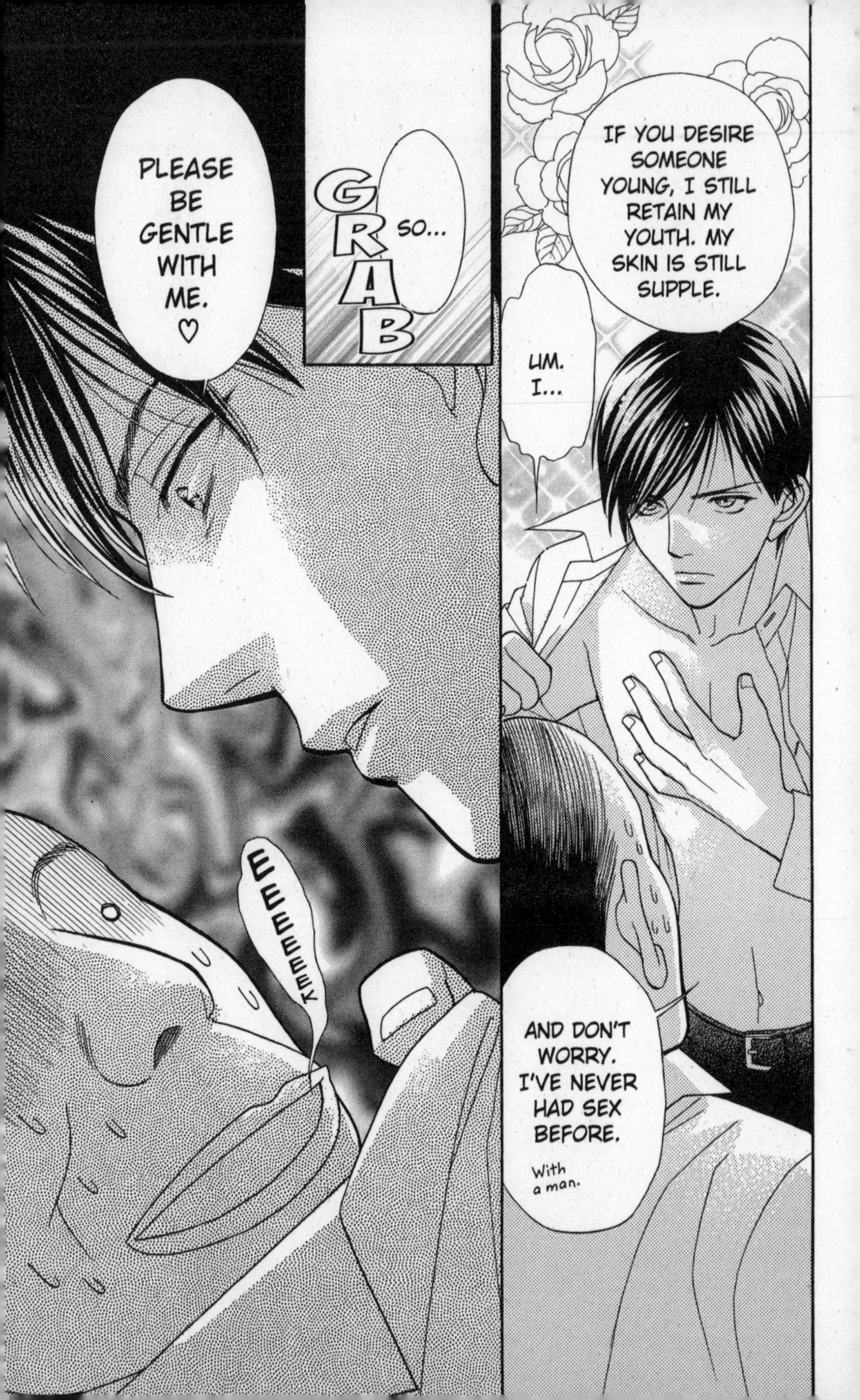
IF YOU DESIRE SOMEONE YOUNG, I STILL RETAIN MY YOUTH. MY SKIN IS STILL SUPPLE.
UM. I...
AND DON'T WORRY. I'VE NEVER HAD SEX BEFORE.
With a man.
SO...
GRAB
PLEASE BE GENTLE WITH ME. ♡
EEEEEEK

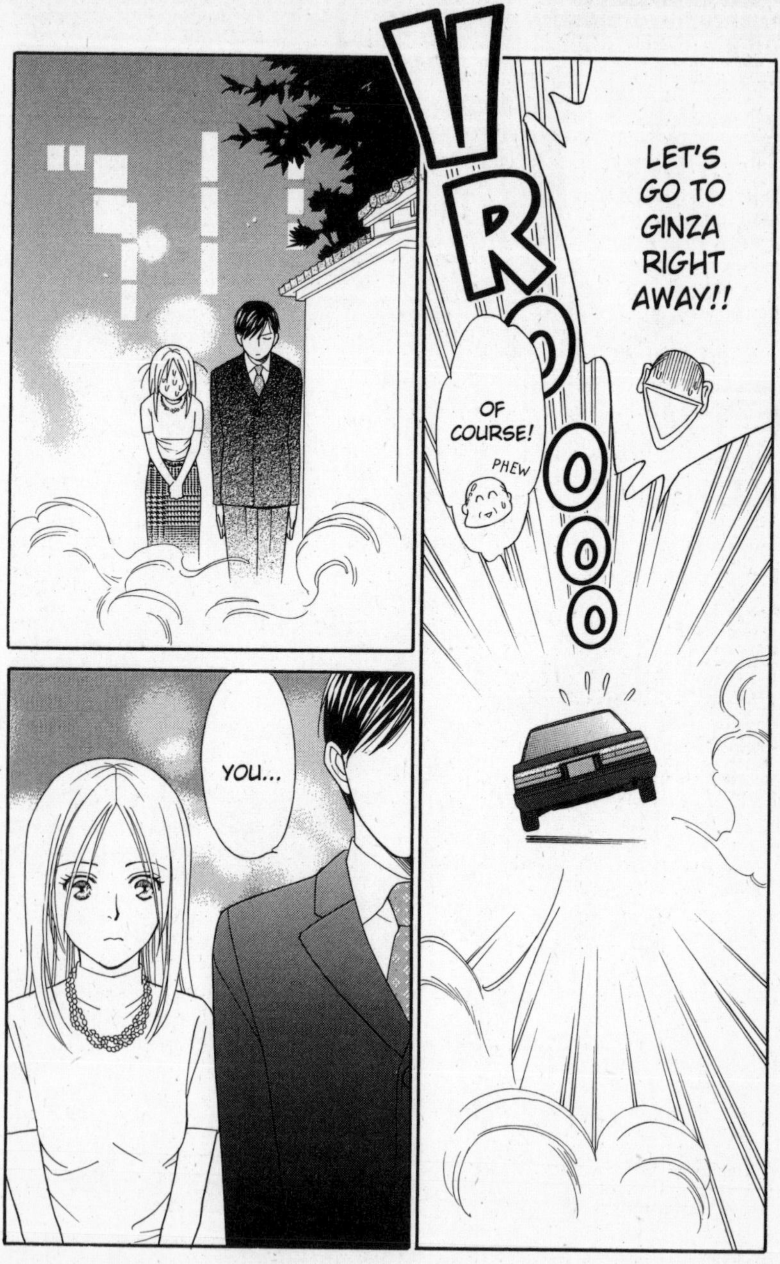
LET'S GO TO GINZA RIGHT AWAY!!
VROOOOOO
OF COURSE!
PHEW
YOU...

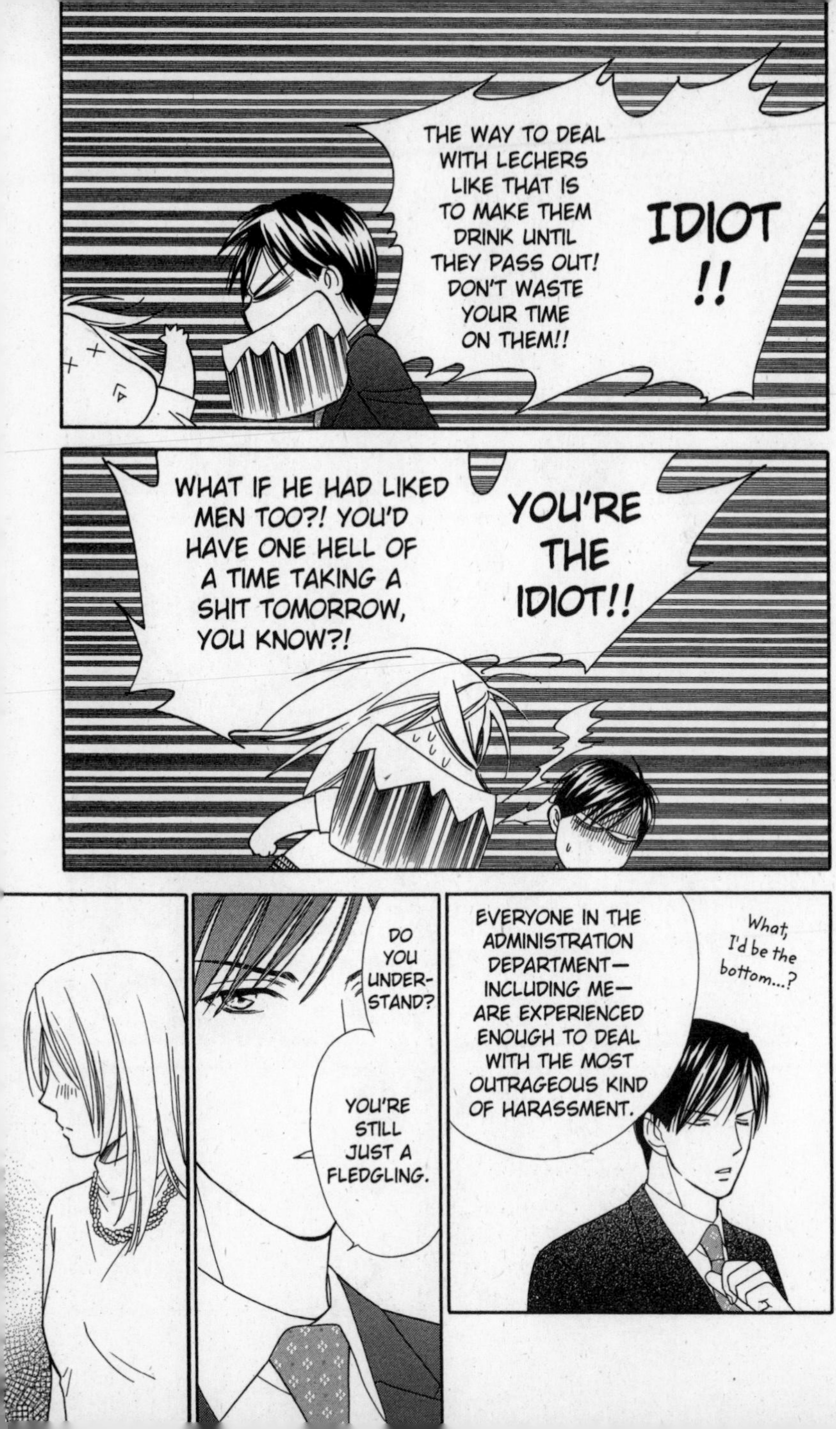
IDIOT!!
THE WAY TO DEAL WITH LECHERS LIKE THAT IS TO MAKE THEM DRINK UNTIL THEY PASS OUT! DON'T WASTE YOUR TIME ON THEM!!
YOU'RE THE IDIOT!!
WHAT IF HE HAD LIKED MEN TOO?! YOU'D HAVE ONE HELL OF A TIME TAKING A SHIT TOMORROW, YOU KNOW?!
What, I'd be the bottom...?
EVERYONE IN THE ADMINISTRATION DEPARTMENT—INCLUDING ME—ARE EXPERIENCED ENOUGH TO DEAL WITH THE MOST OUTRAGEOUS KIND OF HARASSMENT.
DO YOU UNDERSTAND?
YOU'RE STILL JUST A FLEDGLING.

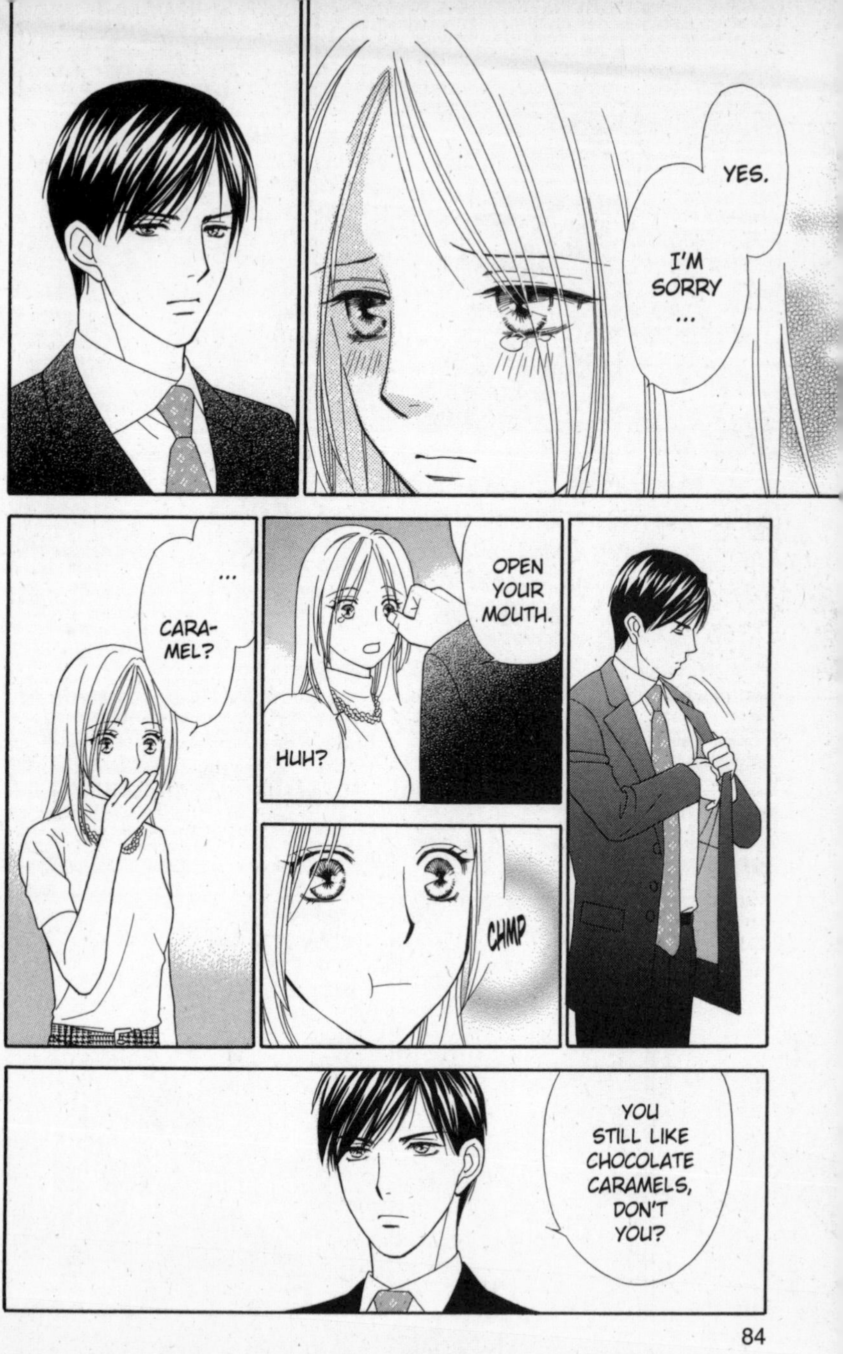
YES.
I'M SORRY ...
OPEN YOUR MOUTH.
HUH?
CHMP
... CARA-MEL?
YOU STILL LIKE CHOCOLATE CARAMELS, DON'T YOU?

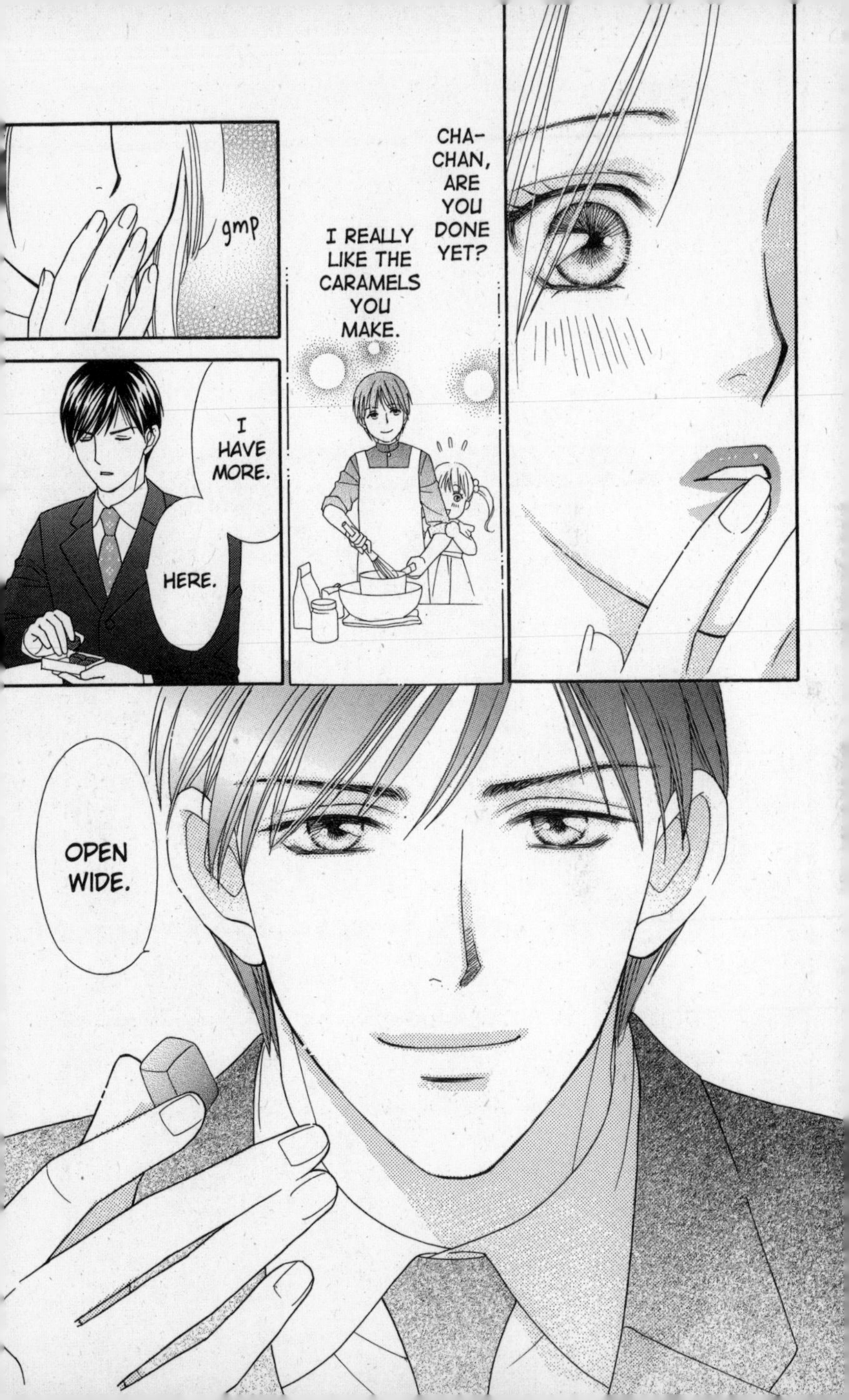
CHA-CHAN, ARE YOU DONE YET?
I REALLY LIKE THE CARAMELS YOU MAKE.
gmp
I HAVE MORE.
HERE.
OPEN WIDE.

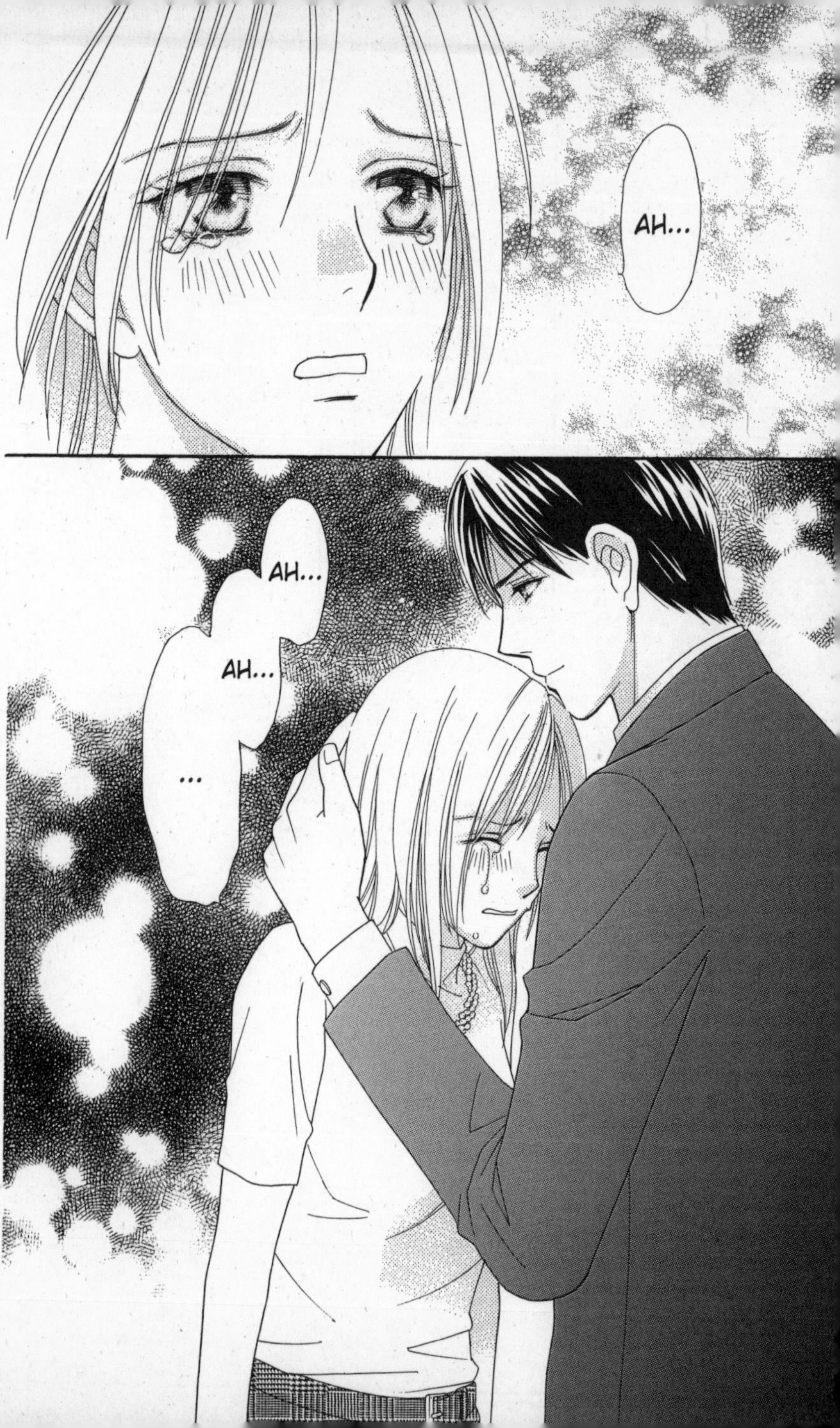
AH...
AH...
AH...
...

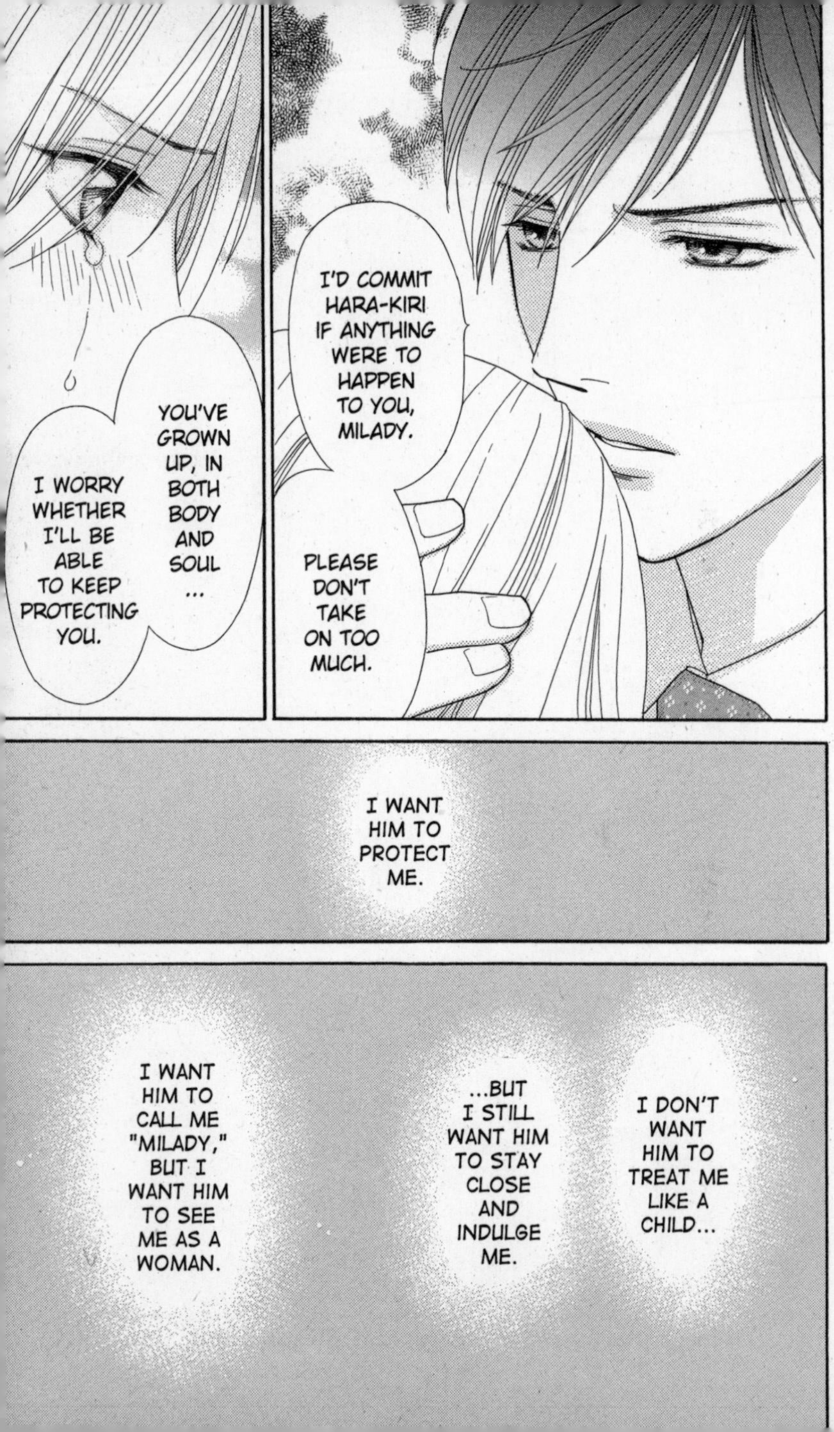
I'D COMMIT HARA-KIRI IF ANYTHING WERE TO HAPPEN TO YOU, MILADY.
PLEASE DON'T TAKE ON TOO MUCH.
YOU'VE GROWN UP, IN BOTH BODY AND SOUL...
I WORRY WHETHER I'LL BE ABLE TO KEEP PROTECTING YOU.
I WANT HIM TO PROTECT ME.
I DON'T WANT HIM TO TREAT ME LIKE A CHILD...
...BUT I STILL WANT HIM TO STAY CLOSE AND INDULGE ME.
I WANT HIM TO CALL ME "MILADY," BUT I WANT HIM TO SEE ME AS A WOMAN.

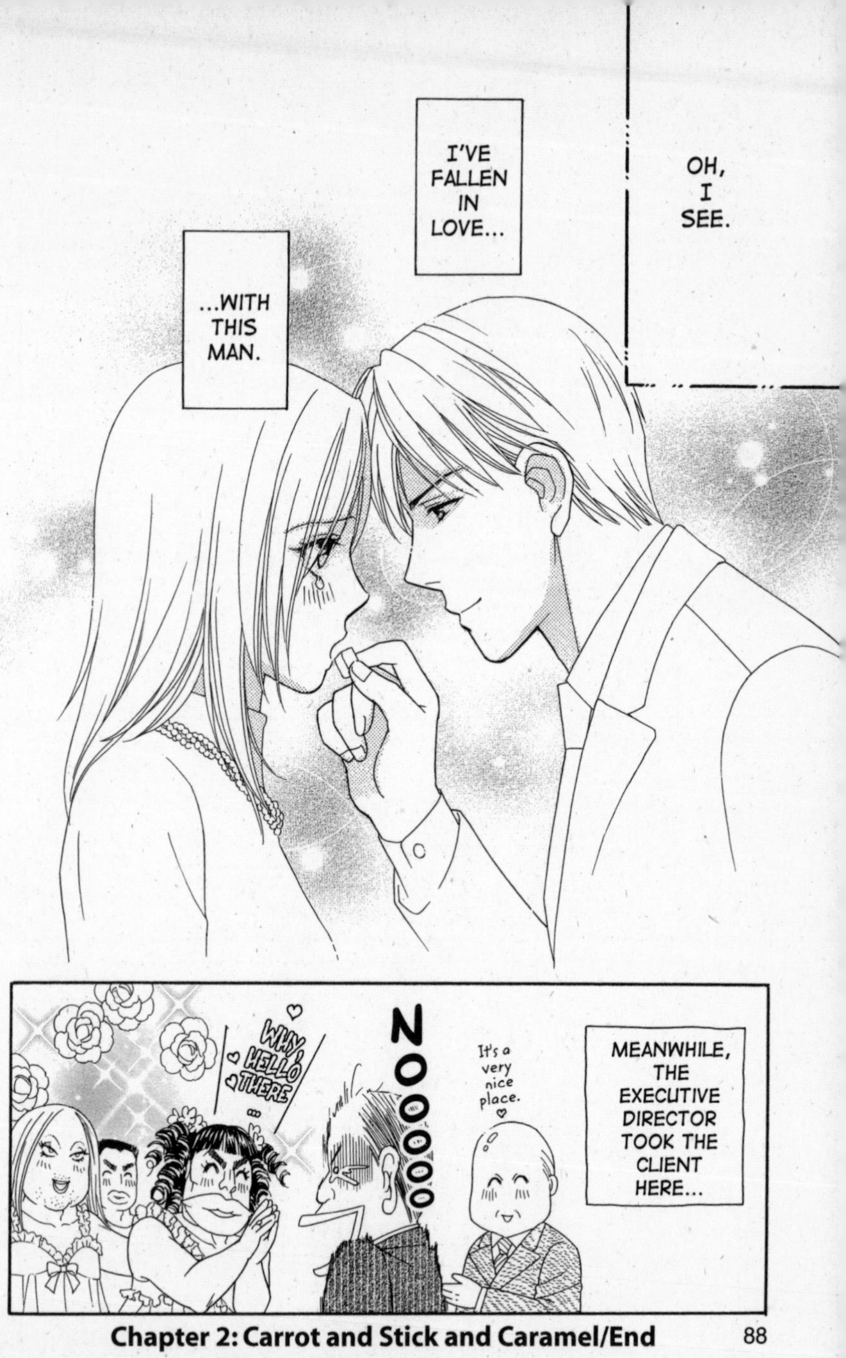
OH, I SEE.
I'VE FALLEN IN LOVE...
...WITH THIS MAN.
MEANWHILE, THE EXECUTIVE DIRECTOR TOOK THE CLIENT HERE...
It's a very nice place.
NOOOOOOO
WHY, HELLO THERE

Chapter 2: Carrot and Stick and Caramel/End

Chapter 3
Secret Assistant

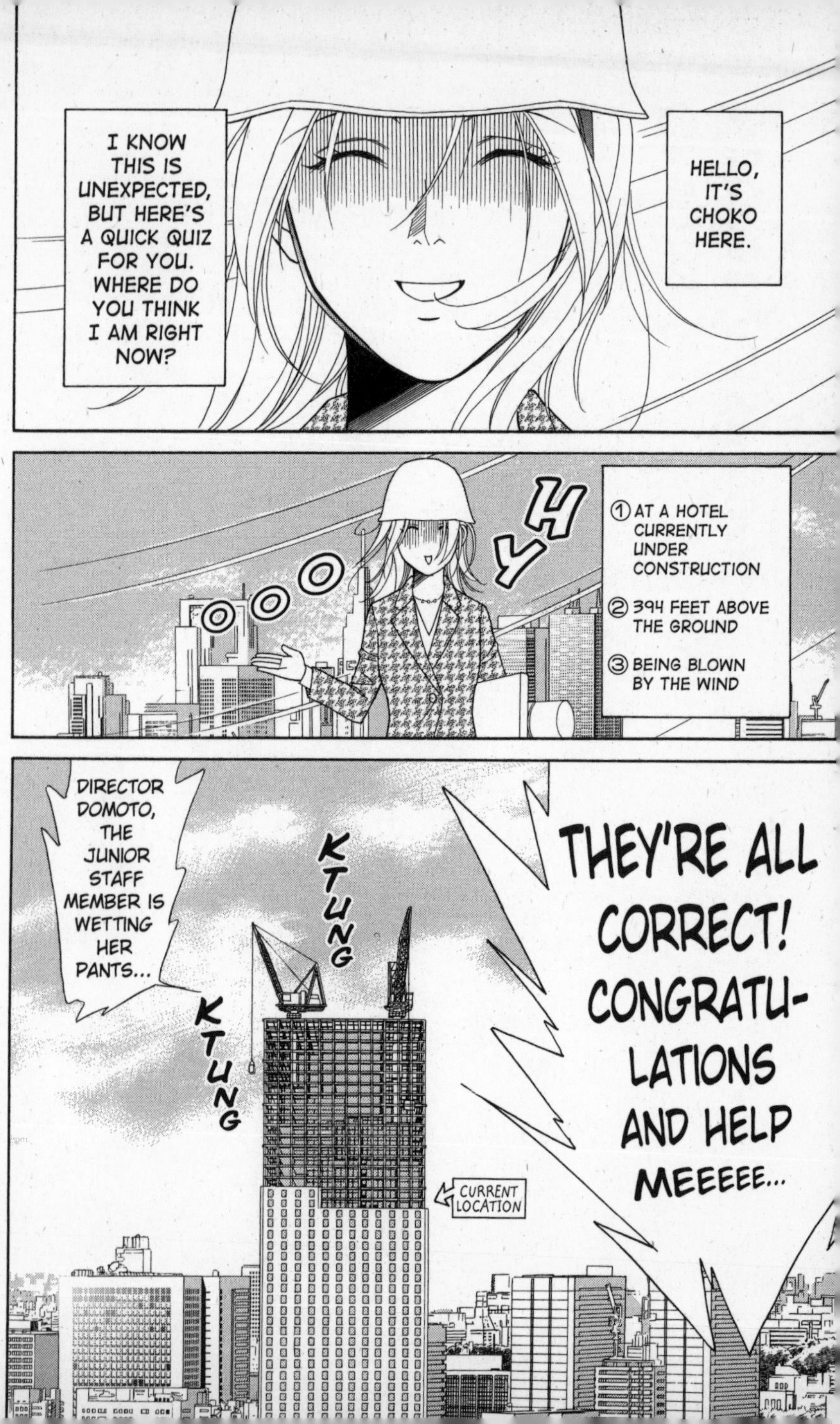
HELLO, IT'S CHOKO HERE.
I KNOW THIS IS UNEXPECTED, BUT HERE'S A QUICK QUIZ FOR YOU. WHERE DO YOU THINK I AM RIGHT NOW?
① AT A HOTEL CURRENTLY UNDER CONSTRUCTION
② 394 FEET ABOVE THE GROUND
③ BEING BLOWN BY THE WIND
HYOOOO
THEY'RE ALL CORRECT! CONGRATU-LATIONS AND HELP MEEEEE...
KTUNG
KTUNG
DIRECTOR DOMOTO, THE JUNIOR STAFF MEMBER IS WETTING HER PANTS...
CURRENT LOCATION

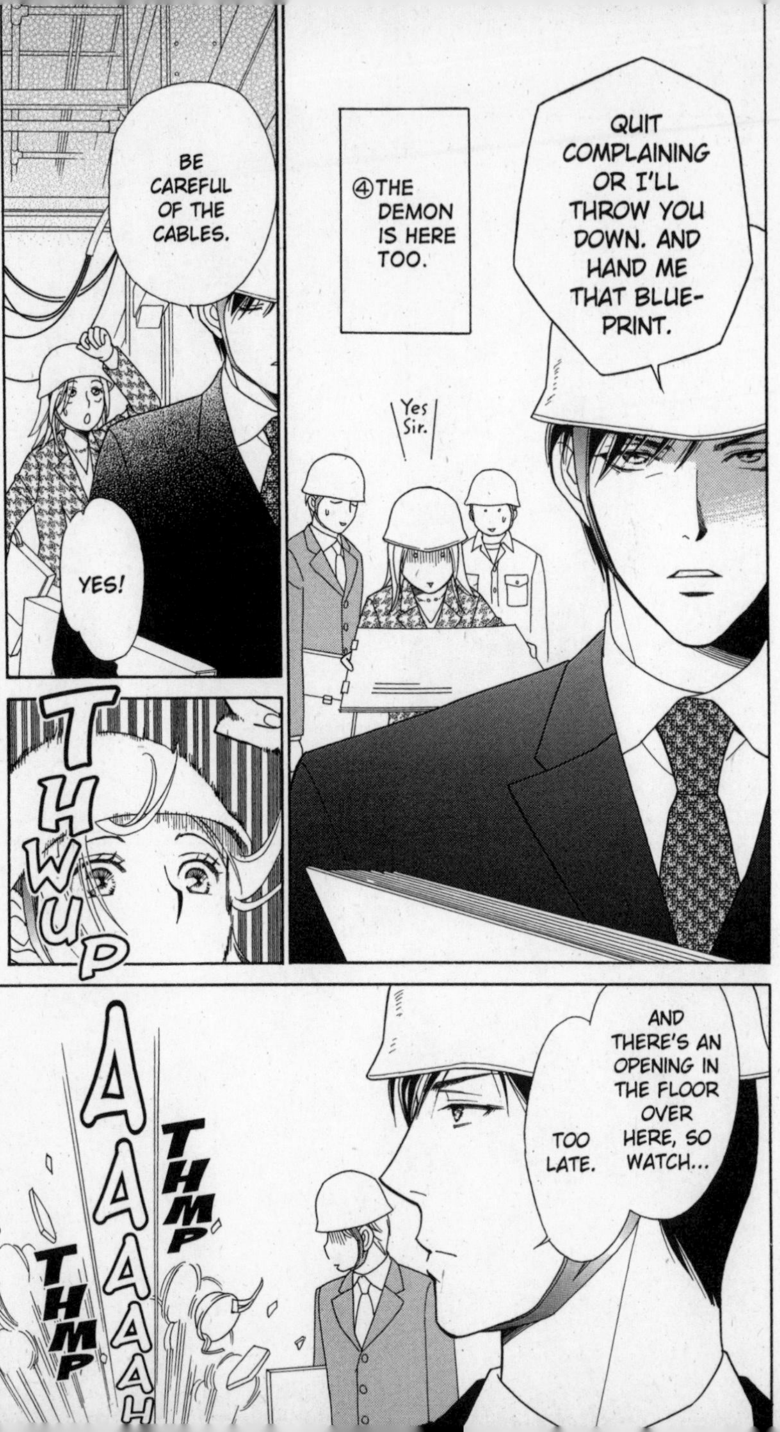
QUIT COMPLAINING OR I'LL THROW YOU DOWN. AND HAND ME THAT BLUE-PRINT.
④THE DEMON IS HERE TOO.
Yes Sir.
BE CAREFUL OF THE CABLES.
YES!
THWUP
AND THERE'S AN OPENING IN THE FLOOR OVER HERE, SO WATCH...
TOO LATE.
THMP
AAAAAH
THMP

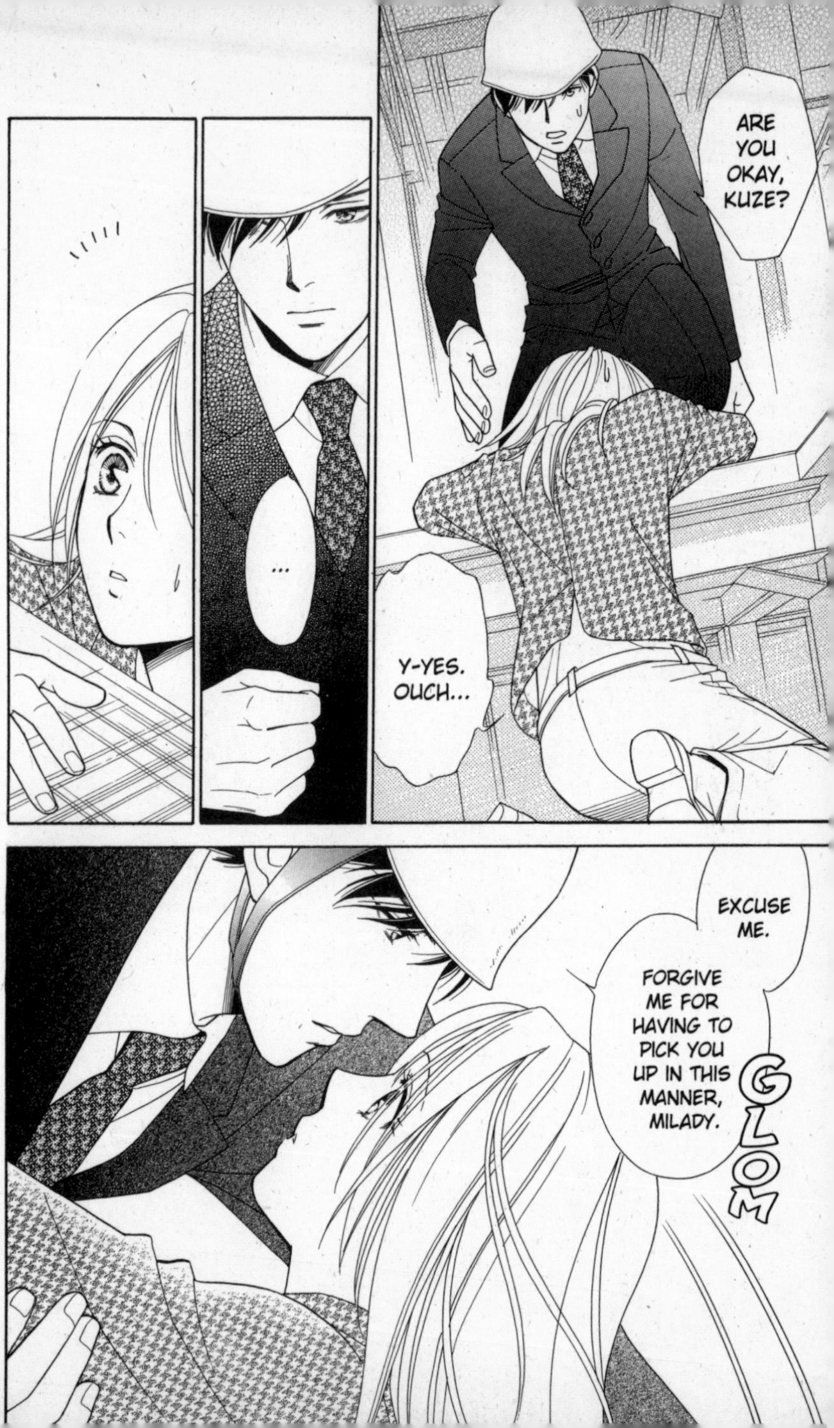
ARE YOU OKAY, KUZE?
Y-YES. OUCH...
...
EXCUSE ME.
FORGIVE ME FOR HAVING TO PICK YOU UP IN THIS MANNER, MILADY.
GLOM

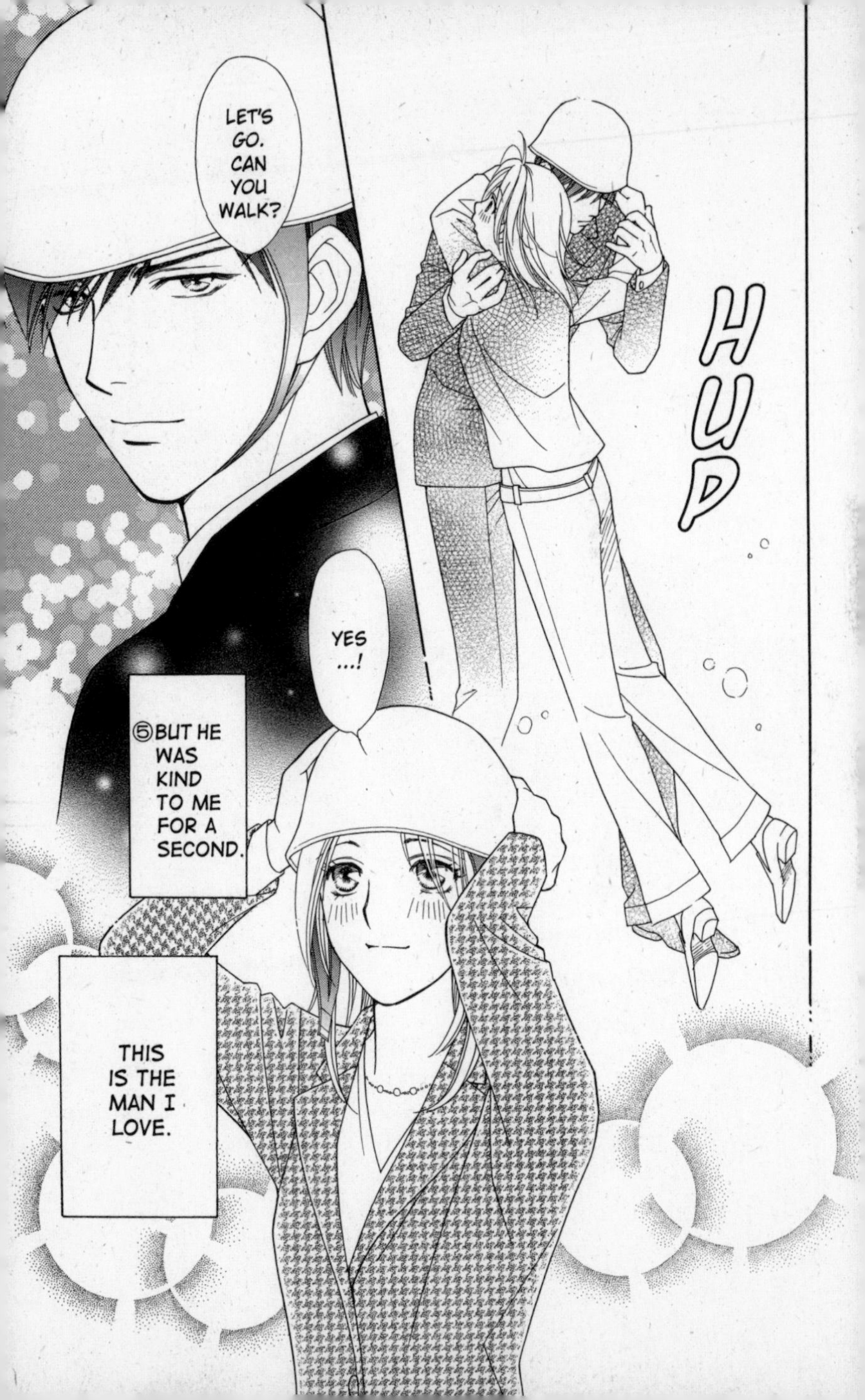
HUP
LET'S GO. CAN YOU WALK?
YES ...!
⑤BUT HE WAS KIND TO ME FOR A SECOND.
THIS IS THE MAN I LOVE.

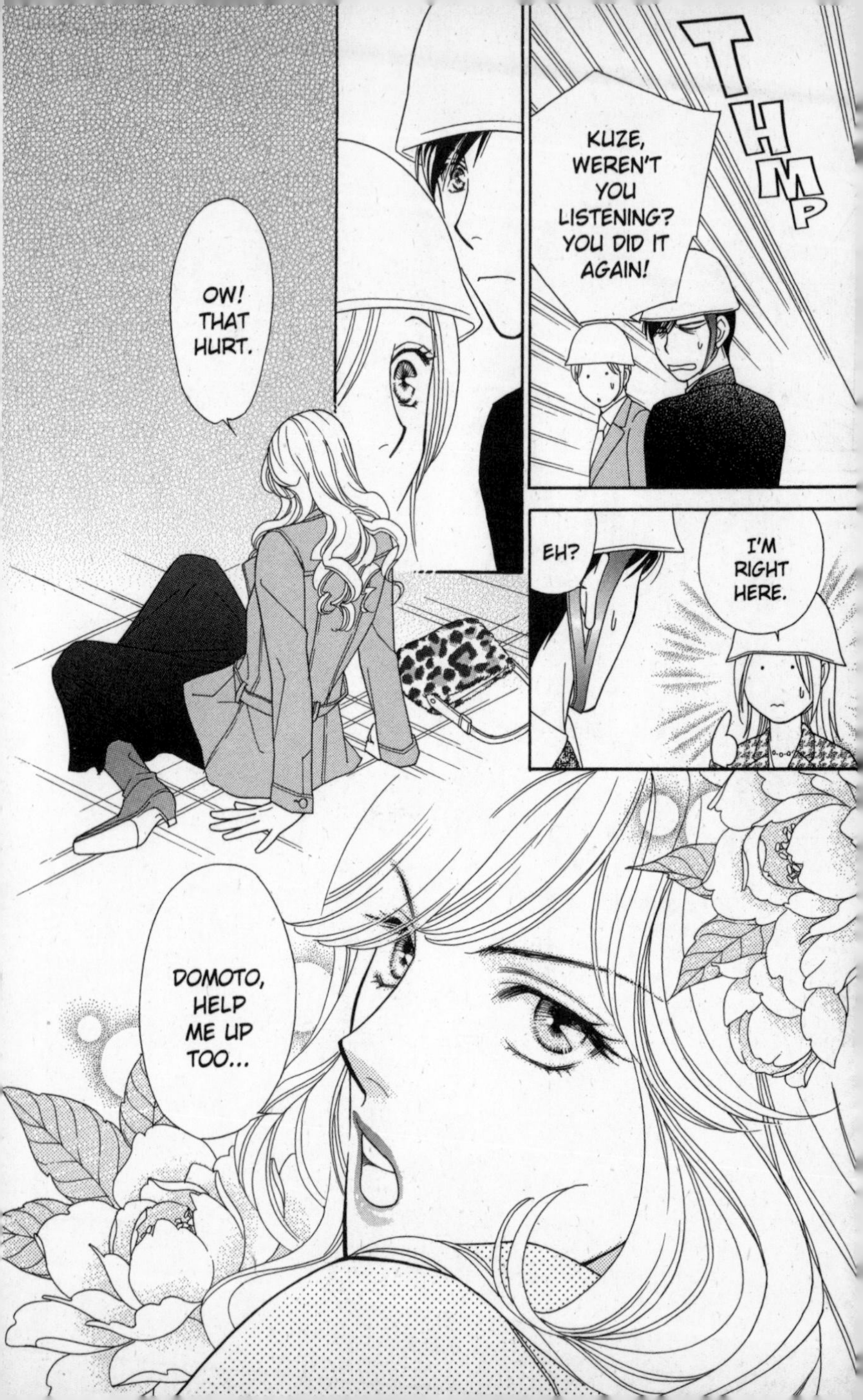
THMP
KUZE, WEREN'T YOU LISTENING? YOU DID IT AGAIN!
I'M RIGHT HERE.
EH?
OW! THAT HURT.
DOMOTO, HELP ME UP TOO...

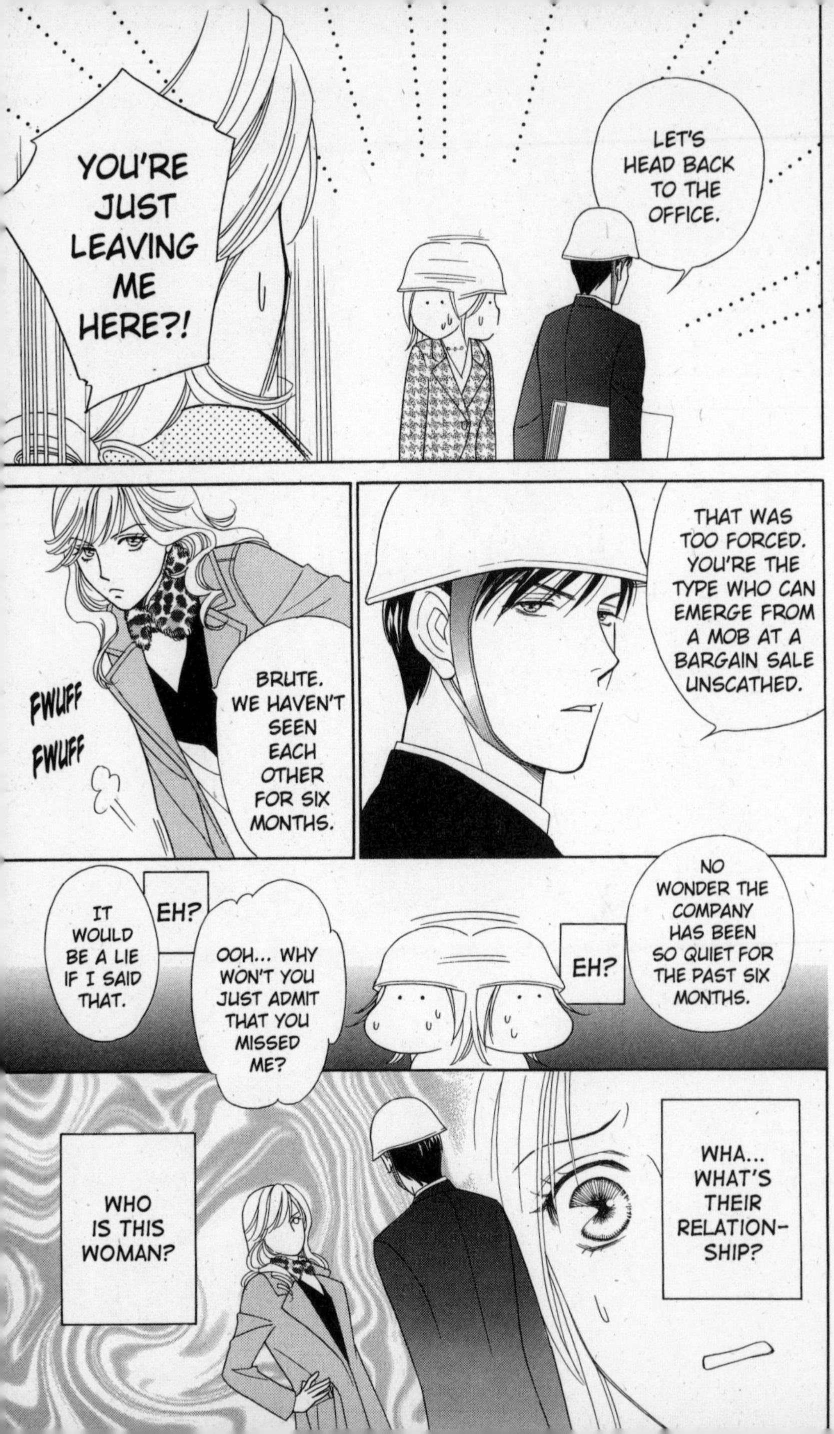
LET'S HEAD BACK TO THE OFFICE.
YOU'RE JUST LEAVING ME HERE?!
THAT WAS TOO FORCED. YOU'RE THE TYPE WHO CAN EMERGE FROM A MOB AT A BARGAIN SALE UNSCATHED.
BRUTE. WE HAVEN'T SEEN EACH OTHER FOR SIX MONTHS.
FWUFF
FWUFF
NO WONDER THE COMPANY HAS BEEN SO QUIET FOR THE PAST SIX MONTHS.
EH?
OOH... WHY WON'T YOU JUST ADMIT THAT YOU MISSED ME?
EH?
IT WOULD BE A LIE IF I SAID THAT.
WHA... WHAT'S THEIR RELATION-SHIP?
WHO IS THIS WOMAN?

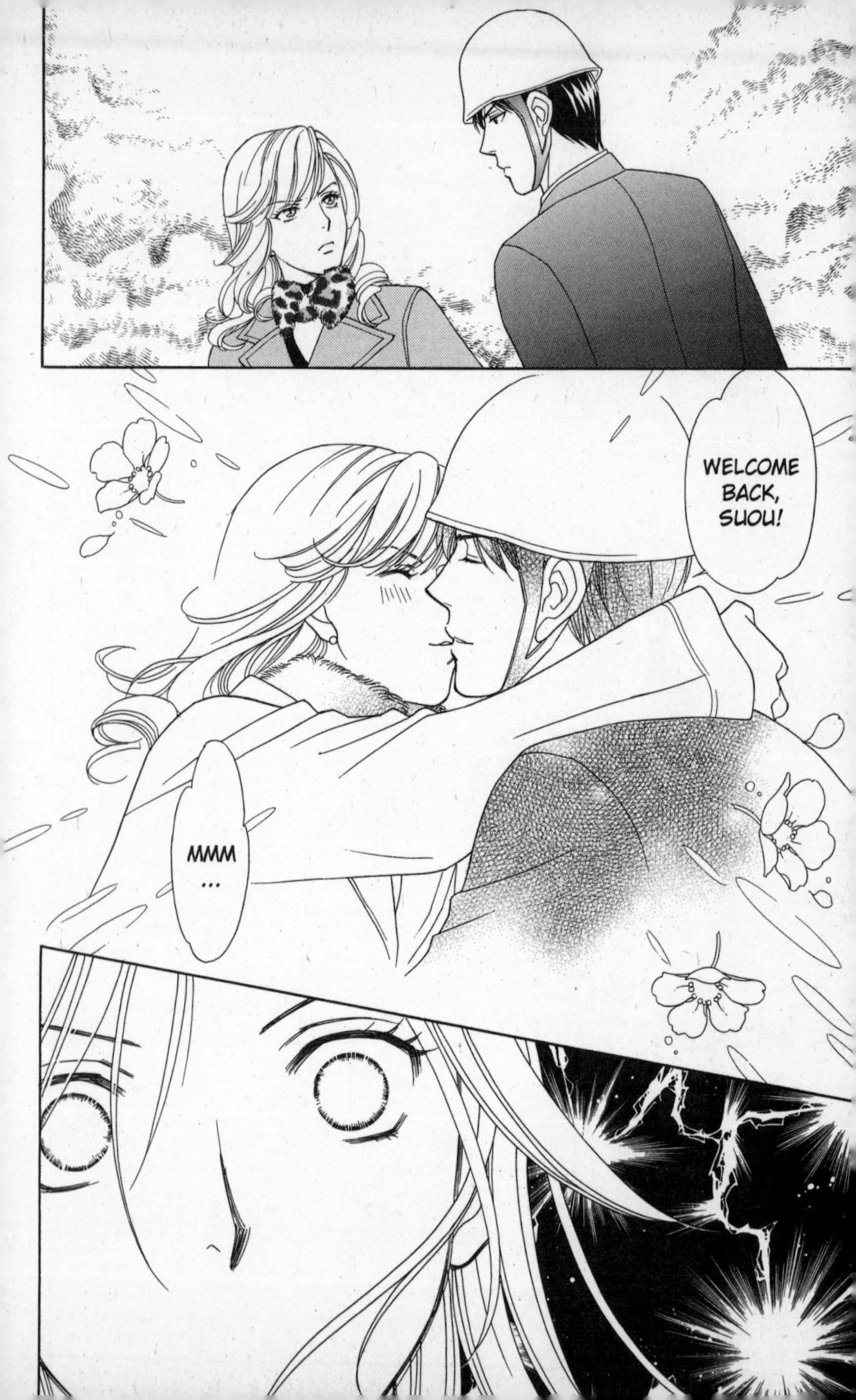
WELCOME BACK, SUOU!
MMM ...

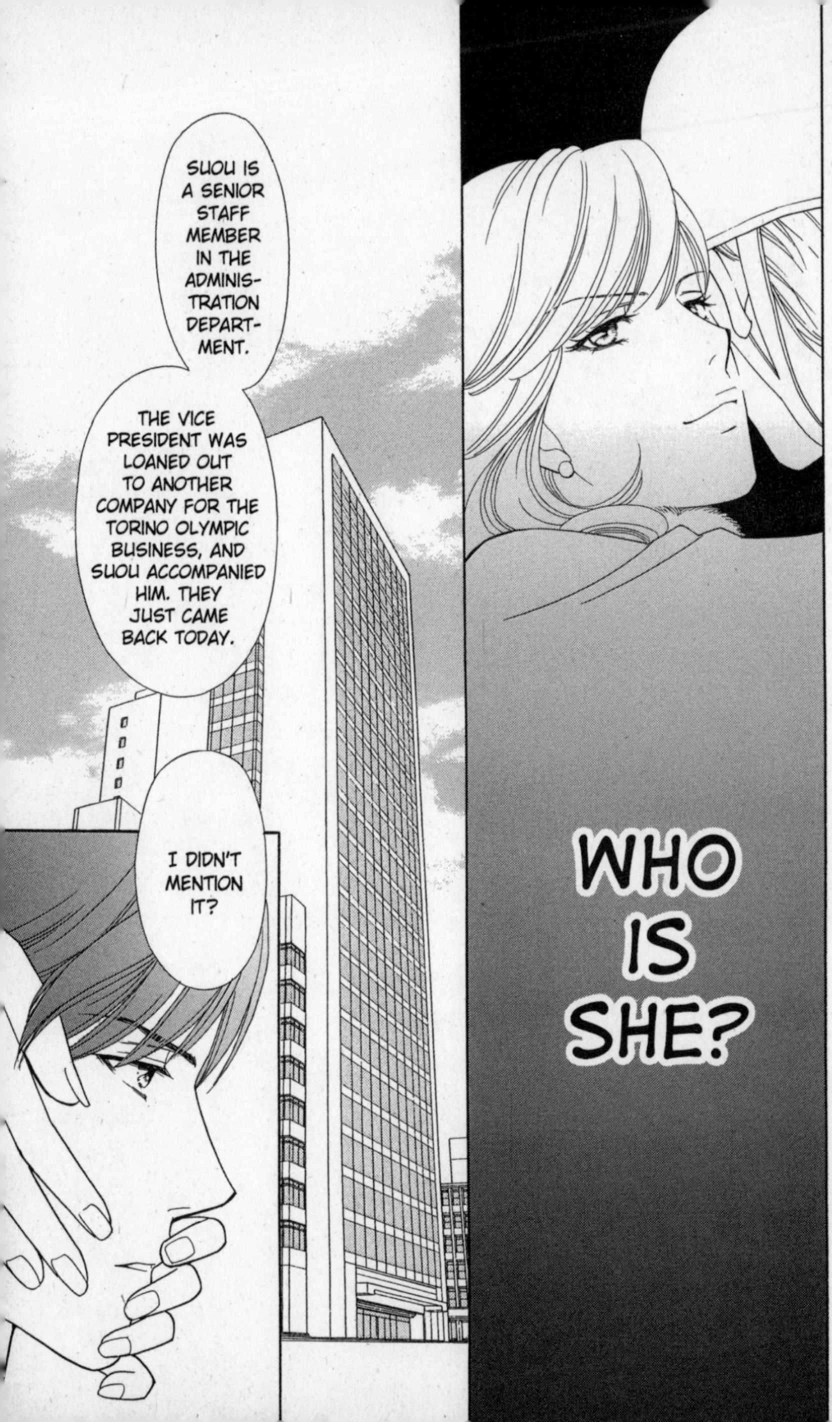
WHO IS SHE?
SUOU IS A SENIOR STAFF MEMBER IN THE ADMINIS-TRATION DEPART-MENT.
THE VICE PRESIDENT WAS LOANED OUT TO ANOTHER COMPANY FOR THE TORINO OLYMPIC BUSINESS, AND SUOU ACCOMPANIED HIM. THEY JUST CAME BACK TODAY.
I DIDN'T MENTION IT?

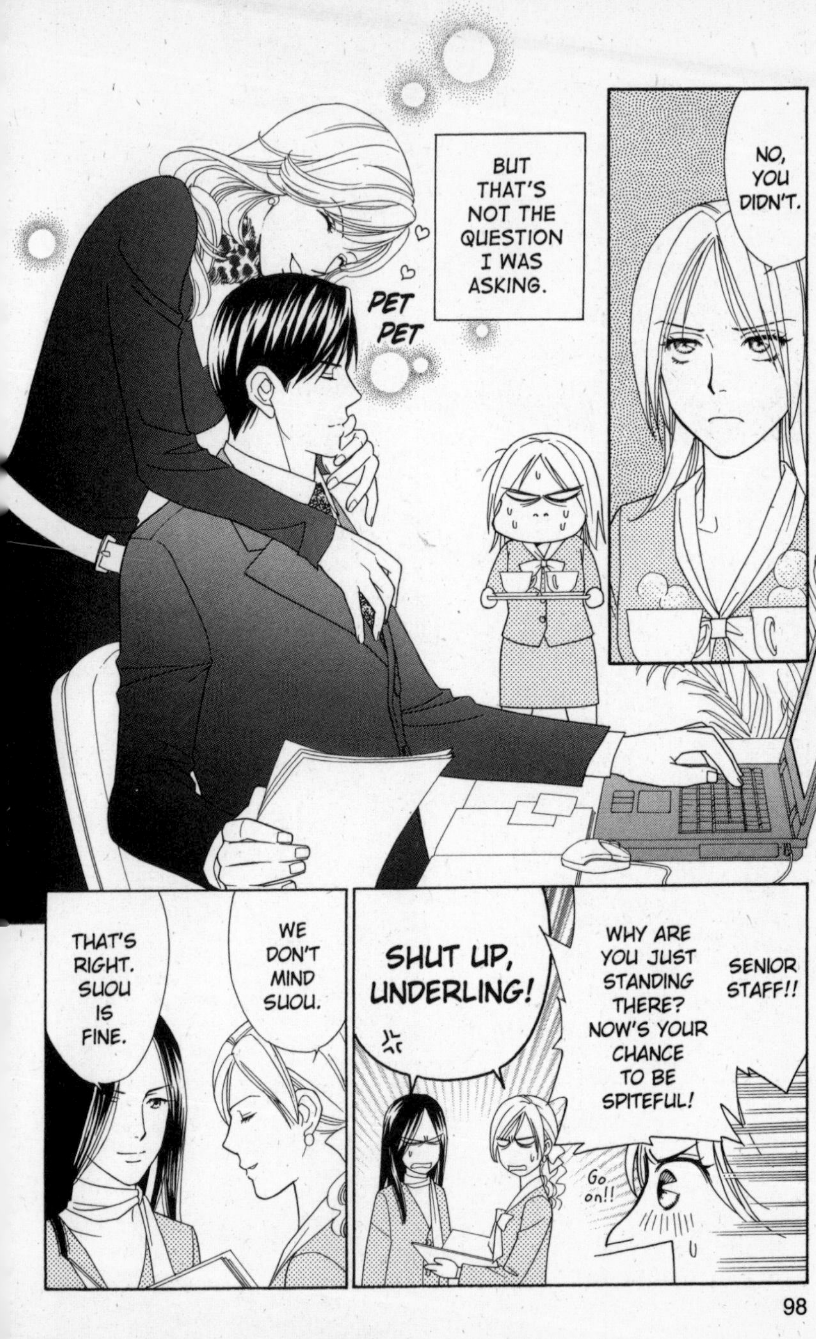
NO, YOU DIDN'T.
BUT THAT'S NOT THE QUESTION I WAS ASKING.
PET PET
SENIOR STAFF!!
WHY ARE YOU JUST STANDING THERE? NOW'S YOUR CHANCE TO BE SPITEFUL!
Go on!!
SHUT UP, UNDERLING!
WE DON'T MIND SUOU.
THAT'S RIGHT. SUOU IS FINE.

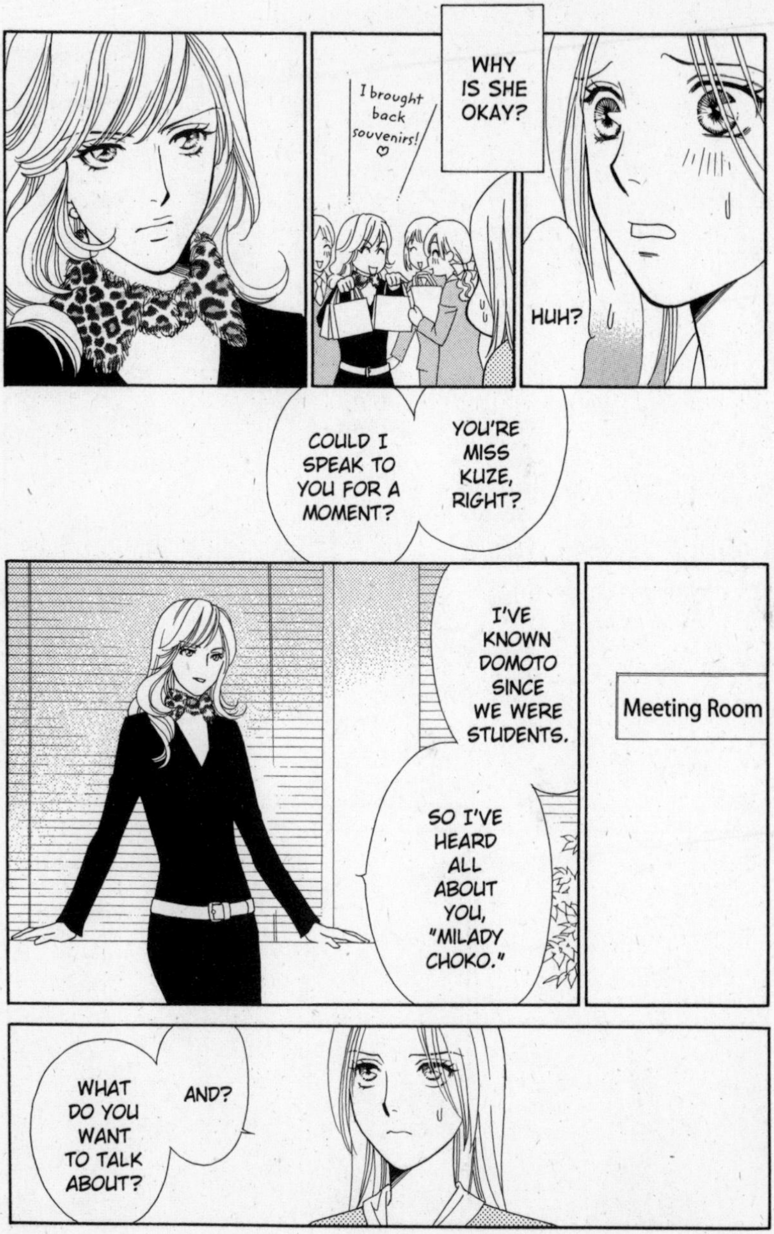
HUH?
WHY IS SHE OKAY?
I brought back souvenirs! ♡
YOU'RE MISS KUZE, RIGHT?
COULD I SPEAK TO YOU FOR A MOMENT?
Meeting Room
I'VE KNOWN DOMOTO SINCE WE WERE STUDENTS.
SO I'VE HEARD ALL ABOUT YOU, "MILADY CHOKO."
AND?
WHAT DO YOU WANT TO TALK ABOUT?

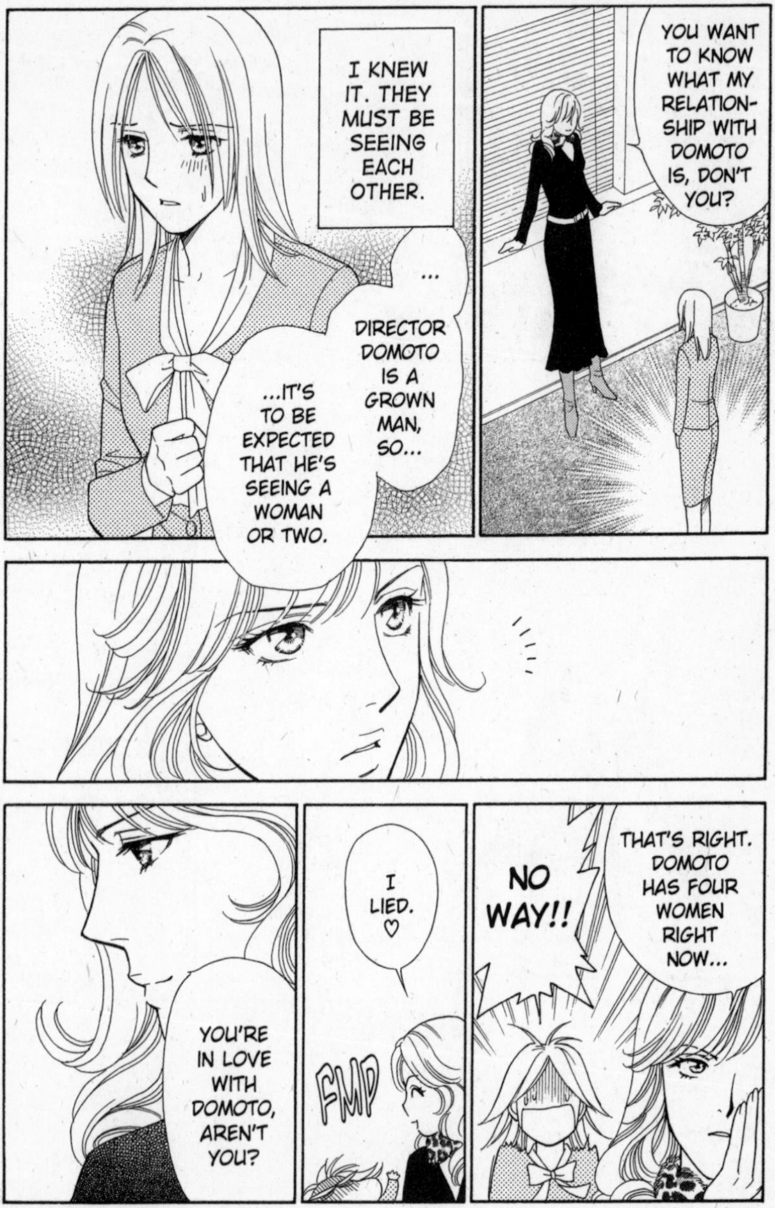

YOU WANT TO KNOW WHAT MY RELATIONSHIP WITH DOMOTO IS, DON'T YOU?
I KNEW IT. THEY MUST BE SEEING EACH OTHER.
...
DIRECTOR DOMOTO IS A GROWN MAN, SO...
...IT'S TO BE EXPECTED THAT HE'S SEEING A WOMAN OR TWO.
THAT'S RIGHT. DOMOTO HAS FOUR WOMEN RIGHT NOW...
NO WAY!!
I LIED. ♡
FMP
YOU'RE IN LOVE WITH DOMOTO, AREN'T YOU?

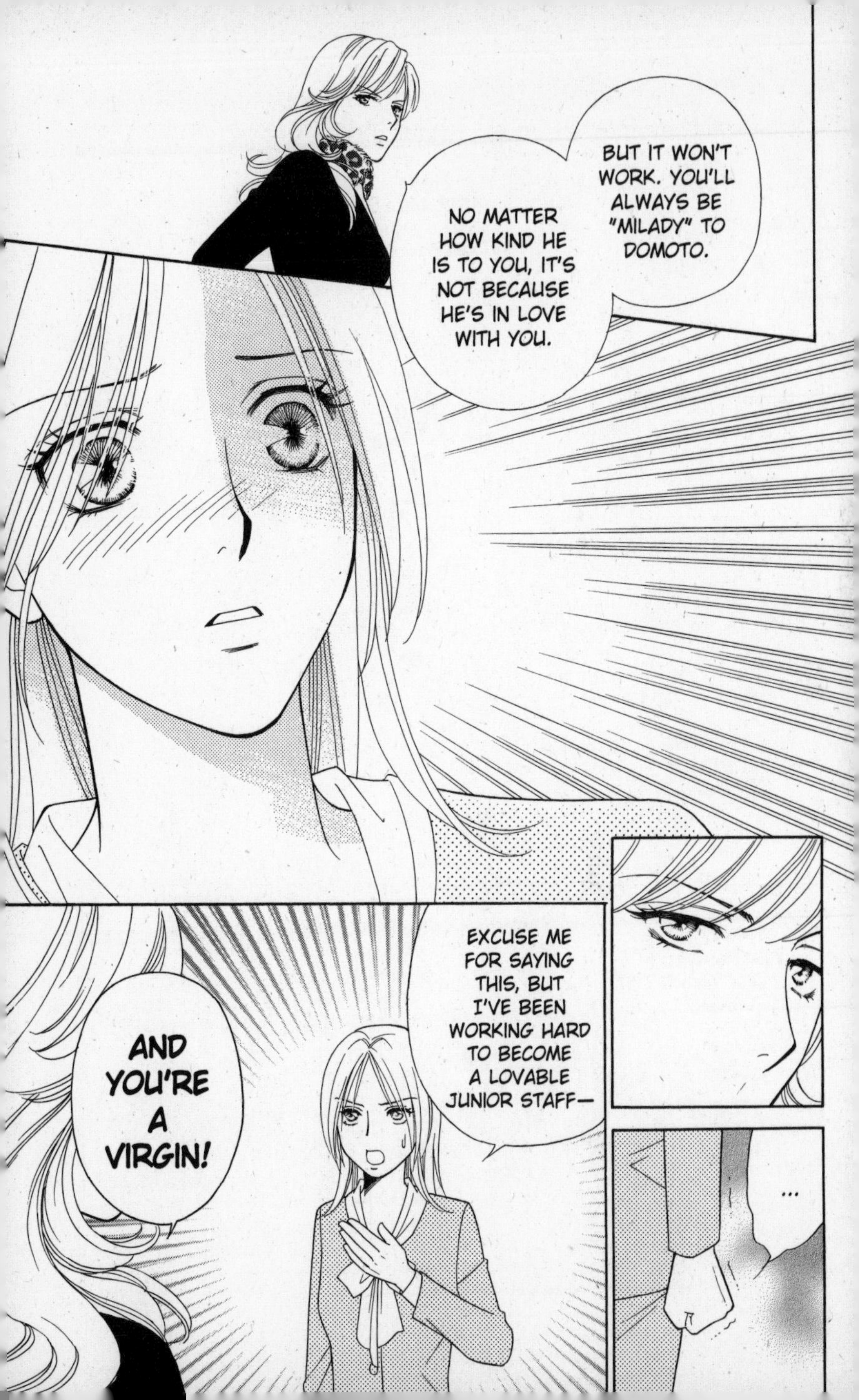
BUT IT WON'T WORK. YOU'LL ALWAYS BE "MILADY" TO DOMOTO.
NO MATTER HOW KIND HE IS TO YOU, IT'S NOT BECAUSE HE'S IN LOVE WITH YOU.
...
EXCUSE ME FOR SAYING THIS, BUT I'VE BEEN WORKING HARD TO BECOME A LOVABLE JUNIOR STAFF—
AND YOU'RE A VIRGIN!

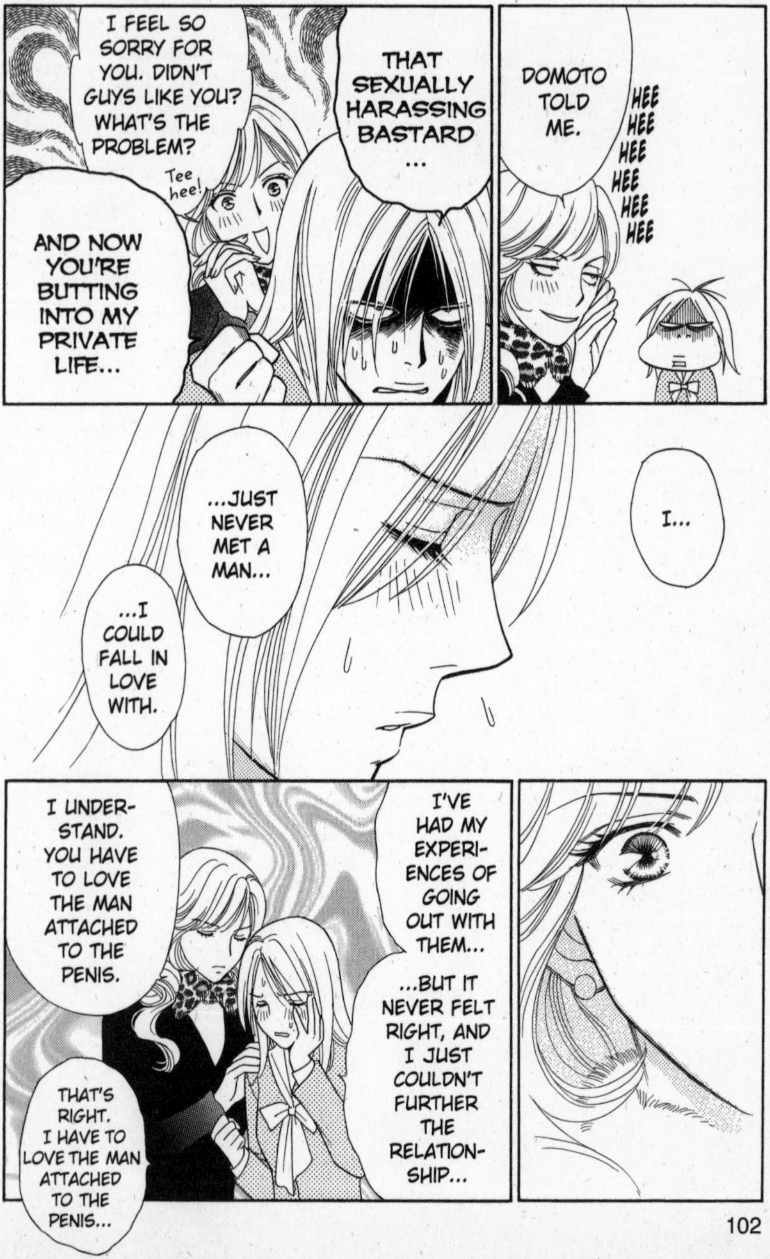
DOMOTO TOLD ME.
HEE HEE HEE HEE HEE HEE
THAT SEXUALLY HARASSING BASTARD...
I FEEL SO SORRY FOR YOU. DIDN'T GUYS LIKE YOU? WHAT'S THE PROBLEM?
Tee hee!
AND NOW YOU'RE BUTTING INTO MY PRIVATE LIFE...
I...
...JUST NEVER MET A MAN...
...I COULD FALL IN LOVE WITH.
I'VE HAD MY EXPERIENCES OF GOING OUT WITH THEM...
...BUT IT NEVER FELT RIGHT, AND I JUST COULDN'T FURTHER THE RELATIONSHIP...
I UNDERSTAND. YOU HAVE TO LOVE THE MAN ATTACHED TO THE PENIS.
THAT'S RIGHT. I HAVE TO LOVE THE MAN ATTACHED TO THE PENIS...

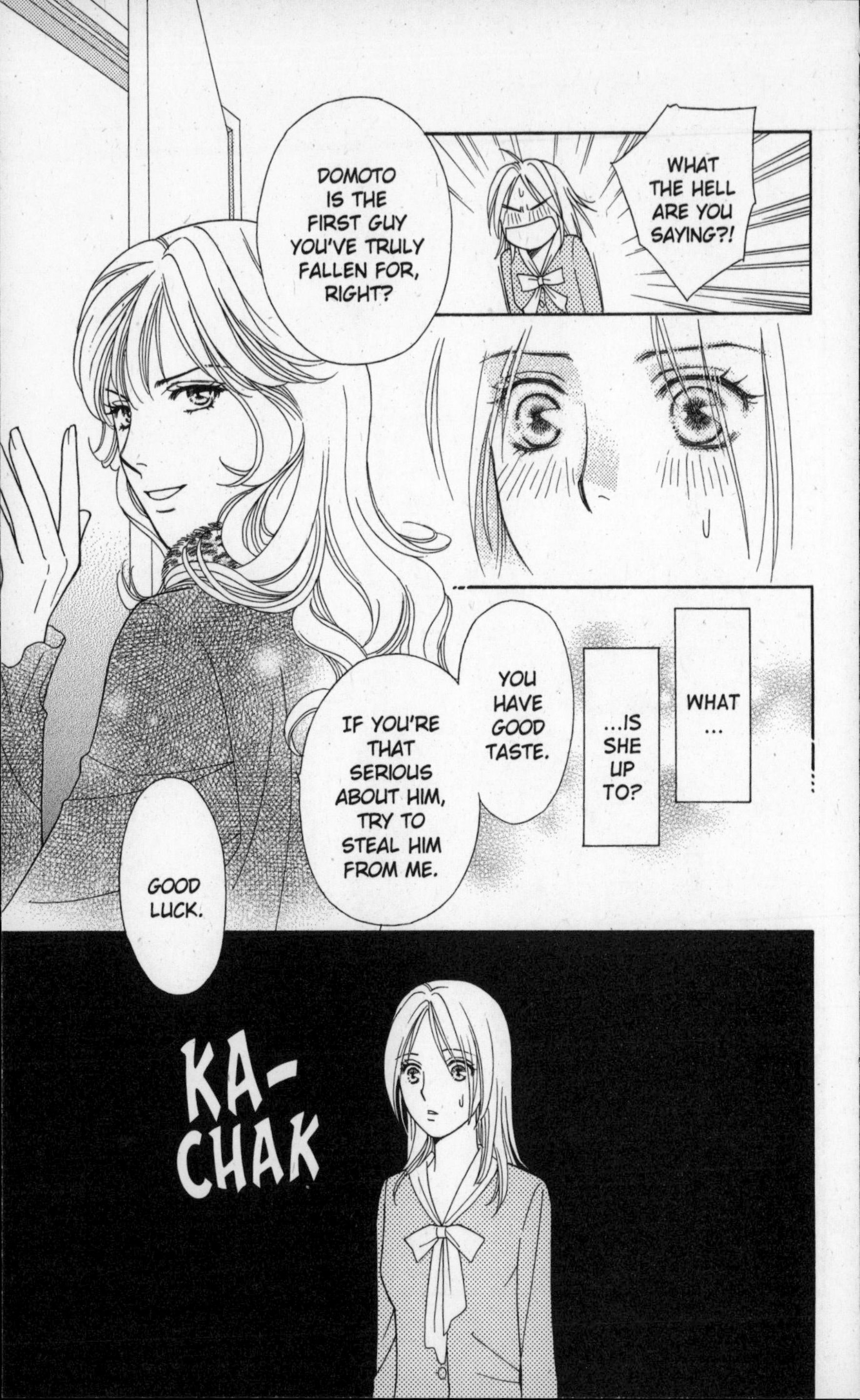
DOMOTO IS THE FIRST GUY YOU'VE TRULY FALLEN FOR, RIGHT?
WHAT THE HELL ARE YOU SAYING?!
WHAT...
...IS SHE UP TO?
YOU HAVE GOOD TASTE.
IF YOU'RE THAT SERIOUS ABOUT HIM, TRY TO STEAL HIM FROM ME.
GOOD LUCK.
KA-CHAK

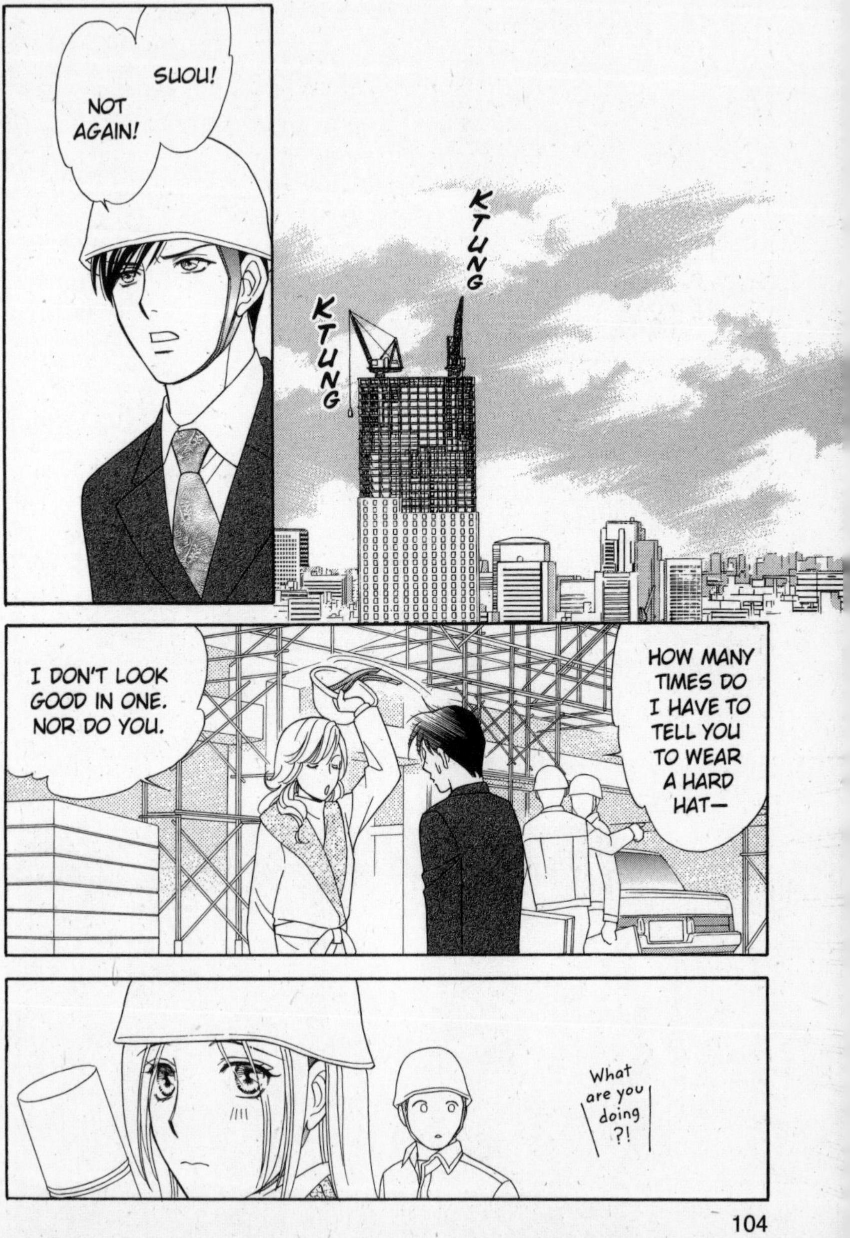
KTUNG
KTUNG
SUOU!
NOT AGAIN!
HOW MANY TIMES DO I HAVE TO TELL YOU TO WEAR A HARD HAT—
I DON'T LOOK GOOD IN ONE. NOR DO YOU.
What are you doing ?!

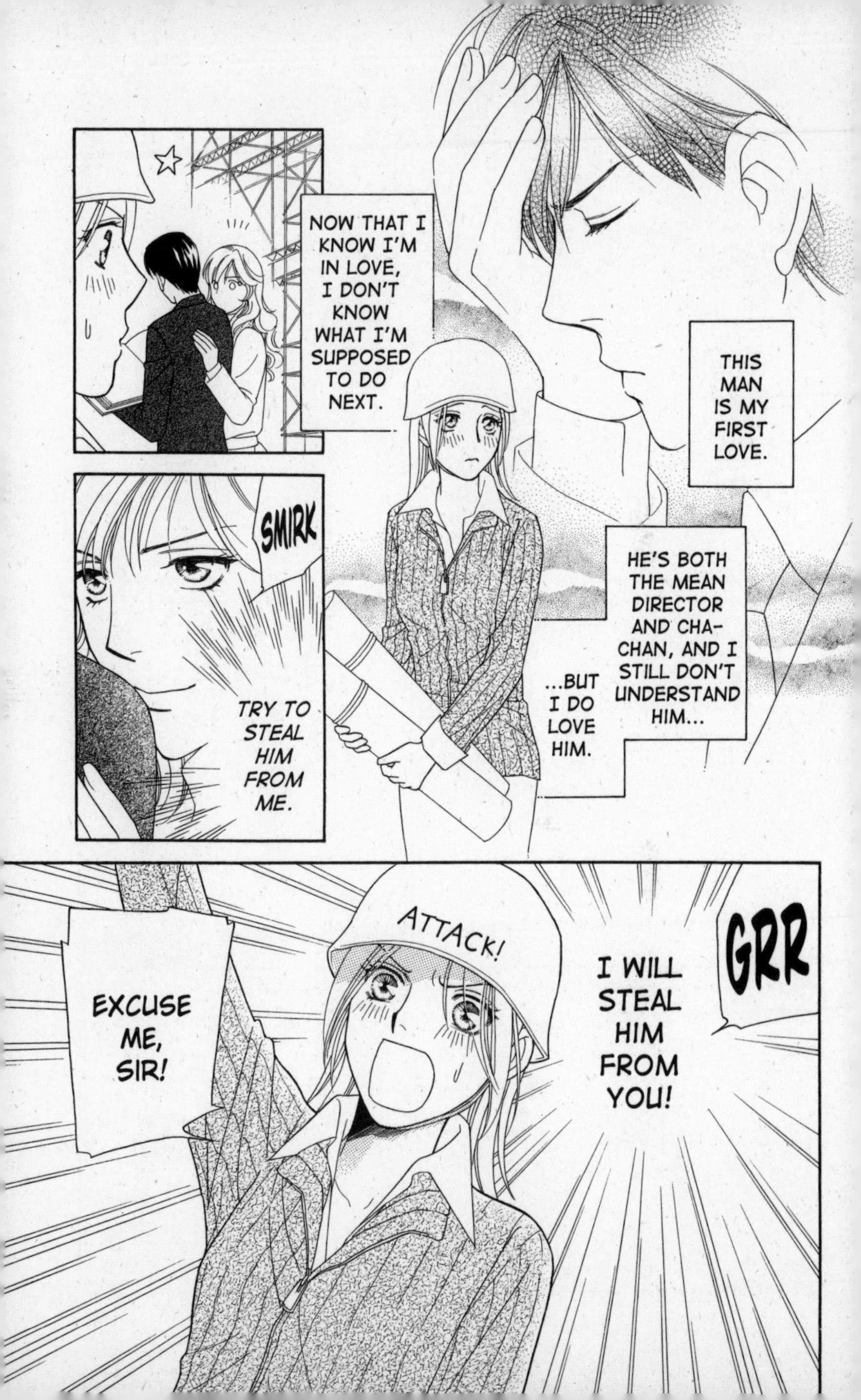
THIS MAN IS MY FIRST LOVE.
HE'S BOTH THE MEAN DIRECTOR AND CHA-CHAN, AND I STILL DON'T UNDERSTAND HIM...
...BUT I DO LOVE HIM.
NOW THAT I KNOW I'M IN LOVE, I DON'T KNOW WHAT I'M SUPPOSED TO DO NEXT.
SMIRK
TRY TO STEAL HIM FROM ME.
GRR
I WILL STEAL HIM FROM YOU!
ATTACK!
EXCUSE ME, SIR!

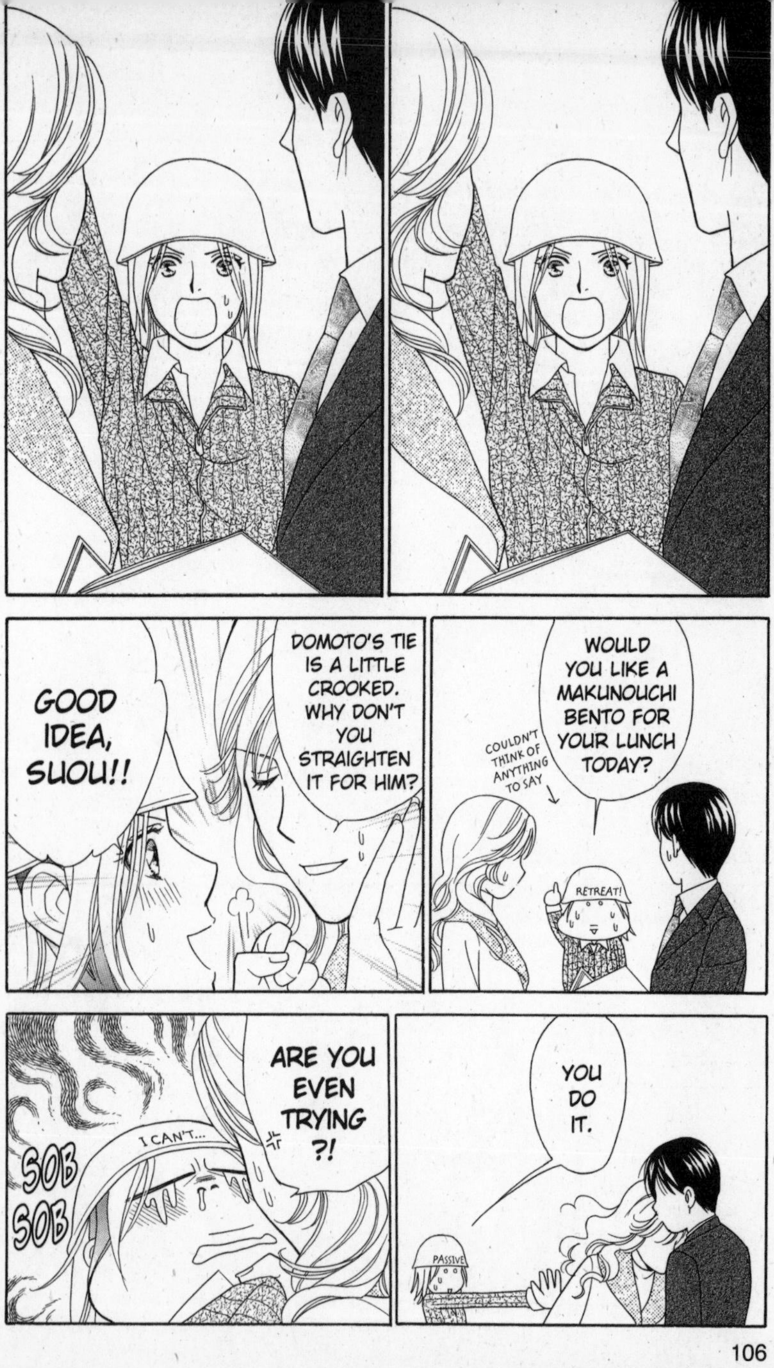
WOULD YOU LIKE A MAKUNOUCHI BENTO FOR YOUR LUNCH TODAY?
COULDN'T THINK OF ANYTHING TO SAY
RETREAT!
DOMOTO'S TIE IS A LITTLE CROOKED. WHY DON'T YOU STRAIGHTEN IT FOR HIM?
GOOD IDEA, SUOU!!
YOU DO IT.
PASSIVE
ARE YOU EVEN TRYING ?!
I CAN'T...
SOB SOB

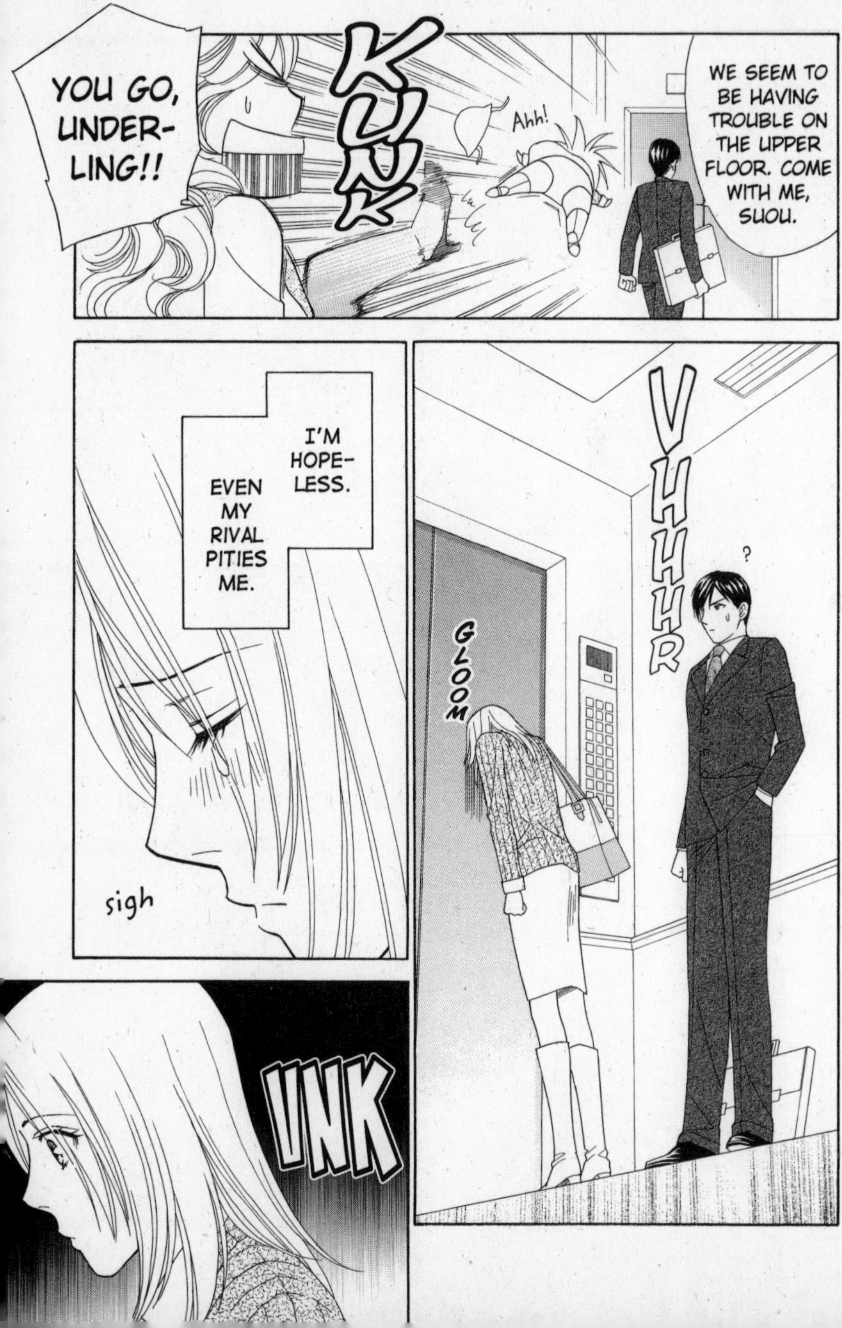
WE SEEM TO BE HAVING TROUBLE ON THE UPPER FLOOR. COME WITH ME, SUOU.
Ahh!
KUNK
YOU GO, UNDER-LING!!
VHHHHR
?
GLOOM
I'M HOPE-LESS.
EVEN MY RIVAL PITIES ME.
sigh
VNK

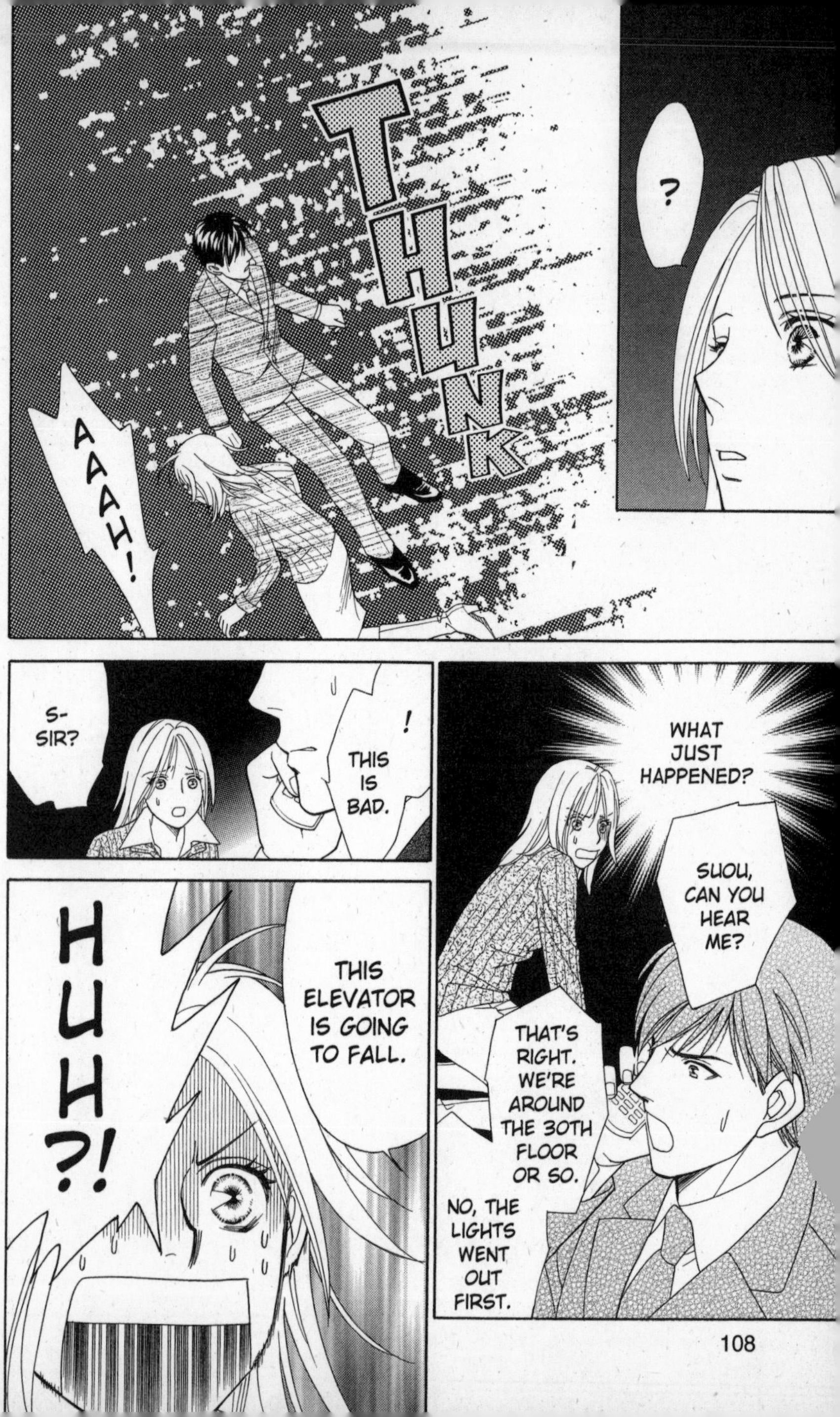
?
THUNK
AAAH!
WHAT JUST HAPPENED?
SUOU, CAN YOU HEAR ME?
THAT'S RIGHT. WE'RE AROUND THE 30TH FLOOR OR SO.
NO, THE LIGHTS WENT OUT FIRST.
!
THIS IS BAD.
S-SIR?
THIS ELEVATOR IS GOING TO FALL.
HUH?!

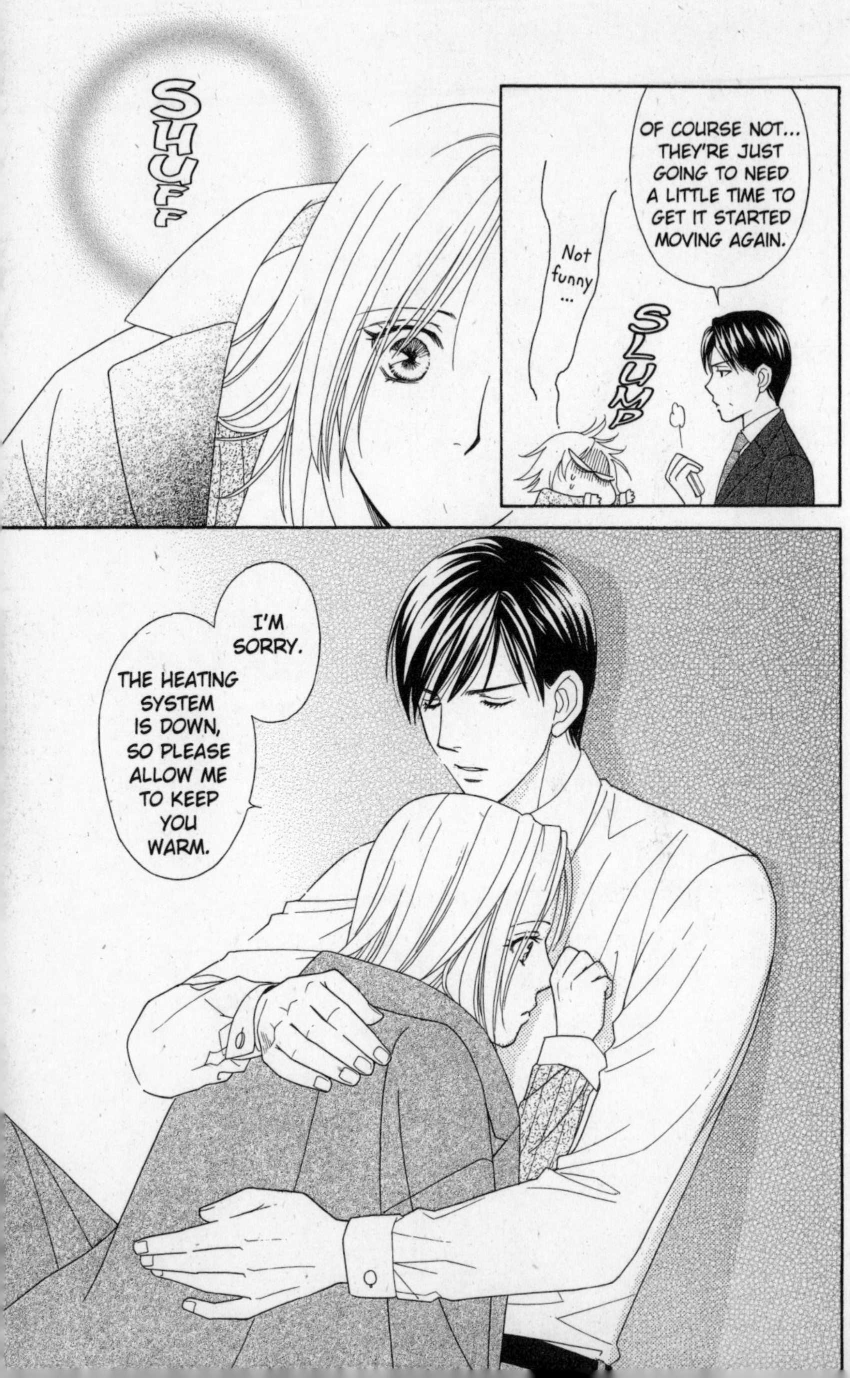
OF COURSE NOT... THEY'RE JUST GOING TO NEED A LITTLE TIME TO GET IT STARTED MOVING AGAIN.
Not funny...
SLUMP
SHUFF
I'M SORRY.
THE HEATING SYSTEM IS DOWN, SO PLEASE ALLOW ME TO KEEP YOU WARM.

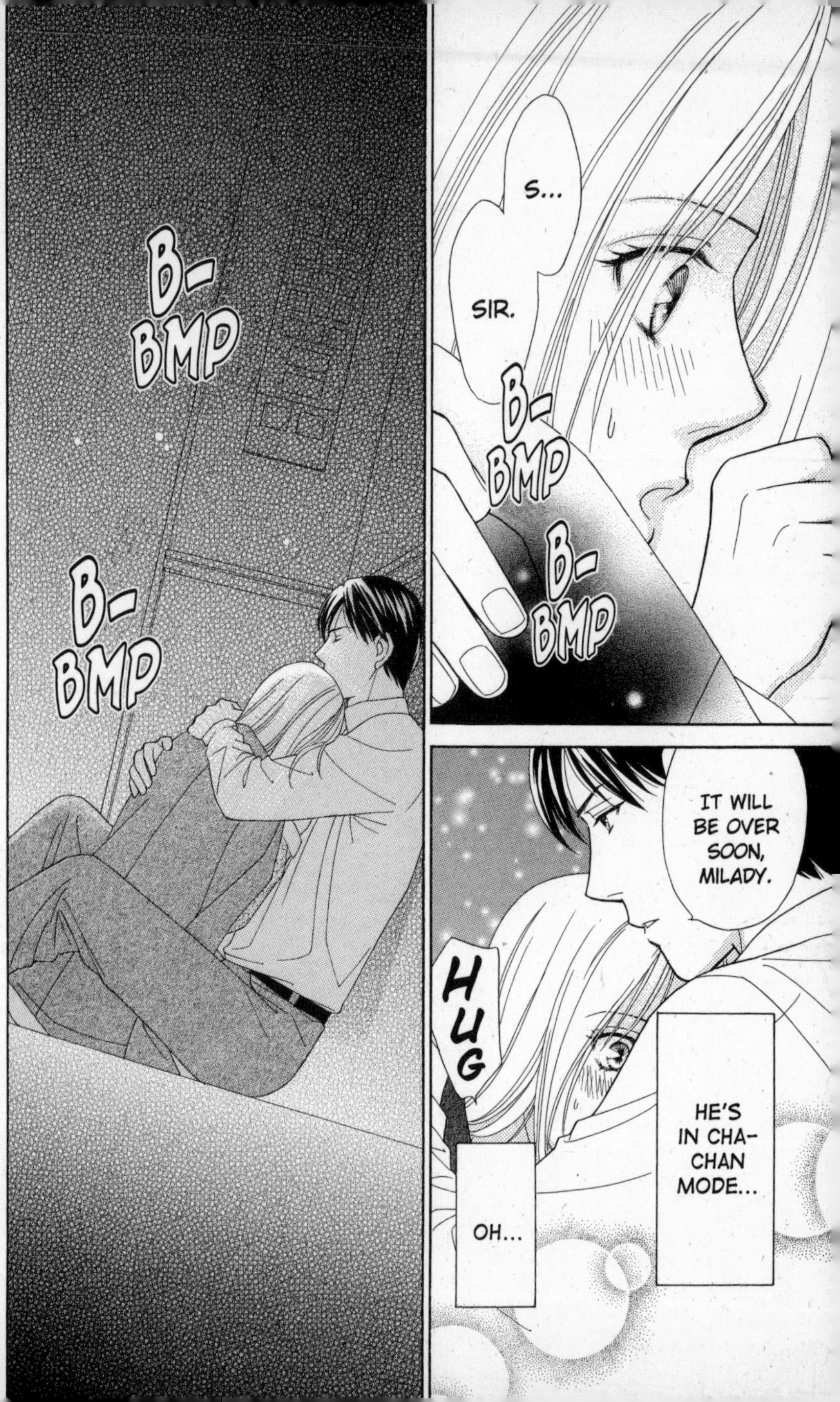
S...
SIR.
B-BMP
B-BMP
IT WILL BE OVER SOON, MILADY.
HUG
HE'S IN CHA-CHAN MODE...
OH...
B-BMP
B-BMP

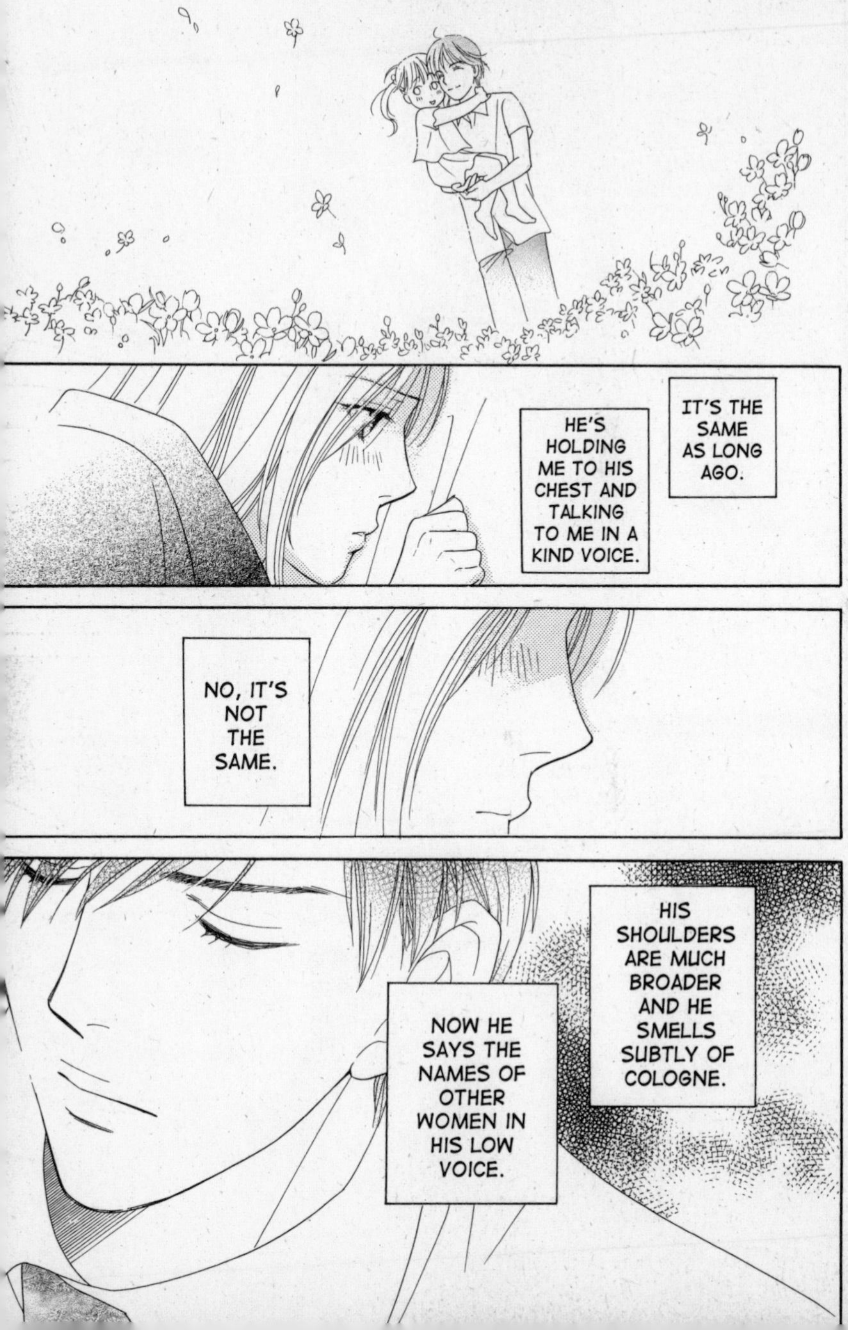
IT'S THE SAME AS LONG AGO.
HE'S HOLDING ME TO HIS CHEST AND TALKING TO ME IN A KIND VOICE.
NO, IT'S NOT THE SAME.
HIS SHOULDERS ARE MUCH BROADER AND HE SMELLS SUBTLY OF COLOGNE.
NOW HE SAYS THE NAMES OF OTHER WOMEN IN HIS LOW VOICE.

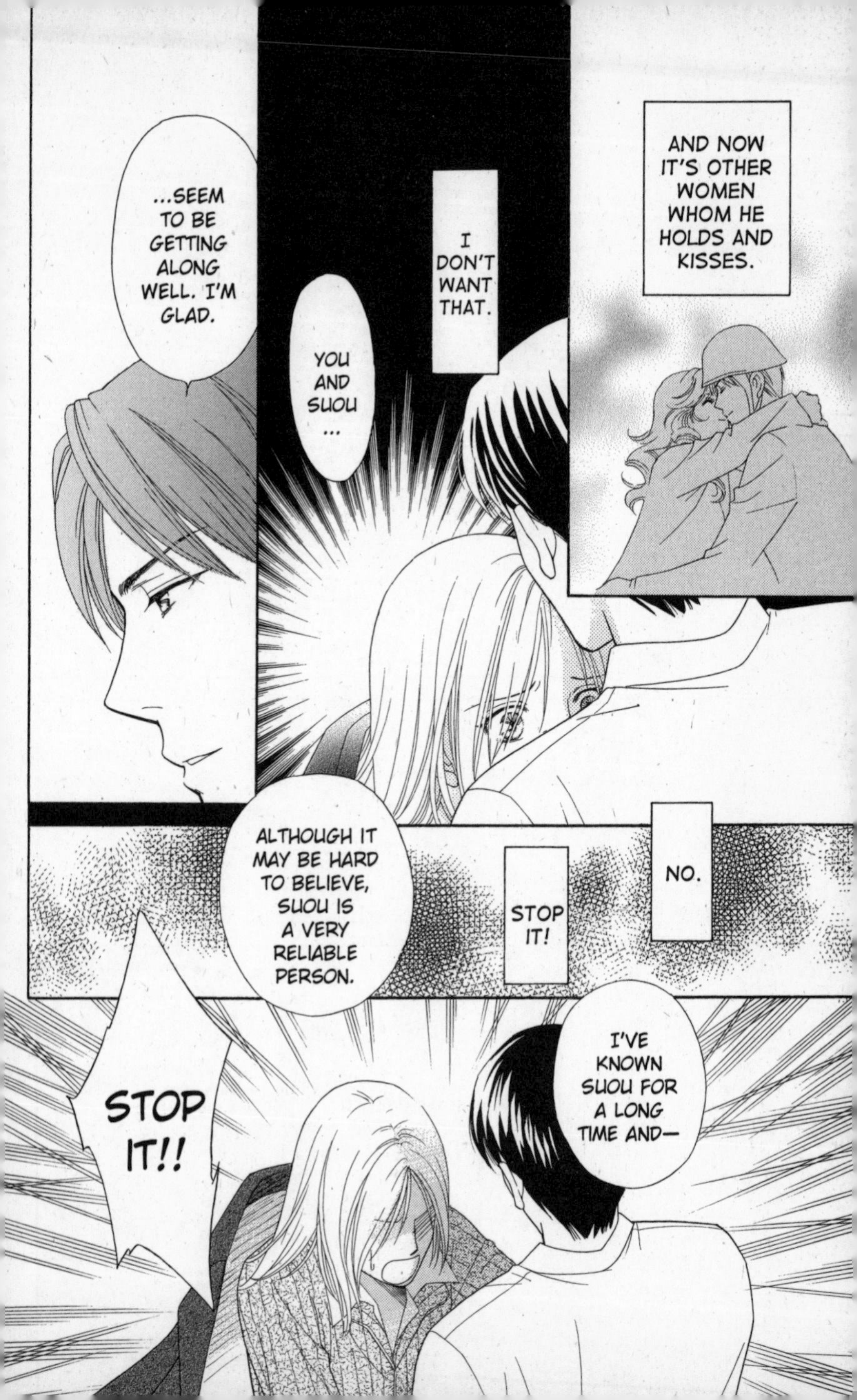
AND NOW IT'S OTHER WOMEN WHOM HE HOLDS AND KISSES.
I DON'T WANT THAT.
YOU AND SUOU ...
...SEEM TO BE GETTING ALONG WELL. I'M GLAD.
NO.
STOP IT!
ALTHOUGH IT MAY BE HARD TO BELIEVE, SUOU IS A VERY RELIABLE PERSON.
I'VE KNOWN SUOU FOR A LONG TIME AND—
STOP IT!!

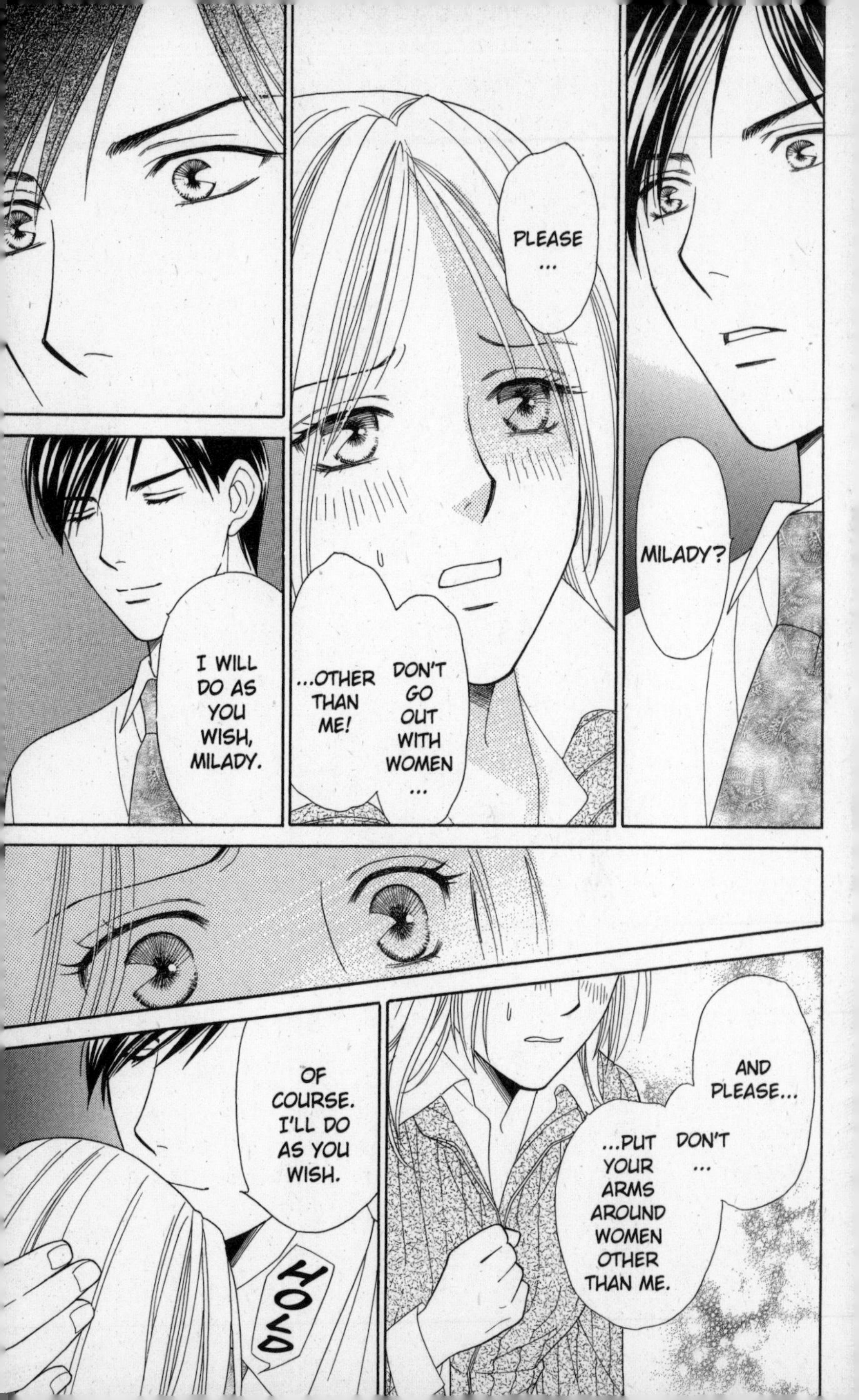
MILADY?
PLEASE ...
DON'T GO OUT WITH WOMEN ...
...OTHER THAN ME!
I WILL DO AS YOU WISH, MILADY.
AND PLEASE...
DON'T ...
...PUT YOUR ARMS AROUND WOMEN OTHER THAN ME.
OF COURSE. I'LL DO AS YOU WISH.
HOLD

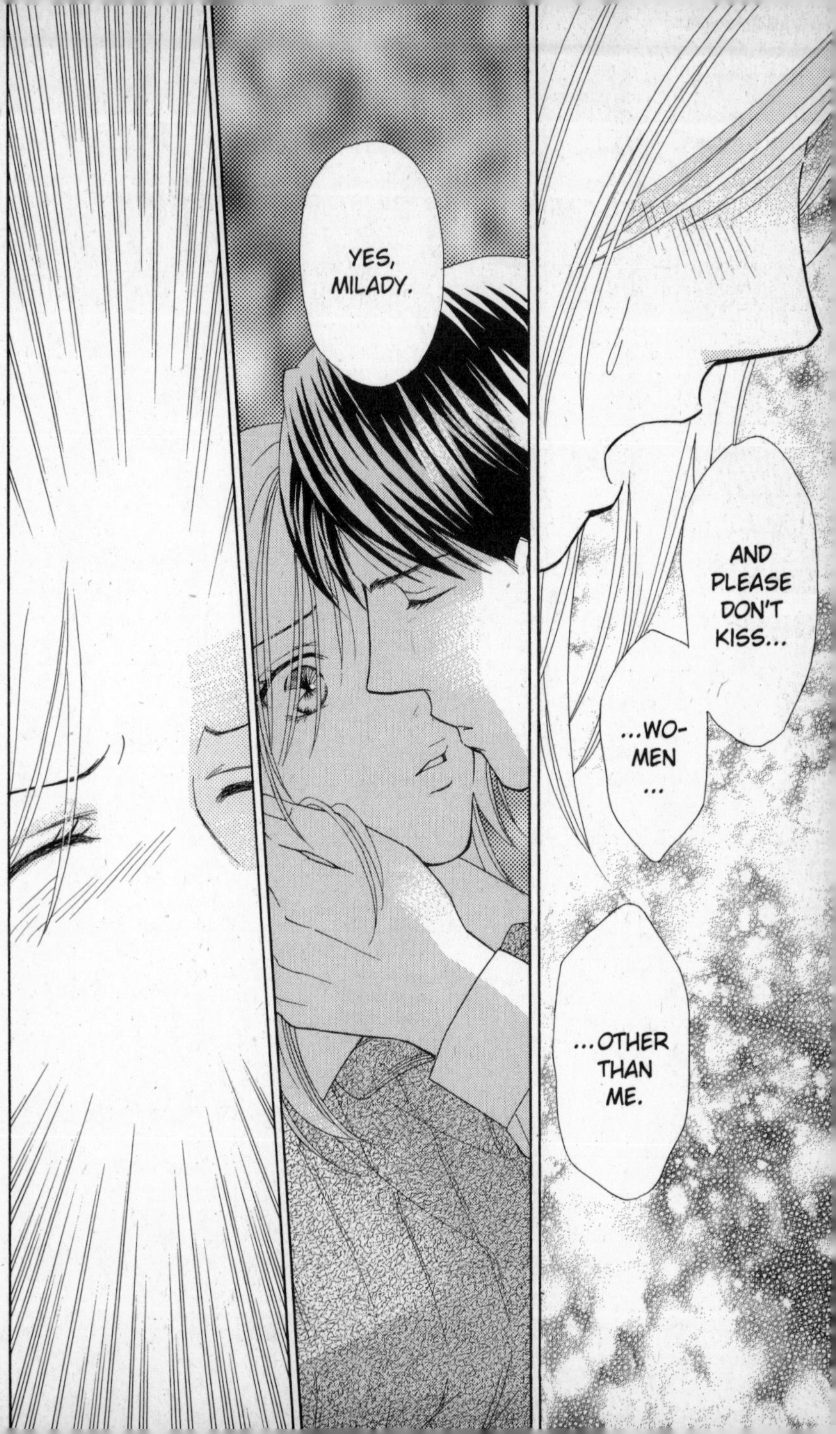
AND PLEASE DON'T KISS...
...WO-MEN ...
...OTHER THAN ME.
YES, MILADY.

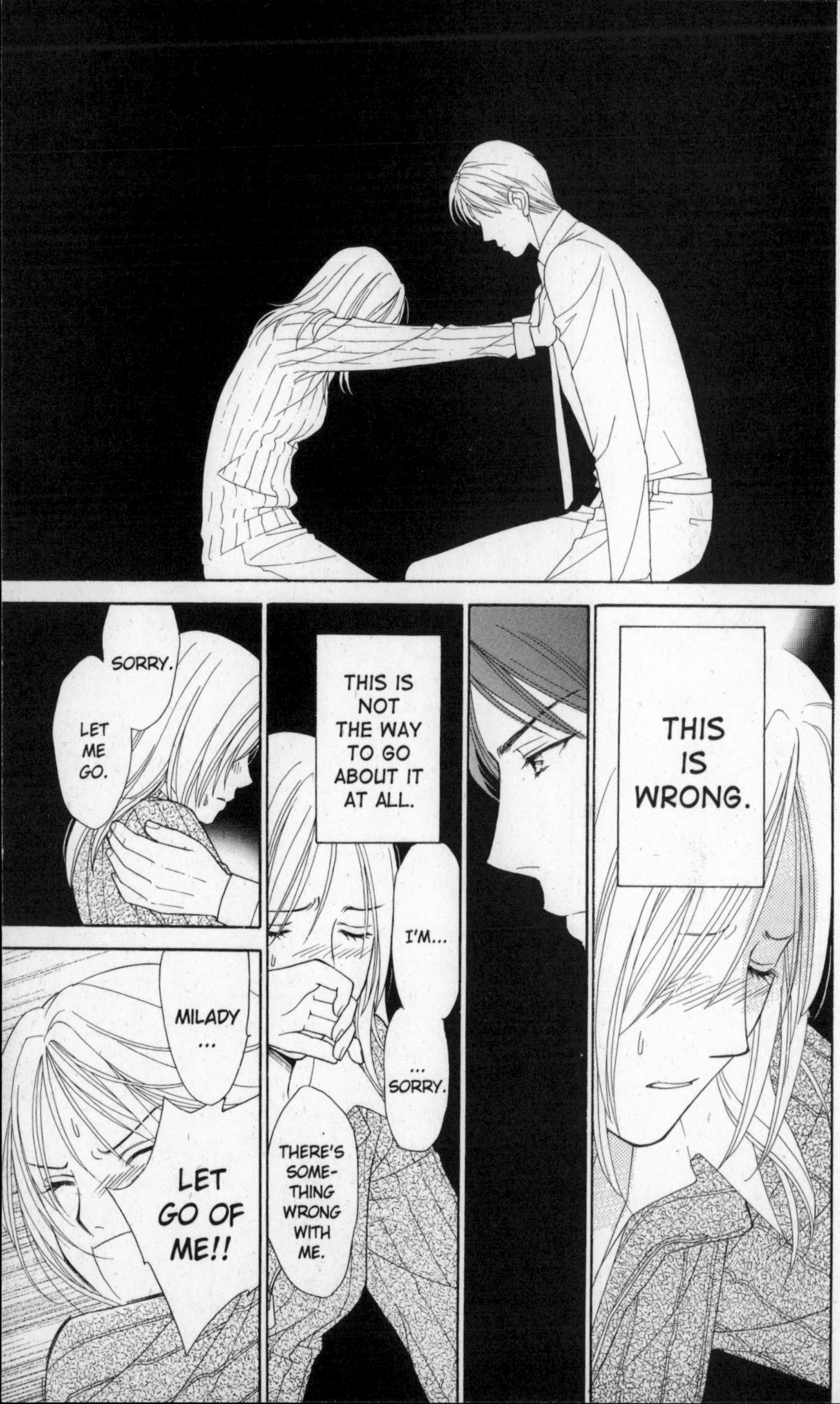
THIS IS WRONG.
THIS IS NOT THE WAY TO GO ABOUT IT AT ALL.
I'M...
... SORRY.
THERE'S SOME-THING WRONG WITH ME.
SORRY.
LET ME GO.
MILADY ...
LET GO OF ME!!

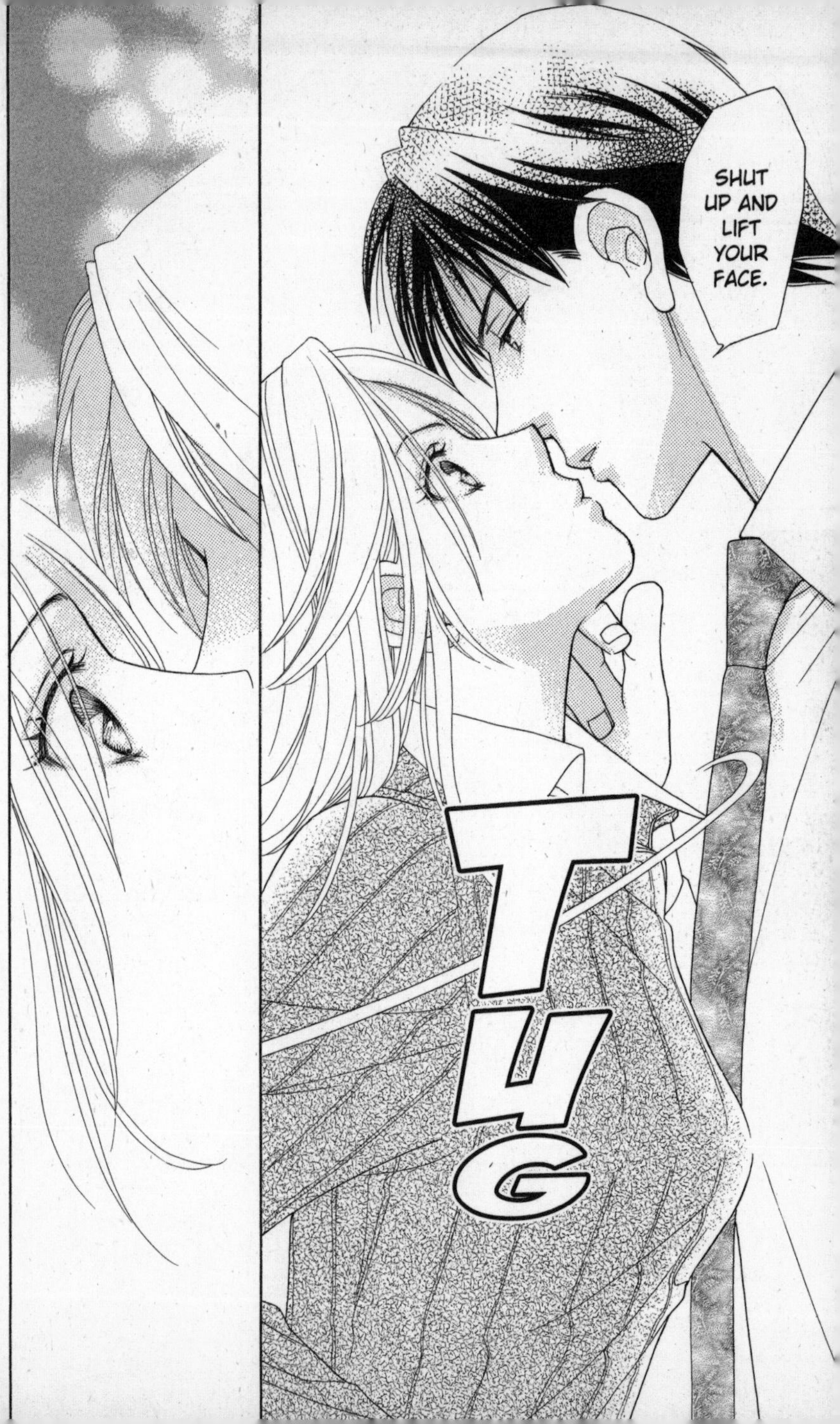
SHUT UP AND LIFT YOUR FACE.
TUG

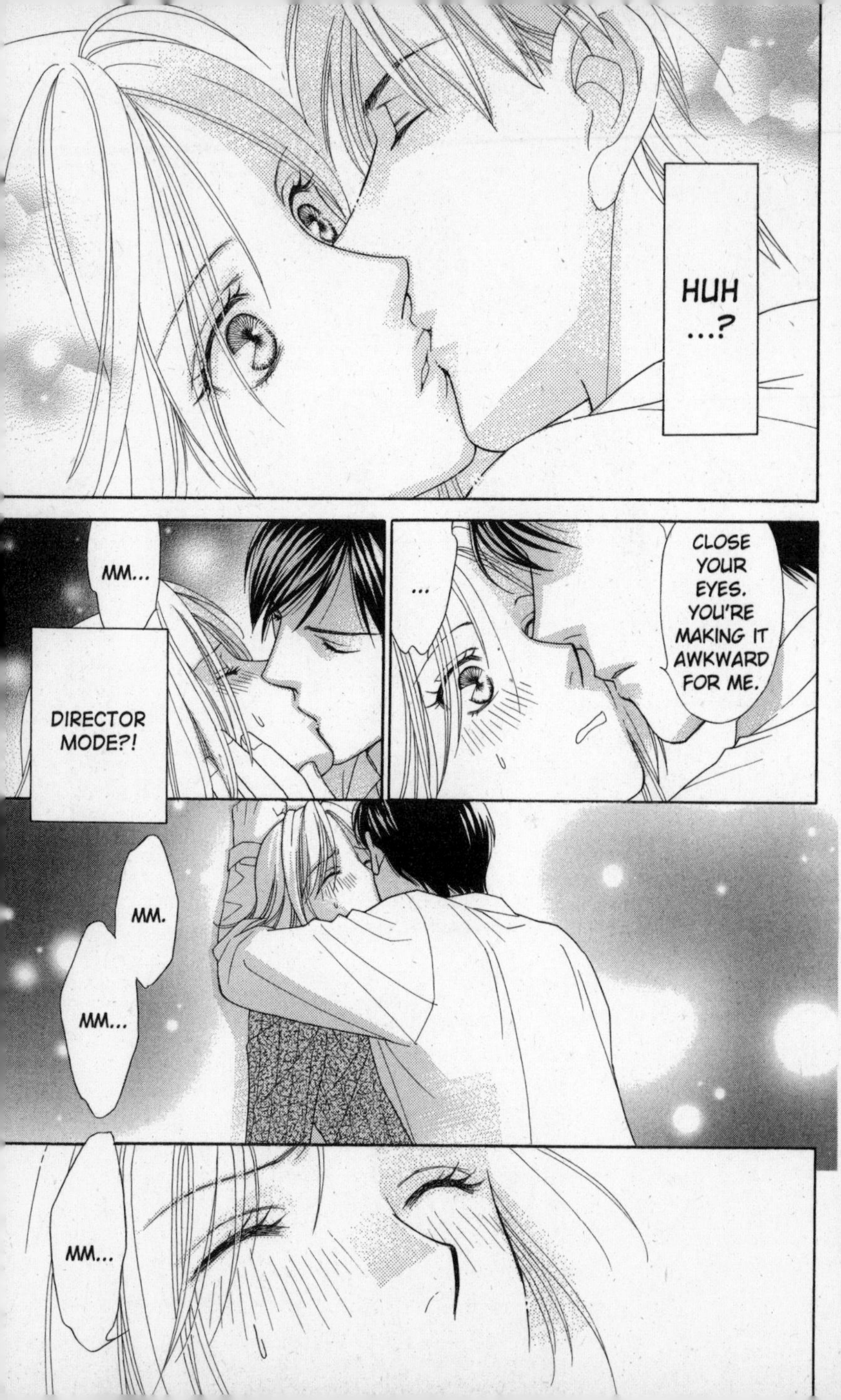
HUH ...?
CLOSE YOUR EYES. YOU'RE MAKING IT AWKWARD FOR ME.
...
MM...
DIRECTOR MODE?!
MM.
MM...
MM...

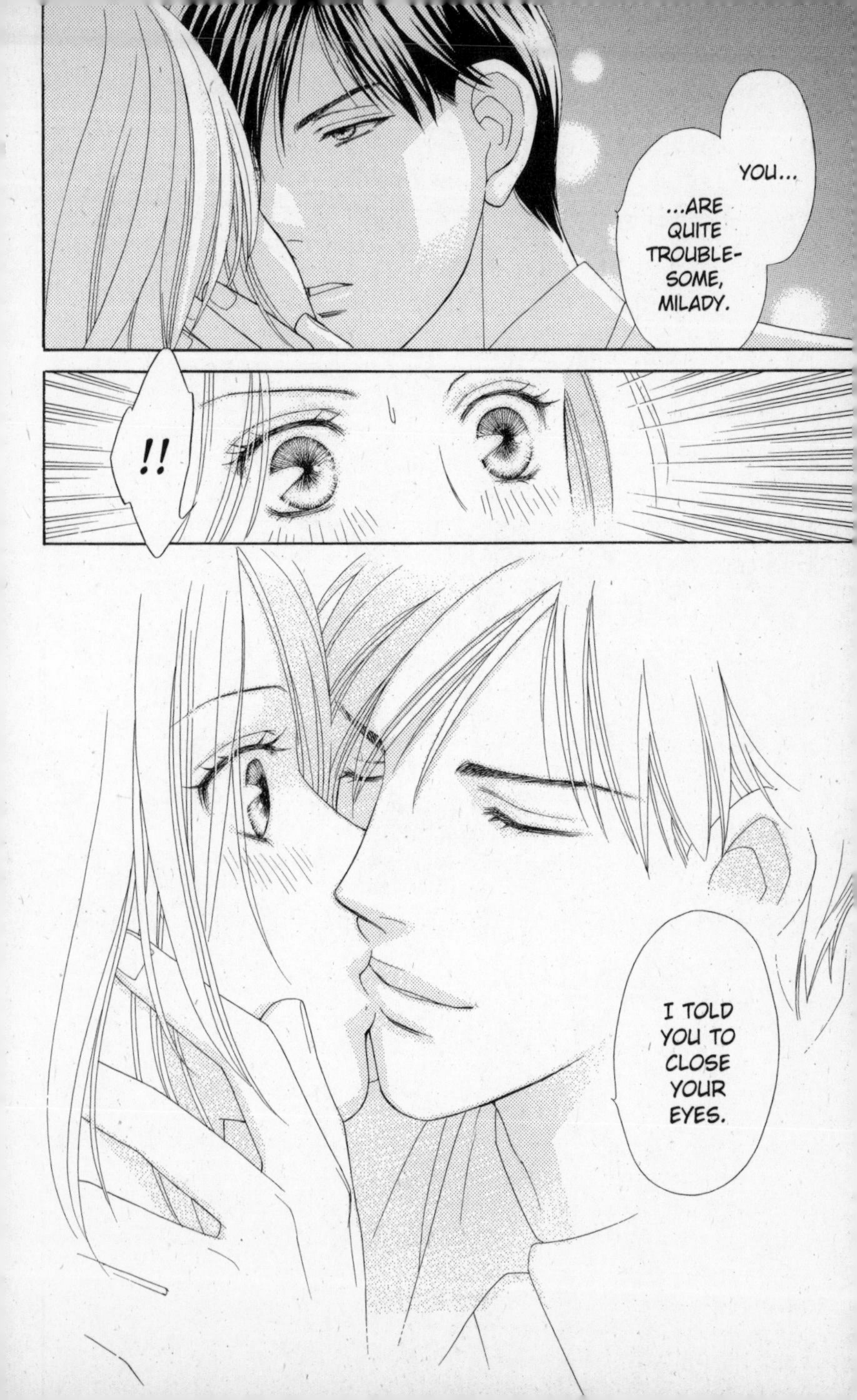
YOU...
...ARE QUITE TROUBLE-SOME, MILADY.
!!
I TOLD YOU TO CLOSE YOUR EYES.

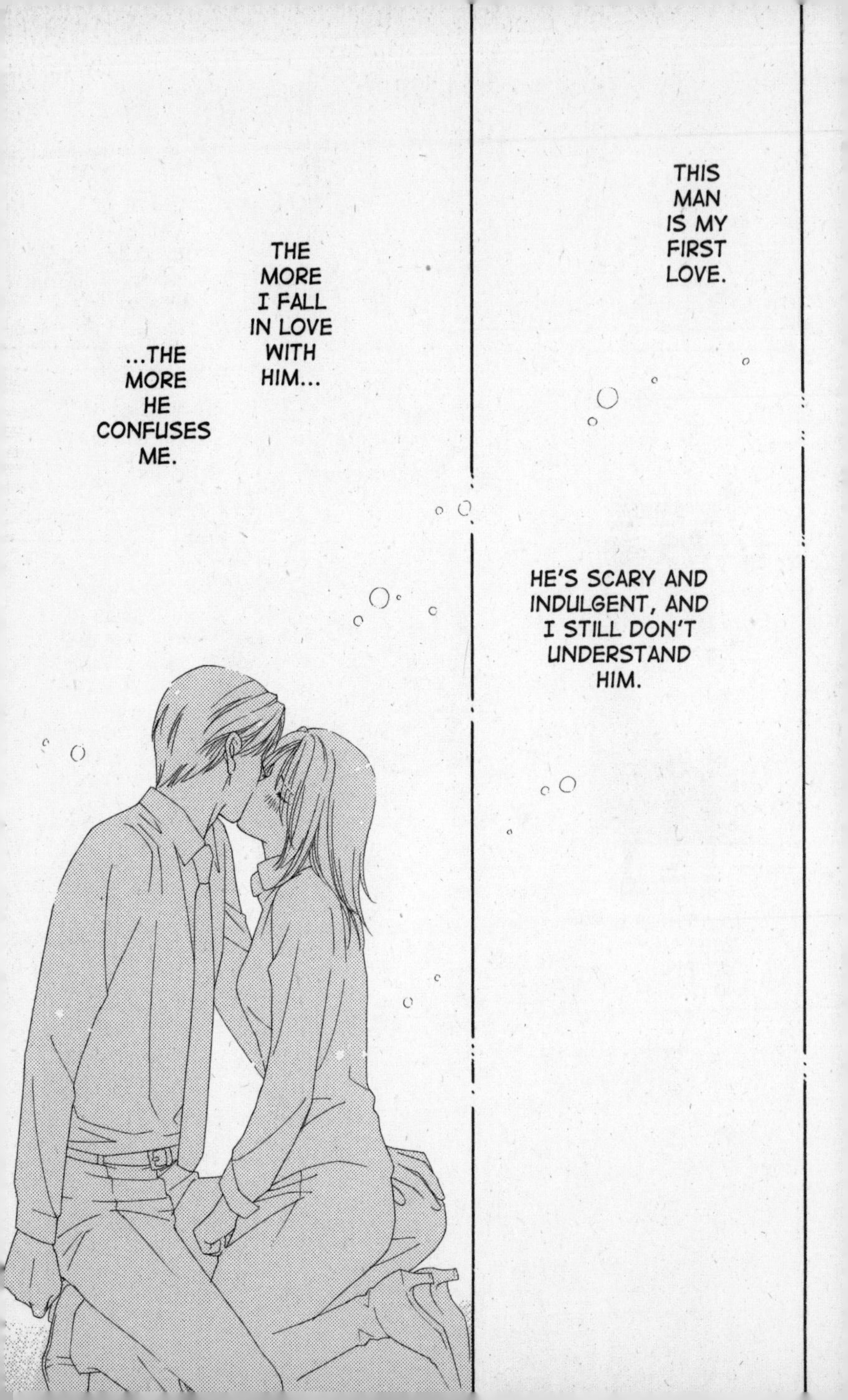
THIS MAN IS MY FIRST LOVE.
HE'S SCARY AND INDULGENT, AND I STILL DON'T UNDERSTAND HIM.
THE MORE I FALL IN LOVE WITH HIM...
...THE MORE HE CONFUSES ME.

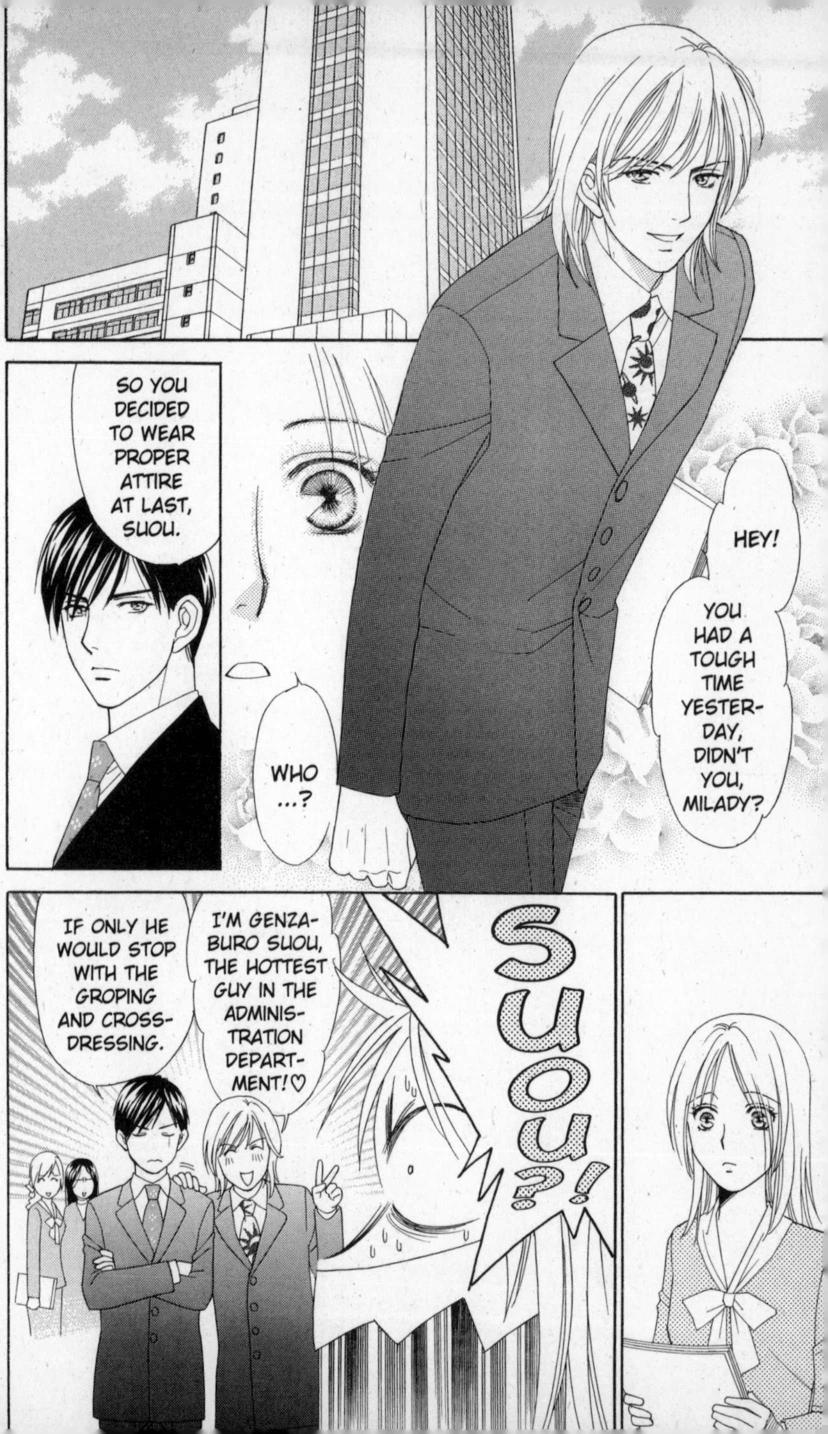

HEY!
YOU HAD A TOUGH TIME YESTER-DAY, DIDN'T YOU, MILADY?
WHO ...?
SO YOU DECIDED TO WEAR PROPER ATTIRE AT LAST, SUOU.
SUOU?!
I'M GENZA-BURO SUOU, THE HOTTEST GUY IN THE ADMINIS-TRATION DEPART-MENT!♡
IF ONLY HE WOULD STOP WITH THE GROPING AND CROSS-DRESSING.

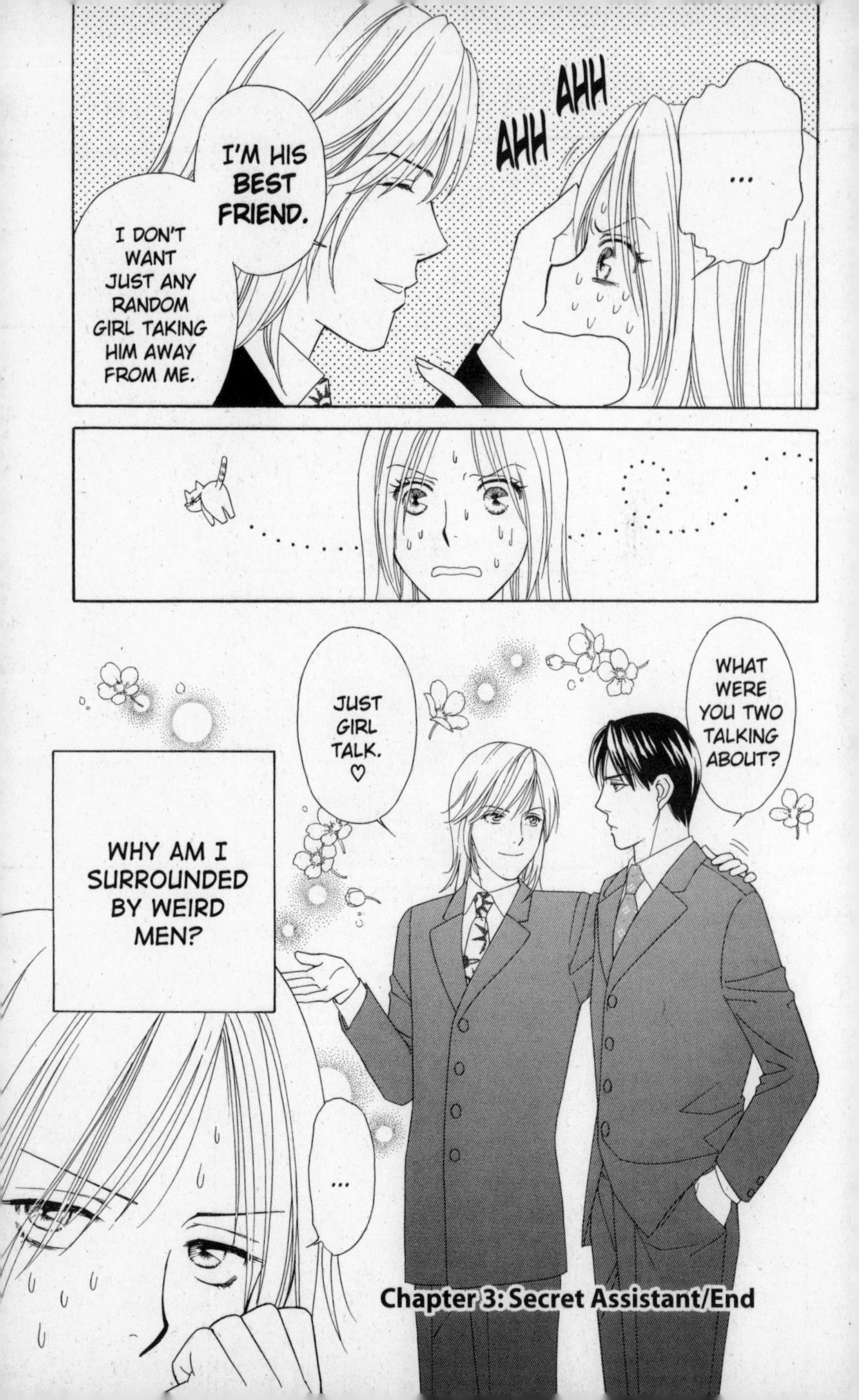
...
AHH AHH
I'M HIS BEST FRIEND.
I DON'T WANT JUST ANY RANDOM GIRL TAKING HIM AWAY FROM ME.
WHAT WERE YOU TWO TALKING ABOUT?
JUST GIRL TALK. ♡
WHY AM I SURROUNDED BY WEIRD MEN?
...
Chapter 3: Secret Assistant/End

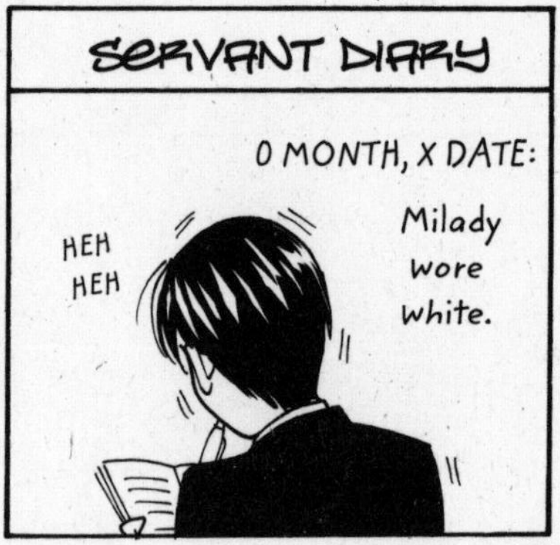
SERVANT DIARY
0 MONTH, X DATE:
Milady wore white.
HEH HEH

*CHECK PAGE 107.

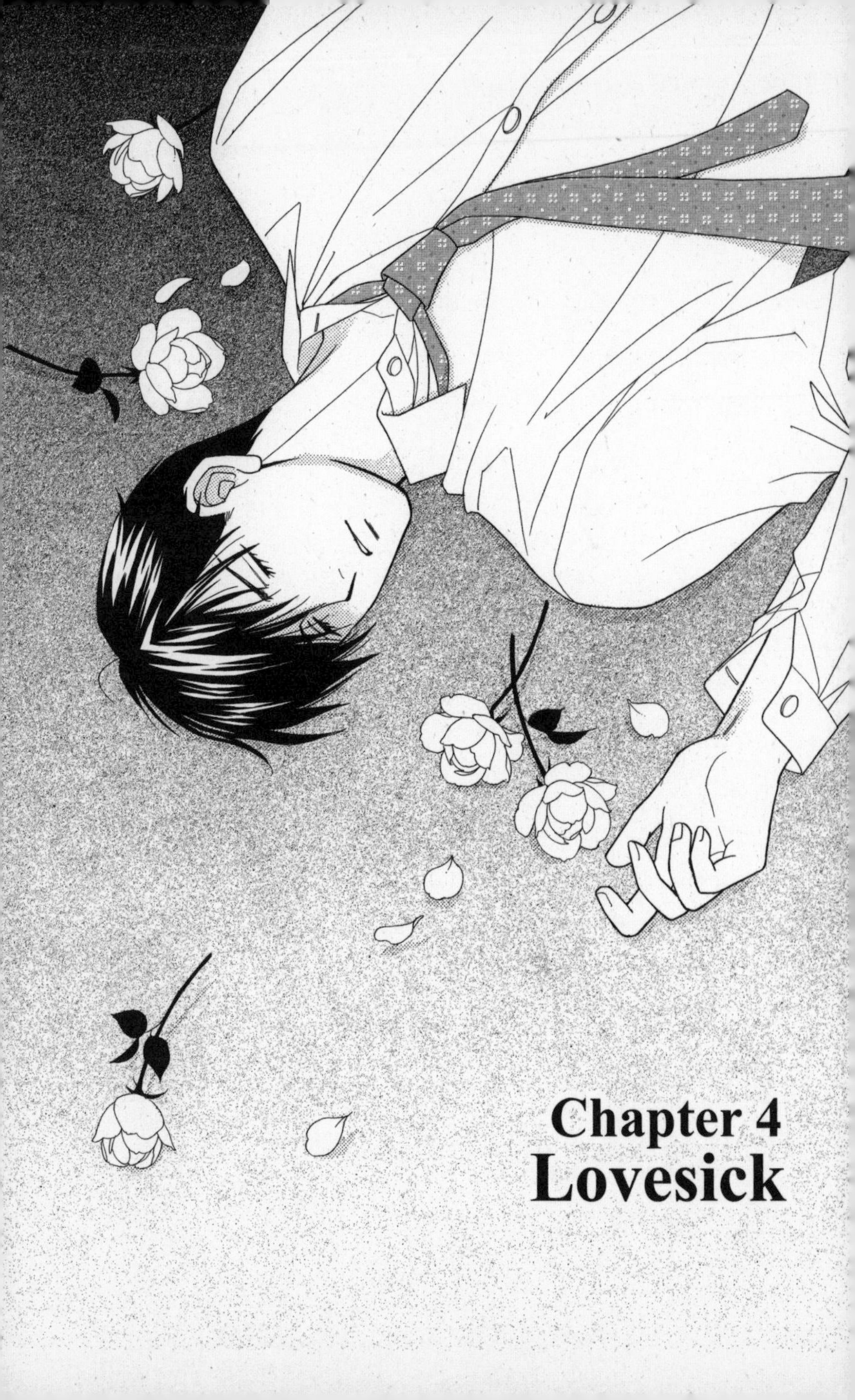

Chapter 4
Lovesick

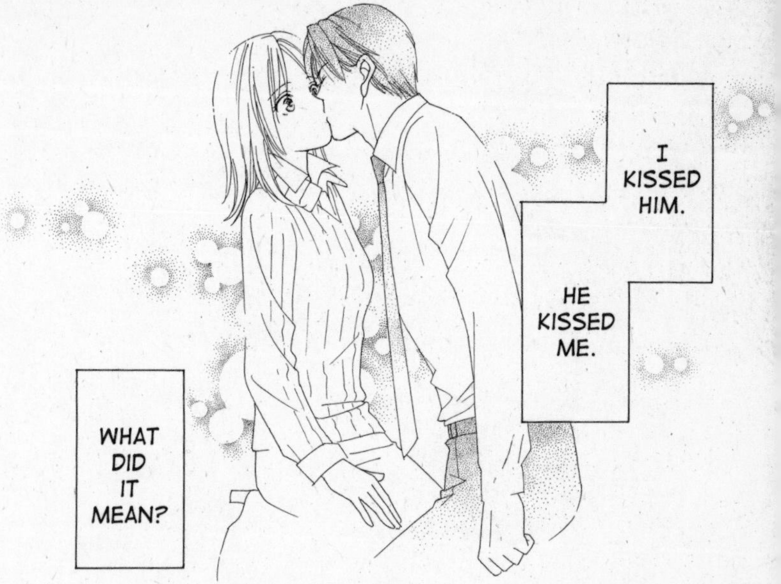
I KISSED HIM.
HE KISSED ME.
WHAT DID IT MEAN?

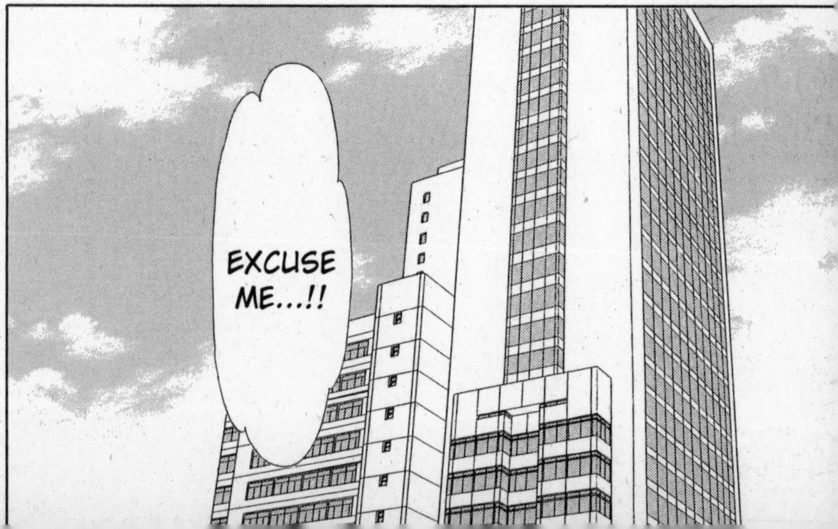
EXCUSE ME...!!

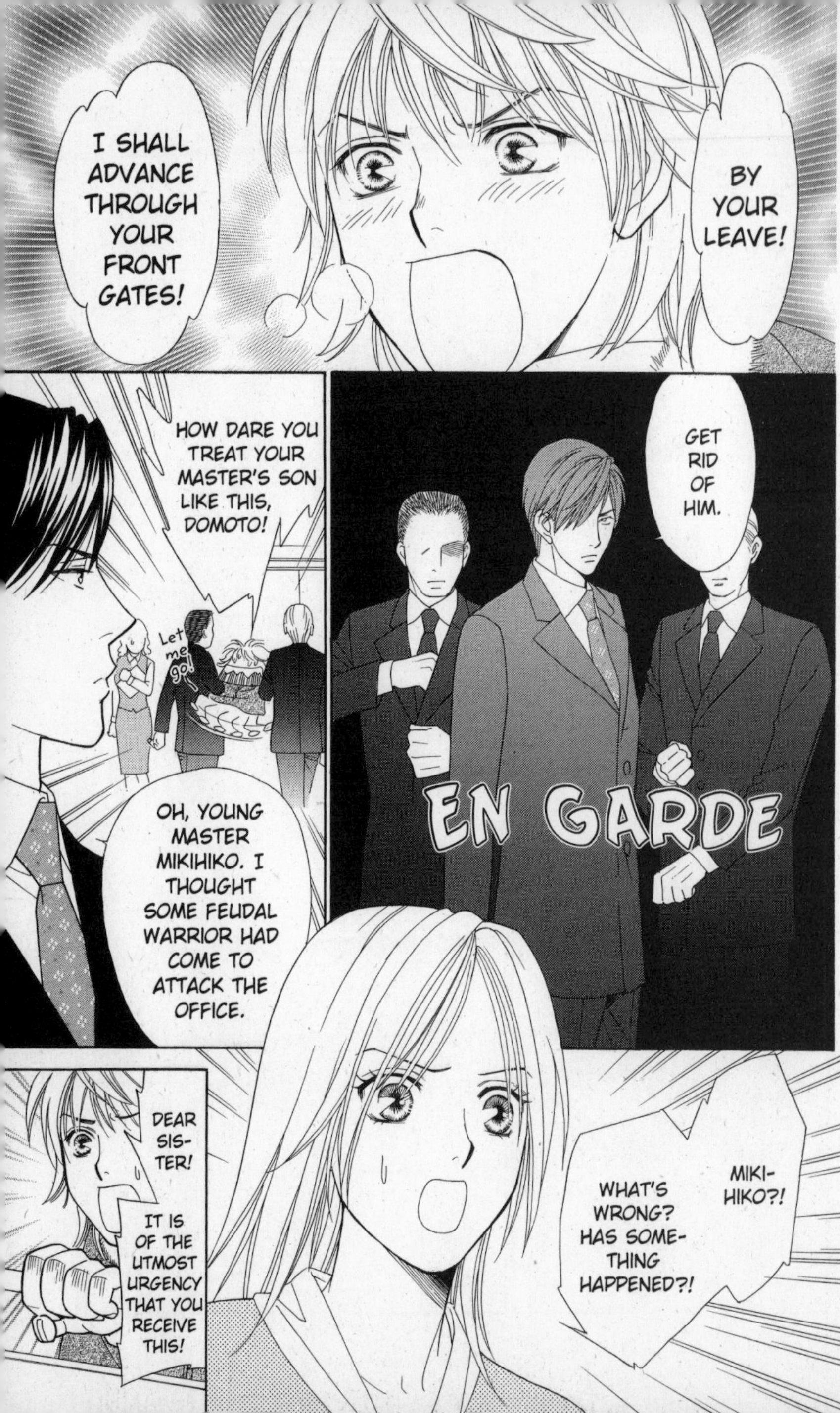

BY YOUR LEAVE!
I SHALL ADVANCE THROUGH YOUR FRONT GATES!
GET RID OF HIM.
EN GARDE
HOW DARE YOU TREAT YOUR MASTER'S SON LIKE THIS, DOMOTO!
Let me go!
OH, YOUNG MASTER MIKIHIKO. I THOUGHT SOME FEUDAL WARRIOR HAD COME TO ATTACK THE OFFICE.
MIKI-HIKO?!
WHAT'S WRONG? HAS SOME-THING HAPPENED?!
DEAR SIS-TER!
IT IS OF THE UTMOST URGENCY THAT YOU RECEIVE THIS!

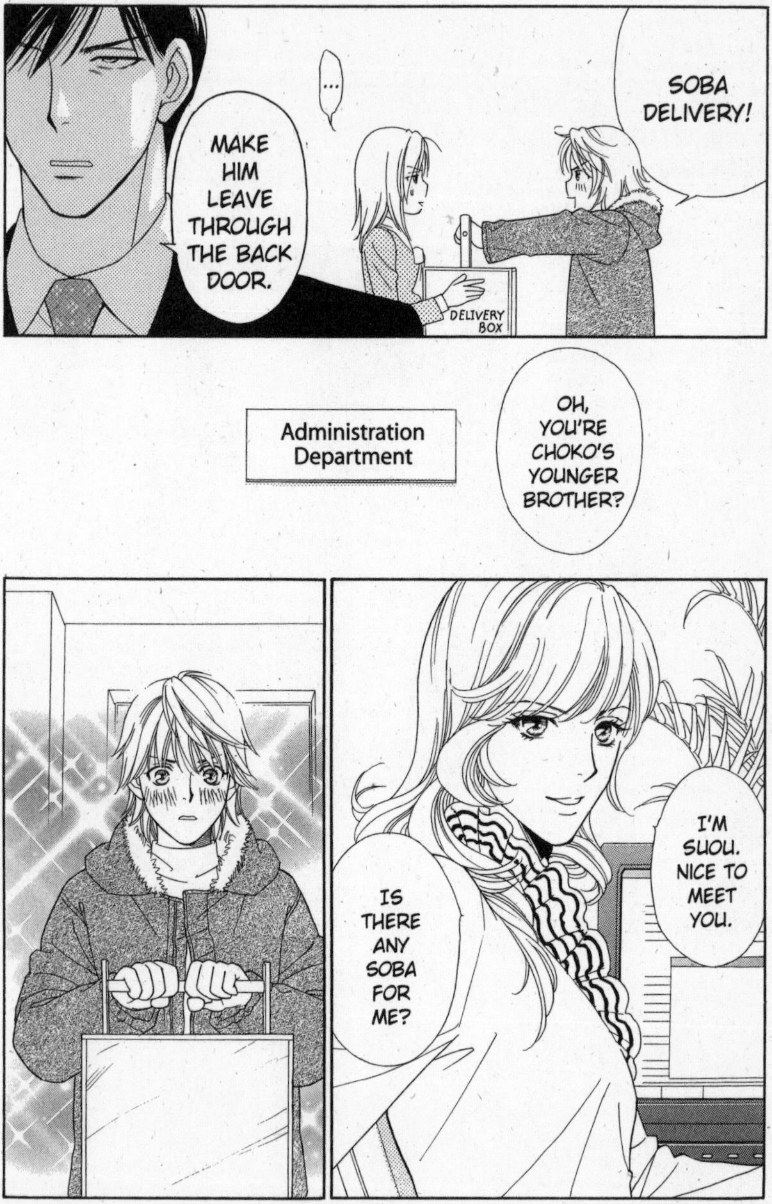
SOBA DELIVERY!
...
DELIVERY BOX
MAKE HIM LEAVE THROUGH THE BACK DOOR.
OH, YOU'RE CHOKO'S YOUNGER BROTHER?
Administration Department
I'M SUOU. NICE TO MEET YOU.
IS THERE ANY SOBA FOR ME?

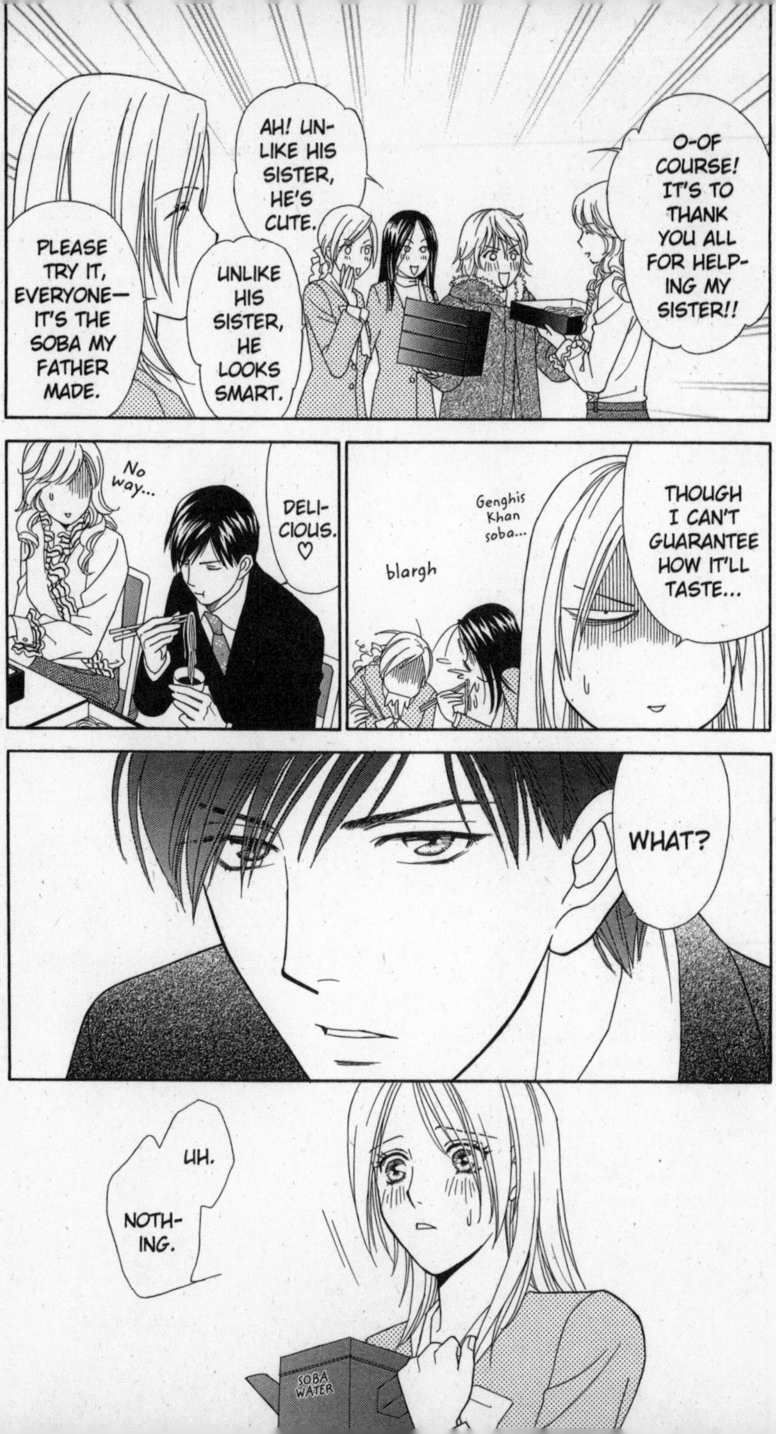
O-OF COURSE! IT'S TO THANK YOU ALL FOR HELPING MY SISTER!!
AH! UNLIKE HIS SISTER, HE'S CUTE.
UNLIKE HIS SISTER, HE LOOKS SMART.
PLEASE TRY IT, EVERYONE— IT'S THE SOBA MY FATHER MADE.
THOUGH I CAN'T GUARANTEE HOW IT'LL TASTE...
Genghis Khan soba...
blargh
DELICIOUS. ♡
No way...
WHAT?
UH.
NOTHING.
SOBA WATER

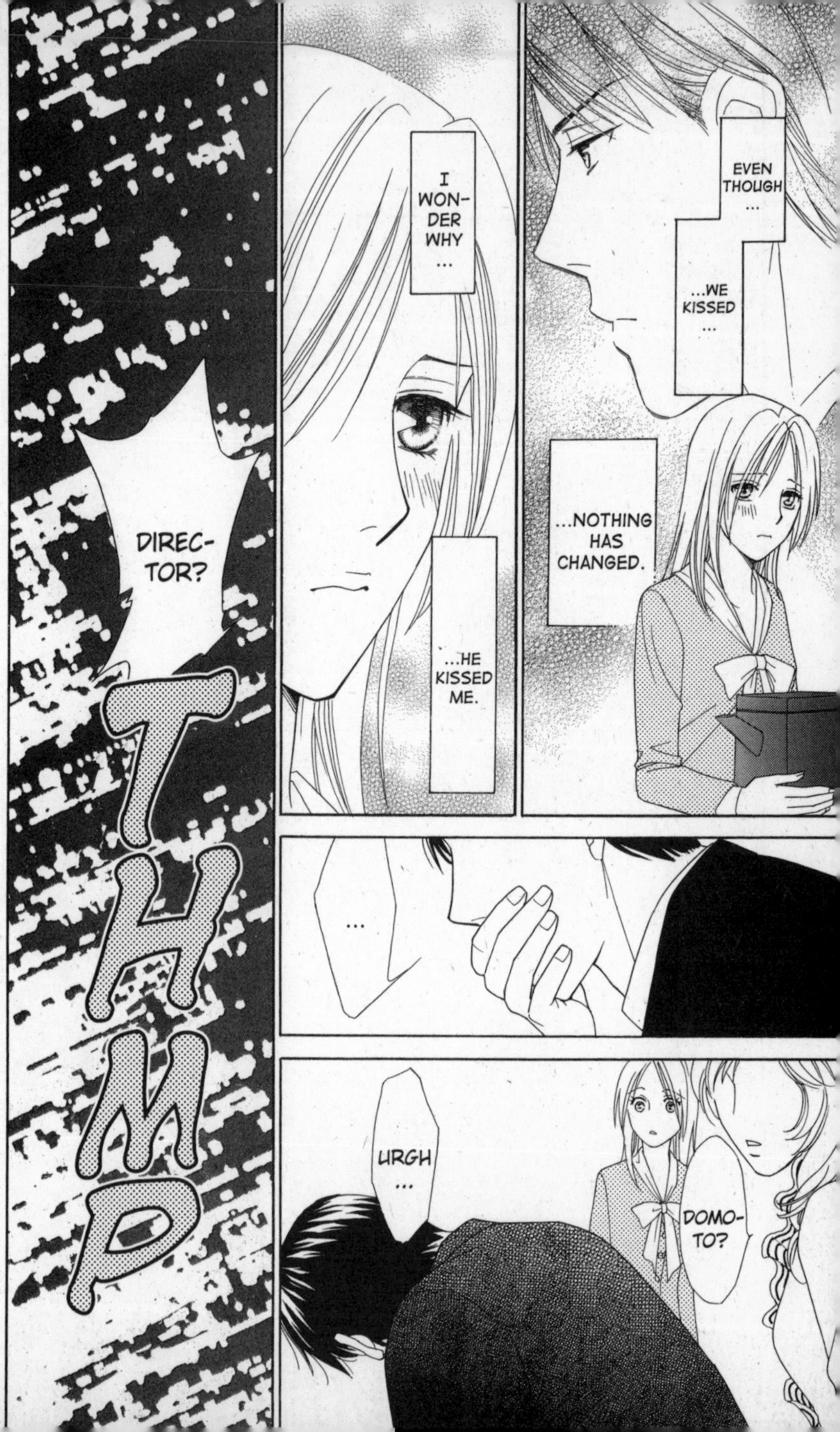
EVEN THOUGH ...
...WE KISSED ...
...NOTHING HAS CHANGED.
I WONDER WHY ...
...HE KISSED ME.
...
URGH ...
DOMOTO?
DIRECTOR?
THUMP

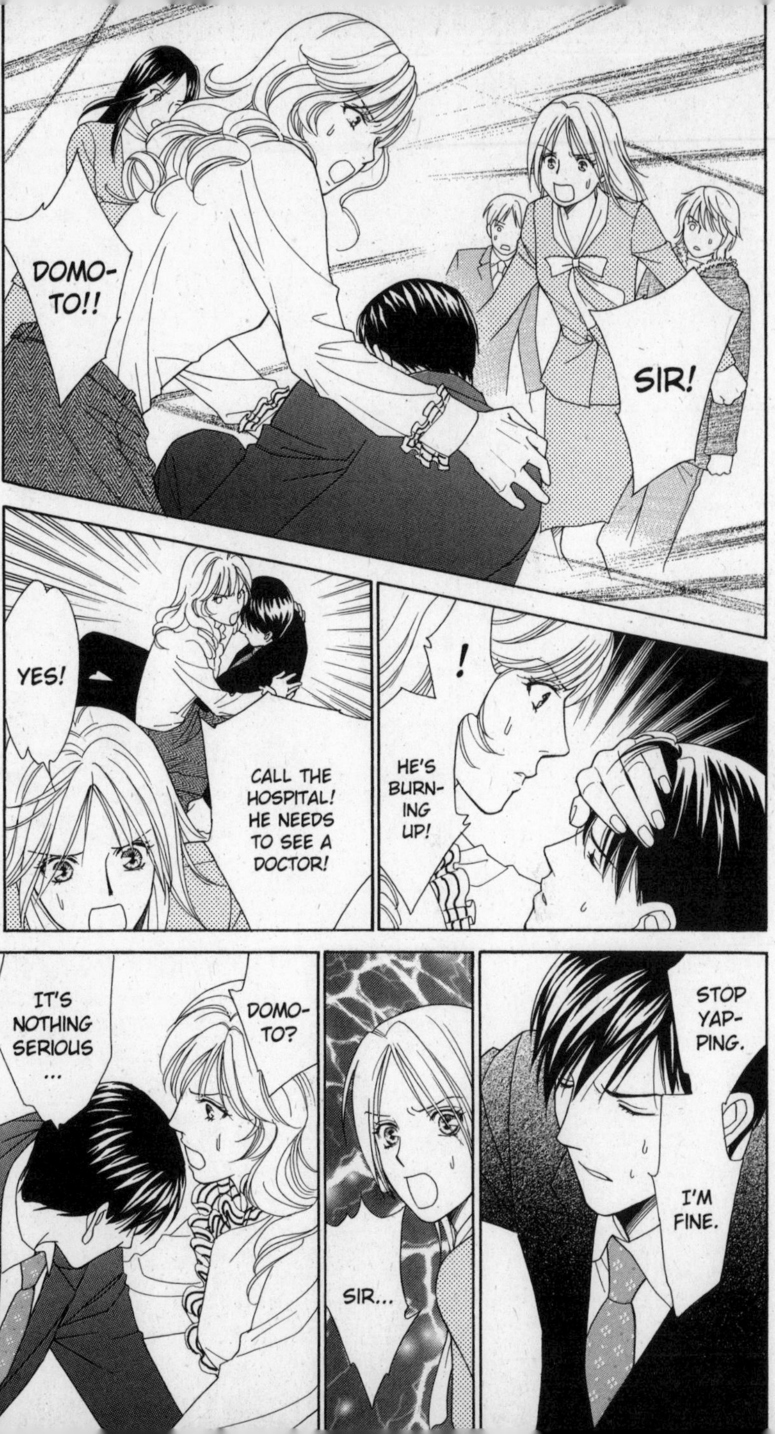
DOMO-TO!!
SIR!
!
HE'S BURN-ING UP!
CALL THE HOSPITAL! HE NEEDS TO SEE A DOCTOR!
YES!
STOP YAP-PING.
I'M FINE.
SIR...
DOMO-TO?
IT'S NOTHING SERIOUS ...

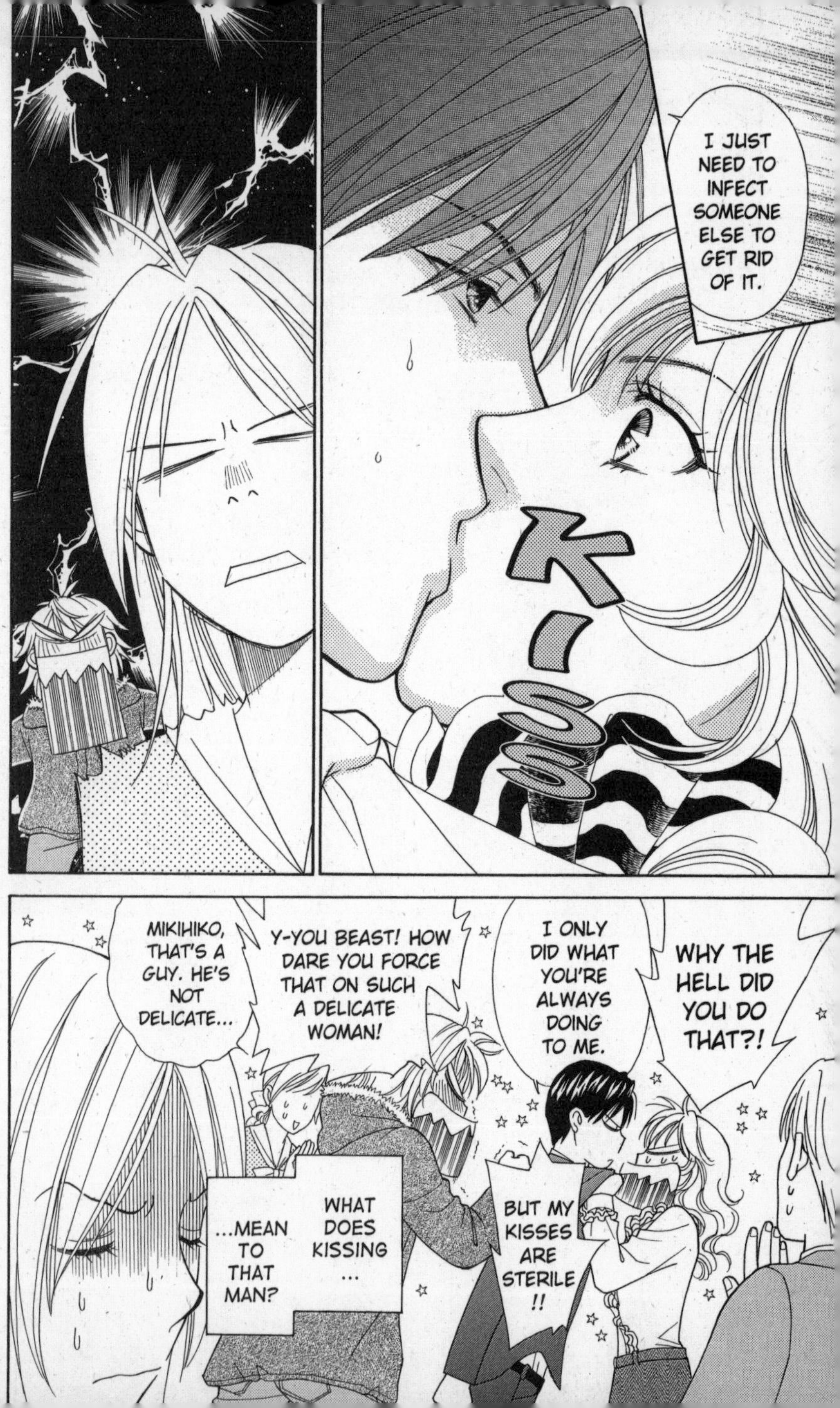
I JUST NEED TO INFECT SOMEONE ELSE TO GET RID OF IT.
KISS
WHY THE HELL DID YOU DO THAT?!
I ONLY DID WHAT YOU'RE ALWAYS DOING TO ME.
Y-YOU BEAST! HOW DARE YOU FORCE THAT ON SUCH A DELICATE WOMAN!
MIKIHIKO, THAT'S A GUY. HE'S NOT DELICATE...
BUT MY KISSES ARE STERILE!!
WHAT DOES KISSING...
...MEAN TO THAT MAN?

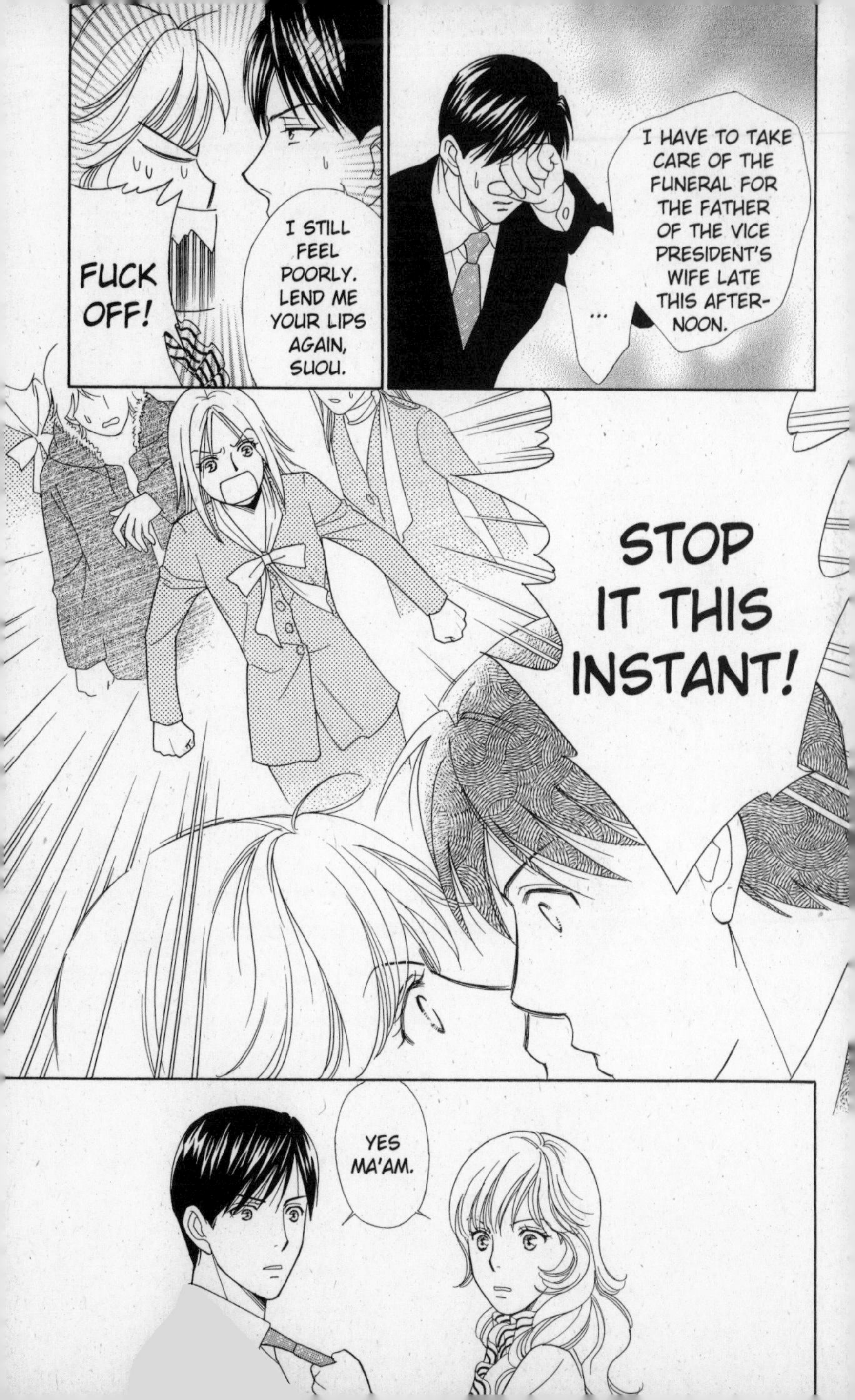
I HAVE TO TAKE CARE OF THE FUNERAL FOR THE FATHER OF THE VICE PRESIDENT'S WIFE LATE THIS AFTER-NOON.
...
I STILL FEEL POORLY. LEND ME YOUR LIPS AGAIN, SUOU.
FUCK OFF!
STOP IT THIS INSTANT!
YES MA'AM.

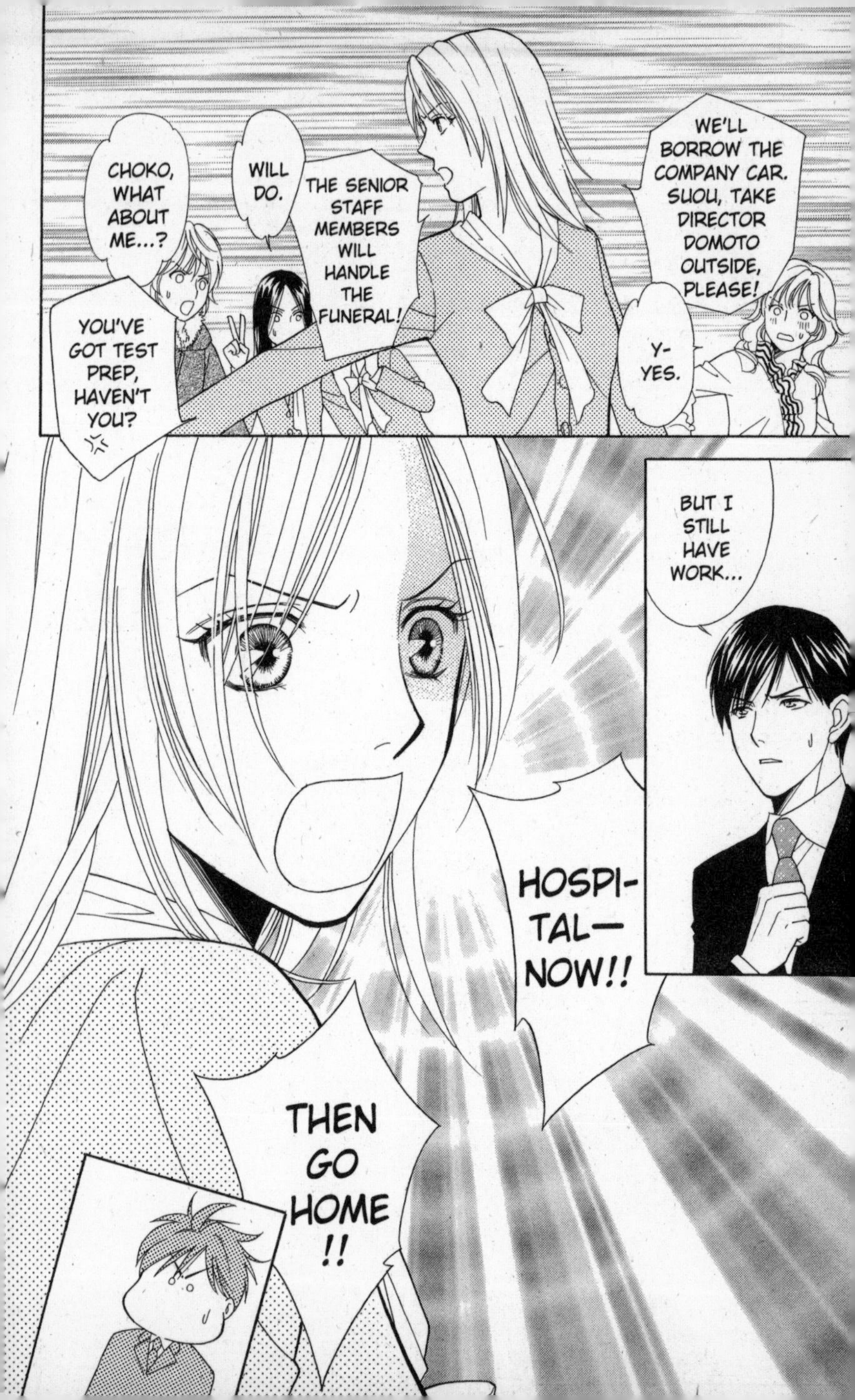
WE'LL BORROW THE COMPANY CAR. SUOU, TAKE DIRECTOR DOMOTO OUTSIDE, PLEASE!
Y-YES.
THE SENIOR STAFF MEMBERS WILL HANDLE THE FUNERAL!
WILL DO.
CHOKO, WHAT ABOUT ME...?
YOU'VE GOT TEST PREP, HAVEN'T YOU?
BUT I STILL HAVE WORK...
HOSPI-TAL—NOW!!
THEN GO HOME!!

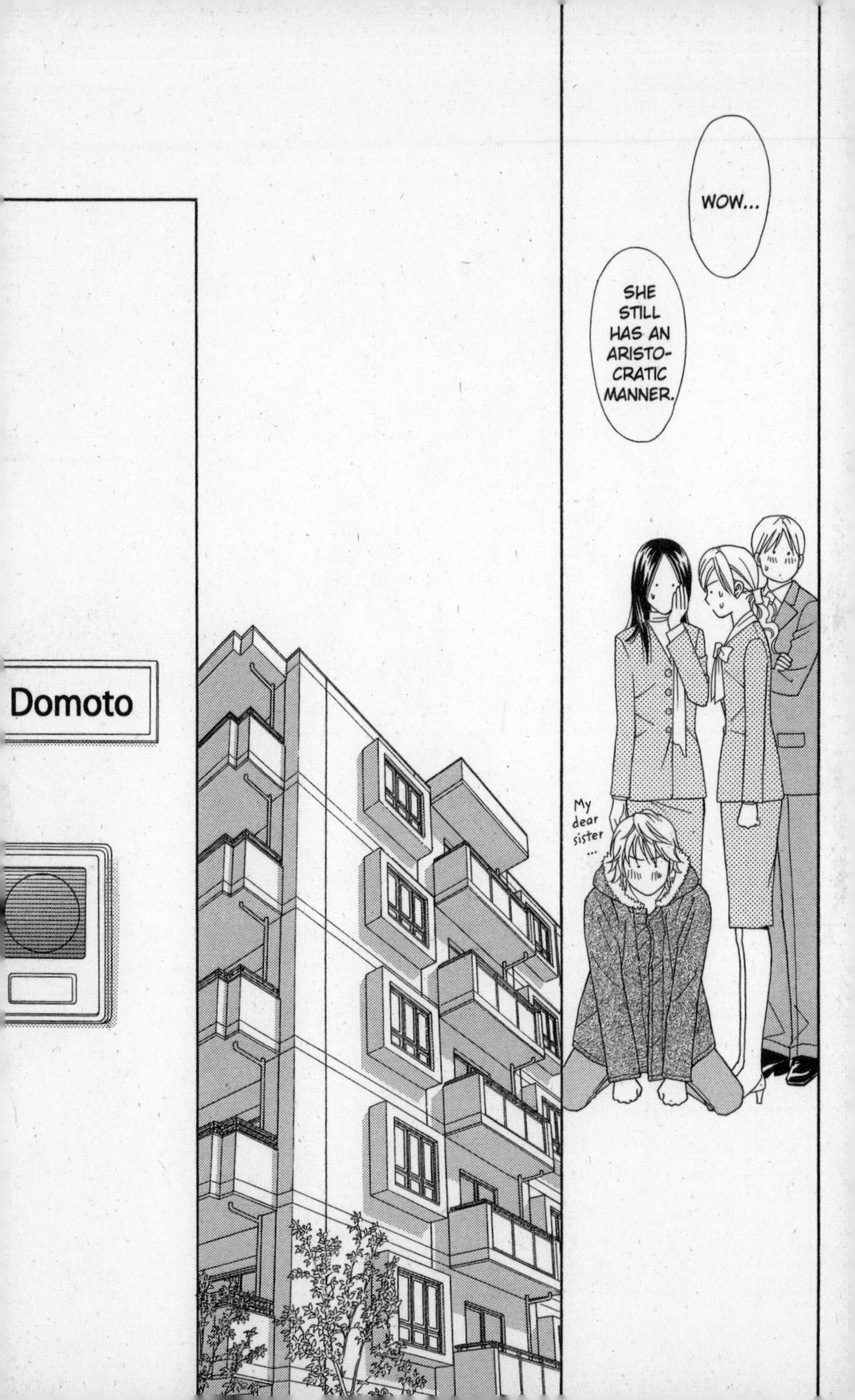
WOW...
SHE STILL HAS AN ARISTO-CRATIC MANNER.
My dear sister ...
Domoto

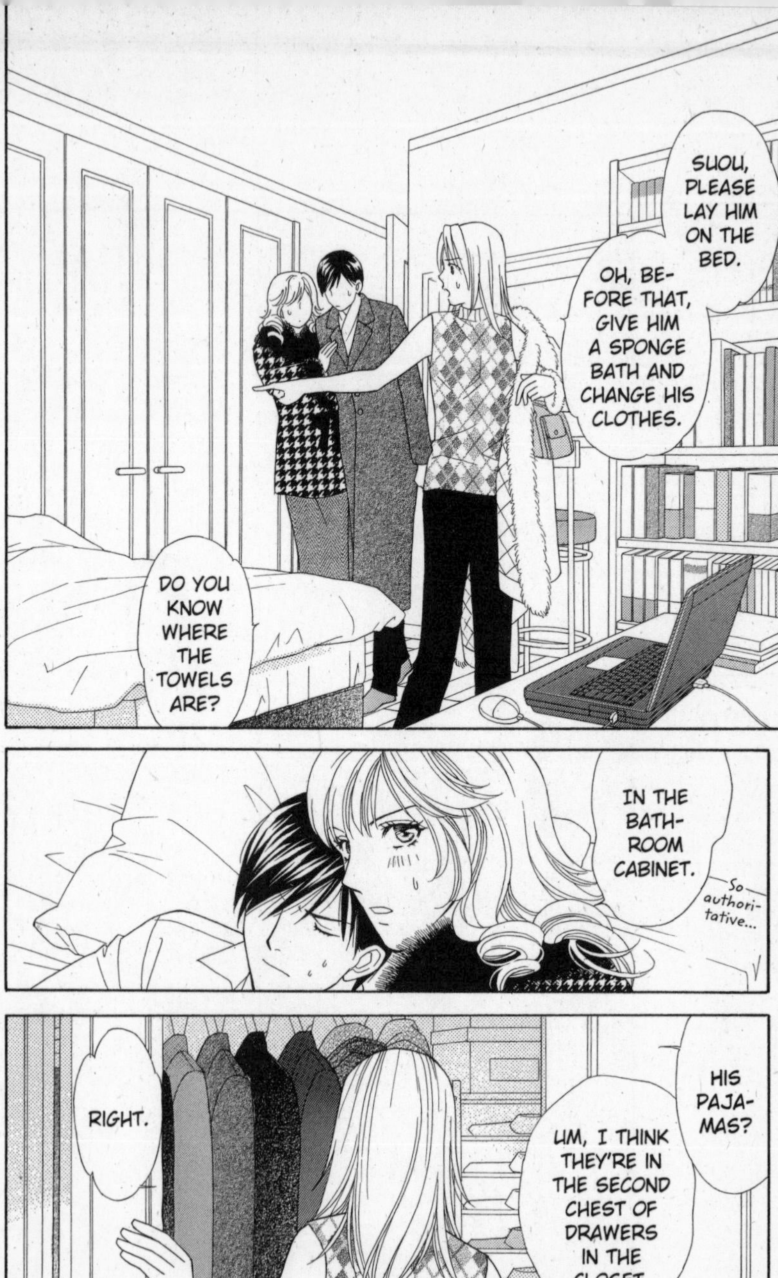
SUOU, PLEASE LAY HIM ON THE BED.
OH, BE-FORE THAT, GIVE HIM A SPONGE BATH AND CHANGE HIS CLOTHES.
DO YOU KNOW WHERE THE TOWELS ARE?
IN THE BATH-ROOM CABINET.
So authori-tative...
HIS PAJA-MAS?
UM, I THINK THEY'RE IN THE SECOND CHEST OF DRAWERS IN THE CLOSET.
RIGHT.

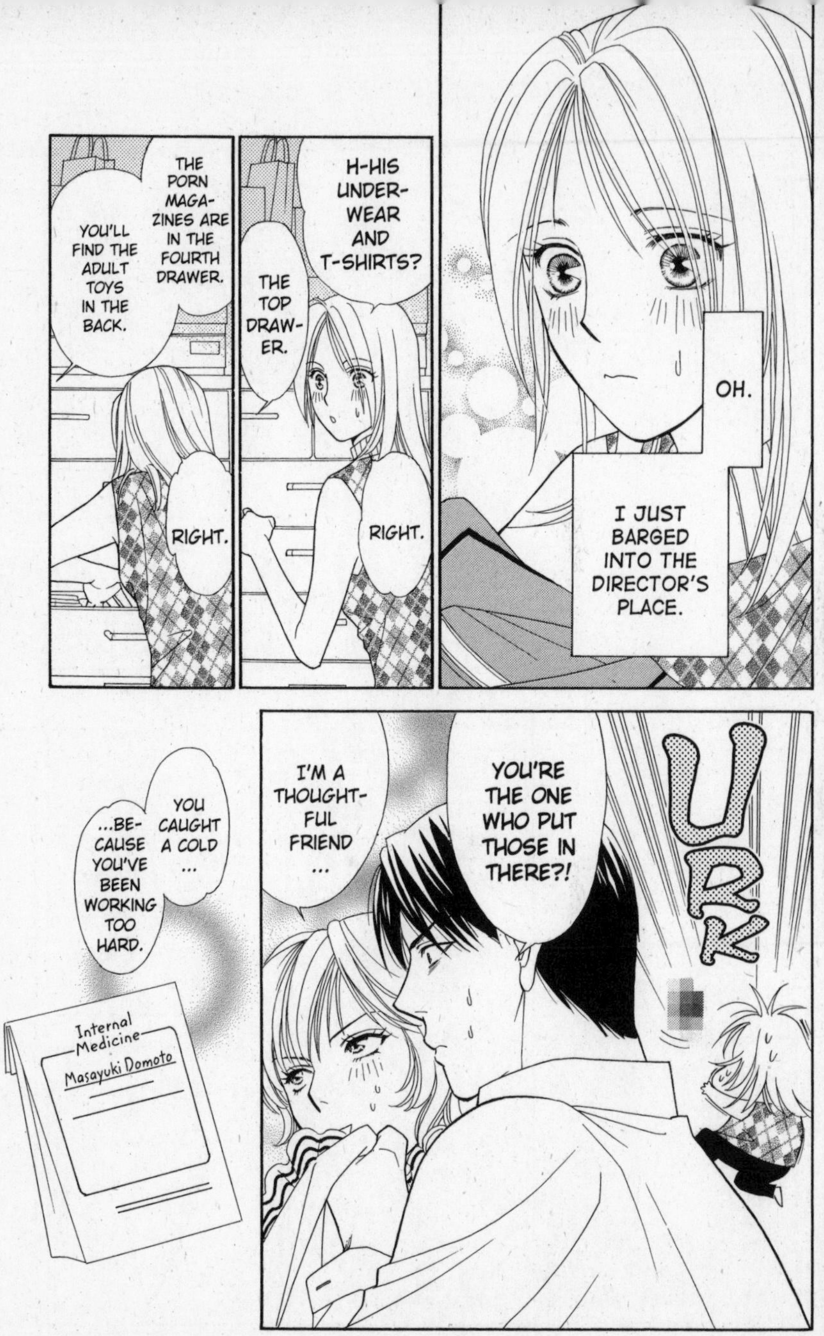
OH.
I JUST BARGED INTO THE DIRECTOR'S PLACE.
H-HIS UNDERWEAR AND T-SHIRTS?
THE TOP DRAWER.
RIGHT.
THE PORN MAGAZINES ARE IN THE FOURTH DRAWER.
YOU'LL FIND THE ADULT TOYS IN THE BACK.
RIGHT.
URK
YOU'RE THE ONE WHO PUT THOSE IN THERE?!
I'M A THOUGHTFUL FRIEND ...
YOU CAUGHT A COLD ...
...BECAUSE YOU'VE BEEN WORKING TOO HARD.
Internal Medicine
Masayuki Domoto

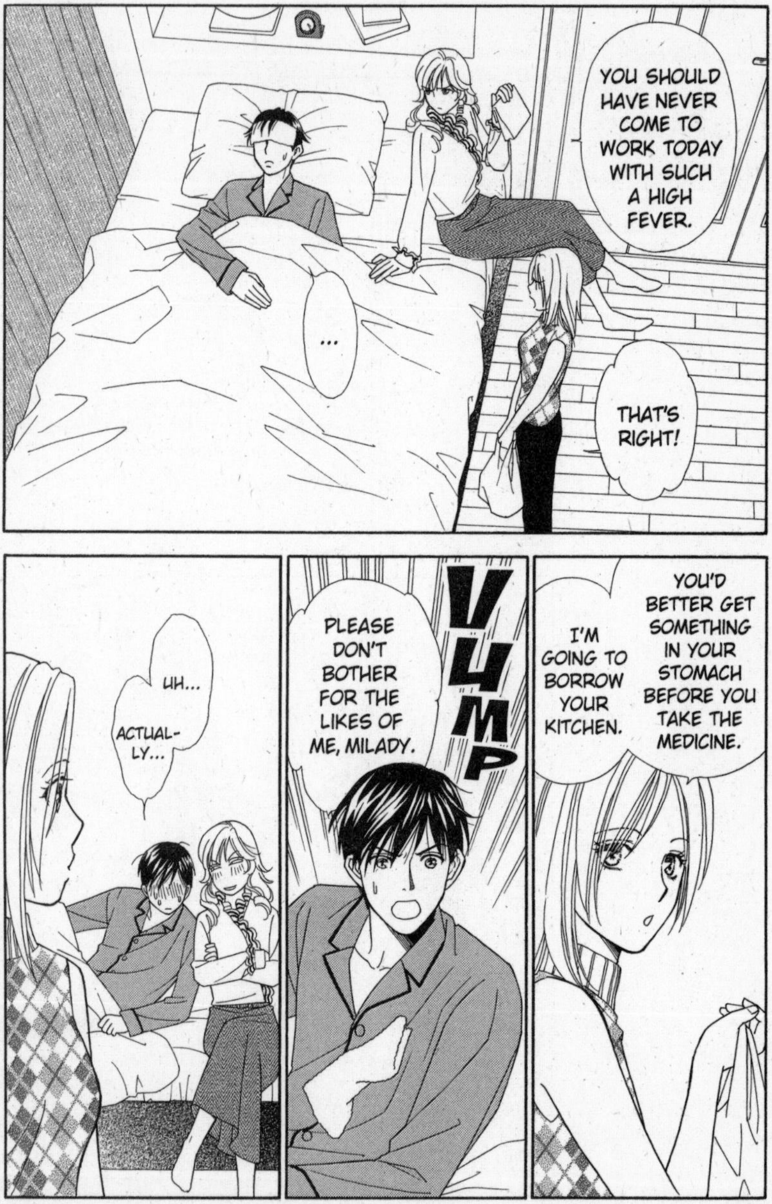
YOU SHOULD HAVE NEVER COME TO WORK TODAY WITH SUCH A HIGH FEVER.
...
THAT'S RIGHT!
YOU'D BETTER GET SOMETHING IN YOUR STOMACH BEFORE YOU TAKE THE MEDICINE.
I'M GOING TO BORROW YOUR KITCHEN.
VUMP
PLEASE DON'T BOTHER FOR THE LIKES OF ME, MILADY.
UH...
ACTUAL-LY...

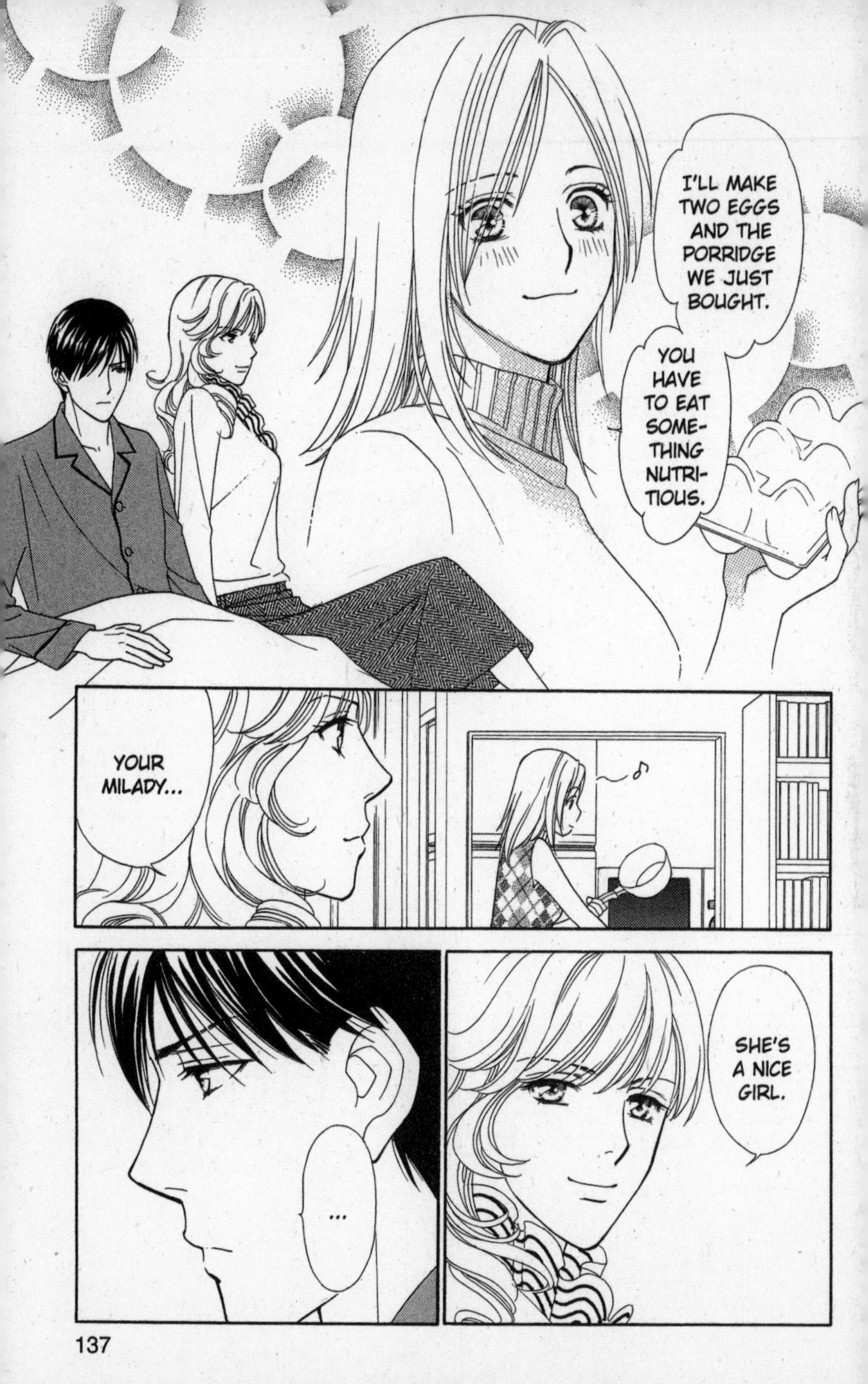
I'LL MAKE TWO EGGS AND THE PORRIDGE WE JUST BOUGHT.
YOU HAVE TO EAT SOME-THING NUTRI-TIOUS.
YOUR MILADY...
SHE'S A NICE GIRL.
...

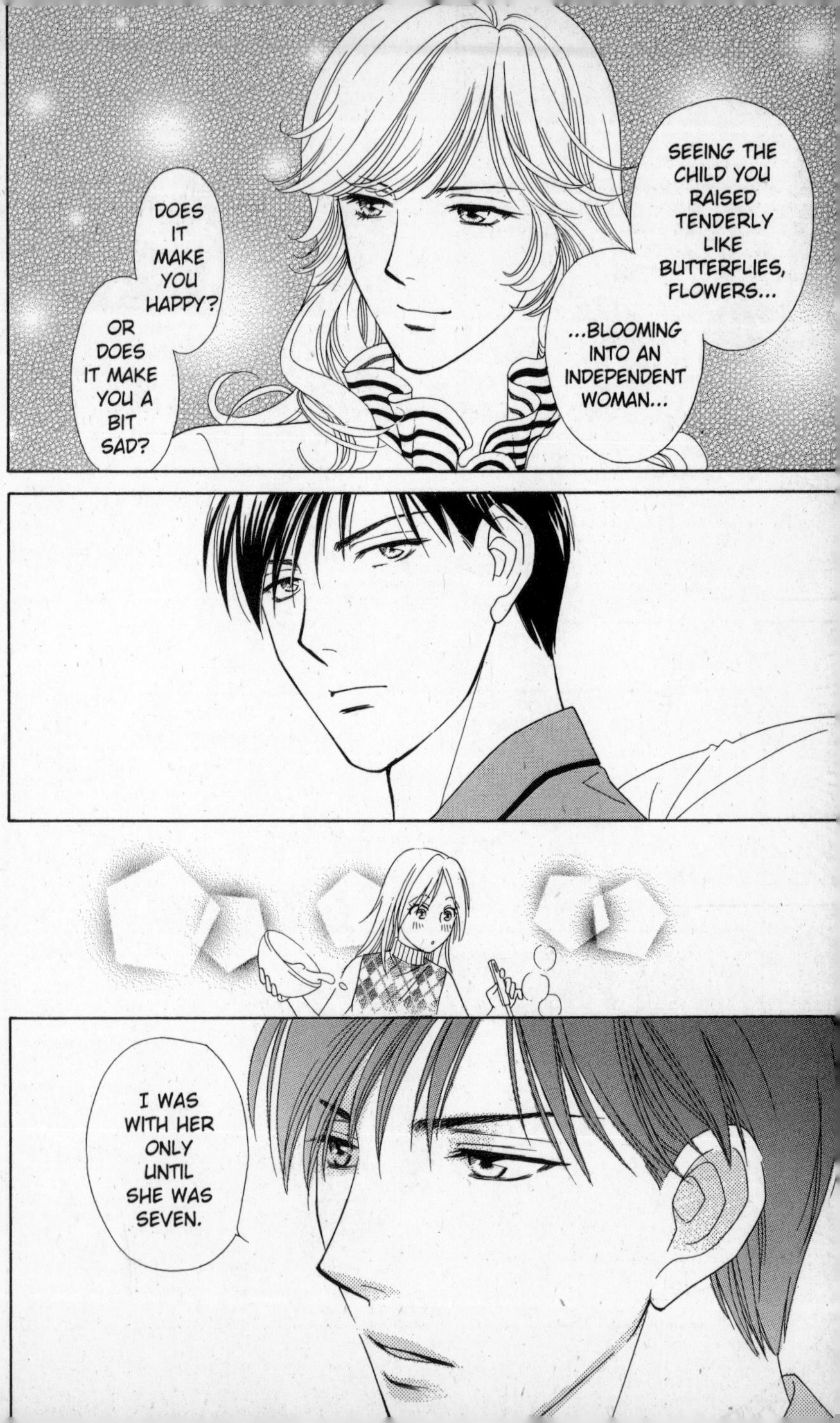
SEEING THE CHILD YOU RAISED TENDERLY LIKE BUTTERFLIES, FLOWERS...
...BLOOMING INTO AN INDEPENDENT WOMAN...
DOES IT MAKE YOU HAPPY?
OR DOES IT MAKE YOU A BIT SAD?
I WAS WITH HER ONLY UNTIL SHE WAS SEVEN.

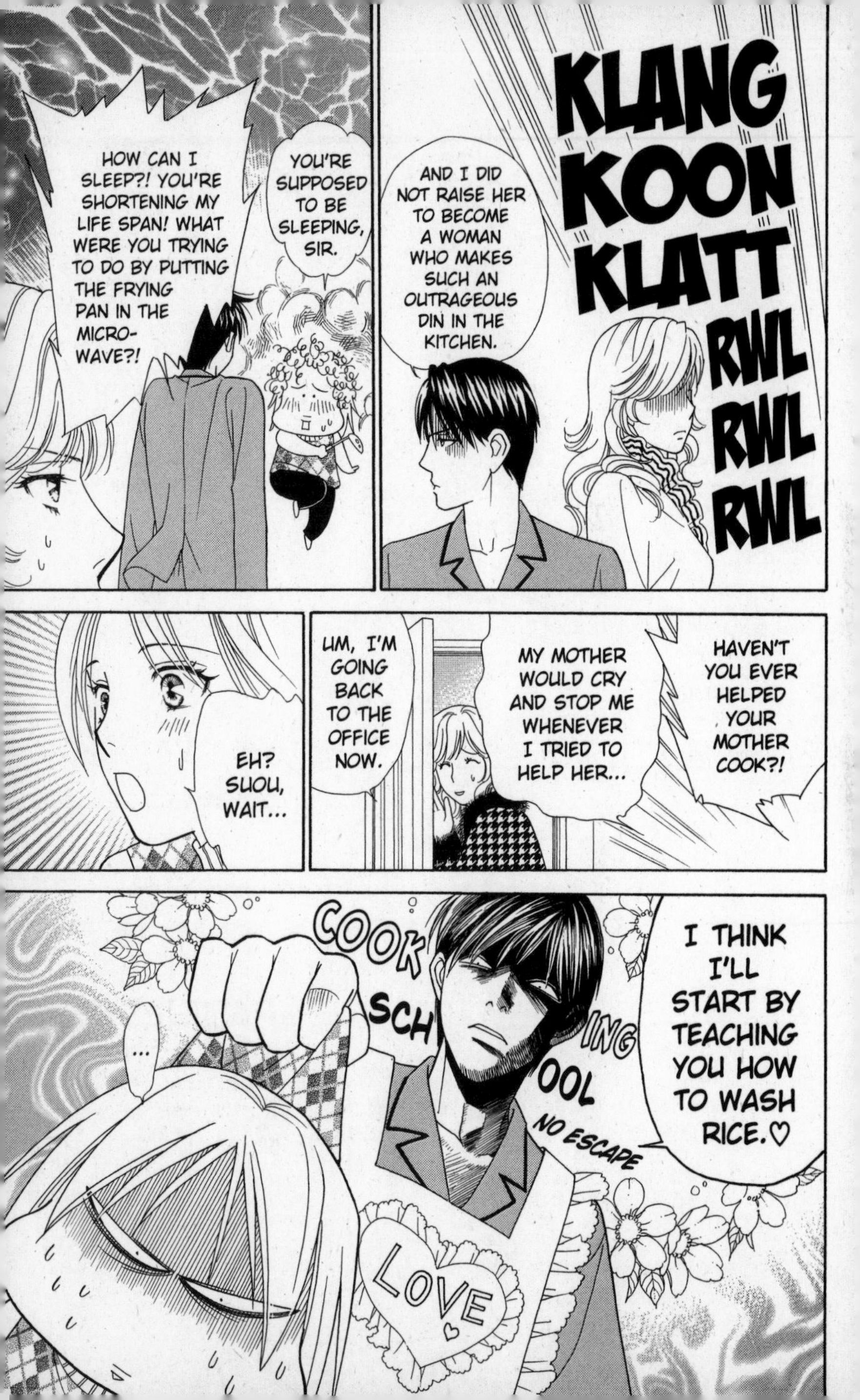
KLANG
KOON
KLATT
RWL
RWL
RWL
AND I DID NOT RAISE HER TO BECOME A WOMAN WHO MAKES SUCH AN OUTRAGEOUS DIN IN THE KITCHEN.
YOU'RE SUPPOSED TO BE SLEEPING, SIR.
HOW CAN I SLEEP?! YOU'RE SHORTENING MY LIFE SPAN! WHAT WERE YOU TRYING TO DO BY PUTTING THE FRYING PAN IN THE MICRO-WAVE?!
HAVEN'T YOU EVER HELPED YOUR MOTHER COOK?!
MY MOTHER WOULD CRY AND STOP ME WHENEVER I TRIED TO HELP HER...
UM, I'M GOING BACK TO THE OFFICE NOW.
EH? SUOU, WAIT...
I THINK I'LL START BY TEACHING YOU HOW TO WASH RICE.♡
COOKING SCHOOL
NO ESCAPE
...
LOVE

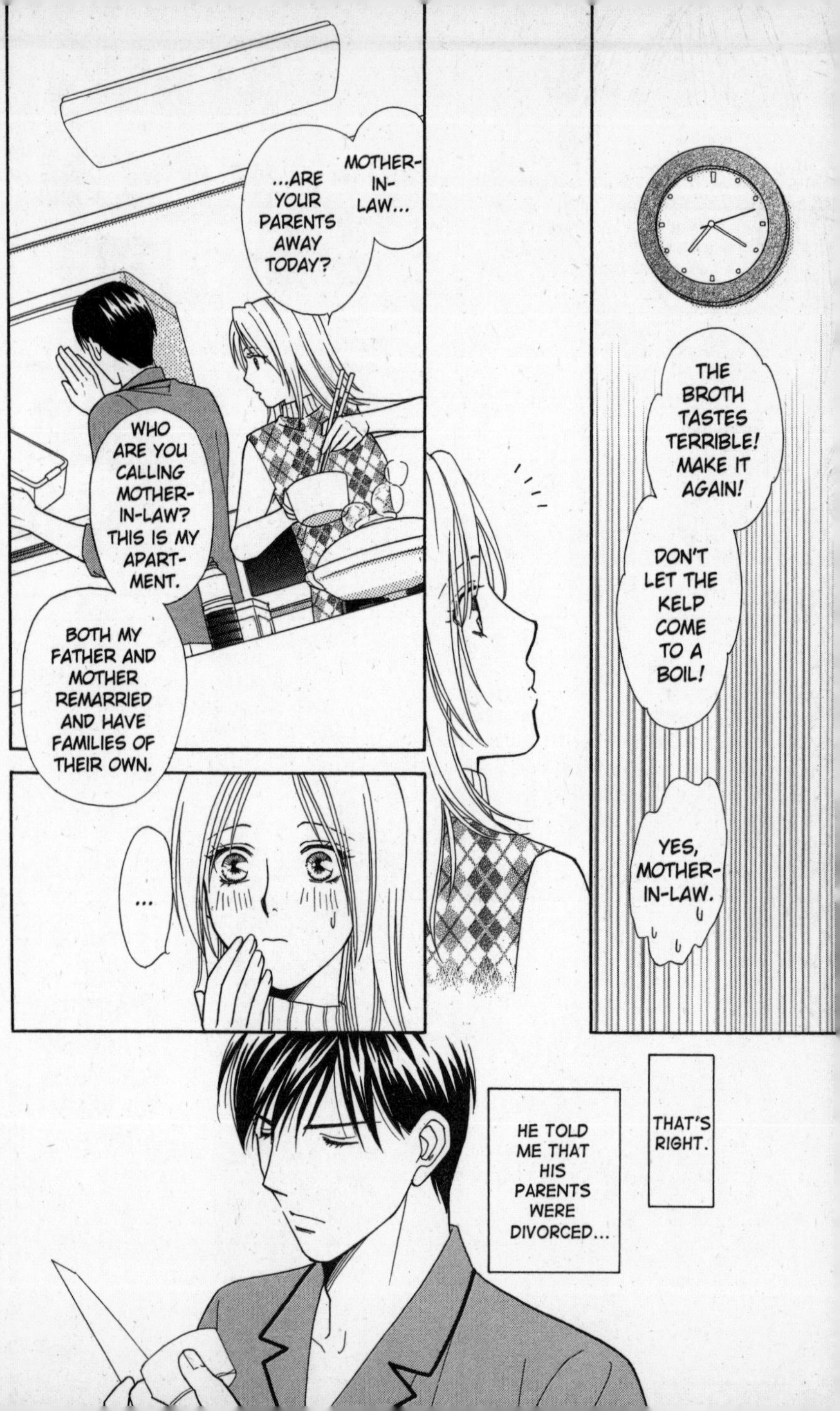
THE BROTH TASTES TERRIBLE! MAKE IT AGAIN!
DON'T LET THE KELP COME TO A BOIL!
YES, MOTHER-IN-LAW.
MOTHER-IN-LAW...
...ARE YOUR PARENTS AWAY TODAY?
WHO ARE YOU CALLING MOTHER-IN-LAW? THIS IS MY APARTMENT.
BOTH MY FATHER AND MOTHER REMARRIED AND HAVE FAMILIES OF THEIR OWN.
...
THAT'S RIGHT.
HE TOLD ME THAT HIS PARENTS WERE DIVORCED...

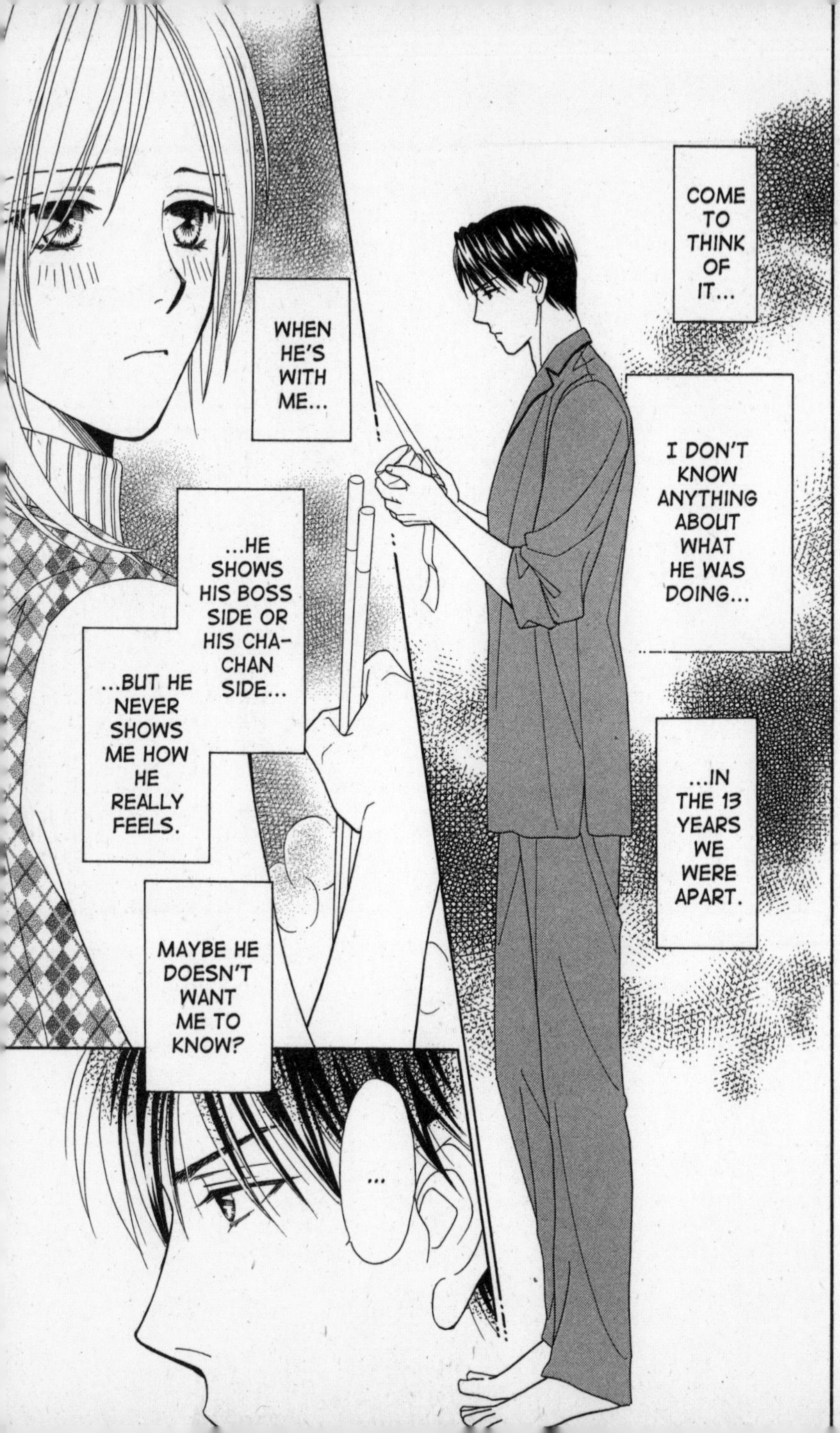
COME TO THINK OF IT...
I DON'T KNOW ANYTHING ABOUT WHAT HE WAS DOING...
...IN THE 13 YEARS WE WERE APART.
WHEN HE'S WITH ME...
...HE SHOWS HIS BOSS SIDE OR HIS CHA-CHAN SIDE...
...BUT HE NEVER SHOWS ME HOW HE REALLY FEELS.
MAYBE HE DOESN'T WANT ME TO KNOW?
...

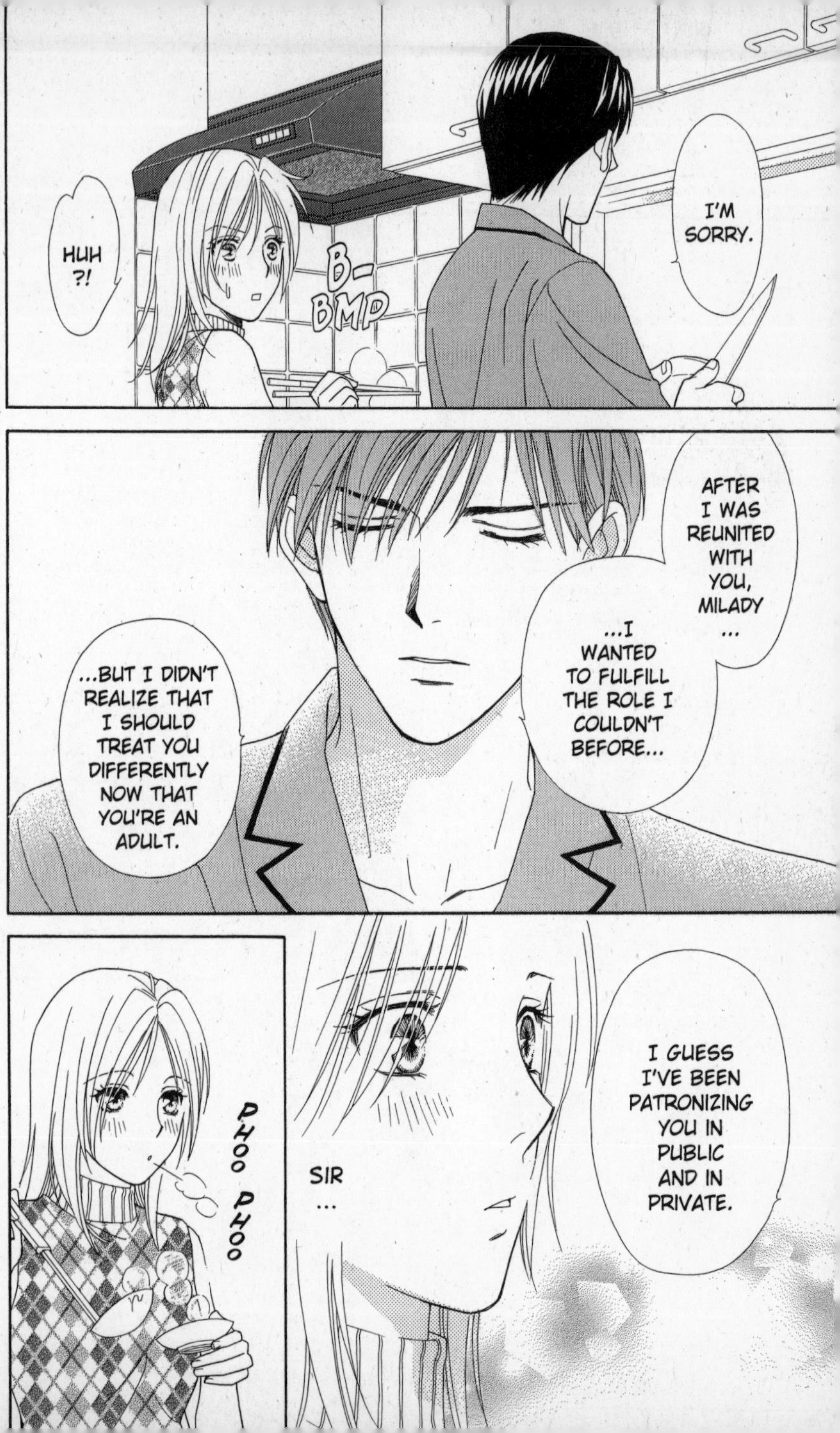
I'M SORRY.
B-BMP
HUH ?!
AFTER I WAS REUNITED WITH YOU, MILADY ...
...I WANTED TO FULFILL THE ROLE I COULDN'T BEFORE...
...BUT I DIDN'T REALIZE THAT I SHOULD TREAT YOU DIFFERENTLY NOW THAT YOU'RE AN ADULT.
I GUESS I'VE BEEN PATRONIZING YOU IN PUBLIC AND IN PRIVATE.
SIR ...
PHOO PHOO

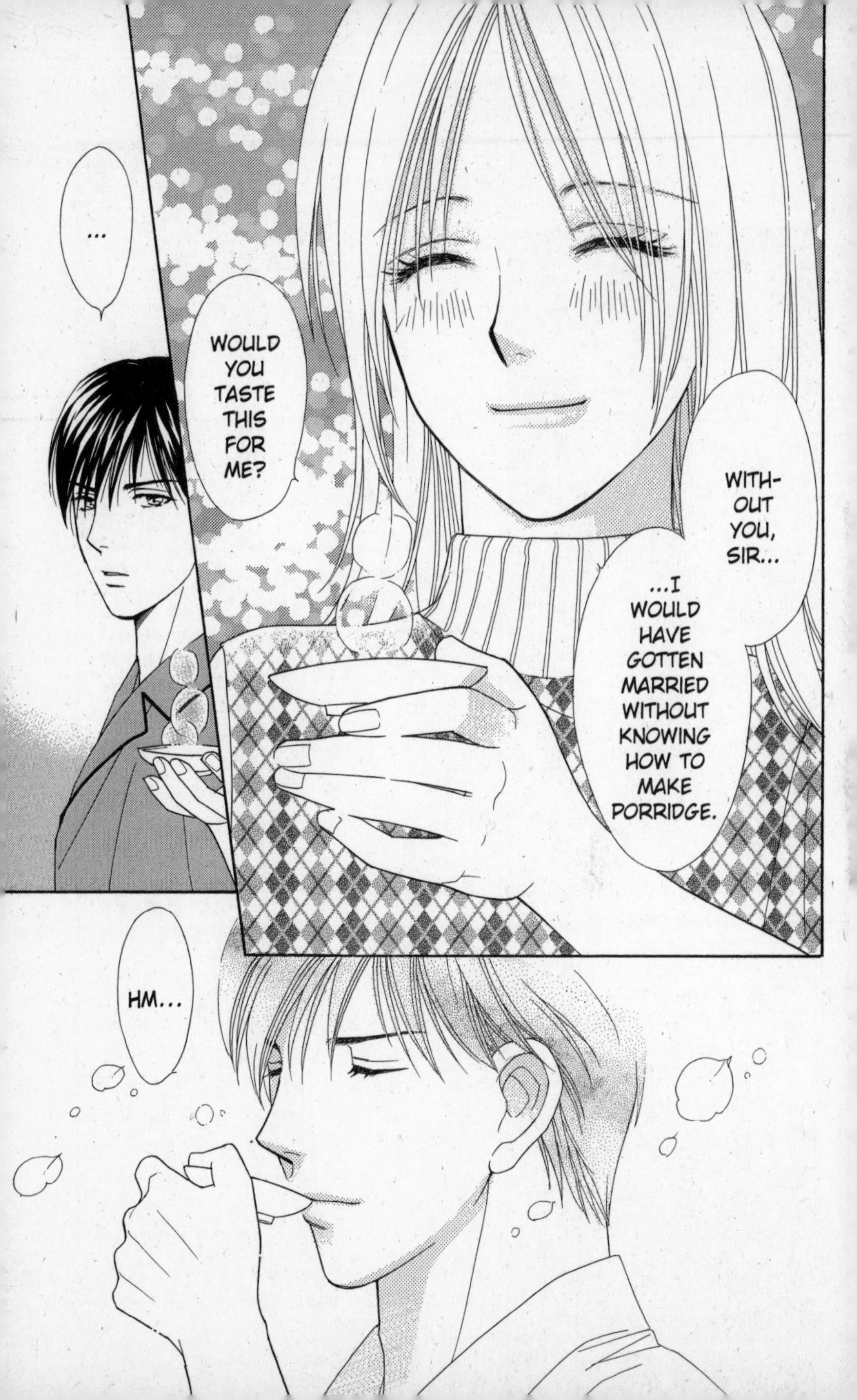
WOULD YOU TASTE THIS FOR ME?
WITH-OUT YOU, SIR...
...I WOULD HAVE GOTTEN MARRIED WITHOUT KNOWING HOW TO MAKE PORRIDGE.
...
HM...

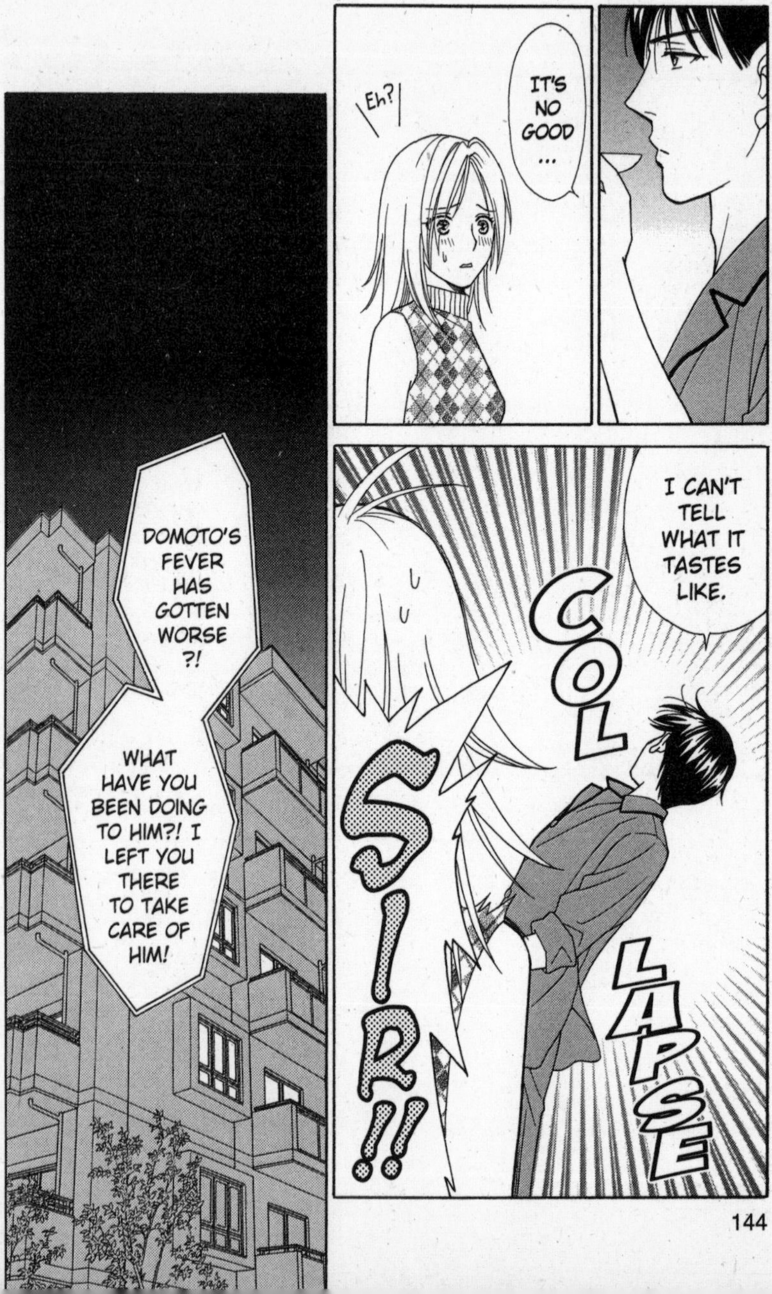
IT'S NO GOOD ...
Eh?
I CAN'T TELL WHAT IT TASTES LIKE.
COL LAPSE
SIR!!
DOMOTO'S FEVER HAS GOTTEN WORSE?!
WHAT HAVE YOU BEEN DOING TO HIM?! I LEFT YOU THERE TO TAKE CARE OF HIM!

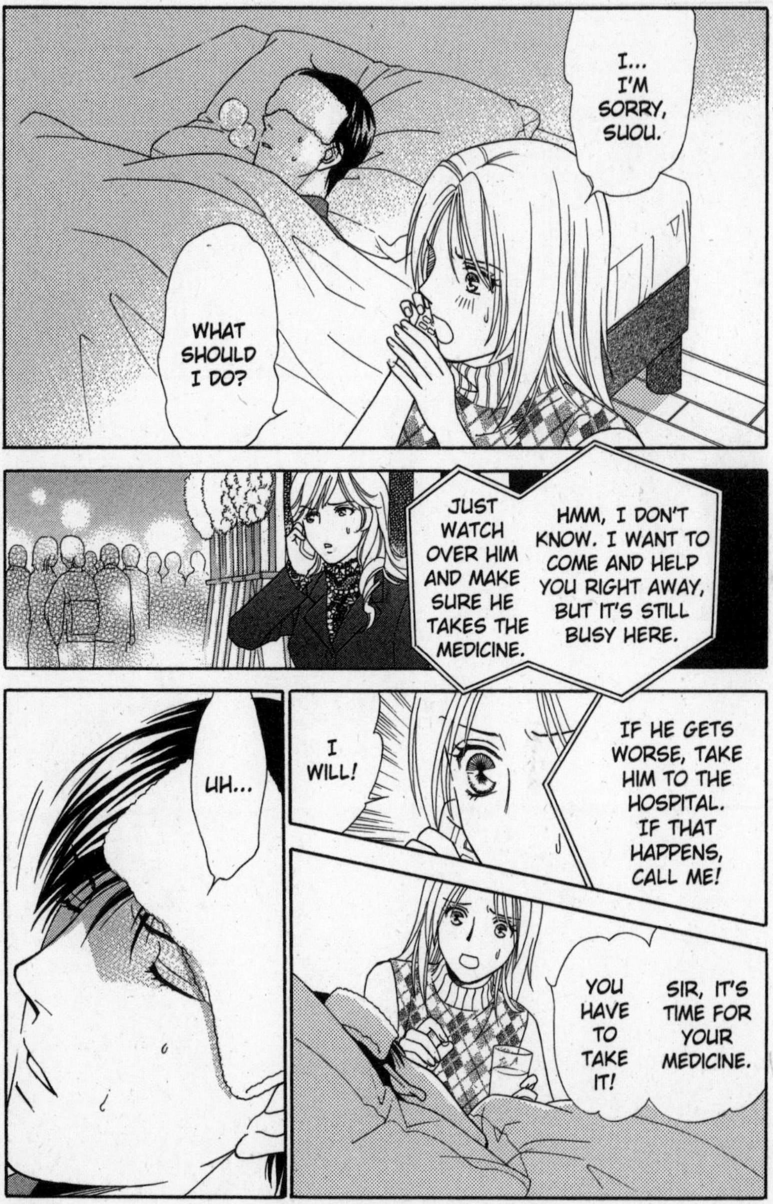
I... I'M SORRY, SUOU.
WHAT SHOULD I DO?
HMM, I DON'T KNOW. I WANT TO COME AND HELP YOU RIGHT AWAY, BUT IT'S STILL BUSY HERE.
JUST WATCH OVER HIM AND MAKE SURE HE TAKES THE MEDICINE.
IF HE GETS WORSE, TAKE HIM TO THE HOSPITAL. IF THAT HAPPENS, CALL ME!
I WILL!
SIR, IT'S TIME FOR YOUR MEDICINE.
YOU HAVE TO TAKE IT!
UH...

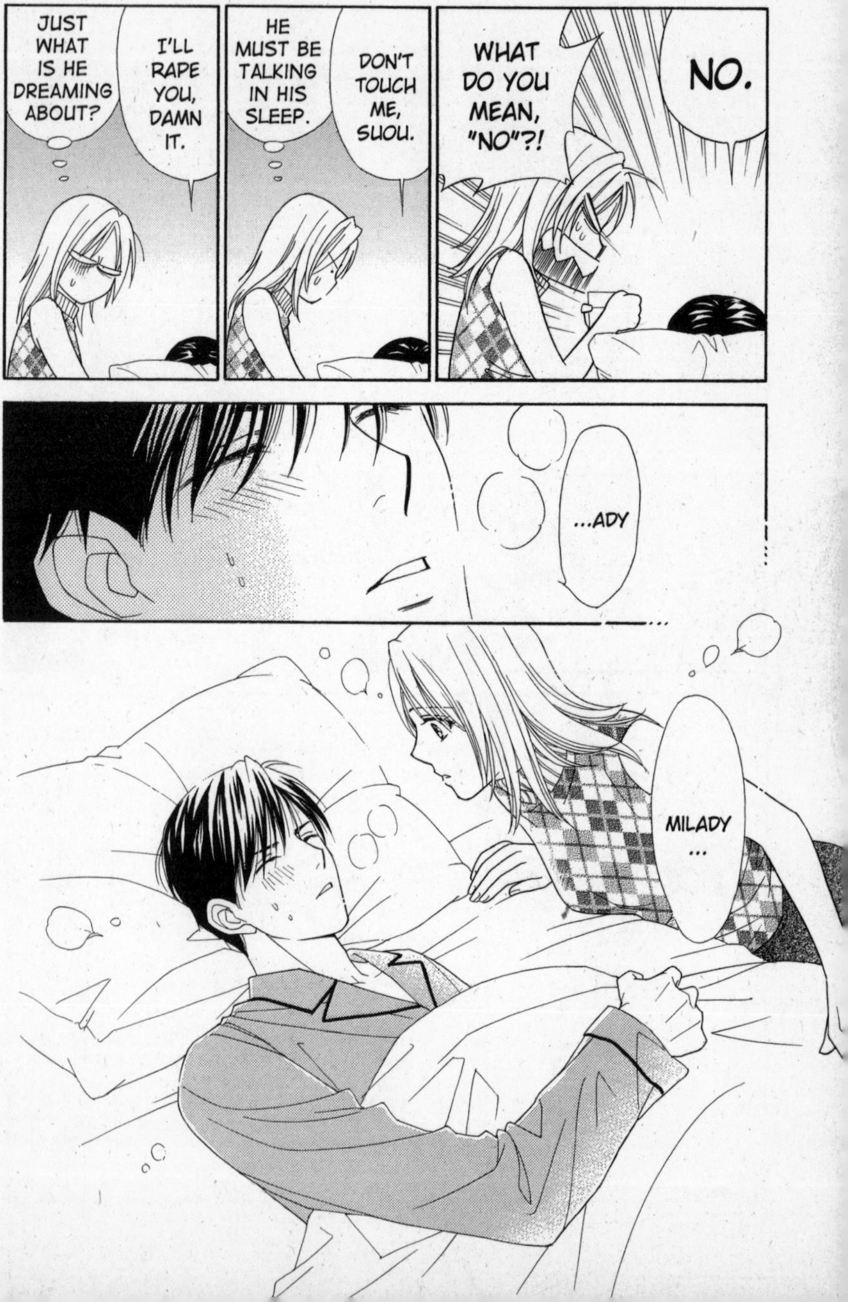
NO.
WHAT DO YOU MEAN, "NO"?!
DON'T TOUCH ME, SUOU.
HE MUST BE TALKING IN HIS SLEEP.
I'LL RAPE YOU, DAMN IT.
JUST WHAT IS HE DREAMING ABOUT?
...ADY
MILADY ...

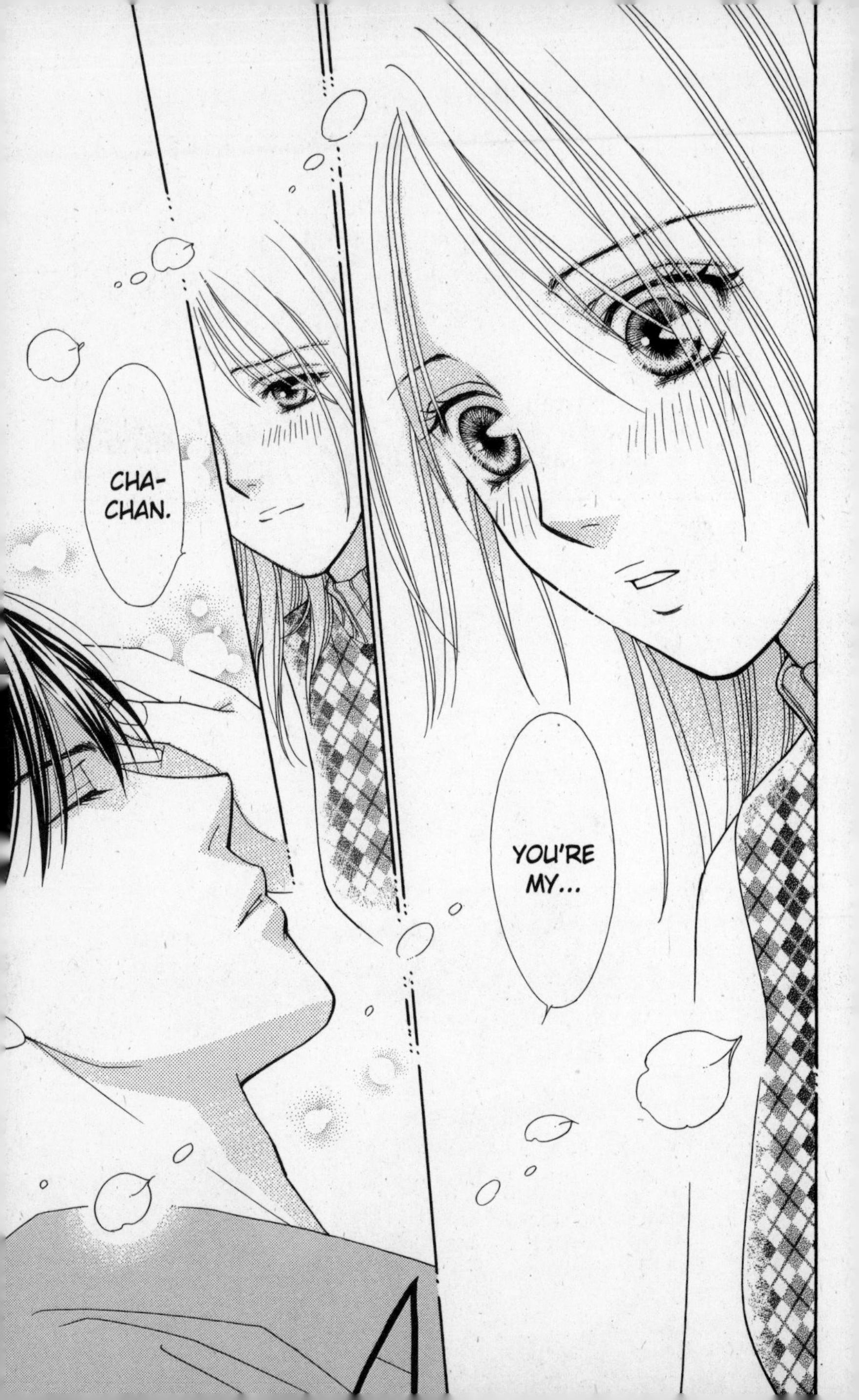
YOU'RE MY...
CHA-CHAN.

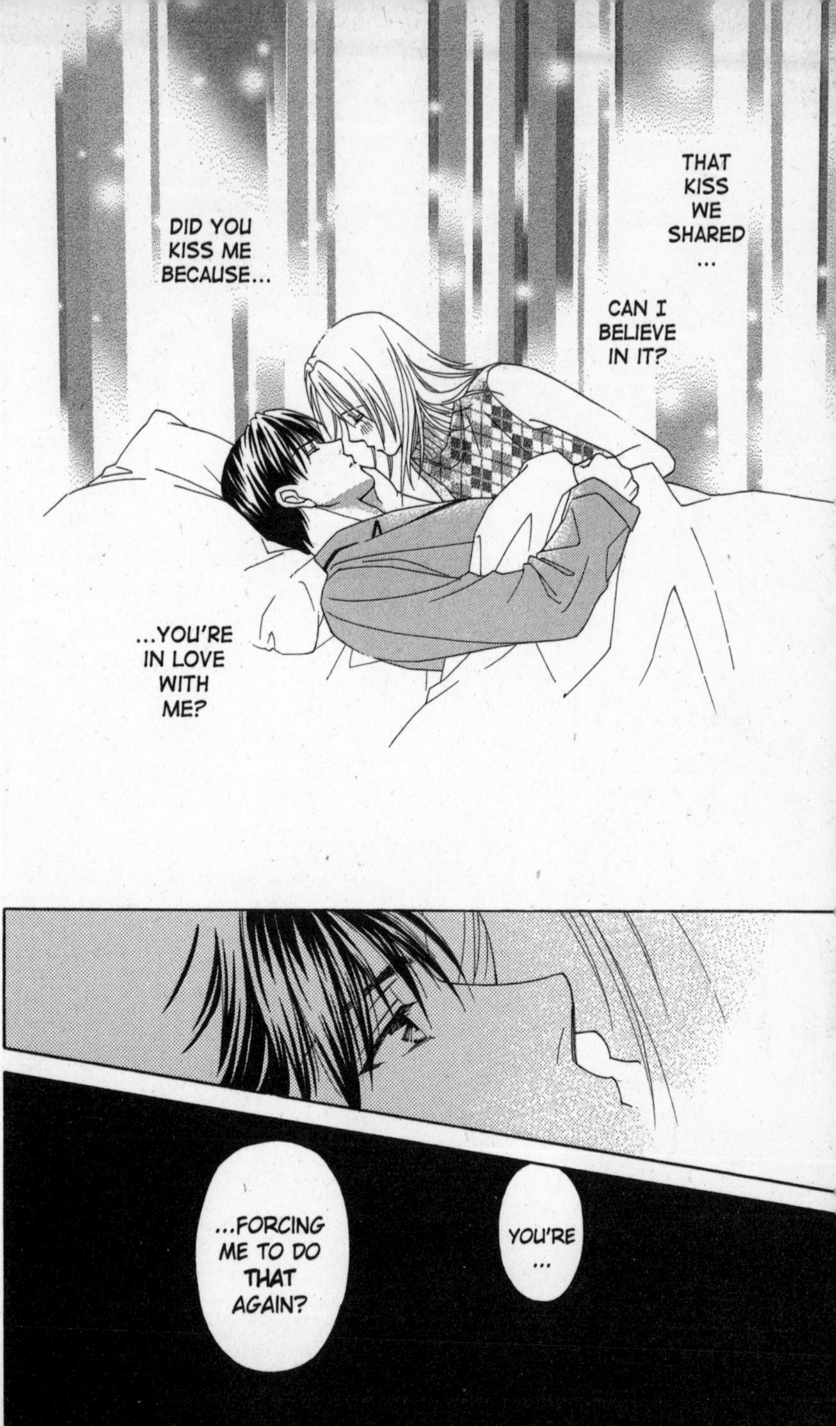
THAT KISS WE SHARED...
CAN I BELIEVE IN IT?
DID YOU KISS ME BECAUSE...
...YOU'RE IN LOVE WITH ME?
YOU'RE...
...FORCING ME TO DO THAT AGAIN?

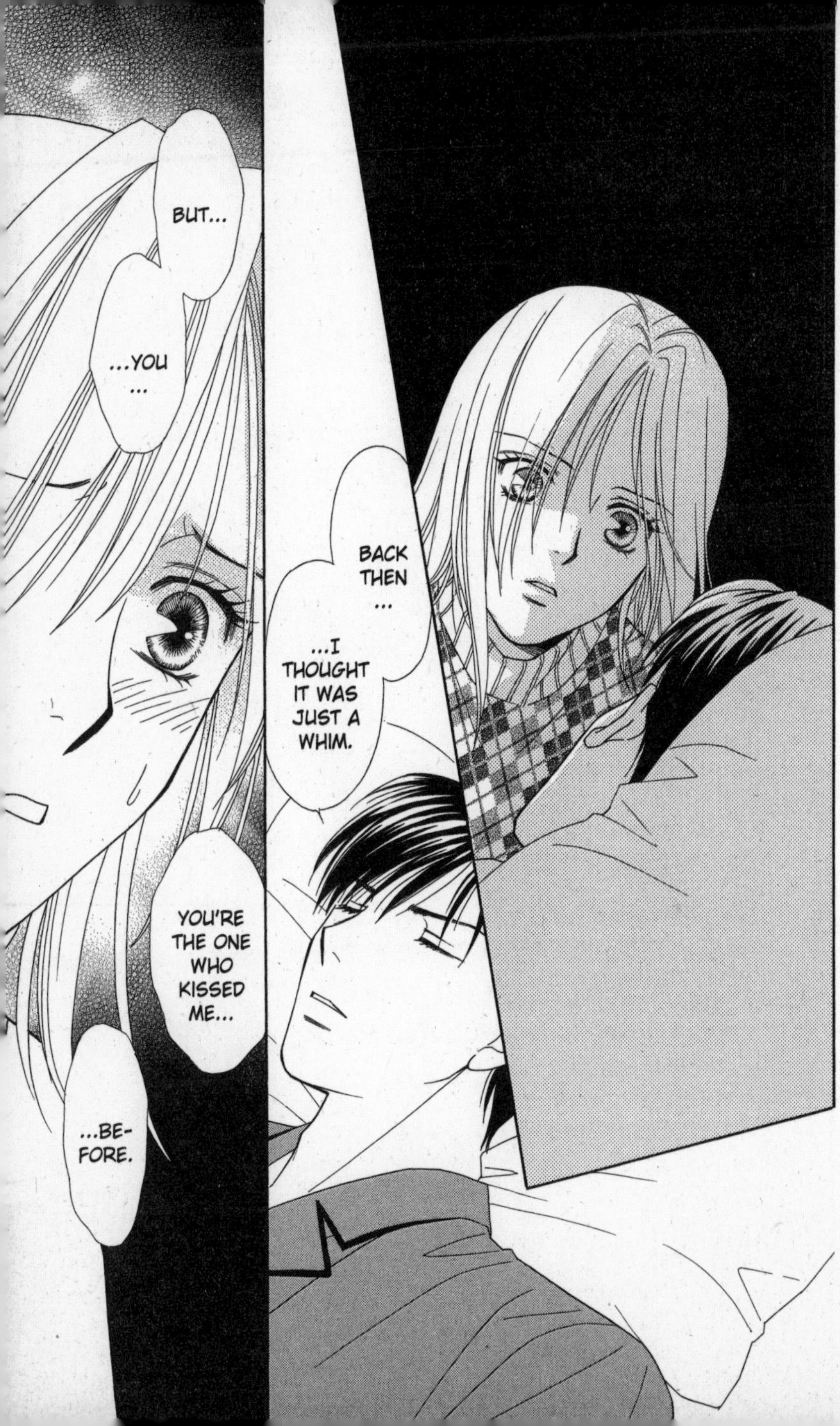
BACK THEN ...
...I THOUGHT IT WAS JUST A WHIM.
BUT...
...YOU ...
YOU'RE THE ONE WHO KISSED ME...
...BE-FORE.

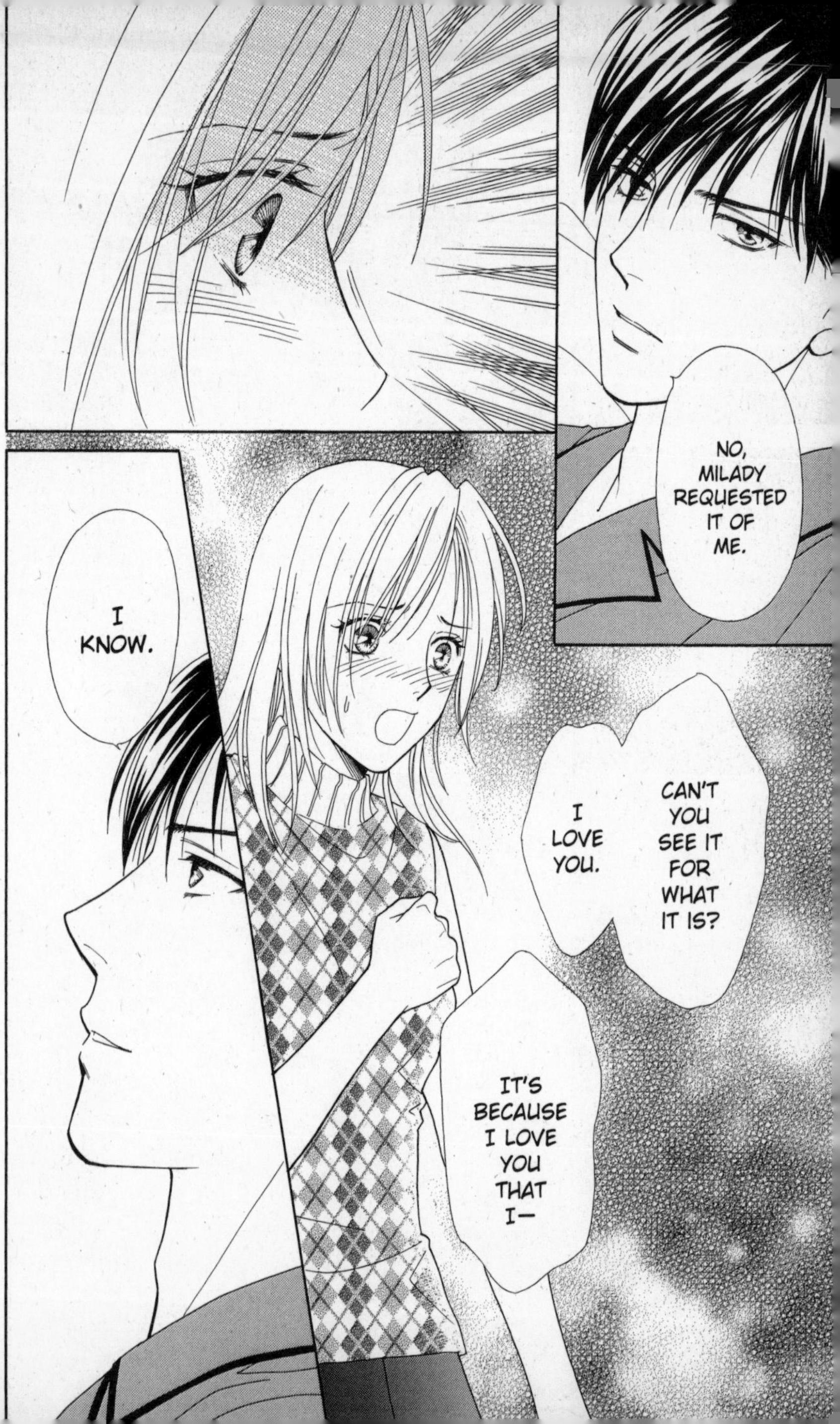
NO, MILADY REQUESTED IT OF ME.
CAN'T YOU SEE IT FOR WHAT IT IS?
I LOVE YOU.
IT'S BECAUSE I LOVE YOU THAT I—
I KNOW.

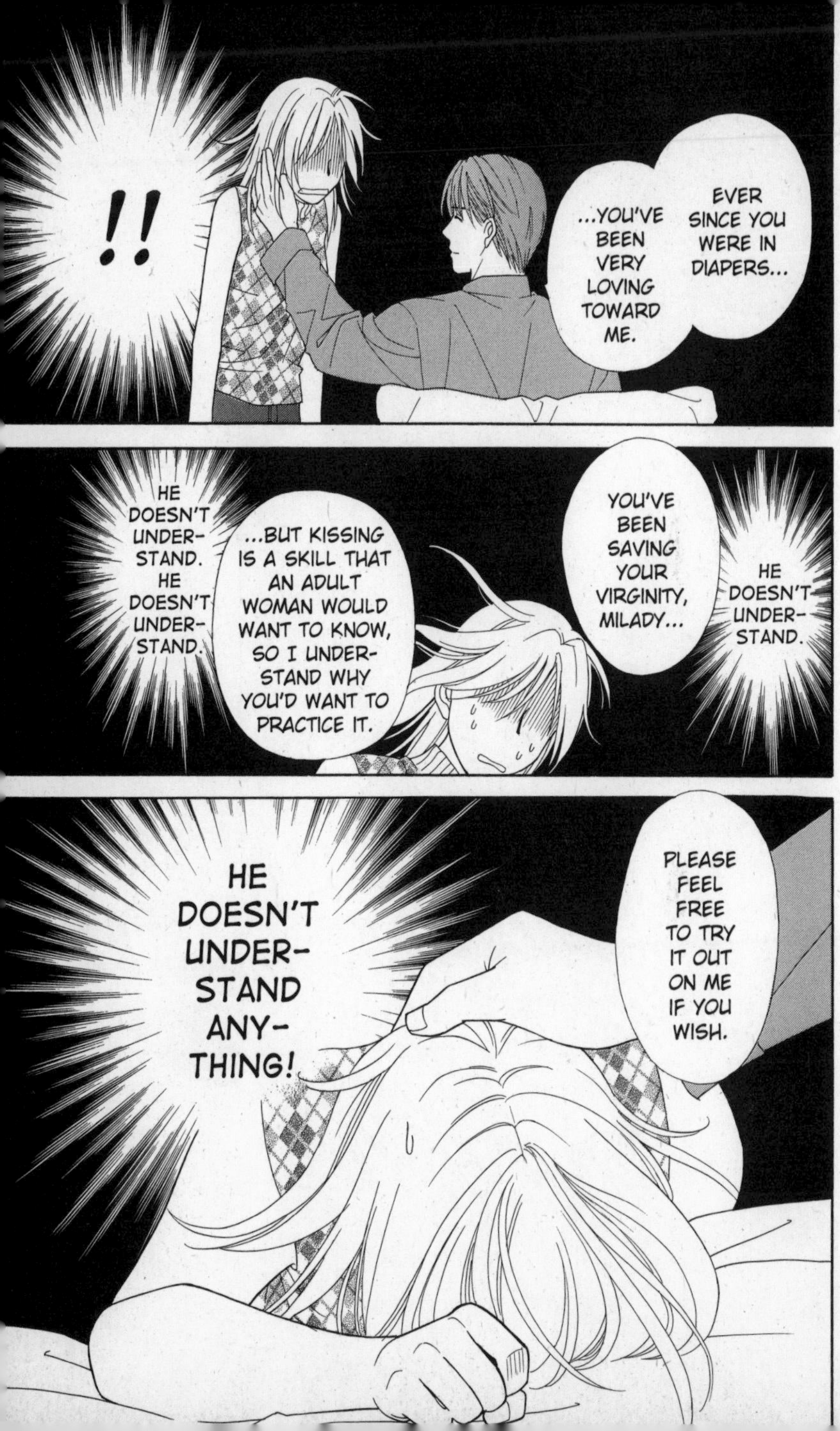
EVER SINCE YOU WERE IN DIAPERS...
...YOU'VE BEEN VERY LOVING TOWARD ME.
!!
HE DOESN'T UNDERSTAND.
YOU'VE BEEN SAVING YOUR VIRGINITY, MILADY...
...BUT KISSING IS A SKILL THAT AN ADULT WOMAN WOULD WANT TO KNOW, SO I UNDERSTAND WHY YOU'D WANT TO PRACTICE IT.
HE DOESN'T UNDERSTAND. HE DOESN'T UNDERSTAND.
PLEASE FEEL FREE TO TRY IT OUT ON ME IF YOU WISH.
HE DOESN'T UNDERSTAND ANYTHING!

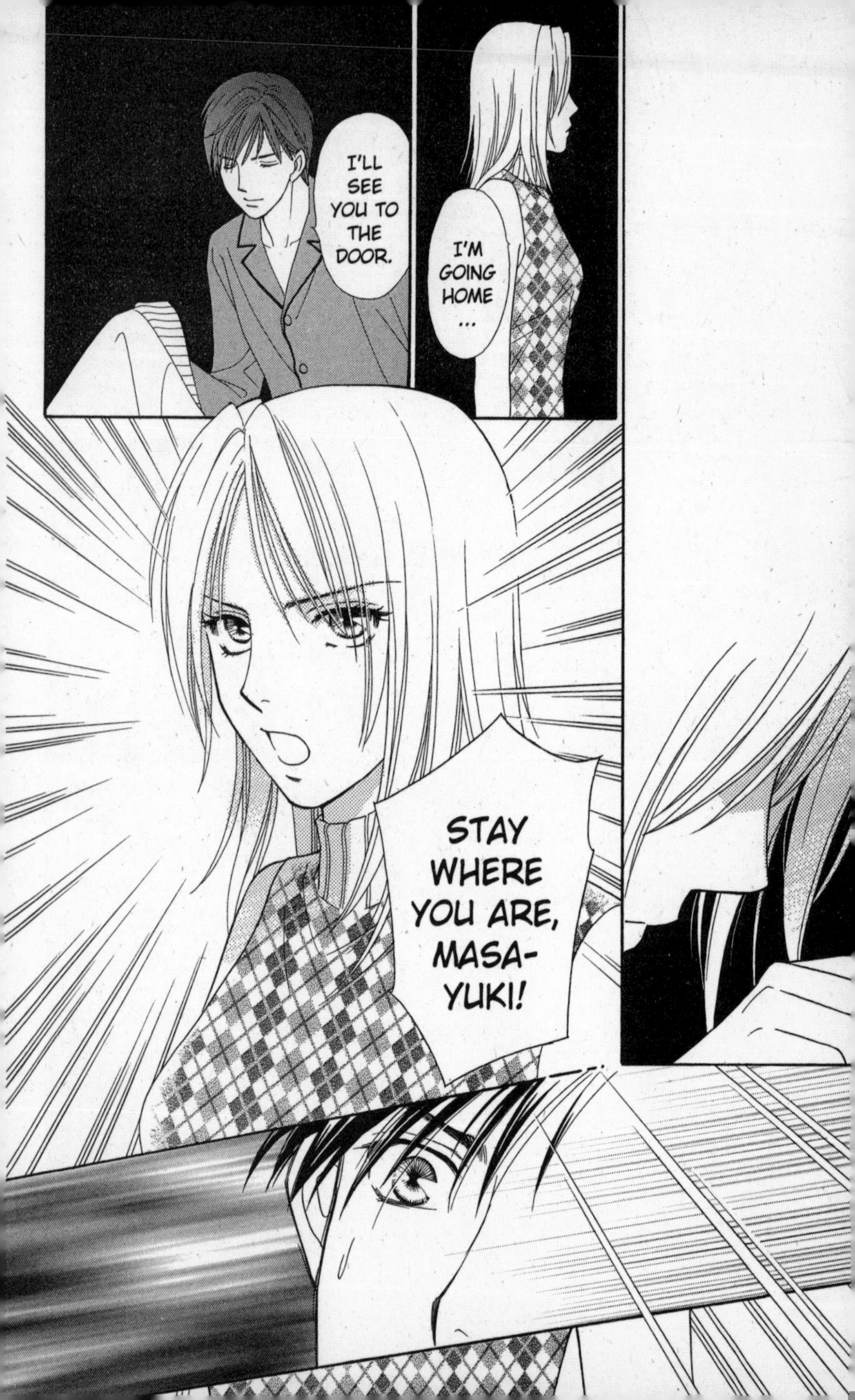
I'M GOING HOME ...
I'LL SEE YOU TO THE DOOR.
STAY WHERE YOU ARE, MASA-YUKI!

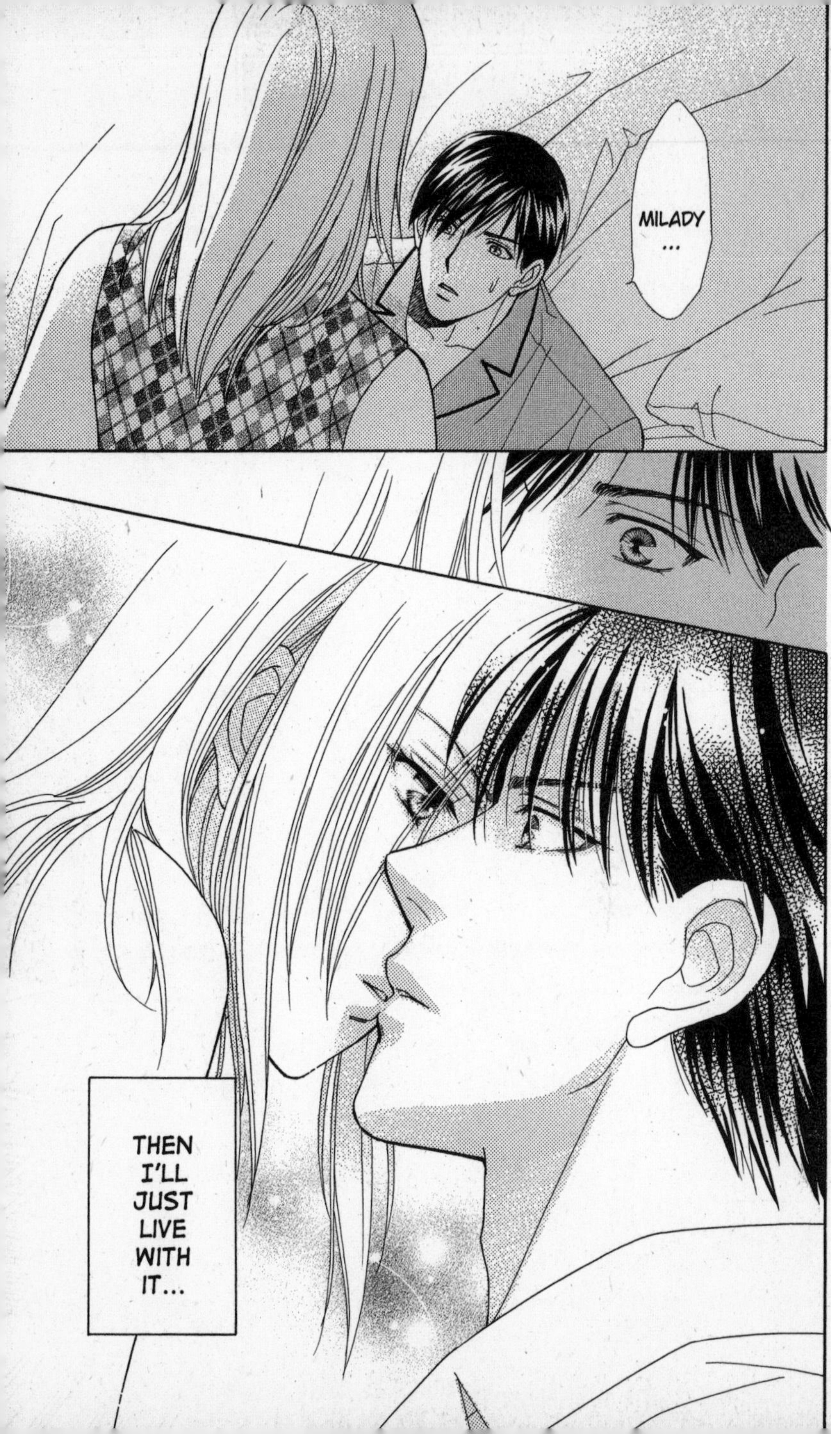
MILADY ...
THEN I'LL JUST LIVE WITH IT...

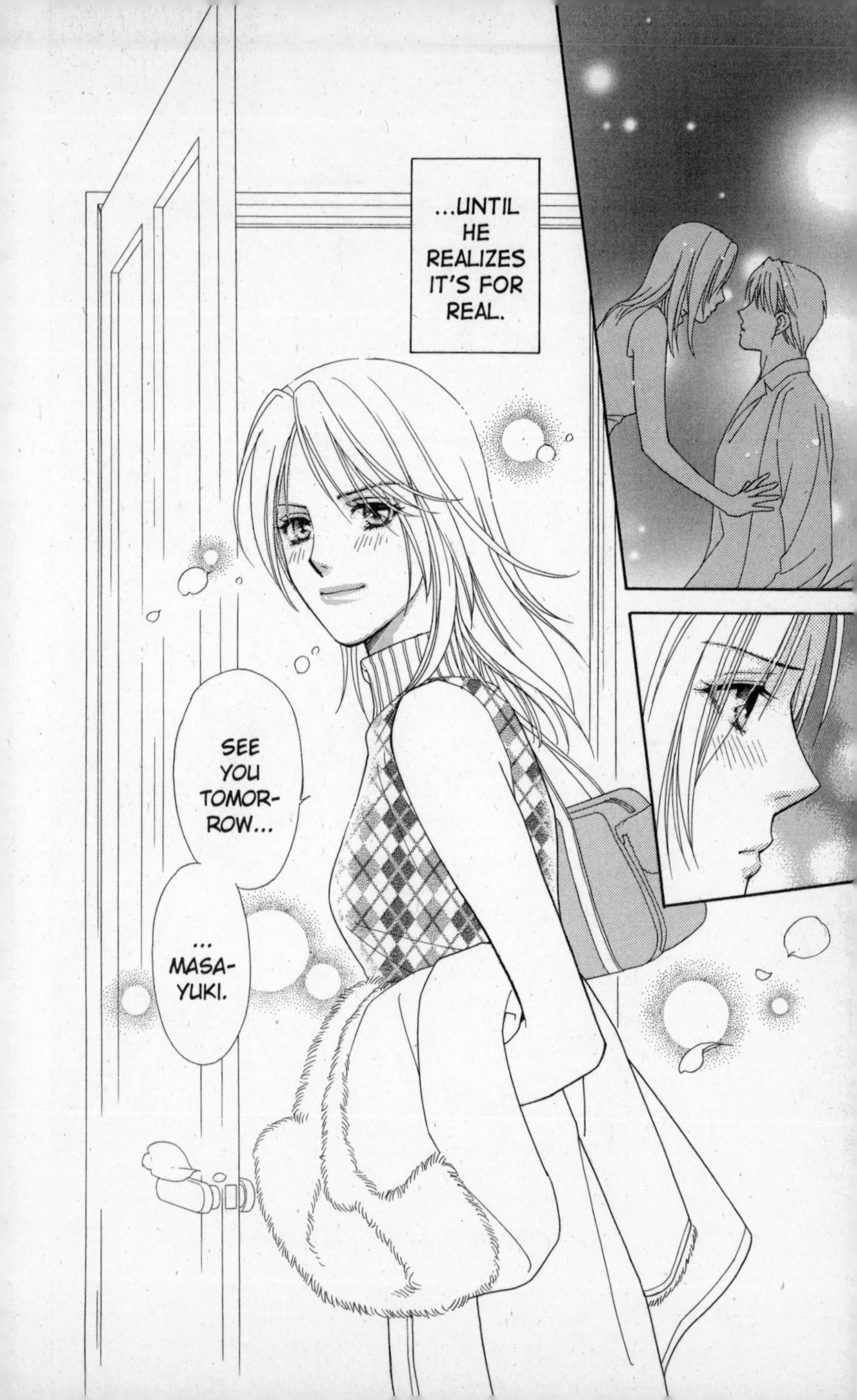
...UNTIL HE REALIZES IT'S FOR REAL.
SEE YOU TOMORROW...
...MASAYUKI.

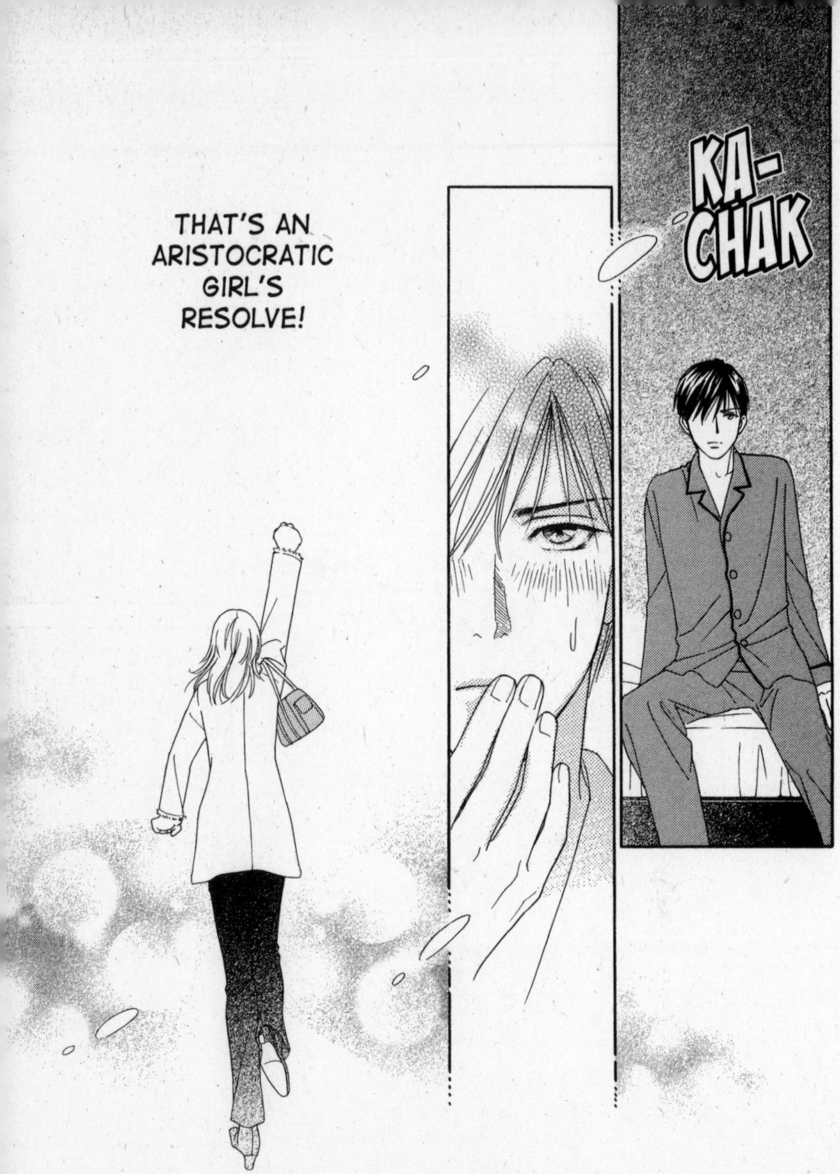
KA-CHAK
THAT'S AN ARISTOCRATIC GIRL'S RESOLVE!

Chapter 4: Lovesick/End

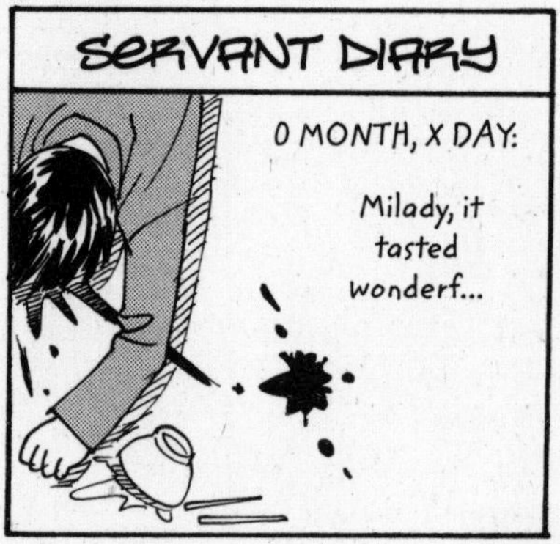
SERVANT DIARY
0 MONTH, X DAY:
Milady, it tasted wonderf...

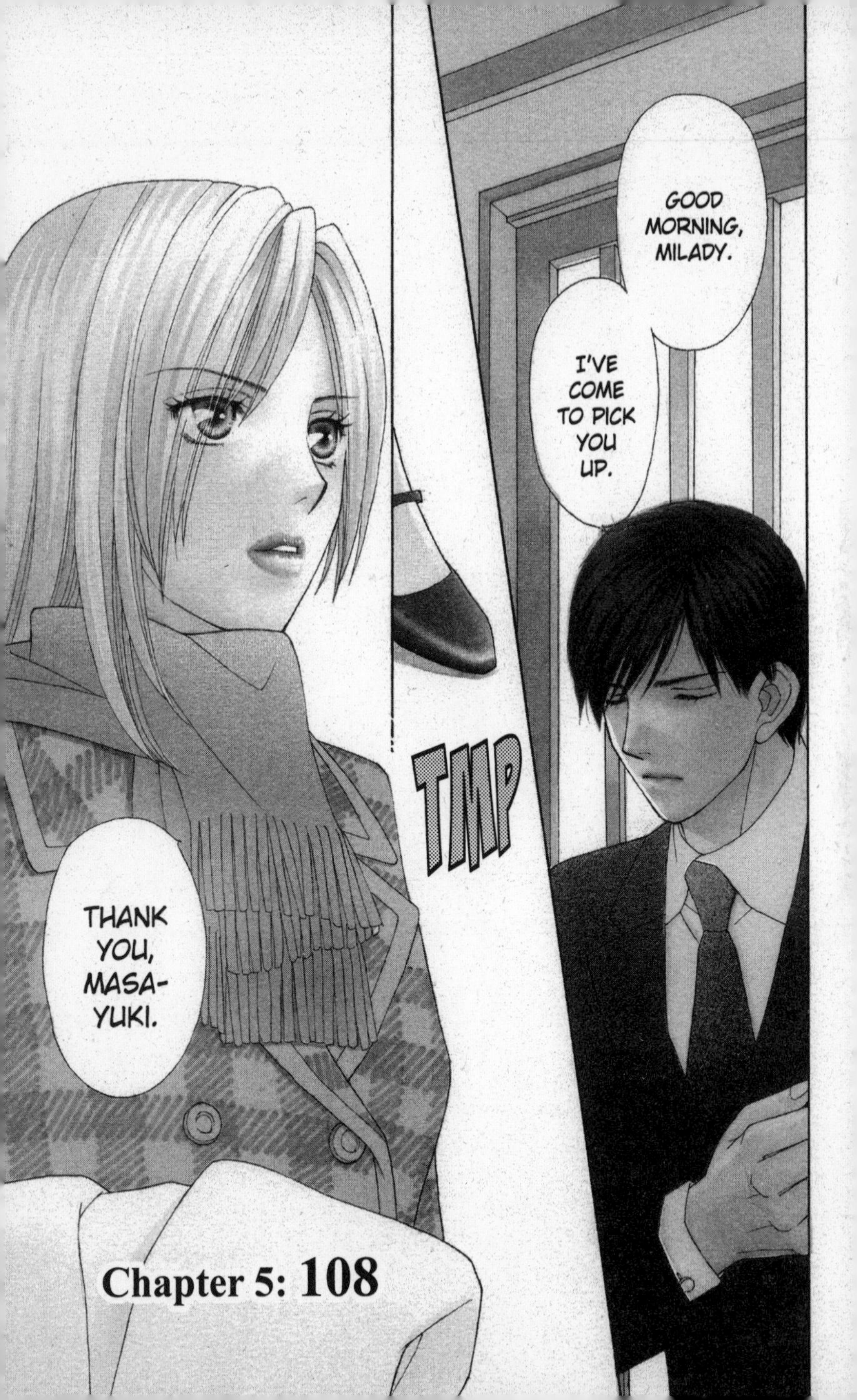
GOOD MORNING, MILADY.
I'VE COME TO PICK YOU UP.
TMP
THANK YOU, MASA-YUKI.

Chapter 5: 108

Chapter 5
108

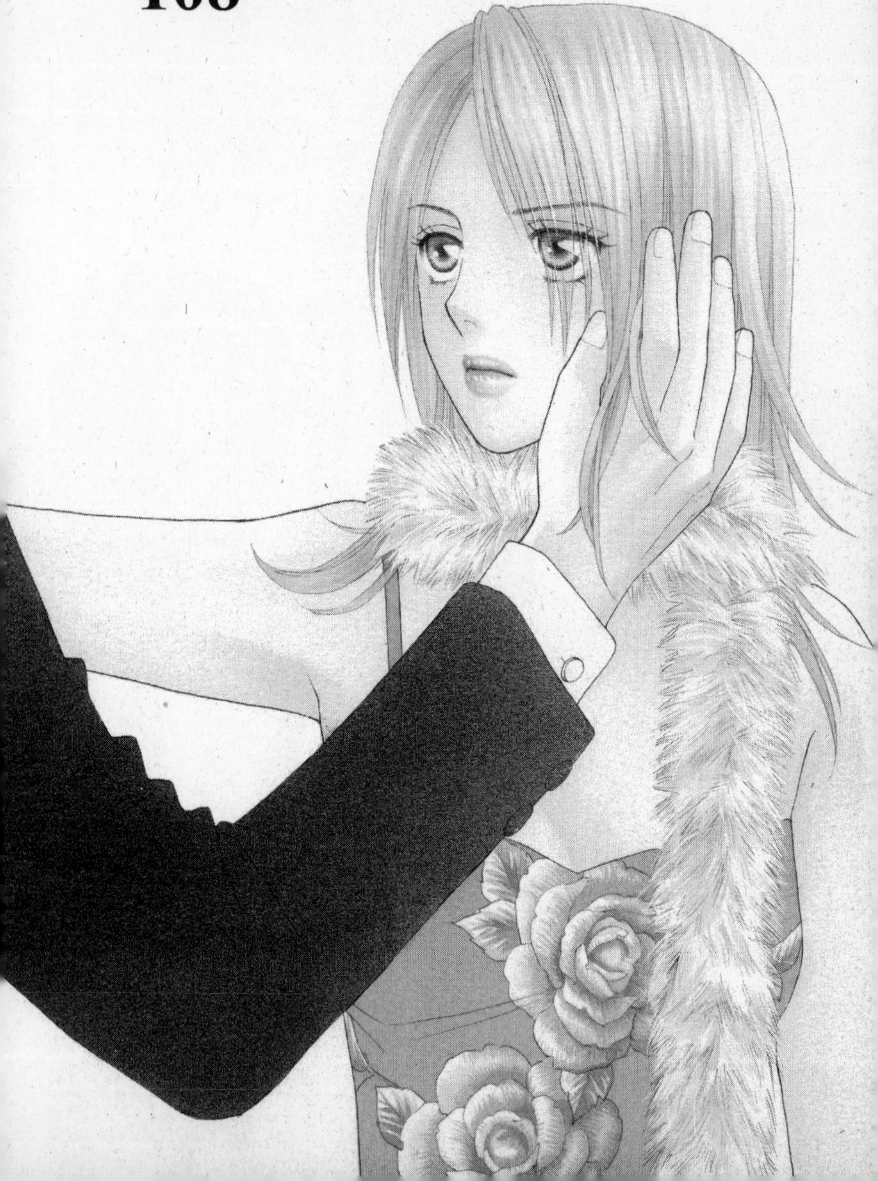

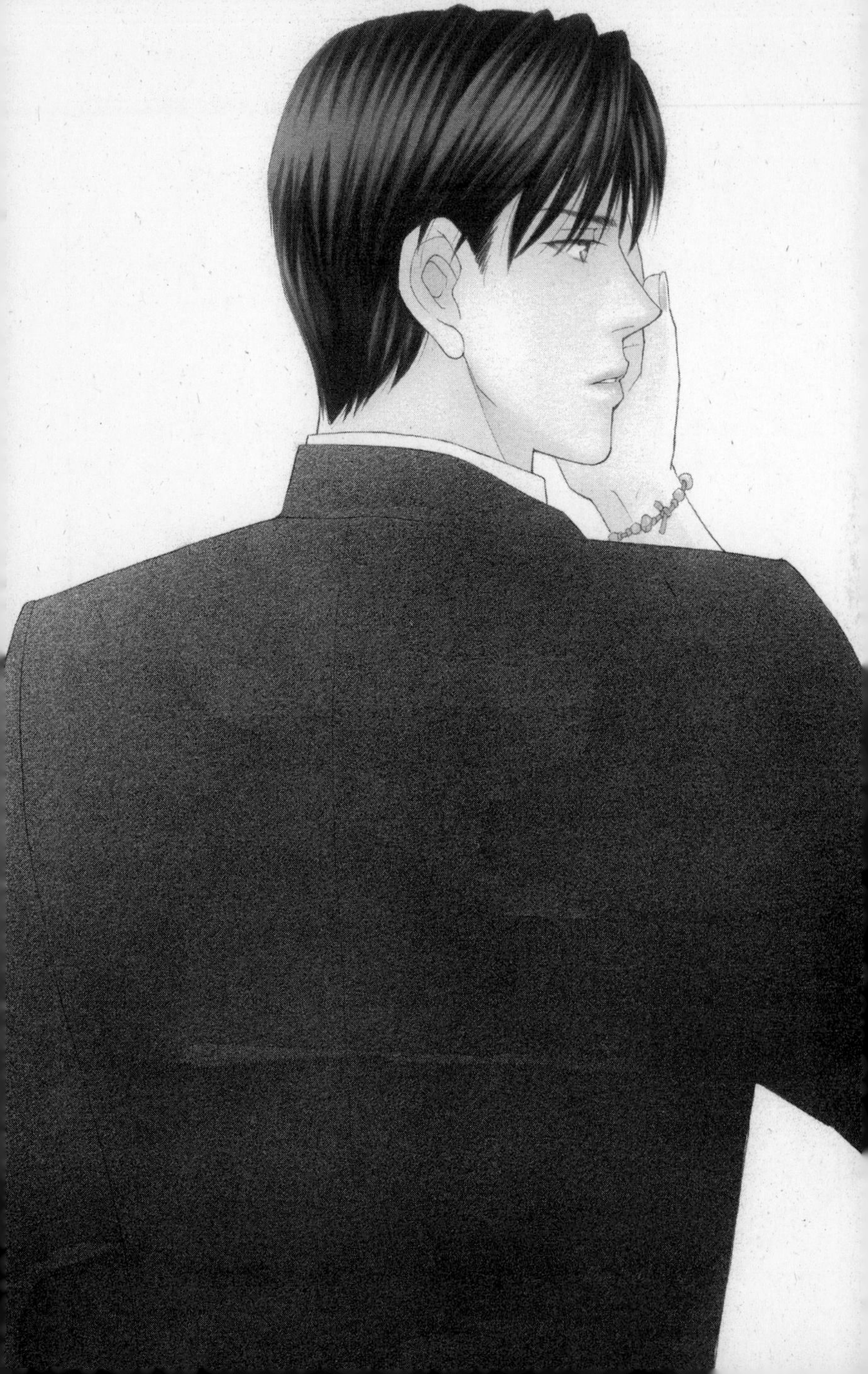

FROM THE AUTHOR

Thank you very much for reading *Butterflies, Flowers* ①...♡ It's Milady and her servant, so I wanted to do something like... Oscar and André—you're the light and I'm your shadow...♪

Rather than a shadow, he's turned into a black hole, and it's growing larger. Why?! Good luck, Milady!

I hope to see you readers again in volume ②. Please let us know what you think about this series.

吉原 由起.
Yuki Yoshihara
2006 ♡.

Nancy Thistlethwaite, Editor
VIZ Media, LLC
295 Bay Street
San Francisco, CA 94133

I wanted to draw something like Reinhard and Kircheis... You know, like Kycilia and M'Quve...
By the way, who'd want to go and see a Four who isn't voiced by Saeko Shimazu, huh...?
Shut up.

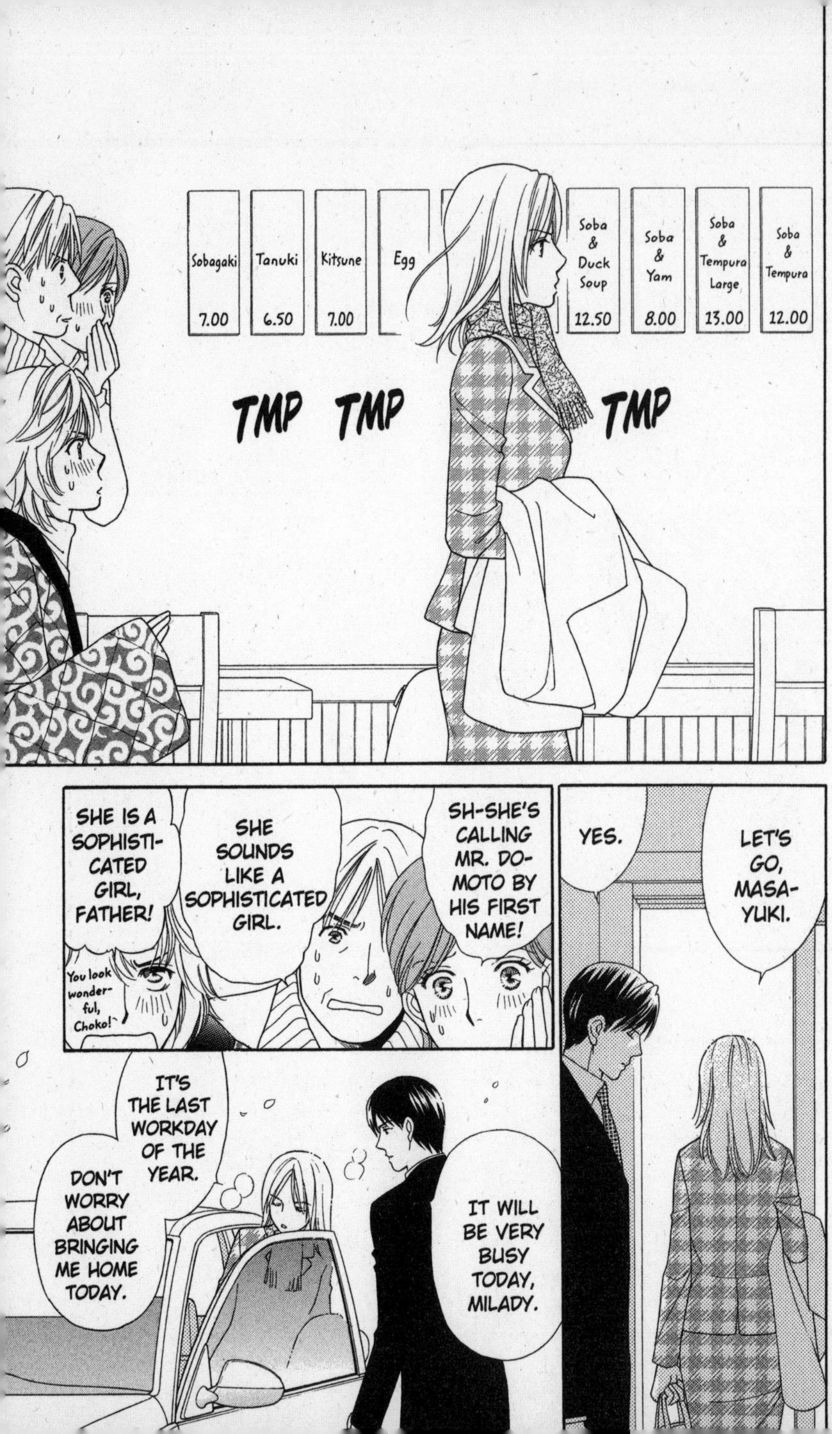
Soba & Tempura 12.00
Soba & Tempura Large 13.00
Soba & Yam 8.00
Soba & Duck Soup 12.50
Egg
Kitsune 7.00
Tanuki 6.50
Sobagaki 7.00
TMP
TMP TMP
LET'S GO, MASA-YUKI.
YES.
SH-SHE'S CALLING MR. DO-MOTO BY HIS FIRST NAME!
SHE SOUNDS LIKE A SOPHISTICATED GIRL.
SHE IS A SOPHISTI-CATED GIRL, FATHER!
You look wonder-ful, Choko!
IT WILL BE VERY BUSY TODAY, MILADY.
IT'S THE LAST WORKDAY OF THE YEAR.
DON'T WORRY ABOUT BRINGING ME HOME TODAY.

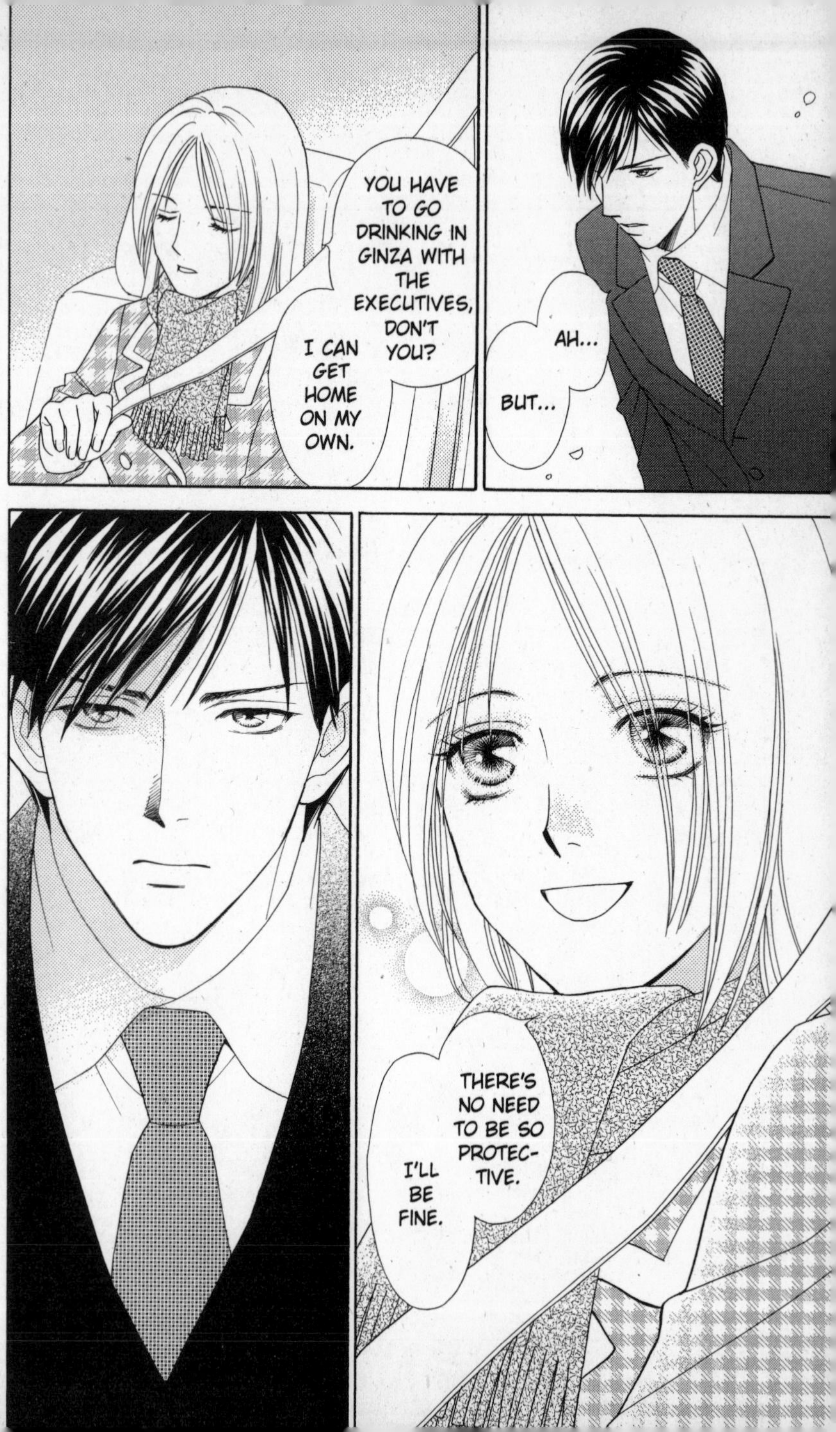
AH...
BUT...
YOU HAVE TO GO DRINKING IN GINZA WITH THE EXECUTIVES, DON'T YOU?
I CAN GET HOME ON MY OWN.
THERE'S NO NEED TO BE SO PROTEC-TIVE.
I'LL BE FINE.

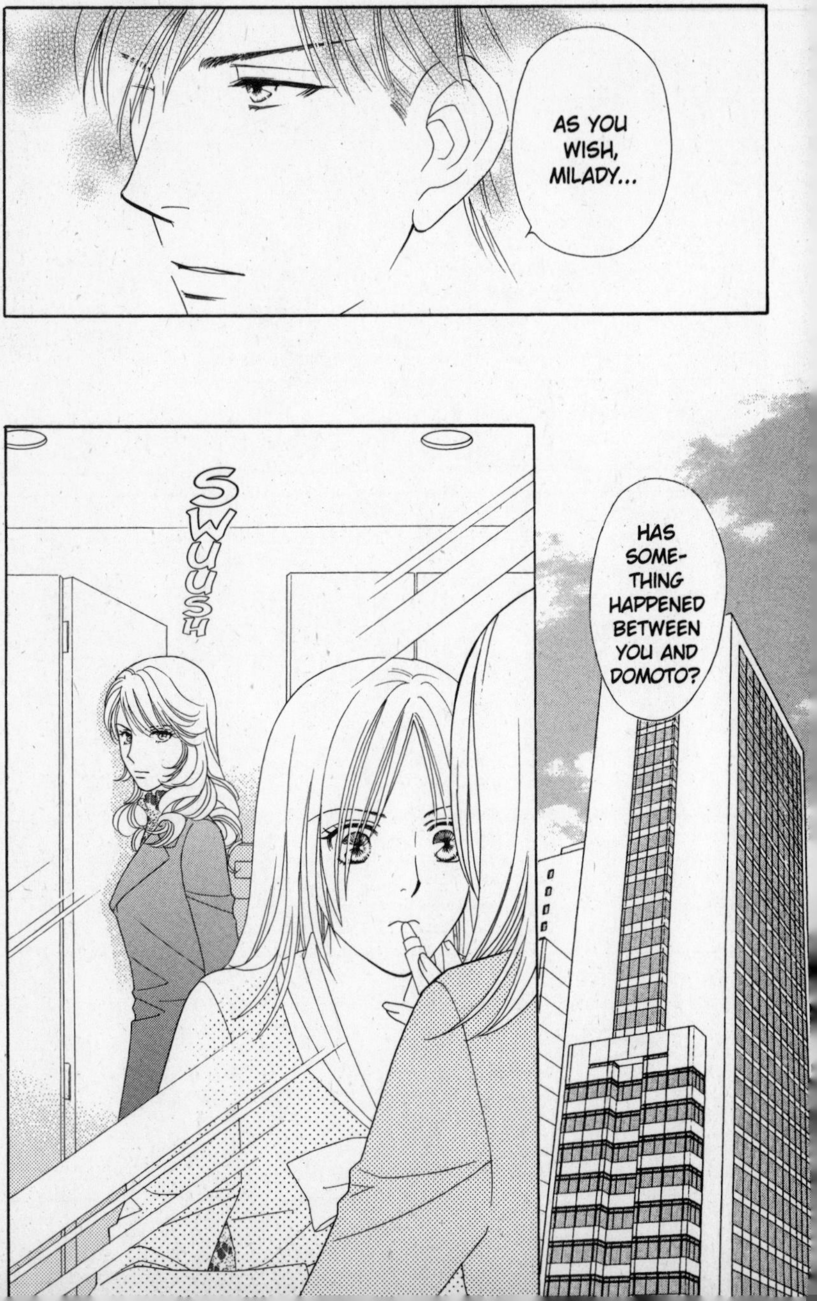
AS YOU WISH, MILADY...
HAS SOME-THING HAPPENED BETWEEN YOU AND DOMOTO?
SWUUSH

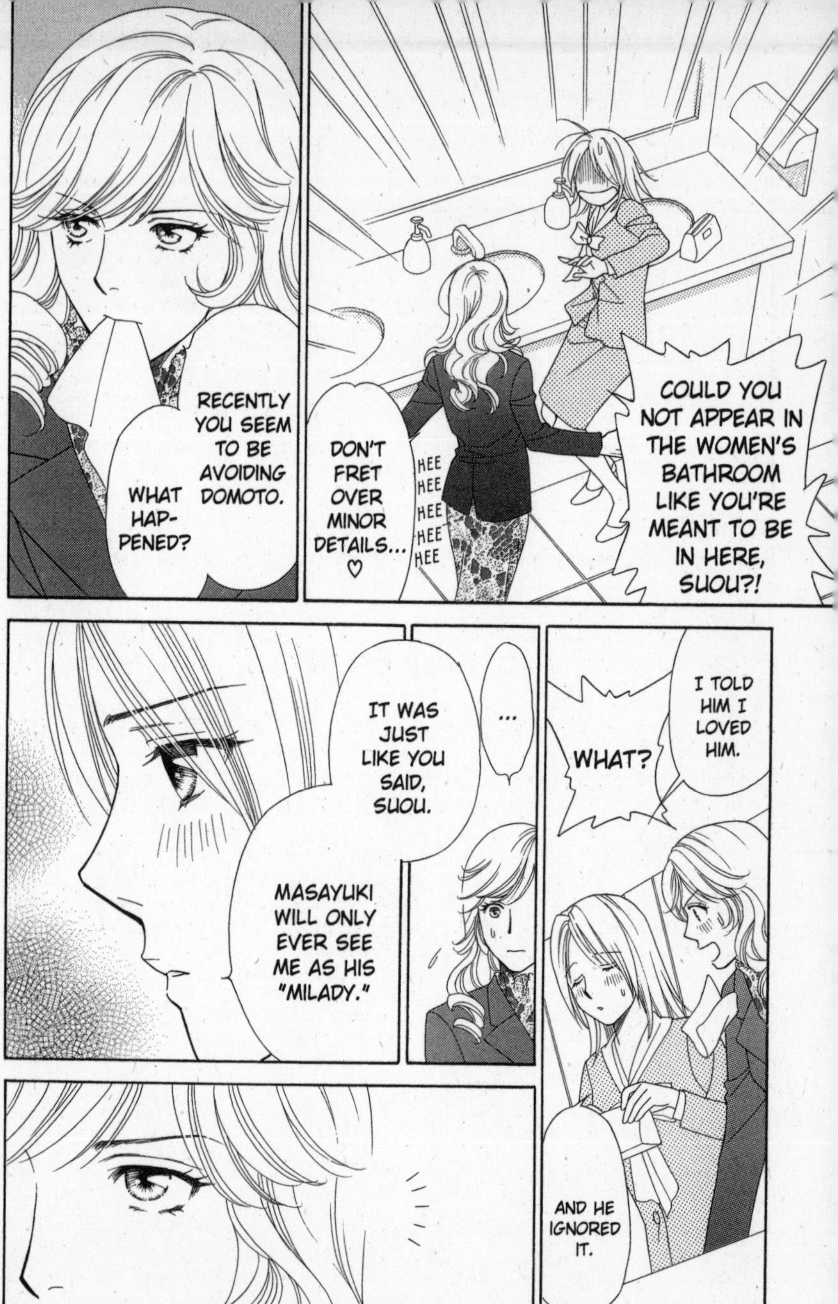
COULD YOU NOT APPEAR IN THE WOMEN'S BATHROOM LIKE YOU'RE MEANT TO BE IN HERE, SUOU?!
HEE HEE HEE HEE HEE
DON'T FRET OVER MINOR DETAILS... ♡
RECENTLY YOU SEEM TO BE AVOIDING DOMOTO.
WHAT HAP-PENED?
I TOLD HIM I LOVED HIM.
WHAT?
AND HE IGNORED IT.
...
IT WAS JUST LIKE YOU SAID, SUOU.
MASAYUKI WILL ONLY EVER SEE ME AS HIS "MILADY."

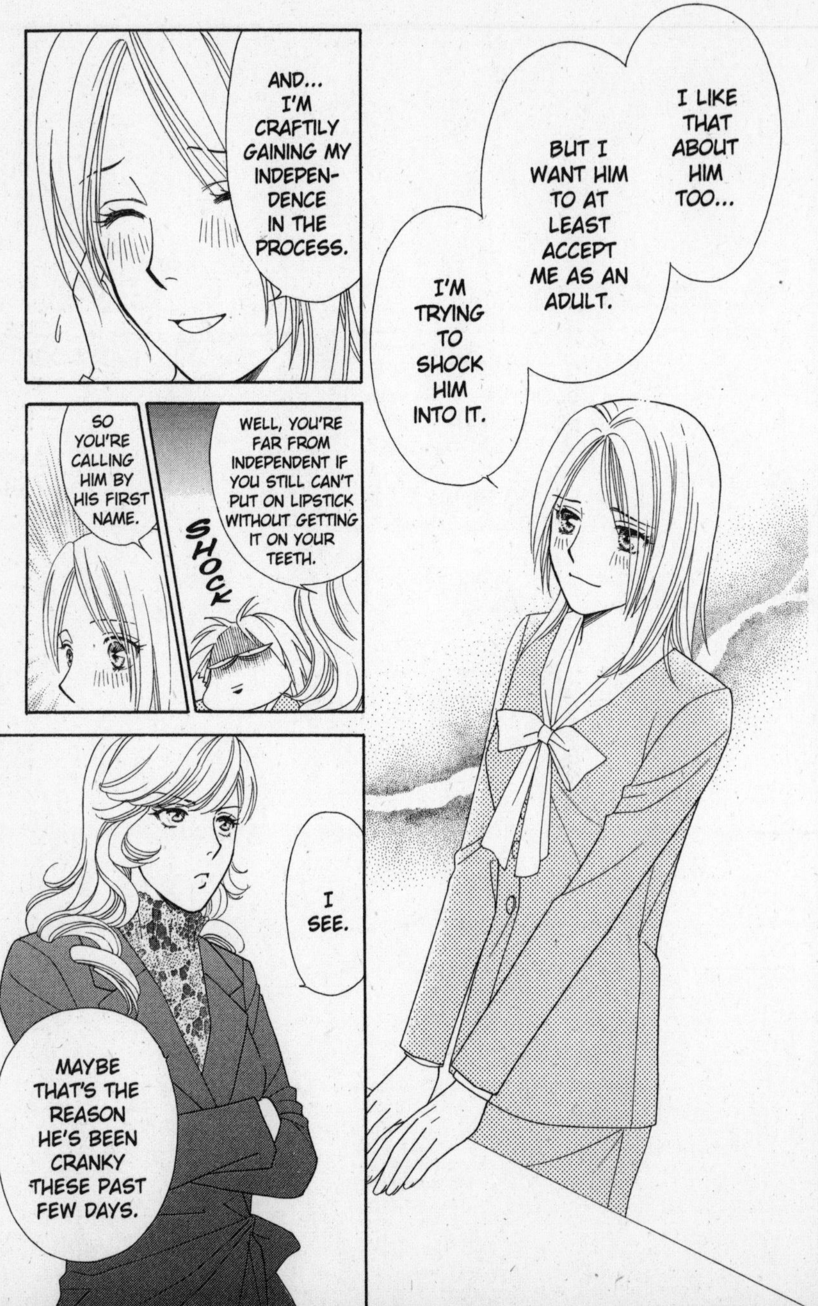
I LIKE THAT ABOUT HIM TOO...
BUT I WANT HIM TO AT LEAST ACCEPT ME AS AN ADULT.
I'M TRYING TO SHOCK HIM INTO IT.
AND... I'M CRAFTILY GAINING MY INDEPEN-DENCE IN THE PROCESS.
WELL, YOU'RE FAR FROM INDEPENDENT IF YOU STILL CAN'T PUT ON LIPSTICK WITHOUT GETTING IT ON YOUR TEETH.
SHOCK
SO YOU'RE CALLING HIM BY HIS FIRST NAME.
I SEE.
MAYBE THAT'S THE REASON HE'S BEEN CRANKY THESE PAST FEW DAYS.

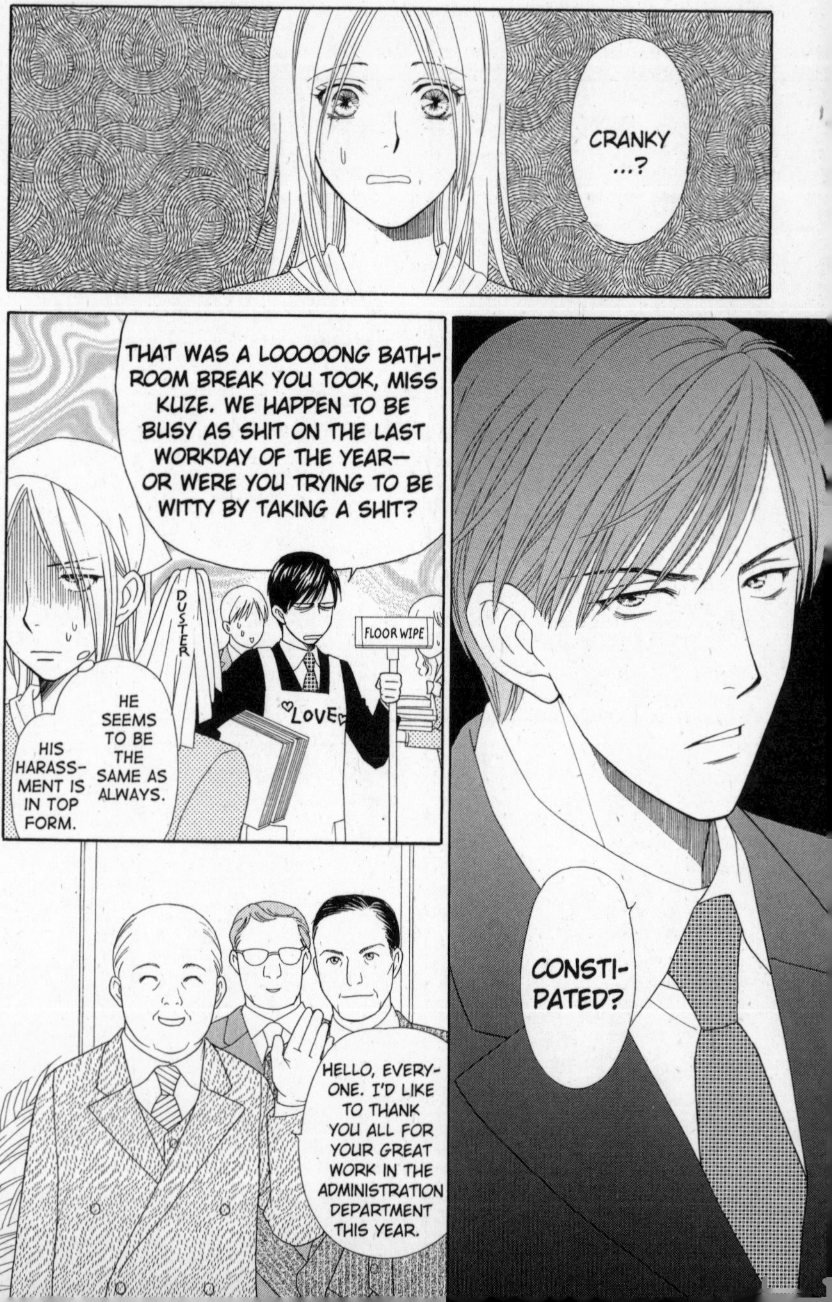
CRANKY ...?
CONSTI-PATED?
THAT WAS A LOOOOONG BATHROOM BREAK YOU TOOK, MISS KUZE. WE HAPPEN TO BE BUSY AS SHIT ON THE LAST WORKDAY OF THE YEAR— OR WERE YOU TRYING TO BE WITTY BY TAKING A SHIT?
FLOOR WIPE
DUSTER
LOVE
HE SEEMS TO BE THE SAME AS ALWAYS.
HIS HARASSMENT IS IN TOP FORM.
HELLO, EVERYONE. I'D LIKE TO THANK YOU ALL FOR YOUR GREAT WORK IN THE ADMINISTRATION DEPARTMENT THIS YEAR.

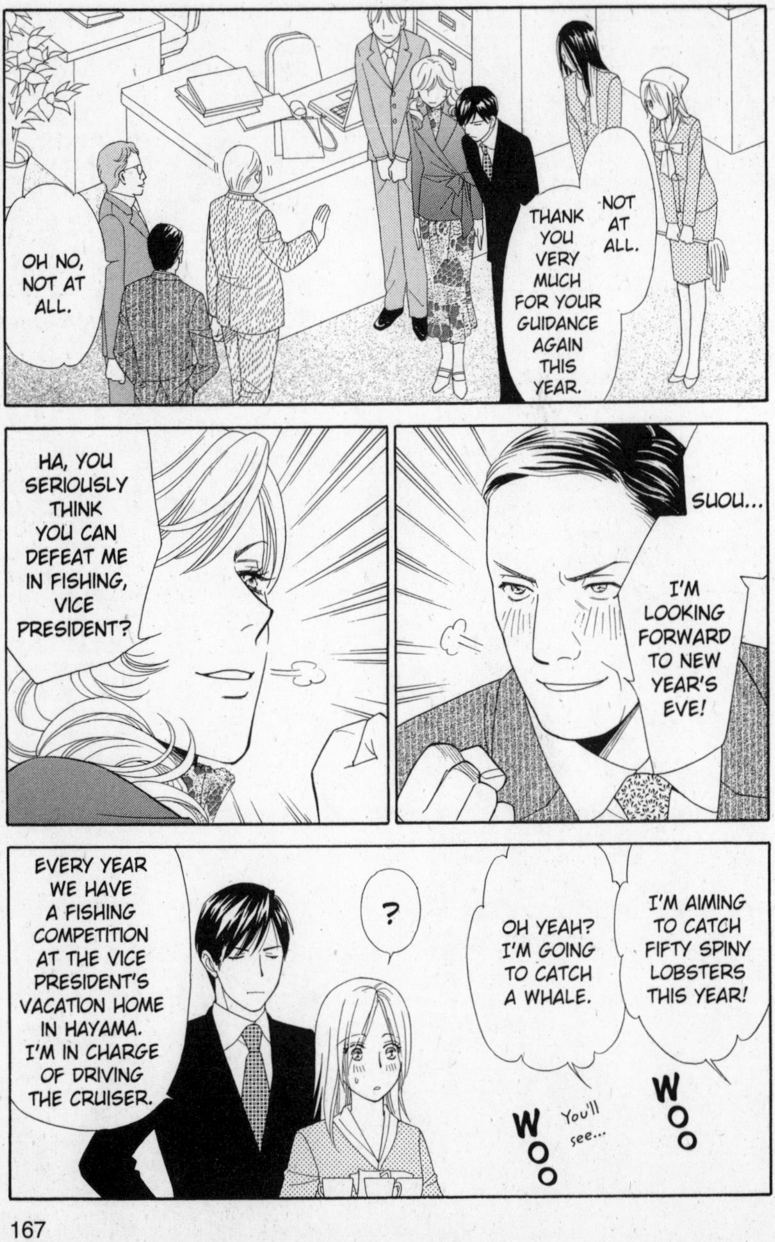
NOT AT ALL.
THANK YOU VERY MUCH FOR YOUR GUIDANCE AGAIN THIS YEAR.
OH NO, NOT AT ALL.
SUOU...
I'M LOOKING FORWARD TO NEW YEAR'S EVE!
HA, YOU SERIOUSLY THINK YOU CAN DEFEAT ME IN FISHING, VICE PRESIDENT?
I'M AIMING TO CATCH FIFTY SPINY LOBSTERS THIS YEAR!
WOO
OH YEAH? I'M GOING TO CATCH A WHALE.
You'll see...
WOO
?
EVERY YEAR WE HAVE A FISHING COMPETITION AT THE VICE PRESIDENT'S VACATION HOME IN HAYAMA. I'M IN CHARGE OF DRIVING THE CRUISER.

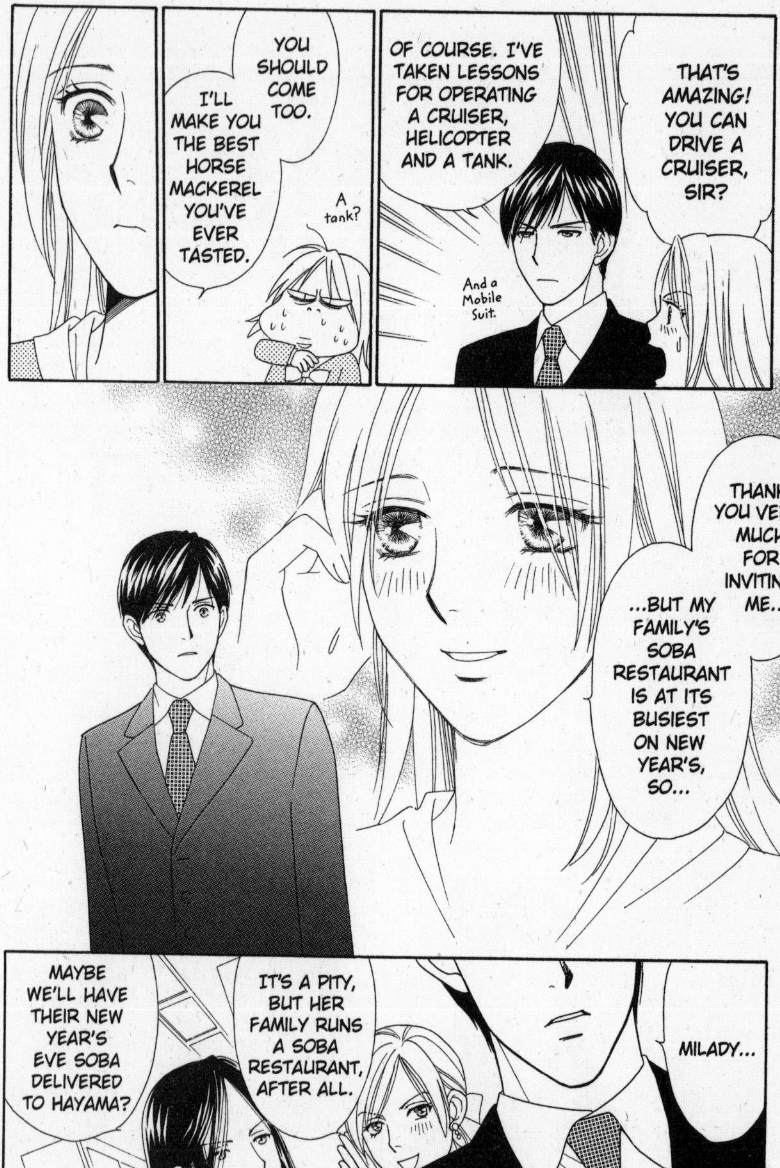
THAT'S AMAZING! YOU CAN DRIVE A CRUISER, SIR?
OF COURSE. I'VE TAKEN LESSONS FOR OPERATING A CRUISER, HELICOPTER AND A TANK.
And a Mobile Suit.
YOU SHOULD COME TOO.
I'LL MAKE YOU THE BEST HORSE MACKEREL YOU'VE EVER TASTED.
A tank?
THANK YOU VERY MUCH FOR INVITING ME...
...BUT MY FAMILY'S SOBA RESTAURANT IS AT ITS BUSIEST ON NEW YEAR'S, SO...
MILADY...
IT'S A PITY, BUT HER FAMILY RUNS A SOBA RESTAURANT, AFTER ALL.
MAYBE WE'LL HAVE THEIR NEW YEAR'S EVE SOBA DELIVERED TO HAYAMA?

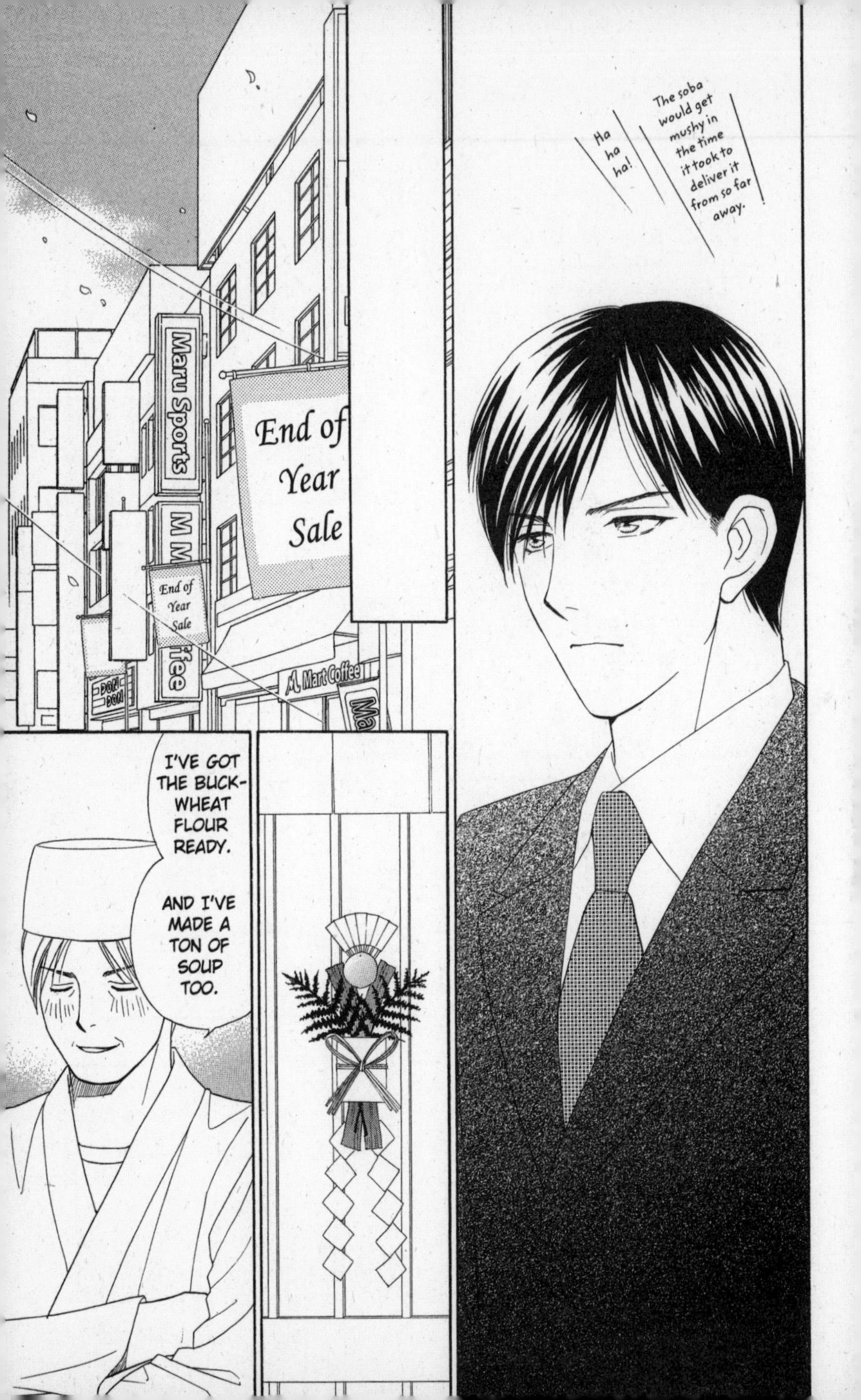

The soba would get mushy in the time it took to deliver it from so far away.
Ha ha ha!
End of Year Sale
Maru Sports
End of Year Sale
Mart Coffee
DON DON
I'VE GOT THE BUCK-WHEAT FLOUR READY.
AND I'VE MADE A TON OF SOUP TOO.

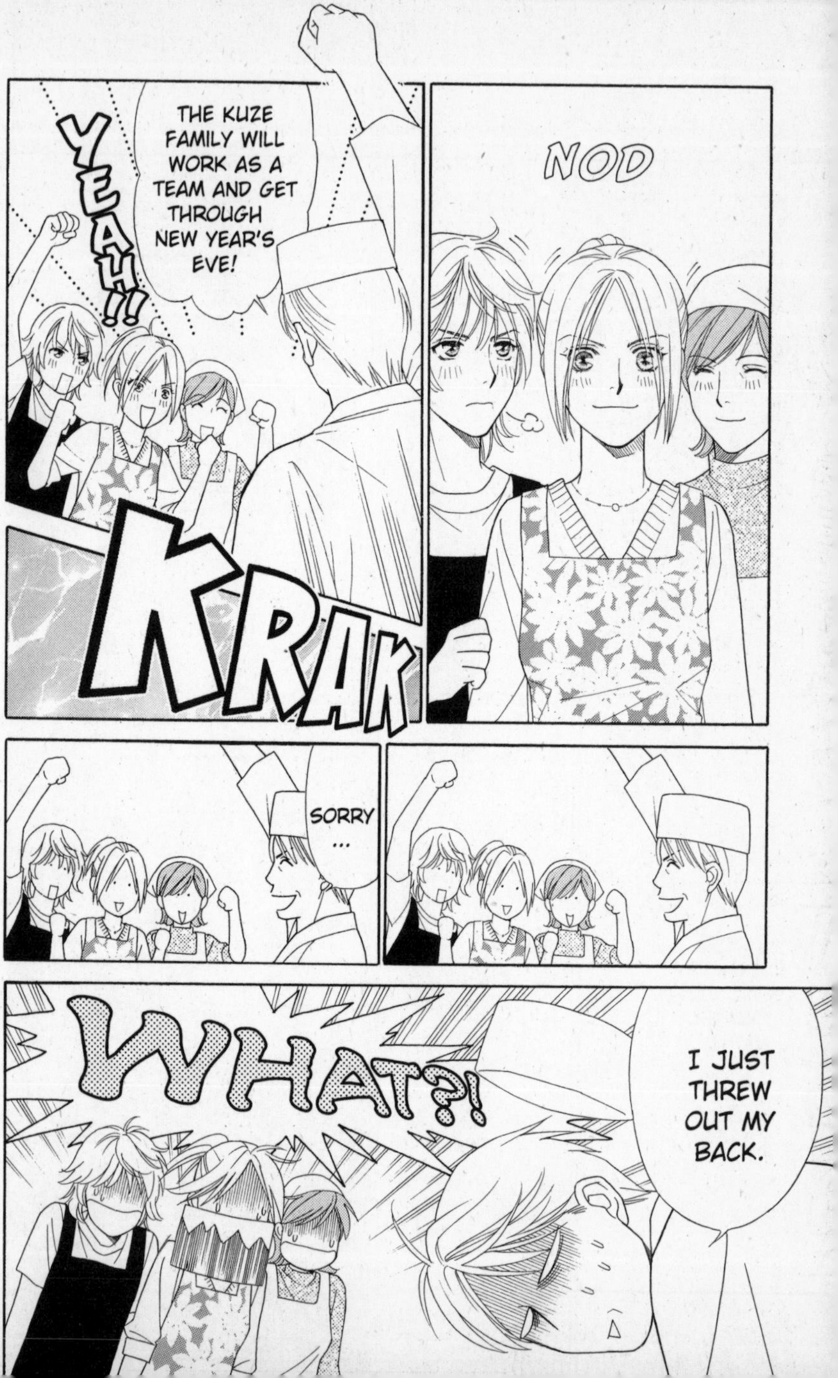
NOD
THE KUZE FAMILY WILL WORK AS A TEAM AND GET THROUGH NEW YEAR'S EVE!
YEAH!!
KRAK
SORRY ...
I JUST THREW OUT MY BACK.
WHAT?!

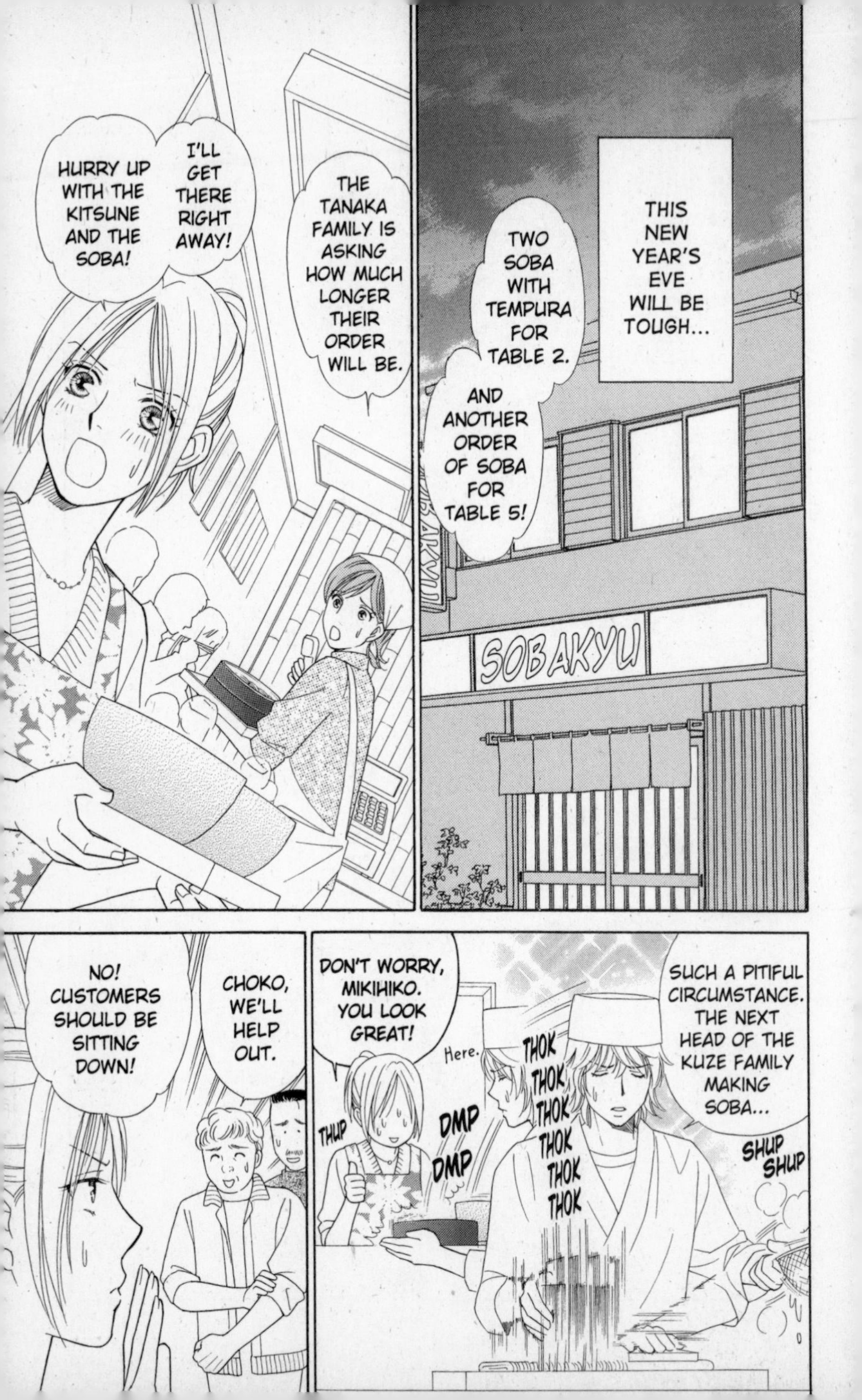
THIS NEW YEAR'S EVE WILL BE TOUGH...
TWO SOBA WITH TEMPURA FOR TABLE 2.
AND ANOTHER ORDER OF SOBA FOR TABLE 5!
SOBAKYU
SOBAKYU
THE TANAKA FAMILY IS ASKING HOW MUCH LONGER THEIR ORDER WILL BE.
I'LL GET THERE RIGHT AWAY!
HURRY UP WITH THE KITSUNE AND THE SOBA!
SUCH A PITIFUL CIRCUMSTANCE. THE NEXT HEAD OF THE KUZE FAMILY MAKING SOBA...
SHUP SHUP
THOK THOK THOK THOK THOK THOK THOK THOK
Here.
DMP DMP
THUP
DON'T WORRY, MIKIHIKO. YOU LOOK GREAT!
CHOKO, WE'LL HELP OUT.
NO! CUSTOMERS SHOULD BE SITTING DOWN!

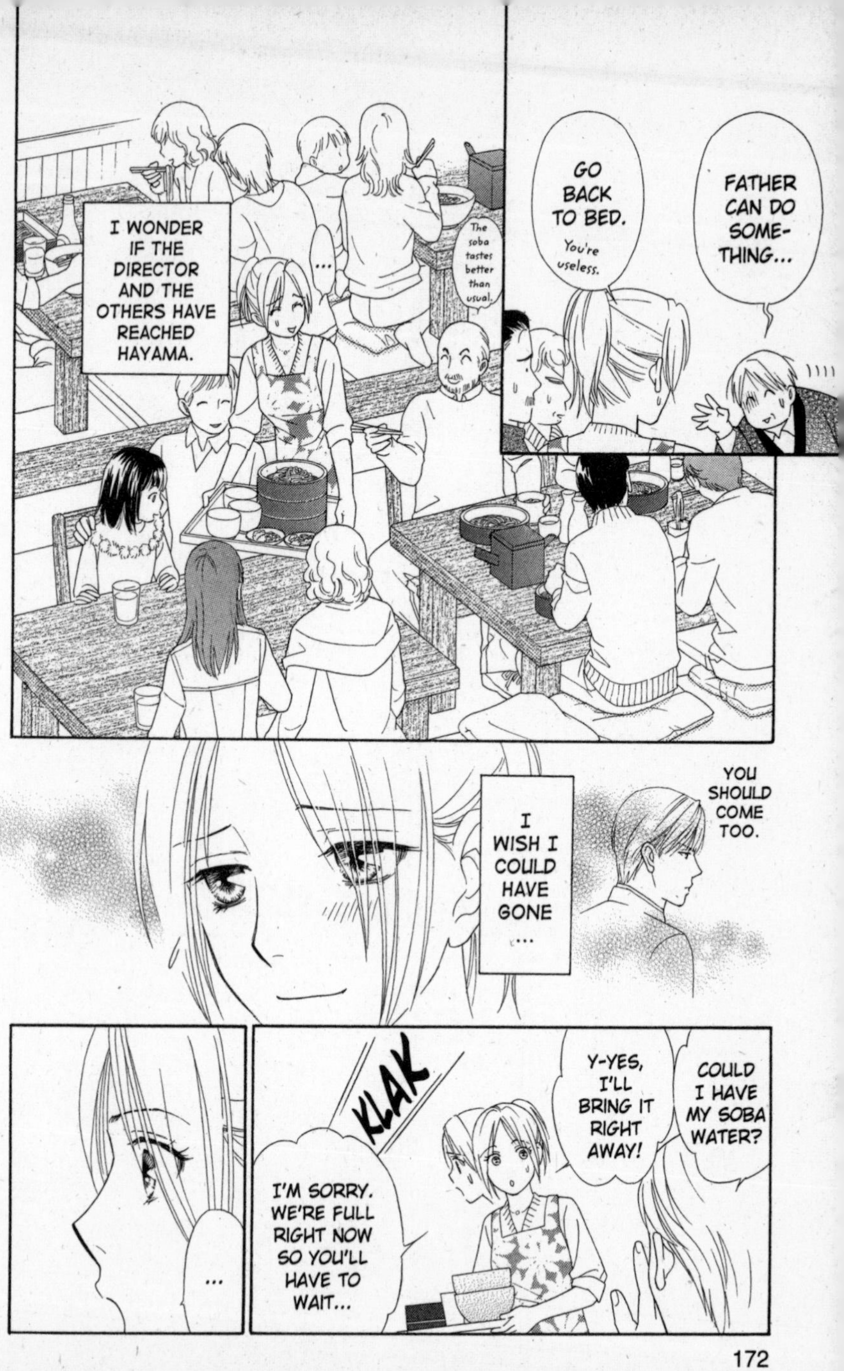
FATHER CAN DO SOME-THING...
GO BACK TO BED.
You're useless.
The soba tastes better than usual.
...
I WONDER IF THE DIRECTOR AND THE OTHERS HAVE REACHED HAYAMA.
YOU SHOULD COME TOO.
I WISH I COULD HAVE GONE...
COULD I HAVE MY SOBA WATER?
Y-YES, I'LL BRING IT RIGHT AWAY!
KLAK
I'M SORRY. WE'RE FULL RIGHT NOW SO YOU'LL HAVE TO WAIT...
...

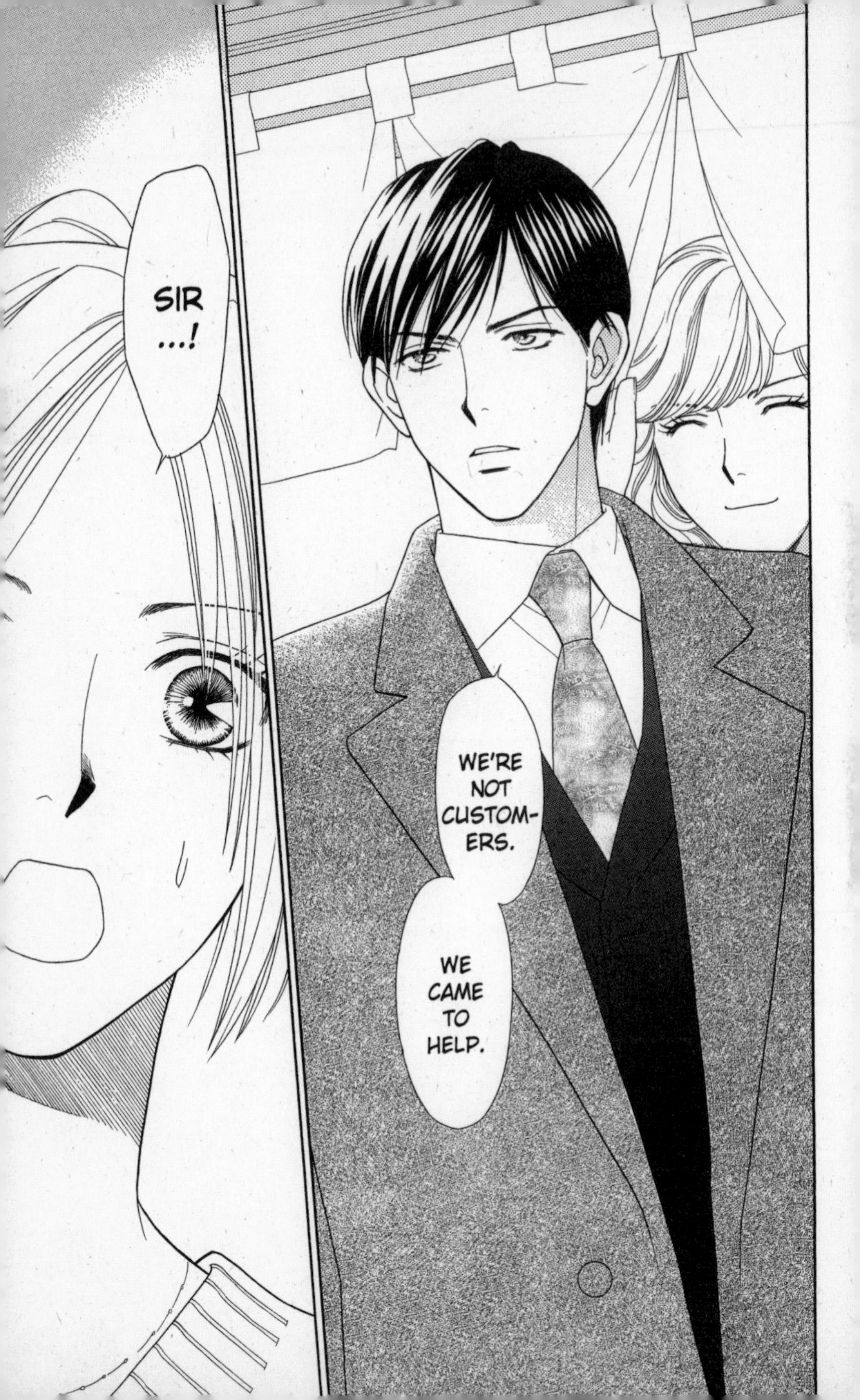
WE'RE NOT CUSTOMERS.
WE CAME TO HELP.
SIR ...!

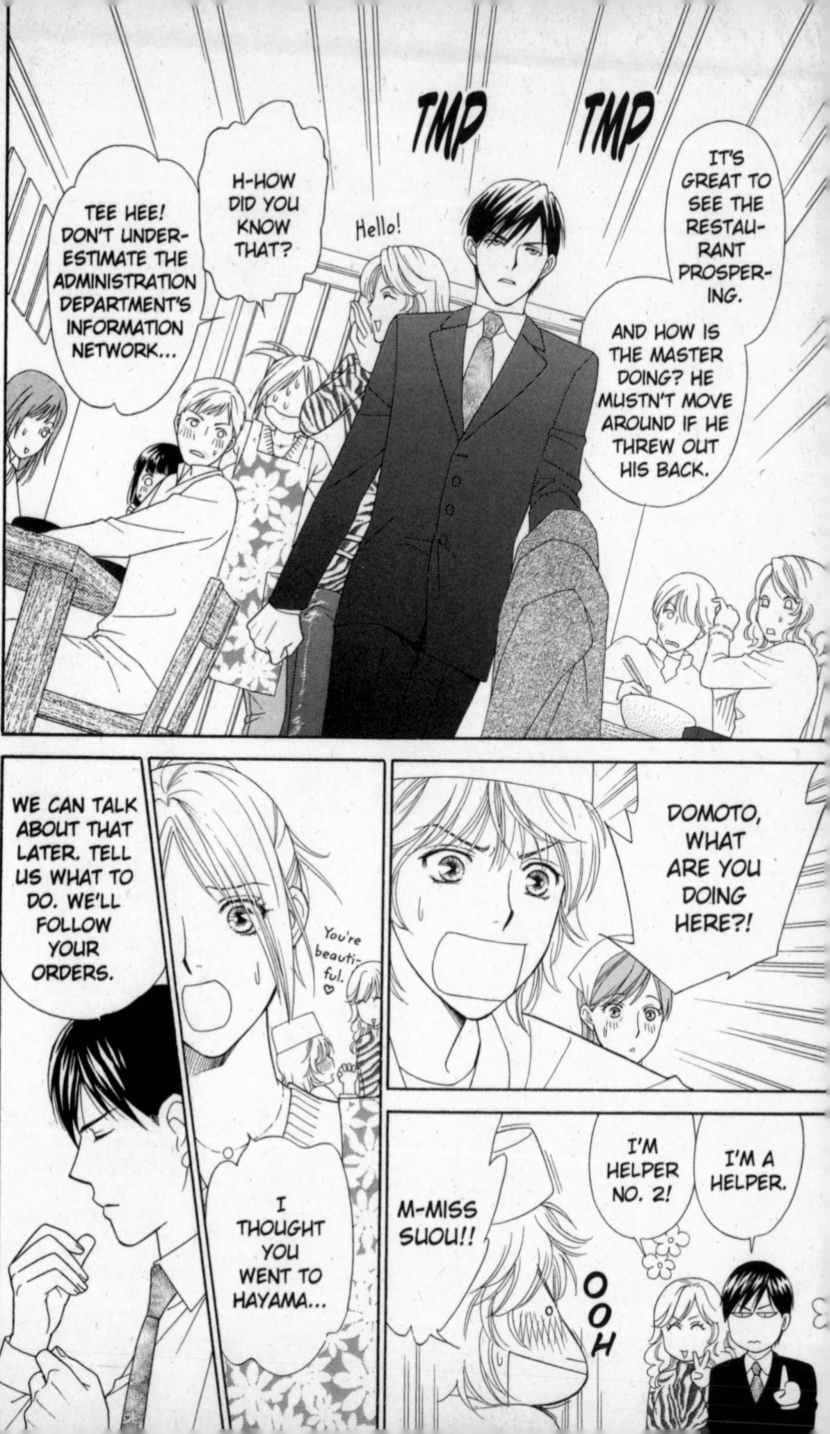
TMP TMP
IT'S GREAT TO SEE THE RESTAURANT PROSPERING.
AND HOW IS THE MASTER DOING? HE MUSTN'T MOVE AROUND IF HE THREW OUT HIS BACK.
H-HOW DID YOU KNOW THAT?
Hello!
TEE HEE! DON'T UNDERESTIMATE THE ADMINISTRATION DEPARTMENT'S INFORMATION NETWORK...
DOMOTO, WHAT ARE YOU DOING HERE?!
I'M A HELPER.
I'M HELPER NO. 2!
M-MISS SUOU!!
OOH
You're beautiful. ♡
I THOUGHT YOU WENT TO HAYAMA...
WE CAN TALK ABOUT THAT LATER. TELL US WHAT TO DO. WE'LL FOLLOW YOUR ORDERS.

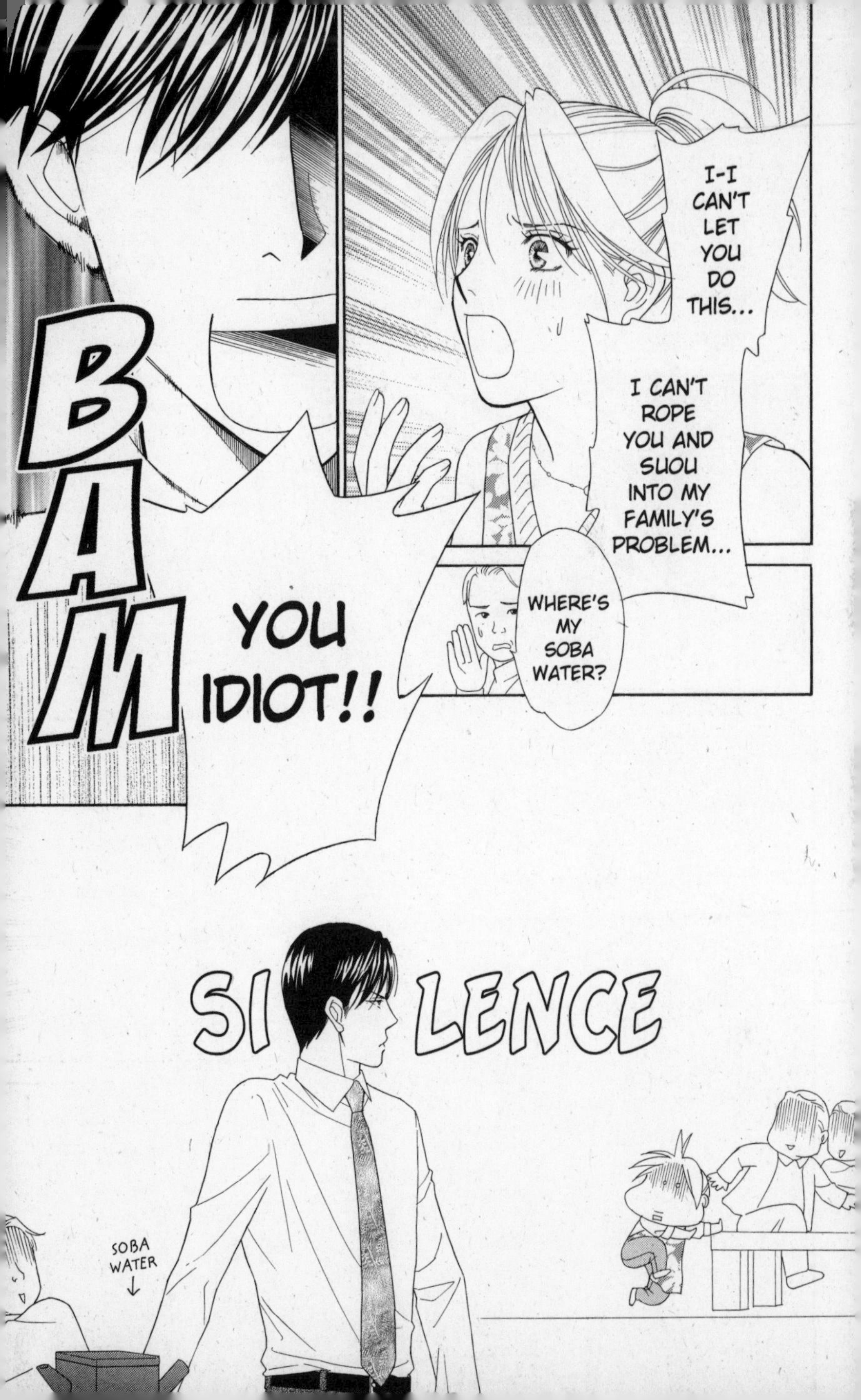
I-I CAN'T LET YOU DO THIS...
I CAN'T ROPE YOU AND SUOU INTO MY FAMILY'S PROBLEM...
WHERE'S MY SOBA WATER?
BAM
YOU IDIOT!!
SILENCE
SOBA WATER

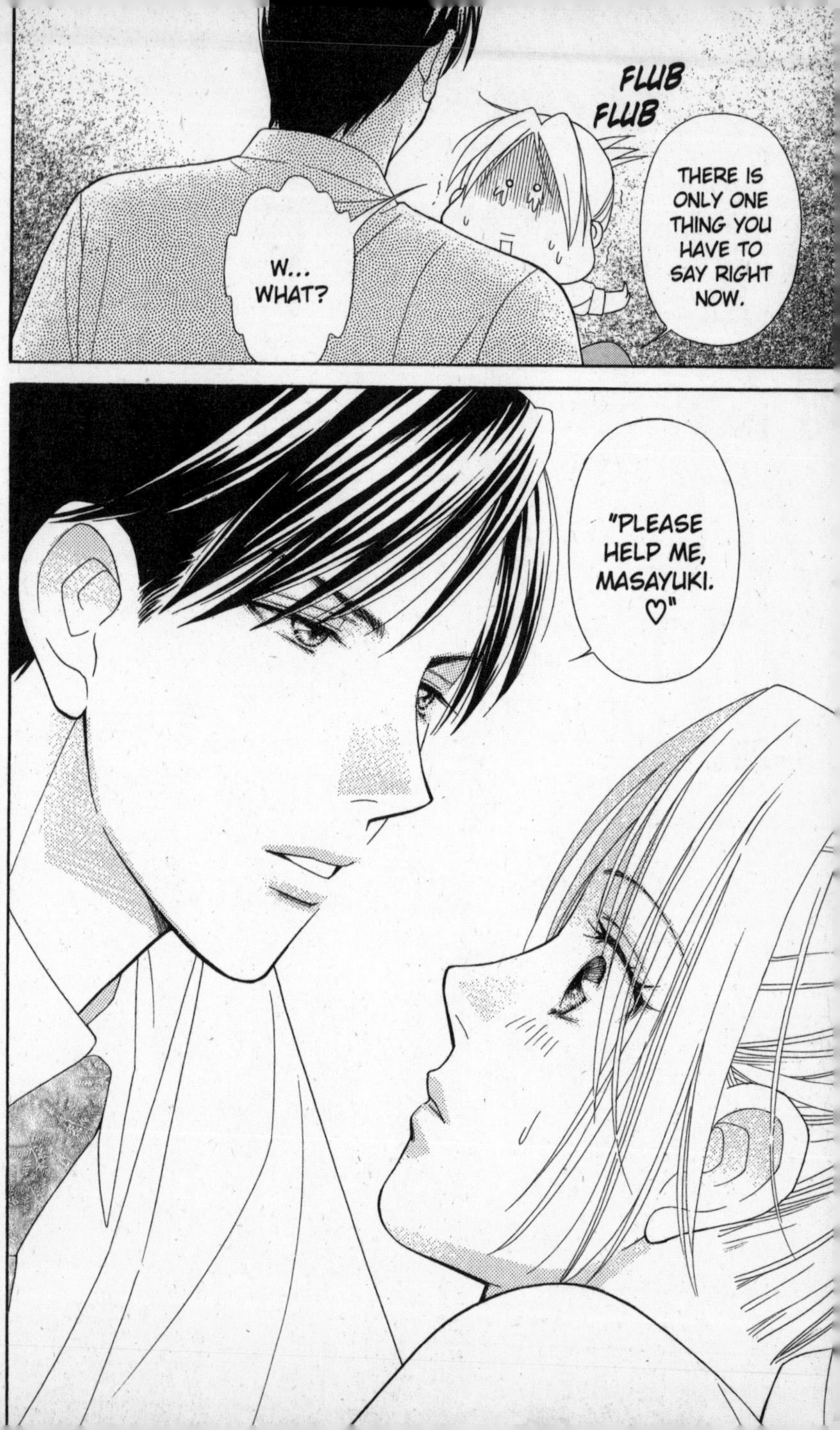
FLUB FLUB
THERE IS ONLY ONE THING YOU HAVE TO SAY RIGHT NOW.
W... WHAT?
"PLEASE HELP ME, MASAYUKI. ♡"

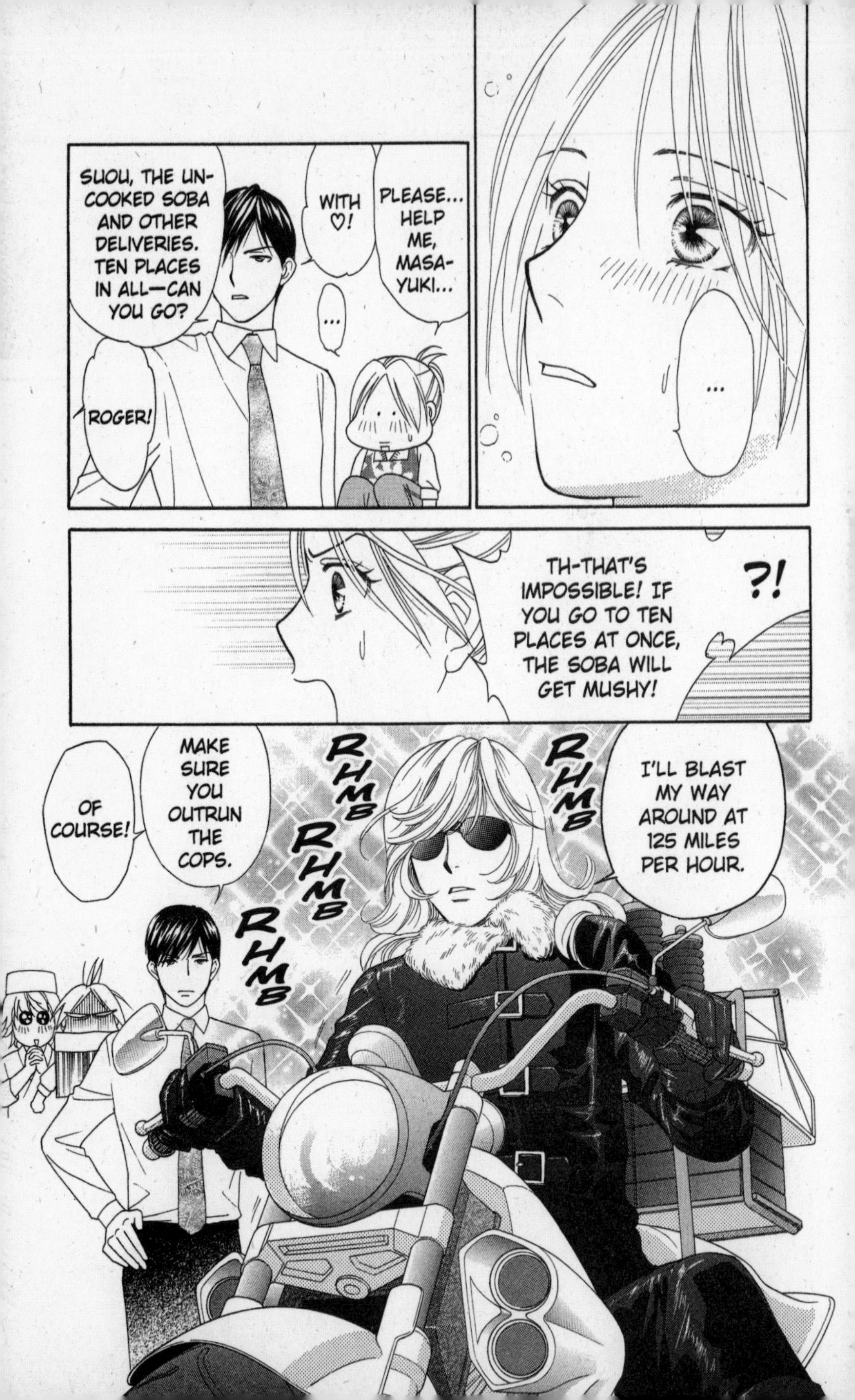
...
PLEASE... HELP ME, MASA-YUKI...
WITH ♡!
...
SUOU, THE UN-COOKED SOBA AND OTHER DELIVERIES. TEN PLACES IN ALL—CAN YOU GO?
ROGER!
?!
TH-THAT'S IMPOSSIBLE! IF YOU GO TO TEN PLACES AT ONCE, THE SOBA WILL GET MUSHY!
I'LL BLAST MY WAY AROUND AT 125 MILES PER HOUR.
RHMB
RHMB
RHMB
RHMB
MAKE SURE YOU OUTRUN THE COPS.
OF COURSE!

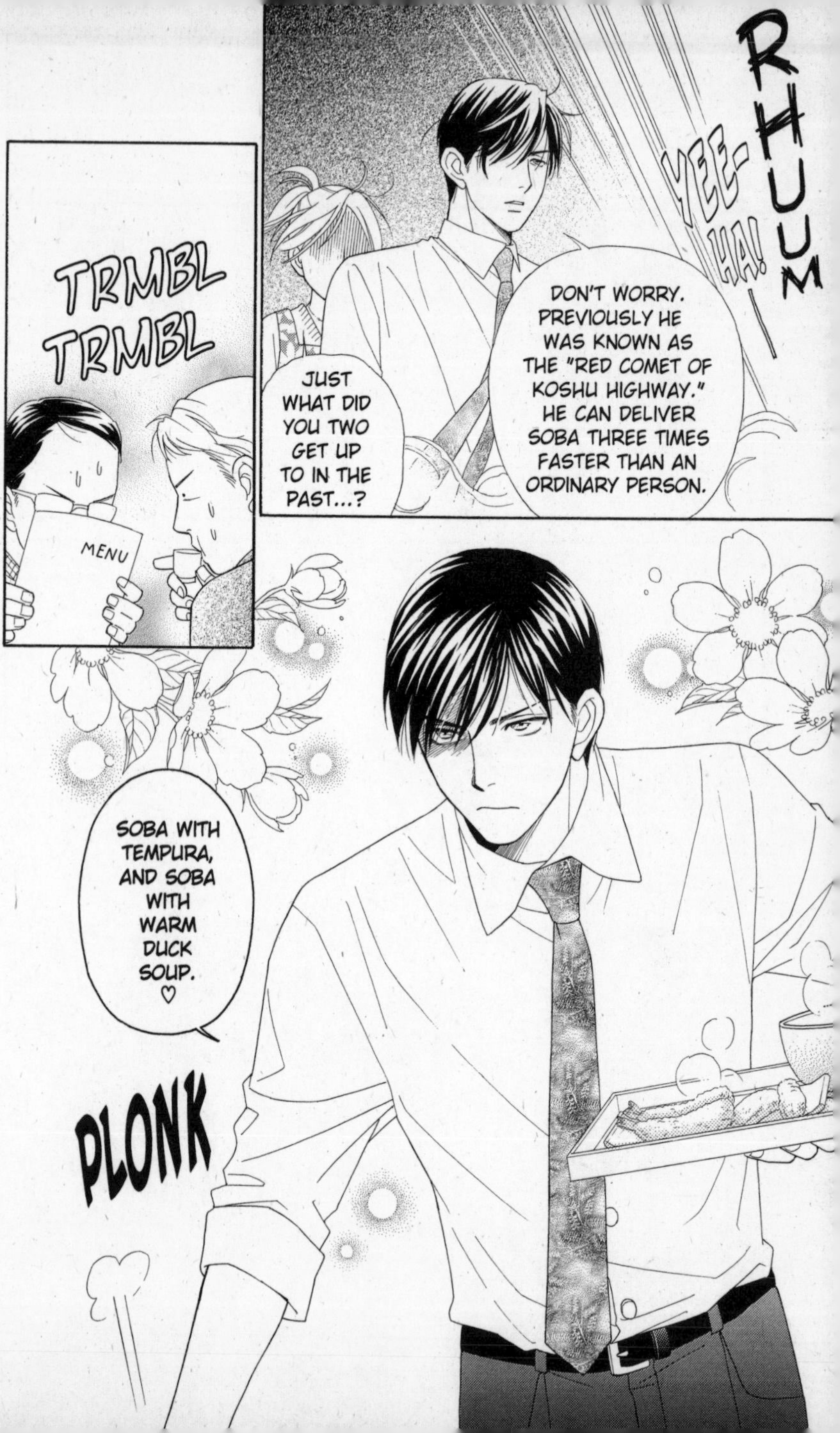
RHUUM—
YEE-HA!
DON'T WORRY. PREVIOUSLY HE WAS KNOWN AS THE "RED COMET OF KOSHU HIGHWAY." HE CAN DELIVER SOBA THREE TIMES FASTER THAN AN ORDINARY PERSON.
JUST WHAT DID YOU TWO GET UP TO IN THE PAST...?
TRMBL TRMBL
MENU
SOBA WITH TEMPURA, AND SOBA WITH WARM DUCK SOUP. ♡
PLONK

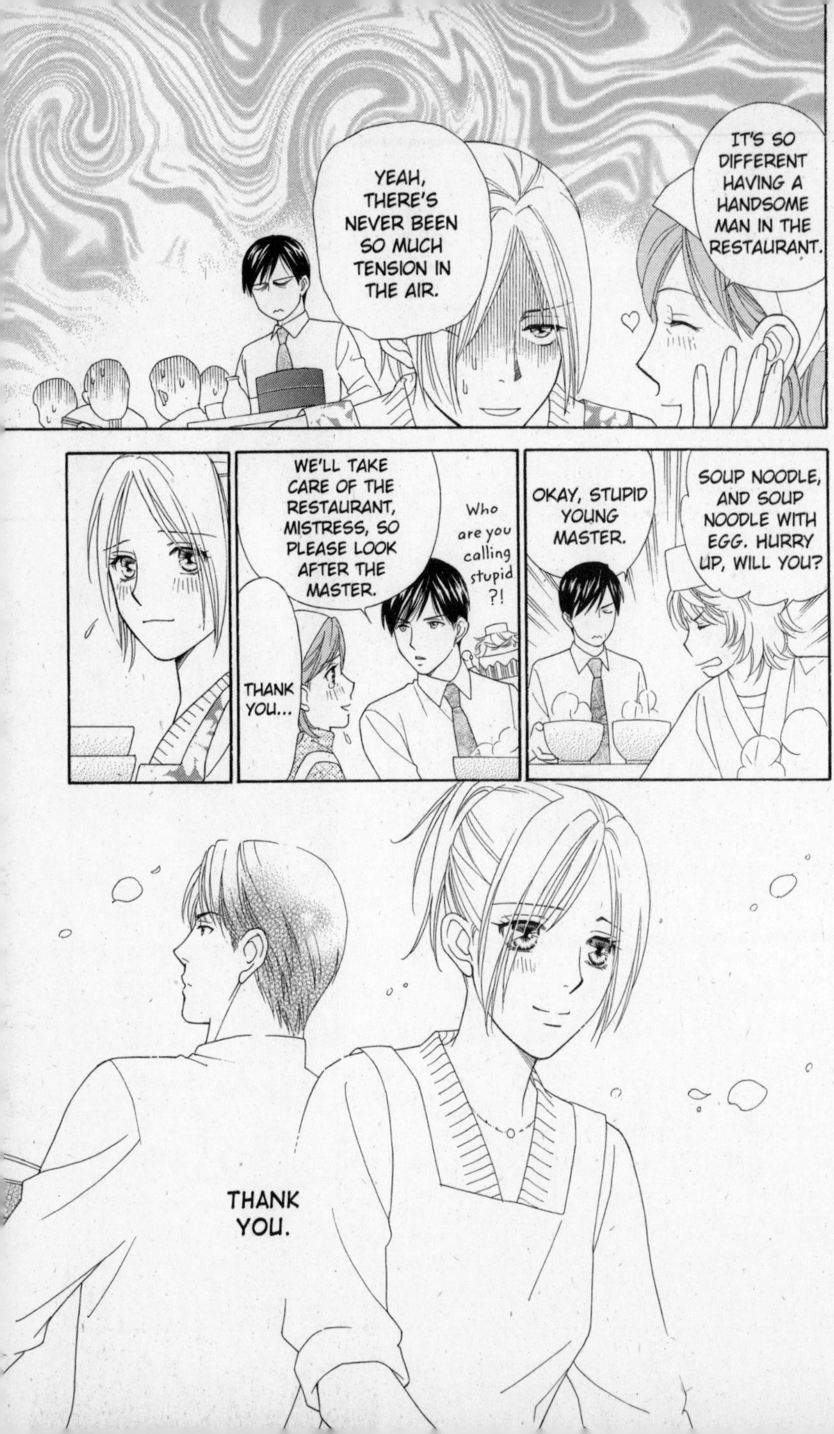
IT'S SO DIFFERENT HAVING A HANDSOME MAN IN THE RESTAURANT.
YEAH, THERE'S NEVER BEEN SO MUCH TENSION IN THE AIR.
SOUP NOODLE, AND SOUP NOODLE WITH EGG. HURRY UP, WILL YOU?
OKAY, STUPID YOUNG MASTER.
Who are you calling stupid ?!
WE'LL TAKE CARE OF THE RESTAURANT, MISTRESS, SO PLEASE LOOK AFTER THE MASTER.
THANK YOU...
THANK YOU.

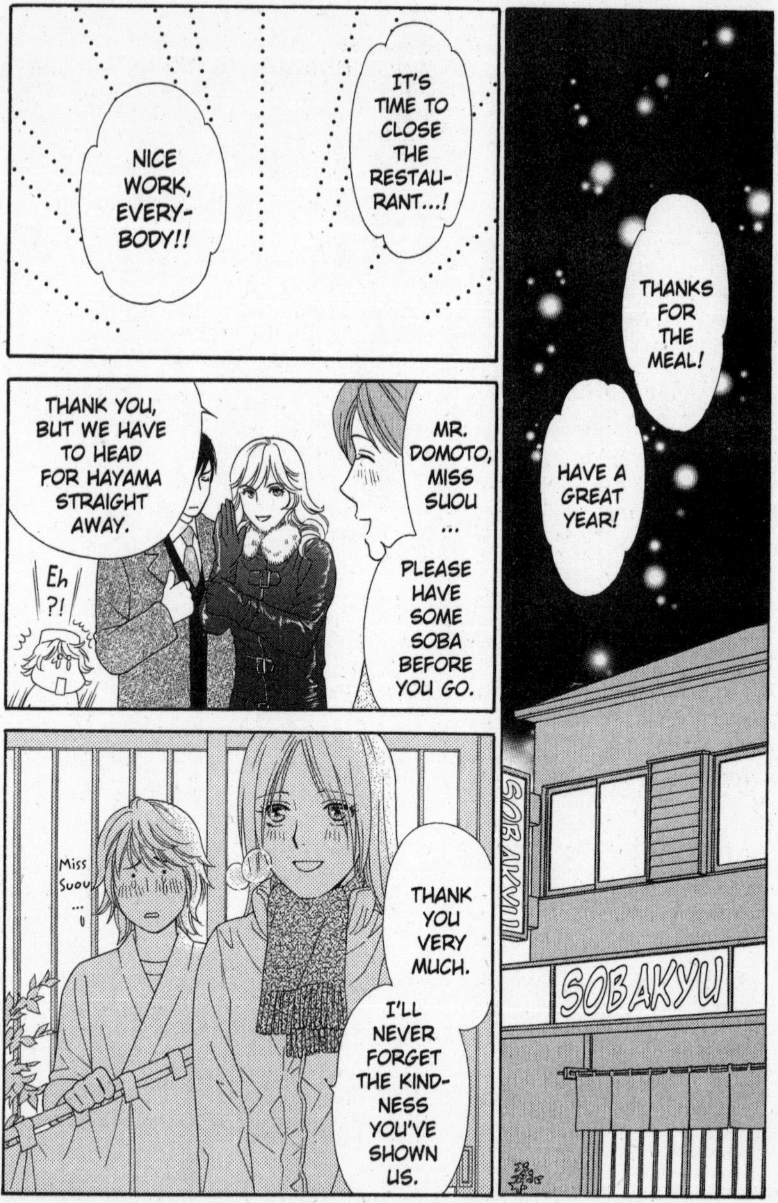
SOBAKYU
THANKS FOR THE MEAL!
HAVE A GREAT YEAR!
SOBAKYU
IT'S TIME TO CLOSE THE RESTAU-RANT...!
NICE WORK, EVERY-BODY!!
MR. DOMOTO, MISS SUOU ...
PLEASE HAVE SOME SOBA BEFORE YOU GO.
THANK YOU, BUT WE HAVE TO HEAD FOR HAYAMA STRAIGHT AWAY.
Eh ?!
THANK YOU VERY MUCH.
I'LL NEVER FORGET THE KIND-NESS YOU'VE SHOWN US.
Miss Suou ...

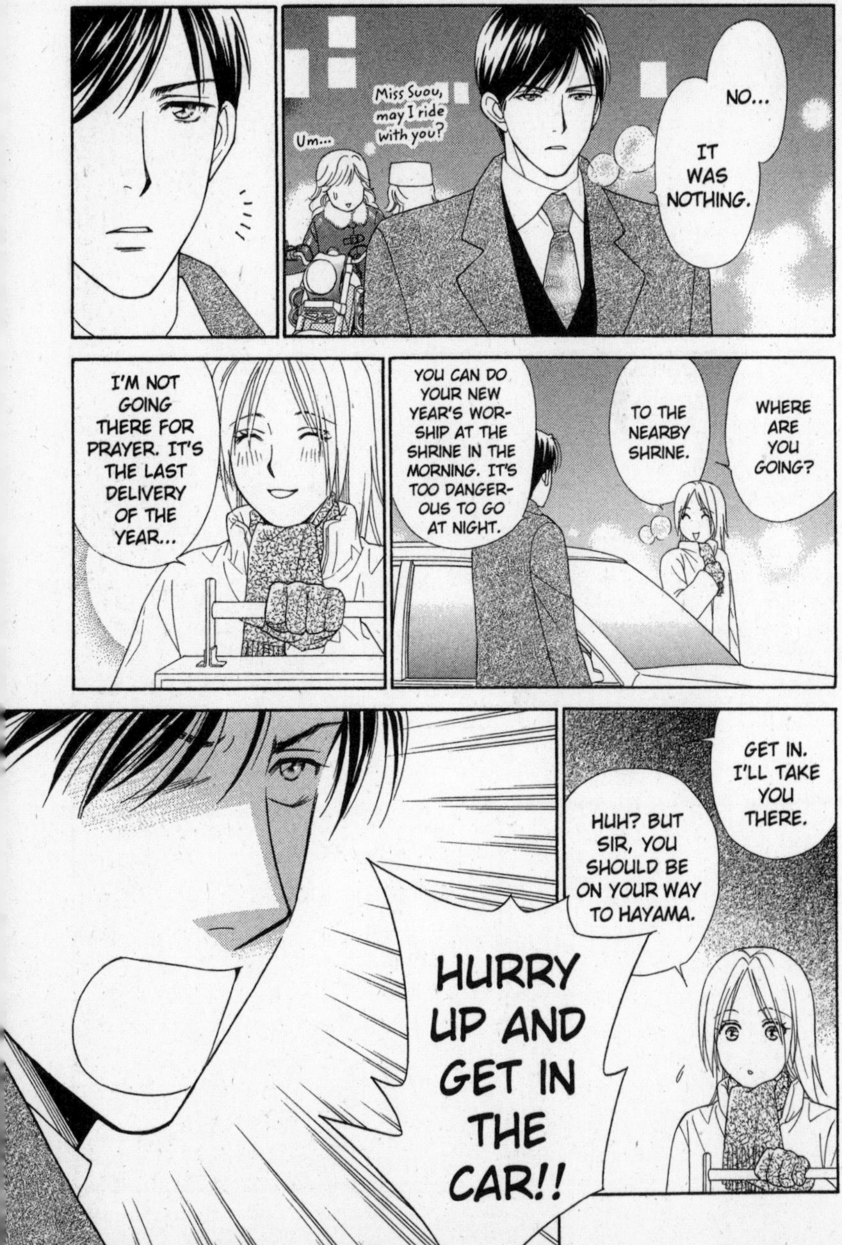
NO...
IT WAS NOTHING.
Miss Suou, may I ride with you?
Um...
WHERE ARE YOU GOING?
TO THE NEARBY SHRINE.
YOU CAN DO YOUR NEW YEAR'S WOR-SHIP AT THE SHRINE IN THE MORNING. IT'S TOO DANGER-OUS TO GO AT NIGHT.
I'M NOT GOING THERE FOR PRAYER. IT'S THE LAST DELIVERY OF THE YEAR...
GET IN. I'LL TAKE YOU THERE.
HUH? BUT SIR, YOU SHOULD BE ON YOUR WAY TO HAYAMA.
HURRY UP AND GET IN THE CAR!!

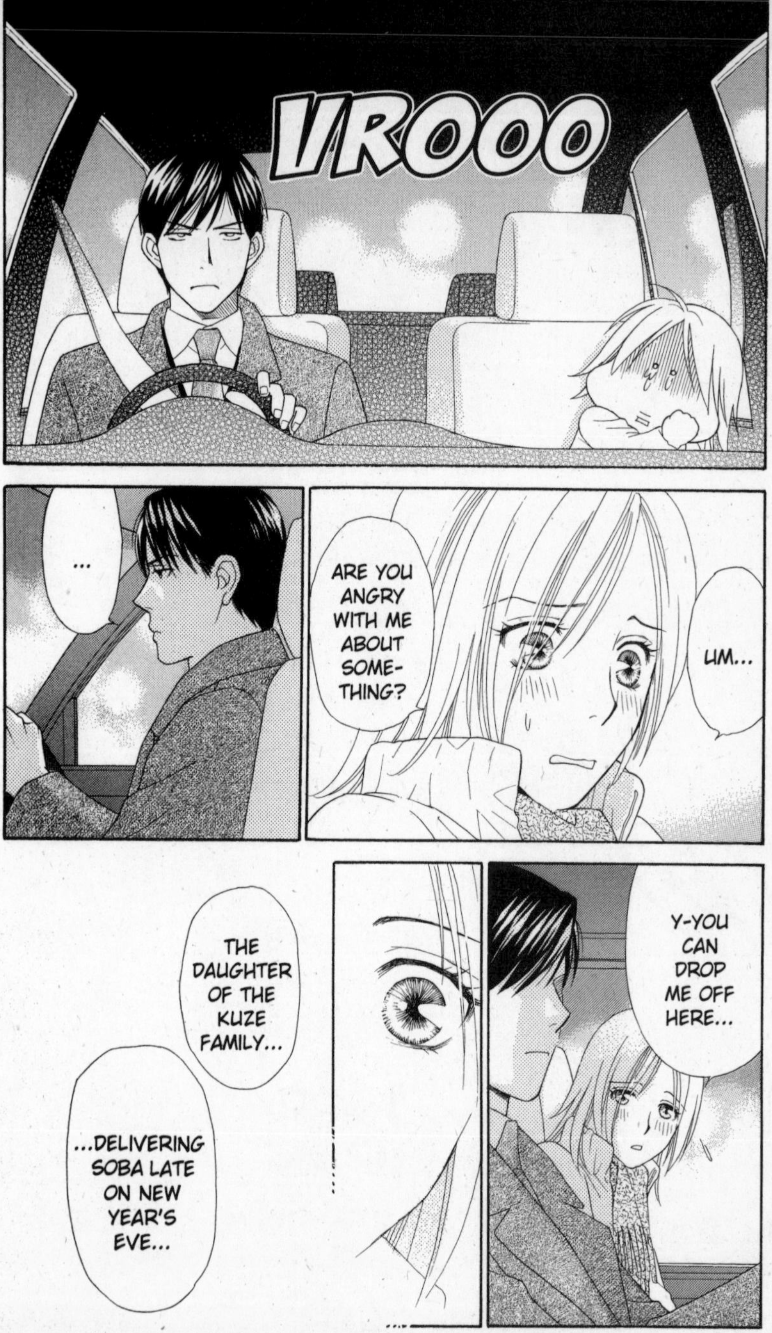
VROOO
UM...
ARE YOU ANGRY WITH ME ABOUT SOME-THING?
...
Y-YOU CAN DROP ME OFF HERE...
THE DAUGHTER OF THE KUZE FAMILY...
...DELIVERING SOBA LATE ON NEW YEAR'S EVE...

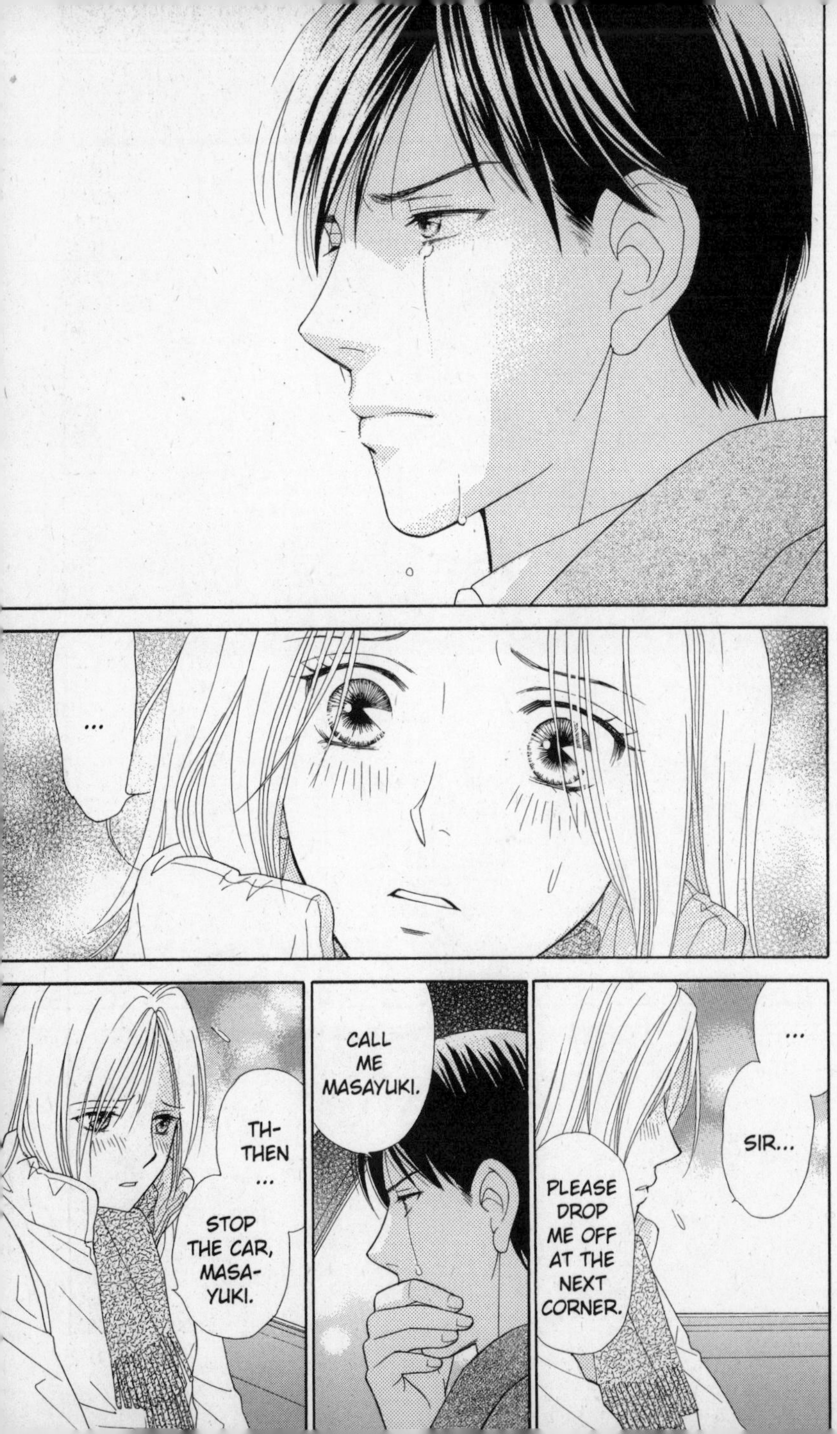
...
...
SIR...
PLEASE DROP ME OFF AT THE NEXT CORNER.
CALL ME MASAYUKI.
TH-THEN ... STOP THE CAR, MASA-YUKI.

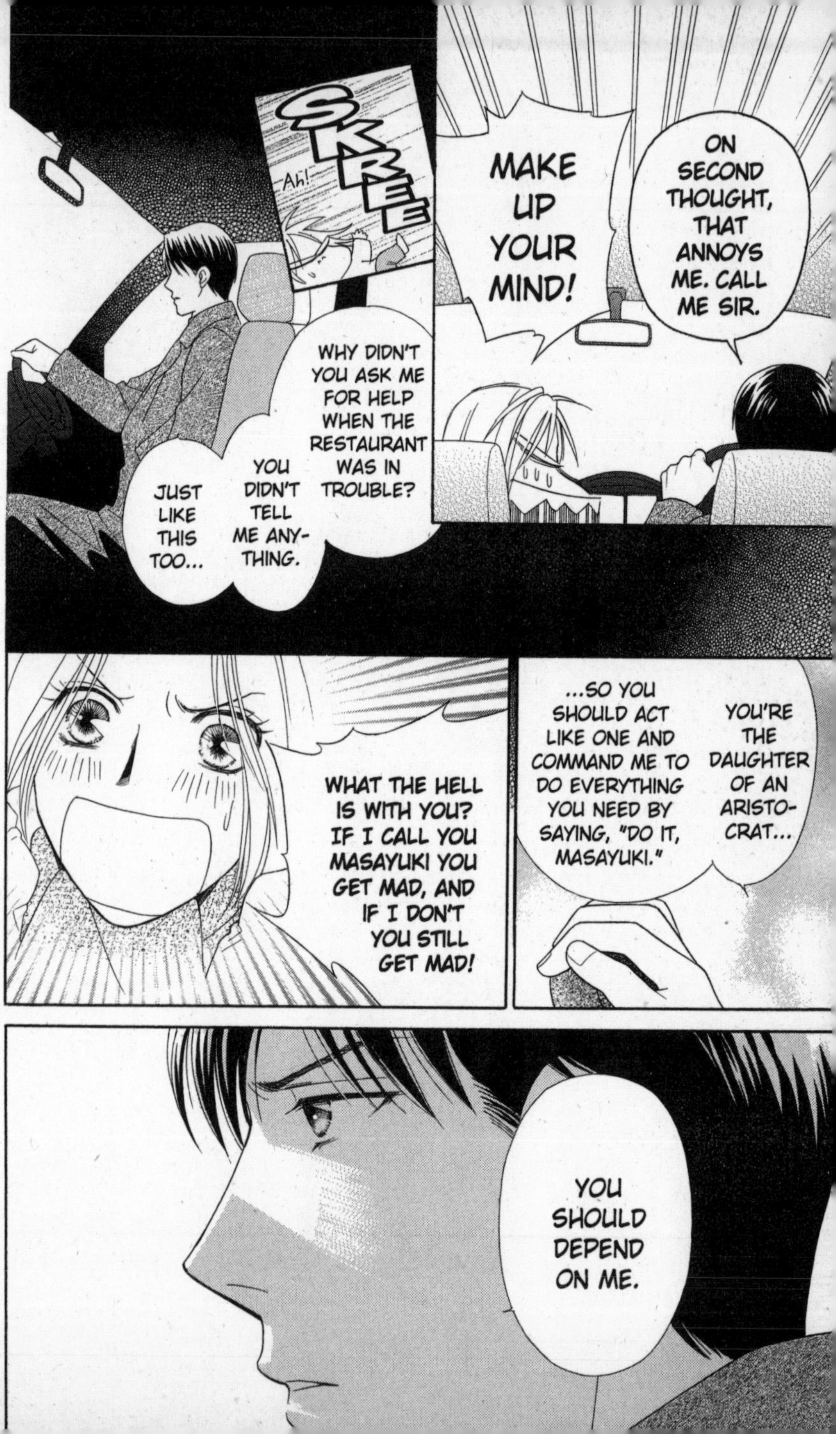
ON SECOND THOUGHT, THAT ANNOYS ME. CALL ME SIR.
MAKE UP YOUR MIND!
SKREE
Ah!
WHY DIDN'T YOU ASK ME FOR HELP WHEN THE RESTAURANT WAS IN TROUBLE?
YOU DIDN'T TELL ME ANY-THING.
JUST LIKE THIS TOO...
YOU'RE THE DAUGHTER OF AN ARISTO-CRAT...
...SO YOU SHOULD ACT LIKE ONE AND COMMAND ME TO DO EVERYTHING YOU NEED BY SAYING, "DO IT, MASAYUKI."
WHAT THE HELL IS WITH YOU? IF I CALL YOU MASAYUKI YOU GET MAD, AND IF I DON'T YOU STILL GET MAD!
YOU SHOULD DEPEND ON ME.

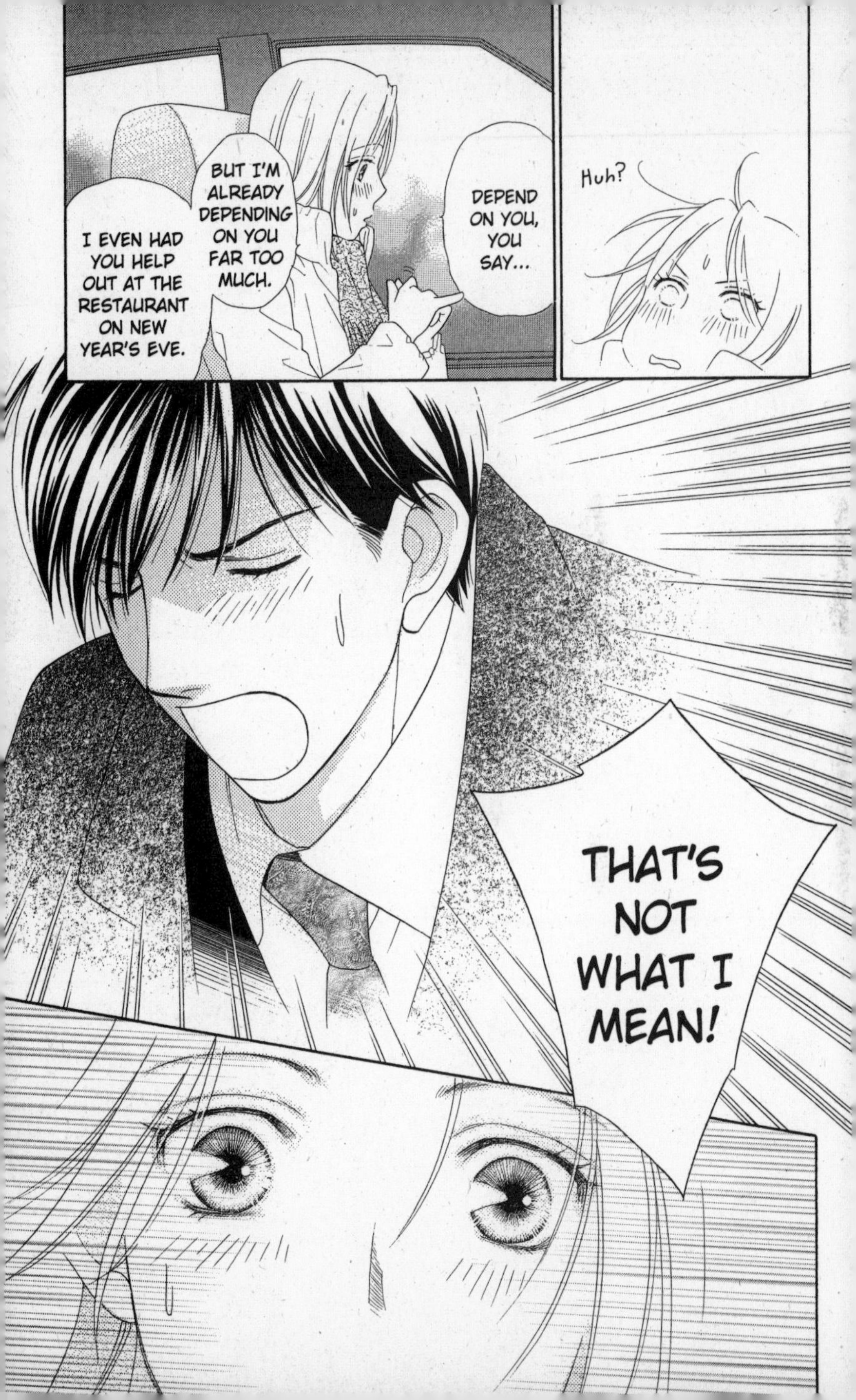
Huh?
DEPEND ON YOU, YOU SAY...
BUT I'M ALREADY DEPENDING ON YOU FAR TOO MUCH.
I EVEN HAD YOU HELP OUT AT THE RESTAURANT ON NEW YEAR'S EVE.
THAT'S NOT WHAT I MEAN!

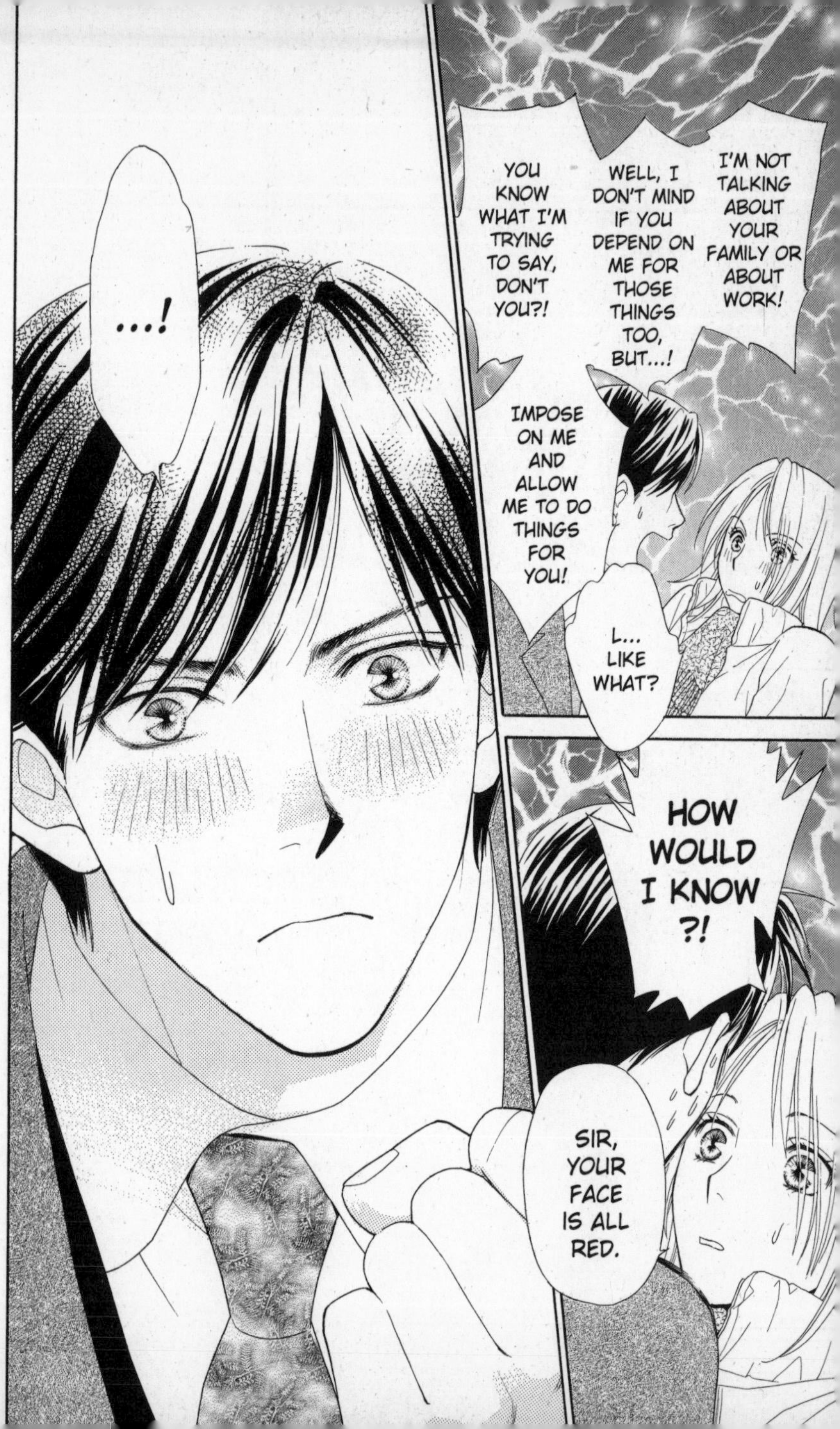
I'M NOT TALKING ABOUT YOUR FAMILY OR ABOUT WORK!
WELL, I DON'T MIND IF YOU DEPEND ON ME FOR THOSE THINGS TOO, BUT...!
YOU KNOW WHAT I'M TRYING TO SAY, DON'T YOU?!
IMPOSE ON ME AND ALLOW ME TO DO THINGS FOR YOU!
L... LIKE WHAT?
HOW WOULD I KNOW ?!
SIR, YOUR FACE IS ALL RED.
...!

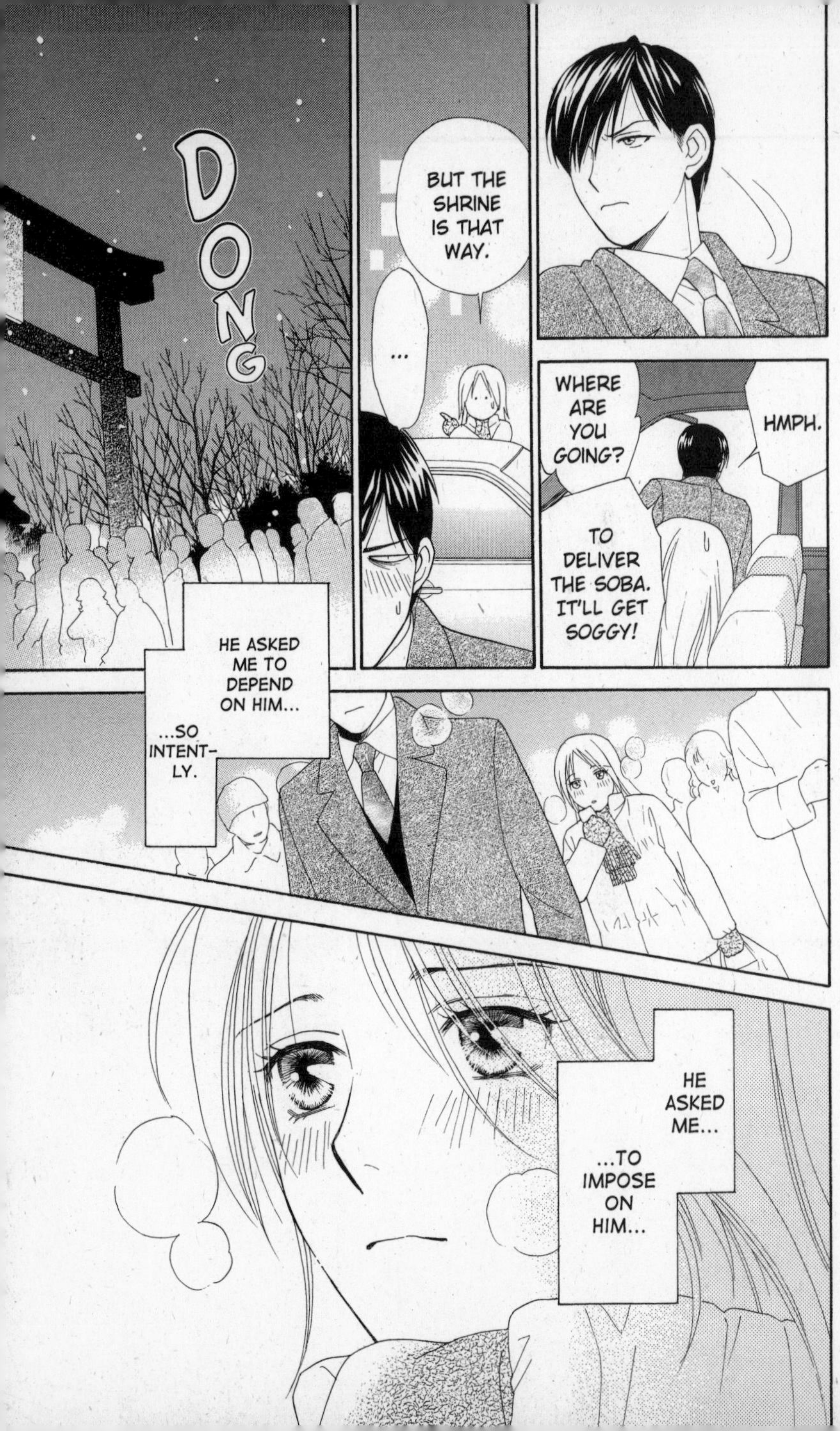
HMPH.
WHERE ARE YOU GOING?
TO DELIVER THE SOBA. IT'LL GET SOGGY!
BUT THE SHRINE IS THAT WAY.
...
DONG
HE ASKED ME TO DEPEND ON HIM...
...SO INTENT-LY.
HE ASKED ME...
...TO IMPOSE ON HIM...

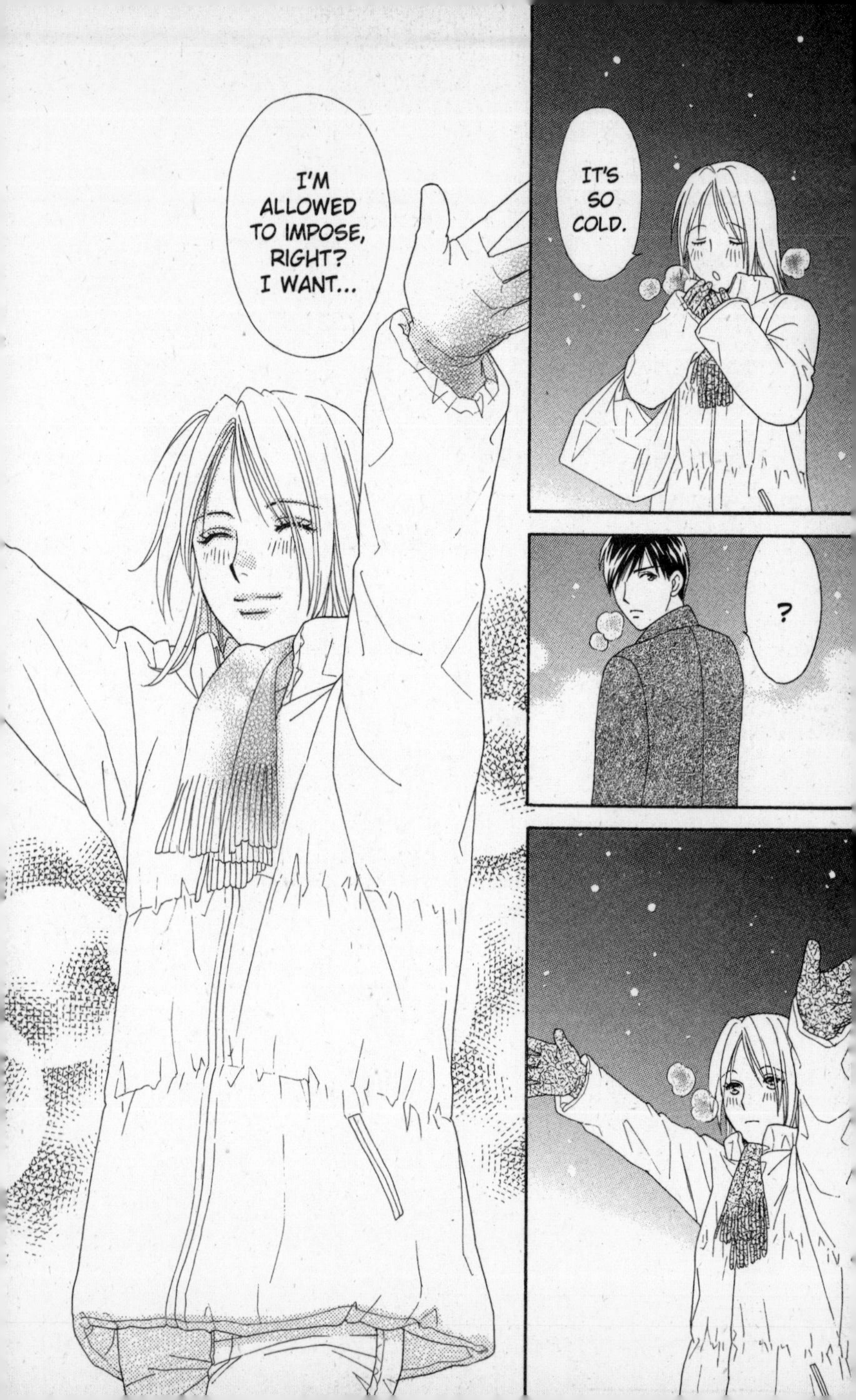
IT'S SO COLD.
?
I'M ALLOWED TO IMPOSE, RIGHT? I WANT...

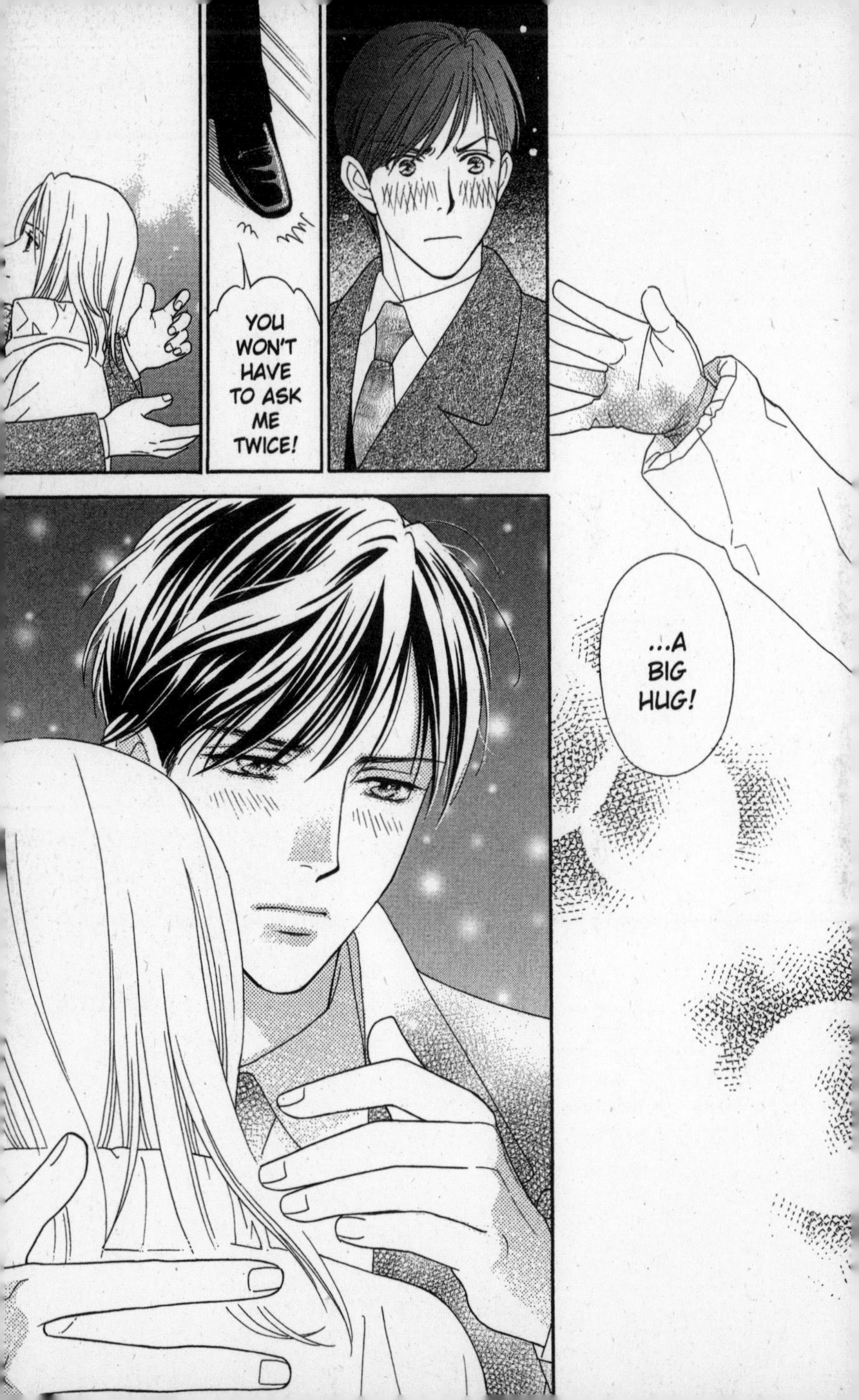
...A BIG HUG!
YOU WON'T HAVE TO ASK ME TWICE!

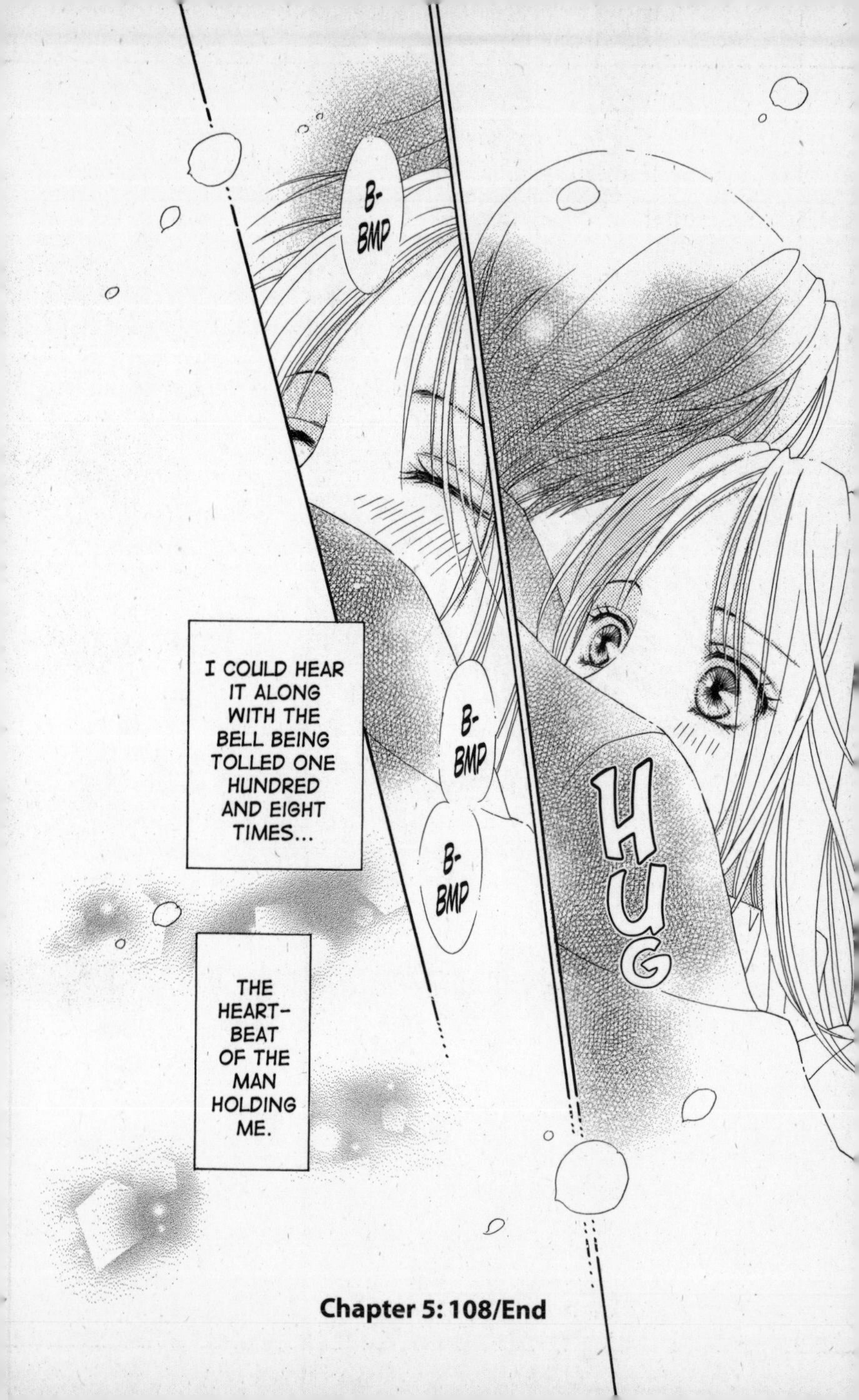
HUG
B-BMP
B-BMP
B-BMP
I COULD HEAR IT ALONG WITH THE BELL BEING TOLLED ONE HUNDRED AND EIGHT TIMES...
THE HEART-BEAT OF THE MAN HOLDING ME.

Chapter 5: 108/End

Butterflies, Flowers

Notes

Chou yo Hana yo (*Butterflies, Flowers*) in Japanese refers to bringing up a child with the utmost care and devotion, as one would delicately raise a flower or butterfly.

Page 13: In the Japanese, Choko's father makes a pun when he mistakenly says that she's too unrefined to attract *yudemen* (boiled noodles) instead of *ikemen* (good-looking men).

Page 17: The poem on pages 17 and 18 is by Emperor Sutoku (1119–1164) of Japan.

Page 65: The Edo period was from 1603 to 1867.

Page 72: The Industrial Revitalization Corporation of Japan provides assistance to companies that have incurred enormous debt.

Page 160: Oscar and André are characters from *The Rose of Versailles*. Reinhard and Kircheis are characters from *Legend of the Galactic Heroes*. Kycilia and M'Quve are characters from *Mobile Suit Gundam*. Saeko Shimazu is a voice actress who played the character Four in the *Mobile Suit Zeta Gundam* TV series, but a different actress played the character in the *Mobile Suit Zeta Gundam: A New Translation* movie trilogy.

Page 168: In the many *Gundam* series, a "Mobile Suit" is a humanoid fighting machine with a pilot. Typical Gundams are 60 feet tall and are used for space combat.

Page 178: Char Aznable, aka the Red Comet, is one of the main characters in *Mobile Suit Gundam*. In the story his machines were reportedly three times faster than normal.

Page 179: In the Japanese version, *wakadaisho* means "young master." Here Masayuki is teasing Mikihiko by saying *baka* (stupid) instead of *waka*.

Page 190: The number 108 is in reference to the number of earthly desires in Buddhism. Starting New Year's Eve, bells are rung at Buddhist temples 108 times to get rid of earthly desires.

About the Author

Yuki Yoshihara was born in Tokyo on February 11. She wanted to become a mangaka since elementary school and debuted in 1988 with *Chanel no Sasayaki*. She is the author of numerous series including *Darling wa Namamono ni Tsuki* and *Itadakimasu*. Yoshihara's favorite band is the Pet Shop Boys, and she keeps her TV tuned to the Mystery Channel.

Butterflies, Flowers
Vol. 1
Shojo Beat Edition

STORY AND ART BY
Yuki Yoshihara

© 2006 Yuki YOSHIHARA/Shogakukan
All rights reserved.
Original Japanese edition "CHOU YO HANA YO"
published by SHOGAKUKAN Inc.

Adaptation/Nancy Thistlethwaite
Translation/Tetsuichiro Miyaki
Touch-up Art & Lettering/Freeman Wong
Design/Hidemi Sahara
Editor/Nancy Thistlethwaite

VP, Production/Alvin Lu
VP, Sales & Product Marketing/Gonzalo Ferreyra
VP, Creative/Linda Espinosa
Publisher/Hyoe Narita

Printed in the U.S.A.

Published by VIZ Media, LLC
P.O. Box 77010
San Francisco, CA 94107

10 9 8 7 6 5 4 3 2 1
First printing, December 2009

Hot Gimmick

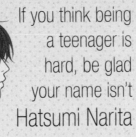

If you think being a teenager is hard, be glad your name isn't Hatsumi Narita

With scandals that would make any gossip girl blush and more triangles than you can throw a geometry book at, this girl may never figure out the game of love!

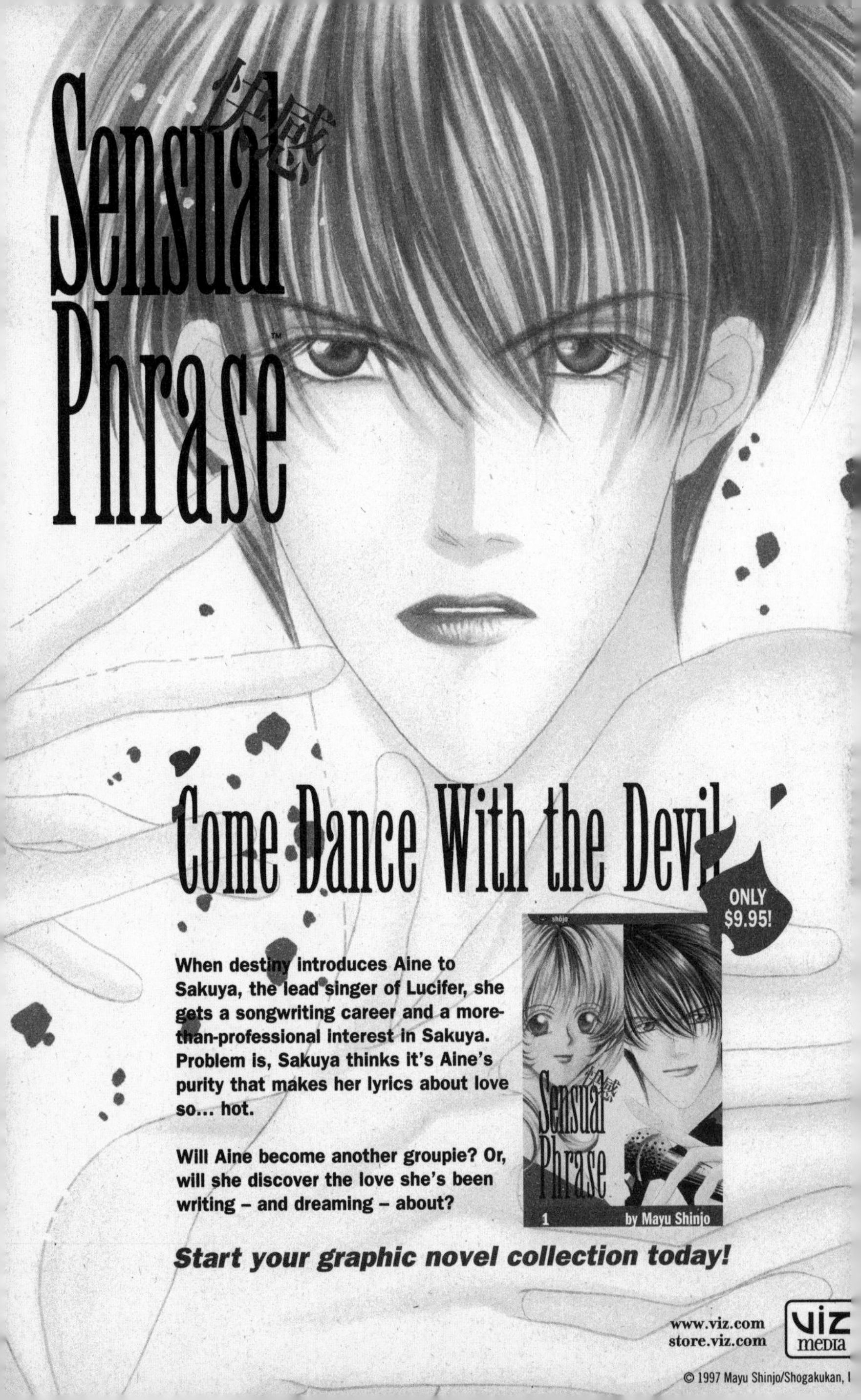
Sensual Phrase™
快感
Come Dance With the Devil
ONLY $9.95!
When destiny introduces Aine to Sakuya, the lead singer of Lucifer, she gets a songwriting career and a more-than-professional interest in Sakuya. Problem is, Sakuya thinks it's Aine's purity that makes her lyrics about love so... hot.
Will Aine become another groupie? Or, will she discover the love she's been writing – and dreaming – about?
shōjo
Sensual Phrase
1
by Mayu Shinjo
Start your graphic novel collection today!
www.viz.com
store.viz.com
VIZ media
© 1997 Mayu Shinjo/Shogakukan, I

TAKE A TRIP TO AN ANCIENT

FUSHIGI YÛGI

FROM THE CREATOR C
ABSOLUTE BOYFRIEND
ALICE 19TH, *CERES:*
CELESTIAL LEGEND,
AND *IMADOKI!*

Tell us what you think about Shojo Beat Manga!

Our survey is now available online. Go to:

shojobeat.com/mangasurvey

Help us make our product offerings better!